Digital Finance and Transformation in the Gulf

Konstantinos Tsanis · Ahmet Faruk Aysan ·
Zhamal Nanaeva
Editors

Digital Finance and Transformation in the Gulf

Fintech, Regulation, and Sustainability

palgrave
macmillan

Editors
Konstantinos Tsanis
Global FinTech & Digital Banking Advisor
International Finance Corporation
Dubai, United Arab Emirates

Ahmet Faruk Aysan
Associate Dean, College of Islamic Studies, Qatar Foundation
Hamad Bin Khalifa University
Doha, Qatar

Zhamal Nanaeva
Researcher
Nordic Centre for Islamic Economy and Finance (NCEIF)
Dubai, United Arab Emirates

ISBN 978-981-92-1587-4 ISBN 978-981-92-1588-1 (eBook)
https://doi.org/10.1007/978-981-92-1588-1

This Palgrave Macmillan imprint is published by the registered company Springer Nature Singapore Pte Ltd.
The registered company address is: 152 Beach Road, #21-01/04 Gateway East, Singapore 189721, Singapore

Contents

List of Contributors

Khalid I. Ahmad College of Law, Hamad Bin Khalifa University (HBKU), Doha, Qatar

Habib Ahmed Durham University Business School, Durham University, Durham, UK;
Department of Islamic Banking, University of Jordan, Amman, Jordan

Wajid Ali Fortune Institute of International Business, Delhi, India

Hamoudah S. Al-Zaini College of Law, Hamad Bin Khalifa University (HBKU), Doha, Qatar

Ilinka Antova University of Sofia "St Kliment Ohridski", Sofia, Bulgaria

Ahmet Faruk Aysan College of Islamic Studies, Hamad Bin Khalifa University, Qatar Foundation, Al-Rayyan, Qatar

Suha Bilquis Aligarh Muslim University, Aligarh, India

Maria Casoria College of Law, Euro University of Bahrain, Manama, Kingdom of Bahrain

Cafer Deniz Department of Economics, Newcastle University, Newcastle, UK;
Graduate School of Healthcare Management, Royal College of Surgeons, Dublin, Ireland;
Department of Economics, University of Us¸Ak, Us¸Ak, Turkey

Meryem Duva Qatar University, Doha, Qatar

Jonathan G. Ercanbrack Reader in Transnational Financial Law, SOAS College of Law, University of London, London, UK

Saib Fakhar New Delhi Institute of Management, New Delhi, India

Abul Hassan School of Business, King Faisal University, Hofuf, Saudi Arabia

Anas Ibrahim Jamous Al-Zahraa University, Jarabulus, Syria

Zhamal Nanaeva Nordic Center for Islamic Economy and Finance, Tallinn, Estonia

Stefan Papastefanou Applied Research Center for Intellectual Assets and the Law in Asia (ARCIALA), Germany and Singapore Management University, Bras Basah, Singapore;
Center for Transnational IP, Media and Technology Law and Policy, Bucerius Law School, Hamburg, Germany

Ali Polat Faculty of Political Science, Department of Economics, Ankara Yildirim Beyazit University, Ankara, Turkey

Mehmet Sahiner School of Business, University of Dundee, Dundee, UK;
Faculty of Economics and Administrative Science, University of Yalova, Yalova, Turkey

Pascal Stiefenhofer Department of Economics, Newcastle University, Newcastle, UK

Muhammad Fazlurrahman Syarif College of Islamic Studies, Hamad Bin Khalifa University, Qatar Foundation, Al-Rayyan, Qatar

List of Figures

List of Tables

PART I

Digital Transformation and Financial Hubs in the Gulf

CHAPTER 1

Gulf Strategic Investments in Finance and Technology for Economic Diversification

Meryem Duva

Introduction

Economic diversification efforts in the GCC have increasingly emphasized knowledge- and technology-based sectors. In line with this shift, the national visions of the GCC countries prioritize non-oil sectors such as finance, advanced technology, and information and communication technologies. In this context, strategic investments through SWFs have emerged as a key instrument for diversification.

SWFs are not new institutions; however, their role in the GCC countries has evolved from managing hydrocarbon revenue surpluses to strategic instruments for long-term development and diversification. This transformation became more evident after the 2008 financial crisis, as shifts in global financial markets led GCC countries to pursue more proactive and global investment strategies.

Accordingly, this study discusses the GCC countries' investments in the finance and technology sectors, especially the fintech sector, and analyses

M. Duva (✉)
Qatar University, Doha, Qatar
e-mail: ma2102059@qu.edu.qa

K. Tsanis et al. (eds.), *Digital Finance and Transformation in the Gulf*,
https://doi.org/10.1007/978-981-92-1588-1_1

their alignment with long-term diversification goals. The analysis focuses on Qatar, Saudi Arabia, and the UAE as a comparative case study.

First, the study examines the process of economic diversification and the national vision documents and identifies each country's economic diversification strategies and the strategic sectors they prioritize. Second, the study examines the investments through the Qatar Investment Authority (QIA), Saudi Arabia's Public Investment Fund (PIF), and the major UAE funds (ADIA and Mubadala) in the finance and technology sectors, especially fintech as a case, based on data collected from official reports, statements, and publicly available sources. Finally, the study evaluates the foreign direct investment (FDI) trends of the countries and the share of the sectors in GDP to assess their alignment with the countries' diversification goals.

Economic Diversification in the Gulf

The economic diversification process in the Gulf has undergone a significant transformation since the early 2000s, as the vulnerabilities associated with rentier economies have become more evident. In response, the GCC countries have introduced long-term national visions to promote economic transformation, in part by reducing dependence on hydrocarbon revenues. These national visions emphasize knowledge- and technology-based sectors in the shift away from hydrocarbon dependency.

Rentierism and Vulnerability to Oil Shocks

The GCC countries are described as rentier states. According to Rentier State Theory,[1] the economy is dependent on *external rents*, such as oil and gas income, and these rents—wealth—are controlled by a small group of society. Consequently, this economic power brings with it political power; thus, it is argued that there is a social contract between *society* and *its rulers*, in which the society minimizes demands for political participation and government accountability in return for economic welfare provided by government through external rents.

[1] Hazem Beblawi and Giacomo Luciani, eds., The Rentier State (London: Croom Helm, 1987), 51–52.

In this context, Giacomo Luciani[2] deepens this theoretical approach and conceptualizes rentier states within the framework of the *allocation state*, highlighting the state's allocative rather than productive function. In allocation states, the economy does not depend on domestic production, and the state functions by allocating external rents.

In this context, since political legitimacy in these countries is largely based on the allocation of wealth generated from hydrocarbon revenues, the decline in oil and gas income may undermine political stability and lead to socioeconomic disruption. Therefore, economic diversification has emerged as a strategic priority for economic development, as well as political and social stability.

In recent decades, economic diversification has become increasingly important for the GCC countries; however, it has developed in two main waves.[3] The early diversification efforts can be traced back to the 1970s, when high revenues from rising oil prices were channeled into infrastructure and industrial investments to support economic development. During the first wave, the GCC countries focused on industrial sectors, such as steel, aluminium, and cement, as part of efforts to restructure their own domestic economies.

In contrast, the second wave in the early 2000s was shaped by fluctuations in oil prices and shifts in global energy markets, particularly the shale gas revolution and the rise of renewable energy, as well as concerns

[2] Giacomo Luciani, "Allocation vs. Production States: A Theoretical Framework," in *The Rentier State*, ed. Hazem Beblawi and Giacomo Luciani (London: Croom Helm, 1987): 63–81.

[3] Omer Naim Kucuk, "Linking Economic Diversification and Regional Investments in the Gulf: Saudi and Emirati Investment Trends in Egypt." Insight Turkey, no.26 (2024): 188.

raised by the "peak oil" theory.[4] These dynamics made strategic restructuring necessary for GCC economies that had long relied on oil revenues as rentier states.

Notably, over the past decades, three major oil price collapses highlighted the need for diversification: the sharp decline in oil prices following the 2008 global financial crisis; the decrease in oil prices between 2014 and 2016 due to expanding shale gas production in the United States; and finally, the sharp collapse in oil prices in 2020 due to the COVID-19 pandemic. Brent crude oil prices fell from around $140 to $45 per barrel in 2008, from $110 to $35 per barrel between 2014 and 2016, to approximately $22 per barrel in 2020.[5]

In response, following the 2008 global crisis, the GCC countries have accelerated the implementation of their long-term development plans, emphasizing sustainable development, economic diversification, and societal welfare. In line with these goals, Qatar introduced its *Qatar National Vision 2030* in 2008,[6] the UAE launched *UAE Vision 2021* in 2010,[7] later the *We the UAE 2031 vision*—and Saudi Arabia announced its *Saudi Vision 2030* in 2016.[8]

[4] The peak oil theory was introduced by M. King Hubbert in 1956. According to this theory, fossil fuel production would follow a bell-shaped curve—reaching a maximum level, so "peak," after which production begins to decline and continue to decrease over time—due to the finite nature of fossil fuel reserves, which took millions of years to form and would not be replenished at a meaningful scale. See: M. King Hubbert, "Nuclear Energy and the Fossil Fuels," Shell Development Company Publication No. 95, presented at the Spring Meeting of the American Petroleum Institute (1956), 1–40. This theory has since evolved in the literature into 'Peak Oil Demand'—a shift from the limits of supply to the limits of demand. In 2000, former Saudi Oil Minister Sheikh Zaki Yamani signaled this shift with the words: "The Stone Age came to an end, not for a lack of stones, and the oil age will end, but not for a lack of oil."

[5] Trading Economics, Brent Crude Oil, https://tradingeconomics.com/commodity/brent-crude-oil.

[6] Government Communication Office, https://www.gco.gov.qa/en/state-of-qatar/qatar-national-vision-2030/our-story/.

[7] The United Arab Emirates' Government portal https://u.ae/en/about-the-uae/strategies-initiatives-and-awards/strategies-plans-and-visions/strategies-plans-and-visions-until-2021/vision-2021.

[8] Saudi Vision 2030, https://www.vision2030.gov.sa/en/explore/story-of-transformation.

National Vision Strategies as a Policy Response

When examining the national visions, although Qatar, the UAE, and Saudi Arabia share the common objective of reducing their dependence on hydrocarbon revenues, each country's economic diversification strategy includes different priorities and sectoral focuses shaped in line with their national visions.

In line with the Qatar National Vision 2030, Qatar prioritizes the transition to a knowledge-based economy.[9] To achieve this, Qatar promotes long-term sustainable development by investing in education, the digital economy, and financial services, as an enabling cluster, as well as manufacturing, logistics, and tourism, as growth clusters.[10]

In line with Saudi Vision 2030, Saudi Arabia has set more institutional and structural transformation objectives; it prioritizes strategic sectors, such as defence, renewable energy, industry, and mining, by investing locally and internationally through the SWFs. In these sectors, localization has been adopted as a priority strategy through strategic investments to increase domestic production capacity and transfer knowledge and technology.[11]

In line with We the UAE 2031 Vision, the UAE prioritizes high-growth potential sectors, including the digital economy, information and communication technologies (ICT), fintech, logistics, and tourism, and aims to achieve global competitiveness in future strategic sectors, such as space exploration and renewable energy.[12]

Accordingly, despite sharing the common goal of reducing dependence on hydrocarbon revenues, the three countries pursue different priorities and sectoral focuses shaped by their national visions. Qatar aims to transition to a knowledge-based economy; Saudi Arabia aims to enhance domestic production and promote knowledge and technology transfer through localization strategies; and the UAE focuses on technology and innovation as key elements of its diversification strategy. This situation demonstrates that the GCC countries have a common goal, but they pursue distinct strategies for economic diversification.

[9] Qatar National Vision 2030, General Secretariat for Development Planning, p. 29.

[10] Planning and Statistics Authority, Third Qatar National Development Strategy 2024–2030, p.16, https://www.npc.qa/en/planning/nds3/Pages/default.aspx.

[11] Saudi Vision 2030, pp. 42–51.

[12] We the UAE 2031 Vision, pp. 29–31.

Knowledge- and Technology-Based Economic Diversification

Economic diversification is often associated with quantitative developments in sectors such as services, industry, manufacturing, and trade in terms of economic growth. However, the sectors based on knowledge and technology are evaluated as a qualitative element for economic development and sustainability in terms of productivity, the digital economy, and the transfer of knowledge and technology.[13]

The knowledge economy is defined by the World Bank as a "one that utilizes knowledge as the key engine of economic growth. It is an economy where knowledge is acquired, created, disseminated, and used effectively to enhance economic development." In this context, a successful transition to a knowledge-based economy involves "*long-term investments in education,*" "*the strengthening of innovation capacity,*" "*developing innovation capability,*" "*modernizing the information infrastructure,*" and "*having an economic environment that is conducive to market transactions.*" These four elements are identified by the World Bank as the core pillars of a knowledge economy.[14]

Considering the objectives of the transition to a knowledge-based economy within the GCC countries' national visions, knowledge-based economic diversification has become a significant element of their strategies. In this context, the literature includes qualitative studies analysing the transition processes of the GCC countries to a knowledge-based economy in line with their national visions and quantitative studies investigating the relationship between technological transformation and economic diversification.

The study conducted by Almoli and Tok[15] examines Qatar's efforts to transition to a knowledge-based economy and discusses their alignment with the country's economic diversification goals within the framework of its national vision and development strategies. The study shows that Qatar has strategically aligned its public policies with the pillars of

[13] Neffati, Mohamed and Rafik Jbir, "The impact of Digitalization and Economic Diversification on Economic Growth: Evidence from Saudi Arabia," Technological and Economic Development of Economy 30 (2024): 1510–1511.

[14] Derek H. C. Chen and Carl J. Dahlman, "The Knowledge Economy, the KAM methodology and World Bank Operations," World Bank (2006): 4.

[15] Ahmed Almoli and M. Evren Tok, "Knowledge-Based Development and Economic Diversification: The Case of Qatar," in H. Miniaoui (Ed.), Economic Development in the Gulf Cooperation Council Countries (Springer, 2020), 43–73.

the knowledge-based economy and provided infrastructure and financial incentive mechanisms through innovation and entrepreneurship ecosystems to facilitate knowledge transfer. According to the analysis of the global indexes utilized in the study—namely the World Economic Forum's Global Competitiveness Index (GCI), the Global Innovation Index (GII), and the Global Entrepreneurship Index (GEI)—Qatar has made significant progress towards knowledge-based development; however, it still faces various limitations in areas such as human capital, market size, creative output, and technology exports. In this context, the study has emphasized the necessity of promoting a research culture, supporting a qualified workforce, strengthening startup skills in education, and enhancing internationalization capacity.

The study conducted by Crupi and Schilirò[16] analyzes the UAE's economic diversification process in the context of the transition to a knowledge- and technology-based economy during the period 2012–2021. It particularly focuses on assessing the effectiveness of the 'Vision 2021' strategy and examines the impact of the policies adopted under this framework on economic diversification. The findings show that the UAE has achieved significant progress in economic diversification efforts during the period 2012–2021, particularly in the growth of non-oil sectors and the increase in exports from these sectors. On the other hand, it emphasized the necessity of developments in education, human capital, the competitiveness of SMEs, and innovation capacity.

The study conducted by Albassam[17] analyses the impact of the nearly forty-year policy process implemented in line with Saudi Arabia's development plans since 1970 on reducing the dependence on hydrocarbon revenues and diversifying its economy. The study demonstrates the limited success of economic diversification efforts, despite the goals set in the development plans, by analysing four key variables: "the oil sector's share of GDP, the private sector's share of GDP, oil exports as a percentage of total exports, and oil revenues as a percentage of total government revenues." In addition, the empirical study conducted by Neffati and

[16] Antonio Crupi and Daniele Schilirò "The UAE Economy and the Path to Diversification and Innovation," International Journal of Business Management and Economic Research (IJBMER), Vol 14 (2023), 2286–2300.

[17] Bassam A. Albassam, 2015. "Economic Diversification in Saudi Arabia: Myth or Reality," Resources Policy, Elsevier, vol. 44 (2015): 112–117.

Jbir[18] analyses the effects of digitalization and economic diversification on economic growth in Saudi Arabia using data for the period 1990–2021. The findings indicate that digitalization and economic diversification affect economic growth both directly and indirectly through non-oil sectors.

Thus, the existing literature reveals that knowledge- and technology-based economic diversification processes have gained growing importance in the GCC countries, focusing on knowledge transfer, innovation, digitalization, and human capital.

Sovereign Wealth Funds as an Instrument of Economic Diversification

Sovereign Wealth Funds (SWFs) are not new institutions; early examples include state-owned funds in the United States, such as the Texas Permanent School Fund, established in 1854, and the Permanent University Fund, established in 1876. However, the first national-level SWF is widely regarded as the Kuwait Investment Authority, established in 1953.[19] In recent years, however, SWFs have emerged as a significant focus of academic debate due to their rising prominence in international financial markets. The importance of SWFs became especially evident after the 2008 global financial crisis, when nine SWFs injected approximately US$71.2 billion into international financial markets.[20] Since then, the assets under management (AUM) of SWFs have grown rapidly, recording an average annual increase of around 7% between 2008 and 2020[21]; a total of 73 new SWFs were also established worldwide between 2010

[18] Neffati, Mohamed and Rafik Jbir, "The impact of Digitalization and Economic Diversification on Economic Growth: Evidence from Saudi Arabia," Technological and Economic Development of Economy 30 (2024): 1510–1511.

[19] Alhashel, "Sovereign Wealth Funds," 2.

[20] Diego López, "SWF 3.0: How Sovereign Wealth Funds Navigated COVID-19 and Changed Forever," Journal of International Business Policy 6, no. 3 (2023): 374.

[21] William L. Megginson, Xin Yue Zhou, and Robert L. Gholson, "The Case against a US Sovereign Wealth Fund," *The Financial Review* 60, no. 1 (February 2025): 6.

and 2022,[22] and by 2025, their total AUM had reached approximately US$13.8 trillion.[23]

During the 2007–2008 global financial crisis, SWFs from GCC countries invested in financial institutions in the US and Europe that were affected by the crisis. To rescue Citigroup, Abu Dhabi Investment Authority (ADIA) invested US$7.6 billion and Kuwait Investment Authority (KIA) US$3 billion; KIA also invested US$2 billion in Merrill Lynch; Qatar Investment Authority (QIA) invested US$0.6 billion in Credit Suisse, and Saudi Arabian Monetary Agency (SAMA) invested US$1.8 billion in UBS; and Saudia Arabia and Singapore Investment Corporation invested US$10 billion in UBS.[24] Thus, during this period, the GCC countries emerged as significant global financial actors and consolidated their presence and influence in international markets.

On the other hand, in the wake of the changing global financial market dynamics after the crisis, the GCC countries demonstrated both the "*intention* and the *capability*"[25] to reposition themselves as active and influential global actors. In this context, the *Late Rentierism* approach, introduced by Matthew Gray,[26] provides a more dynamic interpretation of rentierism by considering the transformation dynamics that have shaped the GCC states over the past two decades. The Late Rentierism approach argues that the traditional assumption—that rentier states are autonomous from society due to the lack of internal taxation—has become increasingly invalid. It suggests that the GCC countries are no longer merely "allocation states;" on the contrary, they are transforming into more active states that respond to new global and local dynamics such as "globalization, new technologies, free trade, investments, social changes, and development imperatives." In this framework,

[22] Statista Research Department, *Statista*, December 18, 2023, https://www.statista.com/.

[23] Global SWF, accessed July 2025, https://globalswf.com/.

[24] Mehmet Asutay, "GCC Sovereign Wealth Funds and Their Role in the European and American Markets," *Equilibri* 12, no. 3 (December 2008): 341.

[25] Kristian Coates Ulrichsen, *The Gulf States in International Political Economy* (New York: Palgrave Macmillan, 2016), 37.

[26] Matthew Gray, *A Theory of "Late Rentierism" in the Arab States of the Gulf* (Doha: Center for International and Regional Studies, Georgetown University School of Foreign Service in Qatar, 2011).

Late Rentierism provides an explanatory theoretical basis for understanding the use of GCC countries' SWFs not merely as instruments for managing surplus revenue, but as strategic instruments for the long-term objectives.

Definition of Sovereign Wealth Funds

Despite the absence of a universally accepted definition, the term 'sovereign wealth fund' was first introduced by Andrew Rozanov in 2005.[27] According to Rozanov, SWFs typically originate from national budget surpluses accumulated over time as a result of "favourable macroeconomic, trade and fiscal positions, coupled with long-term budget planning and spending restraint."[28] Later in 2008, according to International Working Group of Sovereign Wealth Funds (IWG), established by the International Monetary Fund (IMF), aiming to facilitate cross-border investment and ensure financial stability, Sovereign Wealth Funds (SWFs) are defined as "*special purpose investment funds or arrangements, owned by the general government. Created by the general government for macroeconomic purposes, SWFs hold, manage, or administer assets to achieve financial objectives, and employ a set of investment strategies which include investing in foreign financial assets.*"[29] Also, according to Generally Accepted Principles and Practices (GAPP), known as "Santiago Principles,"[30] SWFs are primarily shaped around three strategic objectives: ensuring economic stability -stabilization funds-, generating savings for future generations, savings funds, and increasing the return on reserves, reserve investment corporations. Within this framework, the SWFs of GCC countries aim to diversify their natural resource revenues through various investments, thereby both providing protection against economic fluctuations and transferring these revenues to future generations.

[27] Sara Bazoobandi, *'The Political Economy of the Gulf Sovereign Wealth Funds: A Case Study of Iran, Kuwait, Saudi Arabia and the United Arab Emirates'* (London: Routledge, 2013): 19.

[28] Andrew Rozanov, "Who Holds the Wealth of Nations?," Central Banking Journal 15, no. 4 (May 2005): 52.

[29] International Working Group of Sovereign Wealth Funds (IWG), retrieved April 12, 2025, from https://www.ifswf.org/what-is-a-sovereign-wealth-fund.

[30] "It is the globally accepted standards for governance, investment and risk management practices of SWFs".

Functions of Sovereign Wealth Funds

The literature highlights two distinct approaches to the function of SWFs. The first approach views SWFs as political tools used by regimes to maintain their own interests and stability.[31] In this context, the lack of transparency and accountability of funds has been discussed for the risks of mismanagement, corruption, and distortions in international financial markets, as well as raising concerns about national security and political influence in host countries.[32] The second approach defines SWFs primarily on economic grounds, highlighting the functions of funds in providing macroeconomic stability against income fluctuations, accumulating assets for future generations, contributing to international financial stability, and supporting economic diversification strategies.[33] The study focuses on the latter approach, examining the use of SWFs as strategic investment tools serving the long-term economic diversification objectives of the GCC countries.

In this context, the next section examines strategic investments made by the SWFs of Qatar, the UAE, and Saudi Arabia in the fintech sector, using publicly available news sources and official announcements. Using a limited number of examples, the analysis aims to present a representative framework that shows how each country positions its SWF investments in line with the economic diversification strategies defined in their national vision documents.

[31] Alexis Montambault Trudelle, "Tools of Regime Stability: The Political Economy of Sovereign Wealth Funds in Gulf Rentier States," *Review of International Political Economy* 31, no. 5 (2024): 1446–1471.

[32] Truman, *Sovereign Wealth Funds*, 6.

[33] Farouk El-Kharouf, Sulayman Al-Qudsi, and Shifa Obeid, "The Gulf Corporation Council Sovereign Wealth Funds: Are They Instruments for Economic Diversification or Political Tools?," *Asian Economic Papers* 9, no. 1 (2010): 124–151; Bazoobandi, *The Political Economy of the Gulf Sovereign Wealth Funds*, 22.

FinTech as a Strategic Diversification Instrument

Qatar Investment Authority (QIA)

Qatar Investment Authority (QIA), with existing investors, invested over $500 million in US-based fintech company SoFi (Social Finance, Inc.) in 2019.[34] SoFi is a financial platform founded by Stanford students that started with student loans and later expanded its services to include personal loans, mortgages, investments, and digital banking. In 2022, the company was approved to become a national bank and reached 10 million members as of 2025.[35] This QIA's investment is part of its vision to build a diversified economy based on technology and innovation.

In 2022, the Qatar Investment Authority (QIA), along with other international investors, participated in Checkout.com's $1 billion Series D funding round. Checkout.com, founded in 2012, is a UK-based financial technology company that provides global payment infrastructure.[36]

Abu Dhabi Investment Authority (ADIA) and Mubadala Investment Company

In 2018, Mubadala Investment Company announced its intention to establish a $400 million fund to invest in leading European technology companies.[37] In line with the UAE's economic diversification objectives, it invests in numerous Europe-based technology ventures, fostering the growth of globally competitive technology firms. With its substantial capital under management, Mubadala stands among the key investors providing strong financial support to the European technology sector.

[34] Qatar Investment Authority, "QIA leads over $500 million strategic growth investment in SoFi," May 29, 2013. https://www.qia.qa/en/Newsroom/Pages/Qatar-Investment-Authority-Leads-Over-$500-Million-Strategic-Growth-Investment-in-SoFi.aspx (Accessed 10 March 2025).

[35] SoFi, https://www.sofi.com/our-story/.

[36] Qatar Investment Authority, "QIA takes part in Checkout.com $1 billion Series D funding round," December 1, 2022, https://www.qia.qa/en/Newsroom/Pages/QIA-takes-part-in-Checkout-com-$1-billion-Series-D-funding-round-.aspx (Accessed 10 Mar 2025).

[37] Mubadala Investment Company, "Mubadala to Launch $400 million European Tech Fund," June 13, 2018, https://www.mubadala.net/en/news/mubadala-launch-400-million-european-tech-fund (Accessed March 10, 2025).

In 2019, from its US$ 400 million European Fund, Mubadala made its first investment in WeFox,[38] a Berlin-based fintech company providing a digital platform for insurance solutions. It has maintained its investment in WeFox by participating in a $400 million investment round in 2022.[39] Mubadala also invested in other significant European fintech companies, including Revolut and Klarna, strengthening its presence in the sector. It invested in UK-based neobank Revolut in a share sale process that took place in 2024. Revolut, founded in 2015, is a global fintech company providing financial services, including foreign exchange transactions, digital wallets, investment solutions, and international money transfers.[40] Also, it acquired an equity stake in Klarna, one of the leading fintech companies based in Sweden that provides financial services, including the "Buy Now, Pay Later" (BNPL) options, by participating in an $800 million financing round in 2022.[41] The UAE's investments in fintech are not limited to European companies but also globally, such as the investment in Mphasis, an India-based IT company offering AI and fintech solutions, by ADIA.[42]

Public Investment Fund

An analysis of Saudi Arabia's fintech investments demonstrates that it strategically focuses on supporting local and regional entrepreneurship. In this context, the US-based 500 Global has launched a new fund called

[38] Fintechnews Middle East, "Abu Dhabi's Mubadala Makes its First Investment from Their US$ 400 Million European Fund," March 6, 2019, https://fintechnews.ae/3514/abudhabi/mubadala-wefox-insurtech/ (Accessed March 12, 2025).

[39] FinanceWorld, "Mubadala investments increase Abu Dhabi's IT portfolio," August 26, 2022, https://thefinanceworld.com/mubadala-investments-increase-abu-dhabis-it-portfolio/ (Accessed March 12, 2025).

[40] FinTech News Network, retrieved 10 Mar 2025, from https://fintechnews.ae/22730/abudhabi/mubadala-investment-revolut/

[41] FinTech Futures, "Klarna lands $800m funding as valuation cut to $6.7bn from $45.6bn last year," July 11, 2022, https://www.fintechfutures.com/venture-capital-funding/klarna-lands-800m-funding-as-valuation-cut-to-6-7bn-from-45-6bn-last-year (Accessed March 10, 2025).

[42] Ephraim Modise, "Strategic Synergies: ADIA & GIC's Co-Investments and the Growing MENA-SEA Collaboration" Apr 2, 2025, https://magnitt.com/news/strategic-synergies-adia-gic-s-co-investments-and-the-growing-mena-sea-collaboration-53983 (Accessed April 5, 2025).

"500 MENA" to invest in "high-growth technology startups" across the MENA region. The fund focuses on startups in the early growth phase in the region to support technological developments. This fund is supported by leading Saudi institutions, the Public Investment Fund (PIF), Jada Fund of Funds, and Saudi Venture Capital (SVC).[43] In addition, the PIF and the Hong Kong Monetary Authority (HKMA) have signed a memorandum of understanding to establish a joint investment fund with a target size of USD 1 billion. The fund aims to support the localization of industries in Saudi Arabia by investing in strategic sectors, including fintech, manufacturing, renewable energy, and healthcare.[44] In this context, Saudi Arabia's investment strategies show that the country focuses on supporting and developing regional and domestic fintech startups as part of its localization strategy instead of directly investing in global and foreign fintech companies.

Comparative Assessment and Macro Indicators

The selected examples demonstrate that Qatar, the UAE, and Saudi Arabia pursue distinct strategic approaches in their investments in the fintech sector in line with the economic diversification goals in their national vision documents. In this context, Qatar pursues more focused and selective fintech investments in line with its vision for a knowledge-based economy; the UAE's emphasis on technology and innovation is evident in its diverse fintech investments across global markets; and Saudi Arabia's localization goal is demonstrated through its investments supporting the development of the domestic fintech sector.

Also, in a comparative analysis of FDI net outflows (% of GDP) 2008–2023 (Fig. 1.1),[45] the UAE's FDI outflows demonstrate the highest and

[43] Fintechnews Middle East, "500 Global Launches New MENA Tech Startup Fund," January 24, 2025, https://fintechnews.ae/23854/fintech/500-global-launches-new-mena-tech-startup-fund/ (Accessed April 1, 2025).

[44] Fintechnews Middle East, "Saudi Arabia and Hong Kong to Form US$1 Billion Investment Fund" November 4, 2024, https://fintechnews.ae/23114/fintech-saudi-arabia/saudi-arabia-and-hong-kong-to-form-us1-billion-investment-fund/ (Accessed April 1, 2025).

[45] World Bank Group, Foreign direct investment, net outflows (% of GDP)—Saudi Arabia, Qatar, United Arab Emirates, https://data.worldbank.org/indicator/BM.KLT.DINV.WD.GD.ZS.

most stable foreign investment rates among the three countries. Particularly after 2014, these rates have been around 4–5% in most years, which has reflected a more stable investment strategy. Qatar's FDI outflows, on the other hand, have followed a more volatile trend over the years. The rates, which reached significant peaks particularly in 2011 and 2016, have declined significantly in the following years and have not been maintained at a stable level. This fluctuating trend could show that Qatar has adopted an investment approach shaped by global market conditions and period-specific dynamics in its foreign investments. Saudi Arabia's FDI outflows, on the other hand, remained relatively low between 2008 and 2015. However, a notable increase has been observed since 2016, which can reflect its Vision 2030 and economic diversification objectives. Despite this upward trend, Saudi Arabia's FDI outflows still remain lower compared to those of the UAE and Qatar.

Qatar

Within the framework of the Qatar National Vision 2030, the finance sector has emerged as one of the key strategic sectors. When Qatar's outward foreign direct investment (OFDI) stocks are examined, it is seen that the finance sector accounted for a considerable share of the total outward investment stock over time. In 2008 and 2009, the "Finance, Insurance, Real Estate and Business Services" sector—of which financial intermediation (banks) was the largest sub-sector—accounted for the largest share of Qatar's OFDI stocks, with a share of 68.1% in 2008 and 57.2% in 2009. According to the 2009 OFDI flow data, this sector accounted for 31.8% of total OFDI flows. Over the ten years following the Qatar National Vision 2030, the finance sector consistently held the largest share of OFDI stocks, with shares ranging from 37 to 47% between 2010 and 2018. This sustained trend reflects the strategic role of the finance sector within the economic diversification goals.[46] In this context, the following Fig. 1.2. illustrates the increasing contribution of the finance and insurance sector to Qatar's GDP, showing its growing importance in Qatar's economy and its strategic role in its economic diversification efforts.

[46] It should be noted that the data were gathered only from privately owned companies and public corporations, National Planning Council, https://www.npc.qa/en/pages/default.aspx (Accessed May 5, 2025).

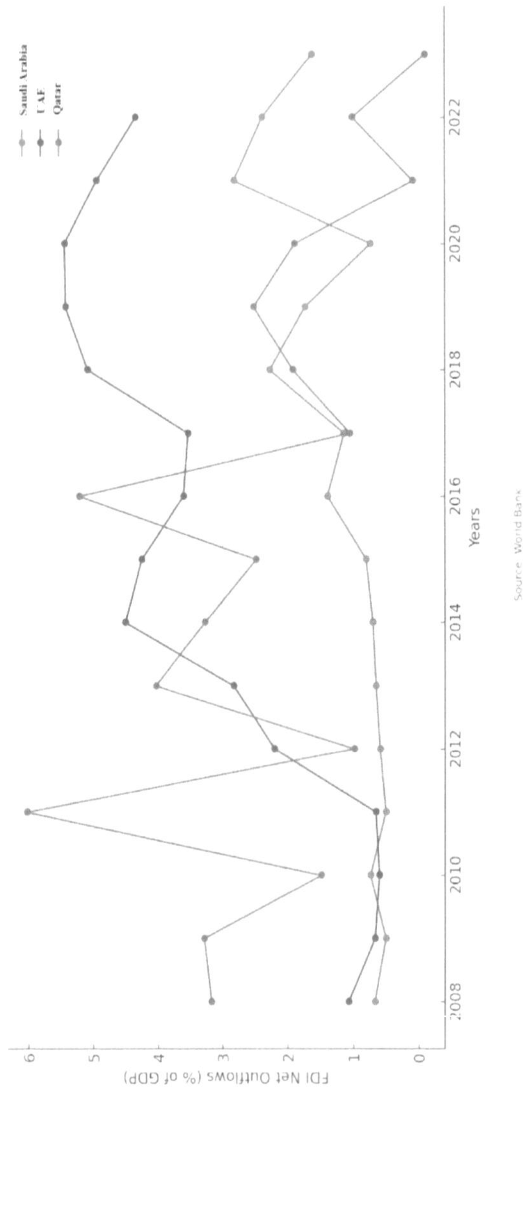

Fig. 1.1 FDI net outflows (% of GDP), 2008–2023

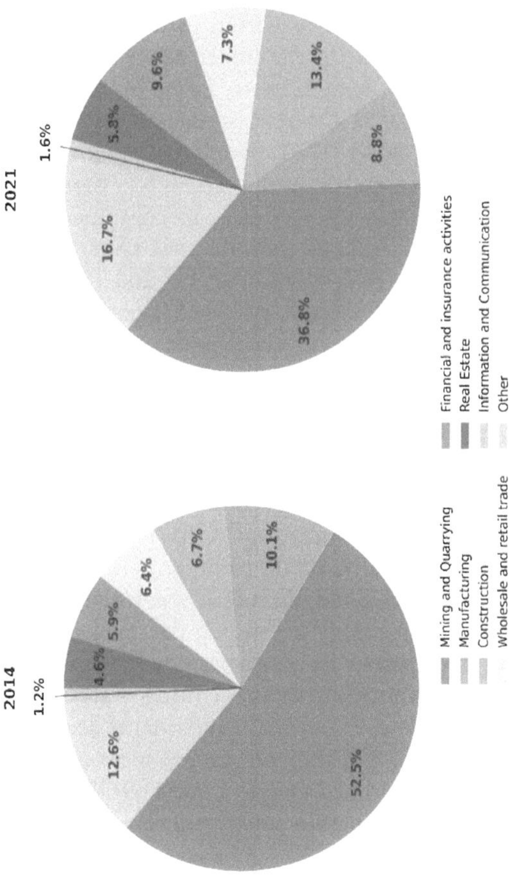

Fig. 1.2 Contribution by sectors to Qatar's GDP (%)

A comparison of data[47] from 2014 and 2021 on the contribution of economic sectors to Qatar's GDP demonstrates that the share of the hydrocarbon sector has considerably decreased from 52.5% to 36.8%. This decline indicates that Qatar's economic diversification efforts have been partially successful. Notably, the increase in the share of the finance and insurance activities from 5.9% to 9.6% is consistent with Qatar's strategically prioritized finance sector within its economic diversification efforts. In addition, the increase in the information and communication sector has remained limited (from 1.2% to 1.6%) but exhibited a steady growth trend. Moreover, 2023 Q4 data indicates that the transformation observed during the 2014–2021 period has continued: while the hydrocarbon sector's share remains stable at 36.8%, the increase in the finance and insurance sector to 13.3% points to continued diversification progress. In summary, the findings indicate that Qatar is progressively reducing its reliance on the hydrocarbon sector and that diversification efforts, especially in the finance sector, have had a noticeable impact.

The United Arab Emirates

Within the framework of its national vision, the UAE aims to transition to a technology- and innovation-based economy. In this context, sectors such as artificial intelligence, the digital economy, and fintech are among the strategic sectors. In this context, the UAE's OFDI flows demonstrate its investment strategy focused on technology and innovation. The UAE's OFDI flows to the United Kingdom show that advanced technology and information technology are among the main sectors. Similarly, communication and information technologies emerge as one of the main sectors in the UAE's OFDI flows to the United States. On the other hand, the UAE's OFDI flows show that investments are not limited to Europe or the United States; on the contrary, they involve a wide range of countries around the world. Indeed, UAE's OFDI flows to India show that e-commerce, information and communication technologies, and the software sector are among the main sectors.[48] Thus, the sectoral

[47] Retrieved October 30, 2025, from https://www.data.gov.qa/explore/dataset/percentage-distribution-of-gross-domestic-product-by-economic-activities-at-current-prices-quarterly/table/

[48] United Arab Emirates, UAE Foreign Direct Investments Dashboard https://www.moec.gov.ae/en/foreign-direct-investment-dashboard (Accessed May 30, 2025).

contributions to GDP of the UAE highlight the influence of the country's technology- and innovation-based investment strategy on its national economy, as illustrated in the following Fig. 1.3.

In the UAE, which has a more diversified economy compared to other GCC countries, the contribution of the hydrocarbon sector to GDP accounts for 24.1% in 2021, down from 32.9% in 2014. The share of the wholesale and retail trade sector in the economy increased from 11.7% in 2014 to 12.8% in 2021, remaining its position as the primary contributor to non-oil GDP. Also, the manufacturing sector, which expanded from 8.1% of GDP in 2014 to 10% in 2021, and the finance sector, with a share of 7.5% of GDP in 2021, are both considerable contributors to non-oil GDP. In addition, despite the low contribution, the increase in the share of the information and communication sector in GDP from 2.5% to 3.1% can be considered as an indicator of the vision prioritizing technology and innovation. These sectoral dynamics can be considered as indicators compatible with the country's national vision objectives in reducing its oil dependency and building a knowledge-based economy.[49]

Saudi Arabia

When Saudi Arabia's foreign direct investment (FDI) trends are examined, a noticeable shift becomes apparent in recent years. The country's outward FDI (FDI outflow) declined from SAR 24 billion in 2017 to SAR 17 billion in 2022, indicating a 28% decrease. In contrast, the total outward FDI stock increased by 52% during the same period, rising from SAR 502 billion to SAR 762 billion. Moreover, the share of FDI outflow in total stock decreased from 4.8% to 2.3%. These developments suggest that Saudi Arabia may have changed its investment approach, giving more importance to national priorities. In line with the goals of Vision 2030, the country seems to focus more on domestic investment, possibly using more resources to support local sectors and strengthen the national economy.[50]

Data on the contribution of economic sectors to Saudi Arabia's GDP (Fig. 1.4) shows that, despite a decrease from 47.2% in 2014 to 44.8%

[49] Federal Competitiveness and Statistics Center, https://fcsc.gov.ae/national-summary-data/ (Accessed May 23, 2025).

[50] Ministry of Investment, Saudi Arabia Foreign Direct Investment Report, January 2024, https://misa.gov.sa/.

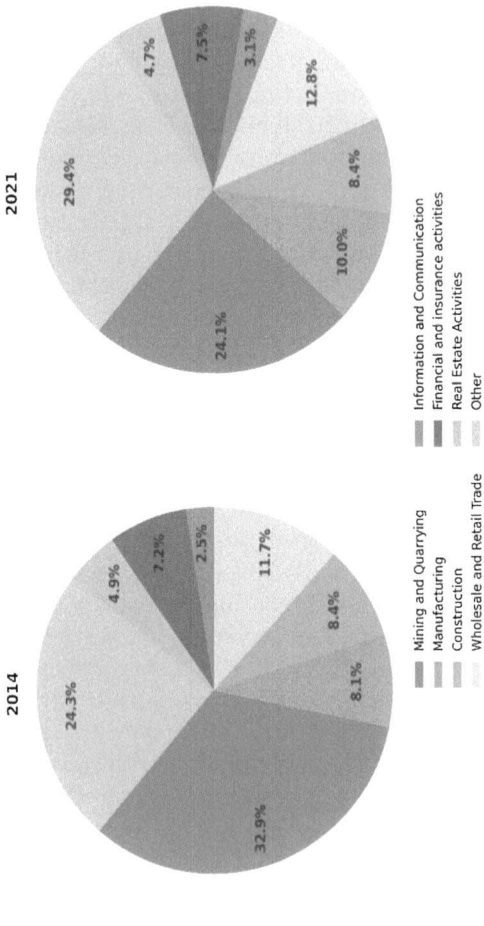

Fig. 1.3 Contribution by sectors to the UAE's GDP (%)

in 2021, there has been no significant decline in the share of the hydrocarbon sector. The service sector considerably contributes to GDP, with key subsectors such as trade, hotels, restaurants, and transportation (with a total share of approximately 11%).[51] However, according to data from 2021, the share of the finance sector accounts for only 4%. Consequently, the effects of Saudi Arabia's economic diversification efforts appear limited; the country's dependence on oil and natural gas remains significant.

Accordingly, an analysis of sectoral contributions to GDP demonstrates that the hydrocarbon sector maintains a dominant share of the economies of these countries; however, there are significant differences among these countries in terms of the extent of economic diversification achieved. In order to evaluate the process of these diversification efforts, the sectoral contribution to GDP data from 2014 to 2021 is analyzed, as the period provides the observation of mid- and long-term developments following the announcement of each country's national vision strategy. According to sectoral contribution to GDP data, the UAE, where the hydrocarbon sector accounted for only 24.1% of GDP in 2021, has a comparatively more diversified economy. Qatar, likewise, has achieved notable success in its economic diversification efforts, reducing the share of the hydrocarbon sector from 52.5% in 2014 to 36.8% in 2021. In contrast, Saudi Arabia still derived 44.8% of its GDP in 2021 from oil and gas, which indicates that the reduction of hydrocarbon dependency remains limited. In Qatar and the UAE, the financial sector plays a strategic role in economic diversification goals by significantly contributing to non-oil GDP. In addition, although the share of information and communication technologies in GDP is limited, the importance given to these areas is increasing. This general picture shows that all three countries aim to reduce hydrocarbon dependency, but the routes they follow and the levels of success they achieve differ. Qatar and the UAE are making faster progress in the transition to a diversified and innovation-focused economic structure.

[51] General Authority for Statistics (GASTAT), retrieved from Sarmad Khan, "Saudi Economy Beats Estimate with 12.2% Q2 growth on higher oil prices," The National, September 8, 2022, https://www.thenationalnews.com/business/economy/2022/09/08/saudi-economy-beats-estimates-with-122-q2-growth-on-higher-oil-prices/.

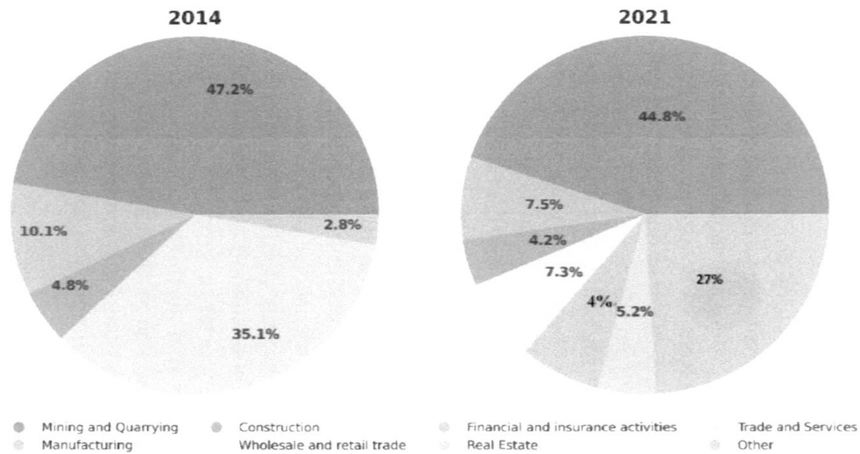

Fig. 1.4 Contribution by sectors to Saudi Arabia's GDP (%)

Conclusion

The GCC countries have increasingly seen economic diversification as a necessary strategy, given the vulnerabilities in their rentier economies. In this context, long-term national visions have identified the main goals and priorities for economic diversification. Therefore, the study aims to examine the GCC countries' investments abroad in finance and technology within the framework of their economic diversification strategies and analyse the extent to which these investments align with the long-term diversification goals of these countries.

The comparative analysis of Qatar, the UAE, and Saudi Arabia demonstrates that, despite their shared goals of decreasing reliance on hydrocarbon revenues, each country adopts distinct strategies and prioritizes different sectors. Qatar prioritizes the education, financial services, and technology and innovation sectors in line with its vision of building a knowledge-based economy, which is reflected in its selective and targeted investments abroad, in fintech. The UAE prioritizes the technology, innovation, and financial services sectors in line with its vision of becoming a global economic and digital hub, which is reflected in its broad and diversified investments abroad in the fintech sector. Saudi Arabia prioritizes the development of technology-based local companies in line with its localization strategies, which is reflected in its investments abroad in fintech sectors to enable technology transfer.

The study also examines macroeconomic indicators to evaluate the outcomes of these strategies. Analyses based on sectoral contributions to GDP suggest that Qatar and the UAE have progressed more effectively in achieving their economic diversification goals, whereas Saudi Arabia continues to rely heavily on hydrocarbon revenues. The financial sector has become increasingly important in terms of its contribution to the GDP in both Qatar and the UAE, with this trend being particularly notable in Qatar. Although still relatively low, the growing share of the information and communication technology sector in both Qatar and the UAE shows that the transition to a knowledge-based economy and digitalization has become a strategic priority.

In conclusion, the findings of the study show the growing importance of fintech investments in the economic diversification strategies of GCC countries and demonstrate that each country adopts distinct investment priorities in line with its national vision.

References

Albassam, Bassam A. "Economic Diversification in Saudi Arabia: Myth or Reality." *Resources Policy* 44 (2015): 112–117.

Alhashel, Bader. "Sovereign Wealth Funds." *International Journal of Economics and Finance* 8, no. 12 (2016): 1–12.

Almoli, Ahmed, and M. Evren Tok. "Knowledge-Based Development and Economic Diversification: The Case of Qatar." In *Economic Development in the Gulf Cooperation Council Countries*, edited by H. Miniaoui, 43–73. Cham: Springer, 2020.

Asutay, Mehmet. "GCC Sovereign Wealth Funds and Their Role in the European and American Markets." *Equilibri* 12, no. 3 (December 2008): 335–354.

Bazoobandi, Sara. *The Political Economy of the Gulf Sovereign Wealth Funds: A Case Study of Iran, Kuwait, Saudi Arabia and the United Arab Emirates.* London: Routledge, 2013.

Beblawi, Hazem, and Giacomo Luciani, eds. *The Rentier State*. London: Croom Helm, 1987.

Chen, Derek H. C., and Carl J. Dahlman. "The Knowledge Economy, the KAM Methodology and World Bank Operations." World Bank, 2006.

Crupi, Antonio, and Daniele Schilirò. "The UAE Economy and the Path to Diversification and Innovation." *International Journal of Business Management and Economic Research (IJBMER)* 14 (2023): 2286–2300.

El-Kharouf, Farouk, Sulayman Al-Qudsi, and Shifa Obeid. "The Gulf Corporation Council Sovereign Wealth Funds: Are They Instruments for Economic Diversification or Political Tools?" *Asian Economic Papers* 9, no. 1 (2010): 124–151.

Federal Competitiveness and Statistics Center. Accessed May 23, 2025. https://fcsc.gov.ae/national-summary-data/.

FinanceWorld. "Mubadala Investments Increase Abu Dhabi's IT Portfolio." August 26, 2022. Accessed March 12, 2025. https://thefinanceworld.com/mubadala-investments-increase-abu-dhabis-it-portfolio/.

Fintech Futures. "Klarna Lands $800m Funding as Valuation Cut to $6.7bn from $45.6bn Last Year." July 11, 2022. Accessed March 10, 2025. https://www.fintechfutures.com/venture-capital-funding/klarna-lands-800m-funding-as-valuation-cut-to-6-7bn-from-45-6bn-last-year.

FinTech News Network. Accessed March 10, 2025. https://fintechnews.ae/22730/abudhabi/mubadala-investment-revolut/.

Fintechnews Middle East. "500 Global Launches New MENA Tech Startup Fund." January 24, 2025. Accessed April 1, 2025. https://fintechnews.ae/23854/fintech/500-global-launches-new-mena-tech-startup-fund/. "Abu Dhabi's Mubadala Makes Its First Investment from Their US$400 Million European Fund." March 6, 2019. Accessed March 12, 2025. https://fintechnews.ae/3514/abudhabi/mubadala-wefox-insurtech/. "Saudi Arabia and

Hong Kong to Form US$1 Billion Investment Fund." November 4, 2024. Accessed April 1, 2025. https://fintechnews.ae/23114/fintech-saudi-arabia/saudi-arabia-and-hong-kong-to-form-us1-billion-investment-fund/.

Global SWF. Accessed July 2025. https://globalswf.com/.

Government Communication Office. Accessed March 2025. https://www.gco.gov.qa/en/state-of-qatar/qatar-national-vision-2030/our-story/.Gray, Matthew. *A Theory of "Late Rentierism" in the Arab States of the Gulf.* Doha: Center for International and Regional Studies, Georgetown University School of Foreign Service in Qatar, 2011.

Hubbert, M. King. "Nuclear Energy and the Fossil Fuels." Shell Development Company Publication No. 95. Paper presented at the Spring Meeting of the American Petroleum Institute, 1956.

International Working Group of Sovereign Wealth Funds (IWG). Accessed April 12, 2025. https://www.ifswf.org/what-is-a-sovereign-wealth-fund.

Kucuk, Omer Naim. "Linking Economic Diversification and Regional Investments in the Gulf: Saudi and Emirati Investment Trends in Egypt." *Insight Turkey* 26 (2024): 188.

López, Diego. "SWF 3.0: How Sovereign Wealth Funds Navigated COVID-19 and Changed Forever." *Journal of International Business Policy* 6, no. 3 (2023): 374–385.

Luciani, Giacomo. "Allocation vs. Production States: A Theoretical Framework." In *The Rentier State*, edited by Hazem Beblawi and Giacomo Luciani, 63–81. London: Croom Helm, 1987.

Megginson, William L., Xin Yue Zhou, and Robert L. Gholson. "The Case Against a US Sovereign Wealth Fund." *The Financial Review* 60, no. 1 (February 2025): 1–25.

Ministry of Investment (Saudi Arabia). *Saudi Arabia Foreign Direct Investment Report.* January 2024. https://misa.gov.sa/.

Modise, Ephraim. "Strategic Synergies: ADIA & GIC's Co-Investments and the Growing MENA–SEA Collaboration." April 2, 2025. Accessed April 5, 2025. https://magnitt.com/news/strategic-synergies-adia-gic-s-co-investments-and-the-growing-mena-sea-collaboration-53983.

Montambault Trudelle, Alexis. "Tools of Regime Stability: The Political Economy of Sovereign Wealth Funds in Gulf Rentier States." *Review of International Political Economy* 31, no. 5 (2024): 1446–1471.

Mubadala Investment Company. "Mubadala to Launch $400 Million European Tech Fund." June 13, 2018. Accessed March 10, 2025. https://www.mubadala.net/en/news/mubadala-launch-400-million-european-tech-fund.

Neffati, Mohamed, and Rafik Jbir. "The Impact of Digitalization and Economic Diversification on Economic Growth: Evidence from Saudi Arabia." *Technological and Economic Development of Economy* 30 (2024): 1508–1525.

Planning and Statistics Authority. *Third Qatar National Development Strategy 2024–2030*. Doha: General Secretariat for Development Planning, 2024. https://www.npc.qa/en/planning/nds3/Pages/default.aspx.

Qatar Investment Authority. "QIA Leads over $500 Million Strategic Growth Investment in SoFi." May 29, 2013. Accessed March 10, 2025. https://www.qia.qa/en/Newsroom/Pages/Qatar-Investment-Authority-Leads-Over-$500-Million-Strategic-Growth-Investment-in-SoFi.aspx. "QIA Takes Part in Checkout.com $1 Billion Series D Funding Round." December 1, 2022. Accessed March 10, 2025. https://www.qia.qa/en/Newsroom/Pages/QIA-takes-part-in-Checkout-com-$1-billion-Series-D-funding-round-.aspx.

Rozanov, Andrew. "Who Holds the Wealth of Nations?" *Central Banking Journal* 15, no. 4 (May 2005): 52–57.

Saudi Vision 2030. *Story of Transformation*. Accessed March 2025. https://www.vision2030.gov.sa/en/explore/story-of-transformation. *Saudi Vision 2030 Document*. Riyadh: Kingdom of Saudi Arabia, 2016, 42–51.

SoFi. "Our Story." Accessed March 10, 2025. https://www.sofi.com/our-story/.

Statista Research Department. *Statista*. December 18, 2023. https://www.statista.com/.

Trading Economics. "Brent Crude Oil." Accessed March 2025. https://tradingeconomics.com/commodity/brent-crude-oil.

Truman, Edwin M. *Sovereign Wealth Funds: Threat or Salvation?* Washington, DC: Peterson Institute for International Economics, 2010.

Ulrichsen, Kristian Coates. *The Gulf States in International Political Economy*. New York: Palgrave Macmillan, 2016.

United Arab Emirates. *UAE Foreign Direct Investments Dashboard*. Accessed May 30, 2025. https://www.moec.gov.ae/en/foreign-direct-investment-dashboard. *Vision 2021*. Accessed March 2025. https://u.ae/en/about-the-uae/strategies-initiatives-and-awards/strategies-plans-and-visions/strategies-plans-and-visions-untill-2021/vision-2021. *We the UAE 2031 Vision*. Abu Dhabi: Government of the United Arab Emirates, 2022, 29–31.

World Bank Group. "Foreign Direct Investment, Net Outflows (% of GDP)—Saudi Arabia, Qatar, United Arab Emirates." Accessed May 7, 2025. https://data.worldbank.org/indicator/BM.KLT.DINV.WD.GD.ZS?end=2023&locations=SA-QA-AE&start=2008&view=chart. *World Bank Open Data—Qatar Economic Activity by Sector*. Accessed May 7, 2025. https://www.data.gov.qa/api/explore/v2.1/catalog/datasets/economic-activity-value-added-by-sector-qatar-in-figures/exports/xlsx?lang=en&timezone=Asia%2FQatar&use_labels=true.

CHAPTER 2

The Evolution of Open Banking in the Gulf Cooperation Council Countries

Maria Casoria

Introduction

Historically, banks have been the primary providers of payment and other financial services, controlling the banking market due to their so-called "data advantage", the absence of alternatives, and the massive amount of trust most customers place in them. This was true until the advent of Open Banking, whose first appearance can be traced back to an investigation conducted in 2016 by the UK Competition and Markets Authority (CMA) that, after scrutinizing the British retail banking market, concluded that older and larger banks did not have to compete hard enough for customers' business, and smaller and newer banks found it difficult to enter or to consolidate their position in the banking market, with the result that customers had to pay more than they should have

M. Casoria (✉)
College of Law, Euro University of Bahrain, Manama, Kingdom of Bahrain
e-mail: maria.casoria3@gmail.com; maria.casoria@eub.edu.bh

K. Tsanis et al. (eds.), *Digital Finance and Transformation in the Gulf*,
https://doi.org/10.1007/978-981-92-1588-1_2

done for accessing banking services and were deprived of the possibility of benefiting from new services.[1]

Open Banking has been described in several ways, although no agreed-upon definition exists. A comprehensive definition has been provided by the Basel Committee on Banking Supervision, which in 2019 defined Open Banking as "the sharing and leveraging of customer-permissioned data by banks with third-party developers and firms to build applications and services, including for example those that provide real-time payments, greater financial transparency options for account holders, marketing and cross-selling opportunities".[2] At its core, Open Banking is disruptive, being a system that enables interoperable payment services by allowing authorized non-banking operators to access customer financial data through the use of a secure technology known as Application Programming Interface (API), to provide two main services, i.e., payment initiation services (PISs) and account information services (AISs), subject to the customer's explicit consent. Therefore, the very idea behind the uptake of Open Banking appears to be fostering greater innovation and competition in the retail banking market, leading to product diversification, more effective user control over their finances and data, broader access to financial services and, for non-business operators, increased consumer welfare.

Despite its incremental success, the reference ecosystem is not exempted from challenges, mainly connected to data protection, cybersecurity concerns, and the interoperability and standardization of the APIs required to offer Open Banking services, challenges which have not prevented the digitalization of banking and financial services from proceeding and from having a ripple effect on other industries. Indeed, after the spread of Open Banking as a consent-driven sharing of bank account customer data, new conceptual and regulatory frameworks have arisen, such as Open Finance, which extends the principles of data sharing to the entire financial sector, including mortgages, savings, pensions, insurance, and investment data, and, more recently, Open Data, a broader data sharing framework which applies the same consent and API-driven

[1] All the investigation documents can be found on the official website of the Competition and Markets Authority. https://www.gov.uk/cma-cases/review-of-banking-for-small-and-medium-sized-businesses-smes-in-the-uk.

[2] Basel Committee on Banking Supervision. (2019). *Report on open banking and application programming interfaces*. https://www.bis.org/bcbs/publ/d486.pdf.

data portability principles to a variety of industries beyond the financial sector, such as utilities, telecoms, and healthcare.[3]

After its initial debut in the UK and the subsequent swift adoption in the European Union with the entry into force of the Second Payment Services Directive, commonly known as PSD2, Open Banking has emerged in other jurisdictions outside the boundaries of the European continent, including the Gulf Cooperation Council (GCC) countries that, as a part of their national economic visions, aim at reducing the dependence on the revenue generated by the exploitation of natural resources, attracting foreign direct investment, diversifying their economies, and promoting financial stability. As a result of this process, the GCC states have embraced the digital disruption in the banking sector and are currently experiencing a dynamic shift in their financial landscape with the adoption of Open Banking, which, alongside the rapid growth of the Fintech industry, is seen as a key enabler to transform the Arabian Gulf into a hub for banking and financial services across the Middle East and North Africa (MENA) region and beyond.

In this context, the chapter provides an overview of the evolution of Open Banking across the GCC. It offers a comparative analysis of the different regulatory initiatives and national strategies implemented by the Arabian Gulf States to support their domestic economic diversification goals, in order to disseminate knowledge about the current state of the art of Open Banking in the GCC, while reflecting on the potential developments in digital banking within this key region of the world. In particular, the author describes the different initiatives undertaken by the GCC governments to promote digital transformation in the payment system, highlights the role played by the various entities operating in the Open Banking ecosystem, discusses why Open Banking services can be a driver for financial inclusion, and theorizes on the expected developments in the GCC in terms of rule of law and enforcement to mitigate the risks associated with the provision of Open Banking services in one of the wealthiest and fastest-developing regions of the world.

[3] Martins Pereira, C. (2025). The uncertain path towards open finance: mutual lessons from the United Kingdom and European Union regulatory approaches. In J. Lee & A. Darbellay (Eds.), *A research agenda for financial law and regulation* (pp. 83–112). Edward Elgar Publishing. https://doi.org/10.4337/9781803929996.00012.

Open Banking Initiatives Across the Gulf Cooperation Council Countries

In the span of almost ten years, Open Banking services have gained a foothold in various countries, although through different policy and regulatory approaches, with some governments mandating the adoption of Open Banking, others supporting the provision of Open Banking services, and a third group allowing industry-led initiatives to shape the market (Colangelo & Khandelwal, 2025).[4] As shown in the map below,[5] most jurisdictions have opted for some form of regulation, either by aligning their legal framework to the prescriptive norms set by the PSS2 or by issuing guidance and recommendations on API standards and specifications, whereas a limited number of states have endorsed a market-driven approach, by enabling data sharing between incumbents and licensed non-traditional banking operators.

[4] Colangelo, G. & Khandelwal, P. (2025). The many shades of Open Banking: a comparative analysis of rationales and models. *Internet Policy Review*, 14 (1). https://doi.org/10.14763/2025.1.1821. See also, University of Cambridge Judge Business School-Cambridge Centre for Alternative Finance. (2024). *The Global State of Open Banking and Open Finance Report*. https://www.jbs.cam.ac.uk/faculty-research/centres/alternative-finance/publications/the-global-state-of-open-banking-and-open-finance-report/.

[5] Open Banking Map. Retrieved on November 22, 2025, from https://www.openbankingmap.com/.

As for the Arab countries, in 2020, the Arab Monetary Fund (AMF) released a report clarifying that Open Banking was, for the most part, still at its early stages of development, yet it was acquiring importance in line with international standards and trends regarding digitalization in the banking sector.[6] One year later, the Arab Regional Fintech Working Group published another important study that contains a list of nine guiding principles that the Arab rulers should follow while implementing Open Banking regulatory regimes.[7] A more recent report of the AMF highlights that Arab nations are actively progressing towards the adoption of Open Banking and Open Finance, and predicts that Open Finance might play a crucial role in promoting financial inclusion in the Arab region.[8] In this scenario, the GCC countries are positioned at the forefront of the ongoing disruption in banking and finance, although the adoption of Open Banking proceeds at varying speed in line with the strategic priorities set by each of the six Arabian Gulf governments.

In the region, Bahrain has established itself as the undisputed pioneer, having been the first to develop an Open Banking-regulated framework and being the home country of the first bank in the MENA region to provide Open Banking services, i.e., the National Bank of Bahrain (NBB). The Central Bank of Bahrain (CBB) first began drafting specific rules in 2017 as a natural consequence of the Regulatory Sandbox launched by the CBB in the same year and issued Open Banking norms in December 2018 as a section of the CBB Rulebook. Such norms, which prescribe the adoption of Open Banking by all retail banks in the Kingdom and regulate Account Information Service Providers (AISPs) and Payment Information Service Providers (PISPs) as examples of "ancillary service providers", in essence, are consistent with the PSD2 and underscore the importance of preserving the security and confidentiality of customers' data in the Open Banking ecosystem.

[6] Arab Monetary Fund. (2020). *A Vision of Open Banking in the Arab World*. https://www.amf.org.ae/en/publications/guiding-principles/open-banking-vision-arab-world.

[7] Arab Regional Fintech Working Group. (2020). *Open Banking Regulatory Principles*. https://www.amf.org.ae/sites/default/files/publications/2021-12/open-banking-regulatory-principles.pdf.

[8] Arab Monetary Fund. (2023). *Guidelines for Effective Open Banking/Finance Adoptions*. https://www.amf.org.ae/sites/default/files/publications/2023-10/Guidelines%20for%20Effective%20Open%20Banking-Finance%20Adoption_0.pdf.

The following step was undertaken in October 2020, when the CBB launched the Open Banking Framework (OBF) to boost the adoption of Open Banking while ensuring a high degree of consistency in the services offered. The OBF enhanced existing procedures and standards in customer experience, security, compliance, API technical specifications, and the overarching governance framework. The following year, in September 2021, the CBB issued a circular setting the requirements for the rollout of the second phase of Open Banking, which included guidelines and standards related to sharing open data, added new business-use cases to the existing list, and set June 2022 as the deadline for the implementation of these requirements by all retail banks (Casoria, 2022).[9]

The latest advancement in the Bahraini Open Banking landscape began in March 2023, when the CBB launched a consultation to extend the scope of Open Banking offerings to legal persons, and continued in October of the same year with a second consultation about the requirements for customer consent and authentication, disclosure by retail bank licensees (Account Servicing Payment Service Providers ASPSPs) and performance reporting of AISPs and PISPs. As a result of the two consultations, the CBB Rulebook has been amended with regard to access to Open Banking services by legal entities, disclosure, reporting, API performance, and the business models of AISPs and PISPs. Moreover, retail bank licensees were asked to coordinate with the BENEFIT Company, a key digital platform to execute financial transactions throughout Bahrain, to implement additional consumer consent and authentication methods at the time of the onboarding. The licensees were also required to submit to the CBB an action plan for the implementation of the new requirements no later than 30 June 2024 since the amendments on the expansion of Open Banking services became effective on 1st September 2024, whereas the rules on reporting and disclosure entered into force on 30th September 2024.[10]

It is noteworthy to mention that, because of the CBB Regulatory Sandbox, which allows FinTech companies to test their technologically advanced solutions in a supervised environment for up to one year until

[9] Casoria, M. (2022). A Comparative Approach to Open Banking and Competition. In *Competition and Payment Services Conference Papers*, 93 (pp. 145–168). https://www.bancaditalia.it/pubblicazioni/quaderni-giuridici/2023-0093/qrg-93.pdf.

[10] Central Bank of Bahrain. (2024). *CBB Rulebook*. https://cbben.thomsonreuters.com/rulebook/open-banking26-may-2024-0.

the product is proven to be technically efficient, beneficial for consumers, and ready to be deployed in Bahrain, several startups have tested their solutions in the Bahraini Sandbox. The Kingdom now hosts important Open Banking service providers, such as Tarabut (previously, Tarabut Gateway), the first and, at the time of its establishment, largest Open Banking platform in the MENA region, which successfully built an API to connect banks and FinTechs located in Bahrain, Saudi Arabia, and the United Arab Emirates.[11]

The most recent developments in the realm of market-driven initiatives are the full Open Banking compliance for corporate APIs powered by Tarabut achieved this year by Al Baraka Islamic Bank, the first bank in Bahrain to acquire such compliance,[12] and the groundbreaking partnership between the BENEFIT Company, Tarabut, and FLOOS, that introduced the first centralized Open Banking authentication solution in Bahrain, streamlining the user experience and enhancing security while setting novel global standards in the sector of digital financial services.[13]

The analysis conducted highlights that the CBB has been instrumental in boosting Open Banking services in the Kingdom. The banking regulator continues to monitor the compliance with its rules by all retail banks, conventional and Islamic, and the authorized Third-party providers (TPPs) to ensure a holistic execution of Open Banking services in the country by all the players involved and further enhance competition, innovation, and efficiency while protecting consumers' interests and supporting the development of customer-centric solutions. Indeed, the fact that Bahrain has been an early mover in the realm of Open Banking has allowed the country to position itself at the forefront of banking and finance in the GCC, attracting a consistent number of Fintech companies to the country, which, in turn, enhanced the Kingdom's reputation as a forward-thinking market for foreign investors.

[11] Bahrain Economic Development Board. (2024, September 4). *Bahrain & Open Banking*. https://www.bahrainedb.com/bahrain-pulse/how-bahrain-is-leading-the-open-banking-revolution-in-the-middle-east.

[12] Al Baraka Islamic Bank. *Al Baraka Islamic Bank the First Bank in Bahrain to Achieve Open Banking Compliance for Corporate APIs—Powered by Tarabut*. https://albaraka.bh/en-gb/press-releases/--8b362267abe9d28887fe26218d31de37/.

[13] Tarabut. (2024, November 27). *Bahrain Leads Global Innovation in Open Banking with The BENEFIT Company, Tarabut and FLOOSS* [Press release]. https://www.tarabut.com/blogs/post/Bahrain-Leads-Global-Innovation-in-Open-Banking-with-The-BENEFIT-Company-Tarabut-and-FLOOSS.

Next in chronological order is Saudi Arabia, Bahrain's closest geographical neighbor. The country has been the second in the GCC to facilitate the adoption of Open Banking in January 2021, when the Saudi Arabian Monetary Authority (SAMA) published an Open Banking Policy (OBP),[14] as part of the Financial Sector Development Program under the Kingdom's 2030 economic vision,[15] to spur economic growth and safeguard financial and monetary stability. Earlier in August 2020, the SAMA had already issued the Payment Service Providers Regulations governing the access to data about payment accounts by AISPs and PISPs on grounds similar to those set by the PSD2, but without mandating to open an API infrastructure. In essence, the OBP provided for a three-phase approach to Open Banking, i.e., a design phase in the first half of 2021, which consisted of devising the ecosystem and defining the Open Banking governance; an implementation phase, which kicked off in the second half of 2021, devoted to the development of defined frameworks, technology building blocks, and rollout activities including testing with financial market participants and enhancement of customer awareness; and the last phase, the go-live, which began in early 2022 when Open Banking was officially launched with a focus on enabling AISs.[16] In the same year the Saudi Council of Ministers approved the National Fintech Strategy with the aim to make the Kingdom a global fintech hub to enhance the economic empowerment of individuals and the society as a whole.[17]

The implementation of Open Banking regulations has been followed by the establishment of an Open Banking Lab in January 2023,[18] which allows banks and Fintechs to collaborate in a controlled environment and, as such, facilitates the development and testing of innovative

[14] SAMA—Saudi Central Bank. (2023). *Open Banking in Saudi Arabia*. https://openbanking.sa/index-en.html.

[15] *Saudi Vision 2030—Financial Sector Development Program*. https://www.vision2030.gov.sa/en/explore/programs/financial-sector-development-program.

[16] SAMA—Saudi Central Bank (2022, February 22). *SAMA issues the Open Banking Framework* [Press release]. https://www.sama.gov.sa/en-us/news/pages/news-794.aspx.

[17] Saudi Ministry of Finance. (2022, June 22). *FSDP Launches FinTech Strategy Implementation Plan* [Press release]. https://www.mof.gov.sa/en/MediaCenter/news/Pages/news_22062022_1.aspx.

[18] SAMA—Saudi Central Bank. (2023, April 1). Saudi Central Bank Launches Open Banking Lab [Press release]. https://www.sama.gov.sa/en-US/News/Pages/news-807.aspx.

Open Banking solutions.[19] The launch of the Open Banking Lab has resulted in several benefits. Firstly, it has accelerated product development by ensuring early compliance of the Open Banking solutions with the national regulatory framework. Secondly, it has fostered collaboration between incumbent banks and Fintech companies, enhancing competition and facilitating the creation of more customer-centric products. Lastly, the fact that the Fintechs operate in a controlled environment increases consumers' confidence in the Open Banking ecosystem.

An updated Open Banking Framework was released in September 2024 focusing on PISs to enhance further the efficiency and security in the provision of digital payment services. According to the SAMA, the revised framework offers a set of guidelines and technical standards based on international best practices to facilitate the provision of Open Banking-enabled services in Saudi Arabia.[20]

In terms of market initiatives, at the time the chapter is written, eleven Open Banking applications are reported to be active in the Kingdom's evolving financial technology market, with the Bahraini-based Tarabut leading the way, but some pioneering platforms competing to offer seamless Open Banking solutions in the Saudi market.[21]

Moving to the United Arab Emirates (UAE), the implementation of a comprehensive regulatory framework for Open Banking has proceeded at a slower pace compared to Bahrain and Saudi Arabia since initially the Central Bank (CBUAE), the Dubai Financial Services Authority (DFSA) operating in the Dubai International Finance Center (DIFC), and the Financial Services Regulatory Authority (FSRA) active in the Abu Dhabi Global Market (ADGM) supported market-led endeavors which were complemented by some sectorial regulations at federal level and by a licensing system for the TPPs primarily located in the free trade areas.

[19] Tarabut. (2023, February 8). *Open Banking in Saudi Arabia: Fuelling Tech Innovation* [Press release]. https://www.tarabut.com/blogs/post/open-banking-in-saudi-arabia-fuelling-tech-innovation.

[20] SAMA—Saudi Central Bank. (2024, February 9). *SAMA announces issuance of second release of Open Banking Framework* [Press release]. https://www.sama.gov.sa/en-US/News/Pages/news-1036.aspx.

[21] Pragmatic Coders. (2025, April 11). *11 Must-Know Open Banking Apps in Saudi Arabia* [Press release]. https://www.pragmaticcoders.com/blog/11-must-know-open-banking-apps-in-saudi-arabia#tarabut-gateway.

In July 2021, for instance, the CBUAE published the Retail Payment Services and Card Schemes Regulation (RPSCS), which licensed nine categories of digital payment services in the UAE, including PISs and AISs, whose providers were given direct or indirect access to the customer data in an efficient and unhindered manner but in the context of a contractual arrangement with the banks and subject to obtaining the customer's explicit consent. The RPSCS contained also a reference to the Central Bank's vision for the adoption of Open Finance. Additionally, in November of the same year, the UAE regulatory authorities issued jointly Guidelines for Financial Institutions Adopting Enabling Technologies regulating the use of APIs for the provision of financial services, although with the disclaimer that the guidelines did not cover Open Banking services (Casoria, 2022).[22]

Despite the initial cautious approach, the UAE currently stand out as the only country in the GCC that has moved a step forward compared to their regional counterparts with the issuance in December 2023 of the Open Finance Regulation (OFR) as a section of the CBUAE Rulebook,[23] in line with the Financial Infrastructure Transformation (FIT) Program launched in February of the same year.[24] The OFR, entered into force in April 2024, includes rules for the provision of Open Banking services and sets norms for the licensing, supervision and operation of an Open Finance Framework in the UAE consisting of a trust framework, an API hub, and common infrastructural services, which provide the Open Finance licensed providers the right to access cross-sectoral sharing of data and initiate transactions on behalf of the users. The list of licensees mandated by the OFR to provide Open Finance services includes a variety of entities, such as banks incorporated in the UAE, both local and branches of foreign banks, commercial and Islamic, finance

[22] Casoria, M. (2022). A Comparative Approach to Open Banking and Competition. In *Competition and Payment Services Conference Papers*, 93 (pp. 145–168). https://www.bancaditalia.it/pubblicazioni/quaderni-giuridici/2023-0093/qrg-93.pdf.

[23] Central Bank of the United Arab Emirates. *CBUAE Rulebook*. https://rulebook.centralbank.ae/en/rulebook/open-finance-regulation.

[24] Central Bank of the United Arab Emirates. (2023, February 12). *CBUAE launches a Financial Infrastructure Transformation Programme to accelerate the digital transformation of the financial services sector* [Press release]. https://www.centralbank.ae/en/news-and-publications/news-and-insights/press-release/cbuae-launches-a-financial-infrastructure-transformation-programme-to-accelerate-the-digital-transformation-of-the-financial-services-sector/.

companies, payment services providers, crowdfunding companies, insurance brokers and companies and any other entity which the CBUAE will deem as a relevant licensee. The granting of licenses for data sharing and initiation services is conceived as a phased process and has already begun with the licensing of banks and insurance companies. This decisive shift from market-led initiatives to a broader Open Finance framework might attract more innovation to the country, given that the UAE is currently the only jurisdiction in the GCC where the principles of digitalization and market openness have expanded beyond the provision of payment-related services.

Regarding implementation initiatives, unlike the market-oriented approach which characterizes both the Bahraini and the Saudi Arabian Open Banking landscape, the UAE has opted for the establishment of a centralized, regulator-led infrastructure for Open Finance activities called AlTareq that is operated by the Central Bank subsidiary Nebras Open Finance LLC.[25] As recently announced, the Fintech company Pay10 is the first non-banking institution to be authorized to offer Open Finance services in the UAE.[26]

The latest regulatory intervention in the GCC is the one undertaken in Oman where the Central Bank (CBO) approved the Regulatory Framework for Open Banking (RFOB) in December 2024, after receiving feedback through a public consultation.[27] The adoption of the RFOB is a consequential step to the release of the Open Banking Data and Information Security Specification rules in December 2023, which established guidelines for a standardized and clear set of actionable security controls

[25] Emirates News Agency—WAM (2924, December 12). *CBUAE board approves establishment of 'Nebras Open Finance', 'Know Your Customer' platform* [Press release]. https://www.wam.ae/en/article/b6nl5sr-cbuae-board-approves-establishment-nebras-open. For an overview of the key features of the Open Finance Framework, *The Open Global Data Tracker*. Retrieved on November 22, 2025, from https://ozoneapi.com/the-global-open-data-tracker/library/cbuae/.

[26] Pincovski, C. (2025, April 24). Pay10 first to launch on UAE's regulated Open Finance infrastructure. *The Payers*. https://thepaypers.com/online-mobile-banking/pay10-first-to-launch-on-uaes-regulated-open-finance-infrastructure--1273267.

[27] For more information, see the website of the Central Bank of Oman. https://cbo.gov.om/. See also, Orme-Clayed, T. (2025, January 3). Oman's Central Bank approves regulatory framework for Open Banking. *Payment Expert*. https://paymentexpert.com/2025/01/03/omans-central-bank-open-banking; Oman News Agency. (2024, December 29). *CBO Approves Regulations for the Banking Deposits Protection Law* [Press release]. https://omannews.gov.om/topics/en/80/show/120309/.

applicable to all participants involved within Oman's Open Banking ecosystem.[28] Earlier initiatives focused on fostering the Fintech industry, since in December 2020 the CBO had established a Fintech Regulatory Sandbox, providing a controlled environment for Fintech companies to test their solutions,[29] and in November 2021, the CBO integrated the Open Banking API Strategy into its broader Fintech Framework and Roadmap, laying the groundwork for the interoperability of financial services and secure data sharing.[30]

Moving to the remaining two regional actors, Kuwait and Qatar, at the time of writing this chapter both countries are still in the process of developing their Open Banking regulations and frameworks. As for Kuwait, the Central Bank of Kuwait (CBK) in November 2018 launched a Regulatory Sandbox, which was subsequently updated in 2019 to expand the range of banking and financial products and services that can be tested, including those related to Open Banking. Information publicly available indicate that the CBK has conducted studies on the need to issue specific regulations for Open Banking and the APIs and has formed an Open Banking Working Group comprising specialists from Kuwaiti banks (Fadlallah, 2023).[31] This process culminated in the issuance of a draft Open Banking

[28] Protiviti Global Business Consulting. (2023, December 2021). *Open Banking Data and Information Security Specification—Central Bank of Oman*. https://cbo.gov.om/Documents/OPRF/CBODataandInformationSecuritySpecification.pdf.

[29] Central Bank of Oman. *CBO Fintech Regulatory Sandbox Framework* https://cbo.gov.om/sites/assets/Documents/English/Fintech/FRSProposalFramework.pdf; Omani Financial Services Authority. *Co- Regulatory Sandbox* https://fsa.gov.om/home/PublicPage/Introduction.

[30] Central Bank of Oman. *Fintech* https://cbo.gov.om/Pages/FinTech.aspx; LexisNexis Middle East. (2023, September 29). *Oman: Central Bank Announces Fintech Roadmap* https://www.lexismiddleeast.com/news/2023-10-02_39.

[31] Fadlallah, H. (2023). Fintech's Financial Products and Regulatory Sandbox. *Kilaw Journal*, 11(4), 31–57. Additional information on the status of the art in Kuwait can be found in *The Global Open Data Tracker*. Retrieved on November 22, 2025, from https://ozoneapi.com/the-global-open-data-tracker/atlas/kuwait/; Handoush, O. Kuwait's Fintech Regulation: A work in progress. *Al Tamimi & Co Law Update*. https://www.tamimi.com/law-update-articles/kuwaits-fintech-regulation-a-work-in-progress/; Pathe, T. (2022, November 25). Central Bank of Kuwait's Regulatory Sandbox to Prioritise ESG Products. *The Fintech Times*. https://thefintechtimes.com/central-bank-of-kuwaits-regulatory-sandbox-to-prioritise-esg-products/; Al-Haroon, B. (2022, August 26). Kuwait to Test an Open Banking Product Within the Fintech Regulatory Sandbox. *Fintech News Middle East*. https://fintechnews.ae/12986/kuwait/kuwait-to-test-an-open-banking-product-within-the-fintech-regulatory-sandbox/.

Regulatory Framework (OBRF) in June of this year, [32] which sets regulatory, supervisory, security, technical, and operational standards for the provision of Open Banking services in the country, in line with best international practices. According to CBK's declarations contained in the press release accompanying the publication of the draft regulations, the OBFR aims to create an infrastructure that enables cooperation between banks and Fintech firms to boost the banking and financial sector and enhance the quality of the services offered to foster the national economy and promote digitalization in line with the "New Kuwait 2035" vision.[33]

Lastly, in Qatar the Central Bank (QCB) has put in place a National Fintech Strategy in 2023, which defines a clear framework for modernizing the financial sector in the state and refers to Open Banking services.[34] According to news publicly available, a specific Open Banking framework should be released by the QCB in 2026.[35] The absence of sectorial regulations has not stopped market-driven initiatives, since the Qatar National Bank (QNB) has taken the lead role by launching its Open Banking platform in 2022, becoming the first bank in the country to offer

[32] Central Bank of Kuwait. *Open Banking*. https://www.cbk.gov.kw/en/supervision/open-banking#:~:text=The%20Open%20Banking%20Regulatory%20Framework,Open%20Banking%20Service%20Providers%20licensed.

[33] Central Bank of Kuwait (2025, June 4). *CBK Issues Draft Open Banking Regulatory Framework* [Press release]. https://www.cbk.gov.kw/en/cbk-news/announcements-and-press-releases/press-releases/2025/06/202506040800-cbk-issues-draft-open-banking-regulatory-framework#:~:text=The%20CBK%20statement%20also%20pointed,promote%20the%20national%20economy%20and.

[34] Qatar Central Bank. *Summary of Fintech Sector Strategy in the State of Qatar*. https://www.qcb.gov.qa/Documents/SuperVision/FENTECHStrategy_EN.pdf.

[35] Fintech on the Rise in Qatar Driven by Increased Adoption of Digital Payments and Strong Government Initiatives (2025, March 24). https://fintechnews.ae/25410/qatar/fintech-on-the-rise-in-qatar-driven-by-increased-adoption-of-digital-payments-and-strong-government-initiatives/#:~:text=Another%20key%20national%20plan%20is,in%20a%20knowledge%2Dbased%20economy.

such services.[36] Additionally, in May 2024, the QNB expanded its offerings by making available to its corporate clients APIs tailored explicitly for their needs.[37]

Despite the steps made towards the establishment of a fully-fledged Open Banking ecosystem, the delayed adoption of a regulatory framework compared to the other regional actors may produce a negative impact on the Qatari banking and financial sector both in terms of decreased competitiveness, since the fact that banking operators predominantly dominate the market and, as a result, product diversification and innovation are limited can act as a deterrent for international Fintech investment, and financial inclusion, given that the almost exclusive reliance on conventional banking operators may prevent access to credit facilities for both vulnerable individuals and Small and Medium-sized Enterprises (SMEs).

The analysis conducted demonstrates that all GCC countries are progressively joining the global wave of digital disruption in banking and finance, albeit at different speeds, as a way to achieve some of the economic diversification goals outlined in their respective national visions and to stimulate economic growth. As regulatory strategies continue to evolve, one item that could be on the agenda of the GCC is the feasibility of establishing a harmonized legal framework for Open Banking, and potentially for Open Finance, at the regional level. Such a framework could enhance their ability to compete with other regions, like the European Union, where the implementation of transnational regulations for the provision of payment services has accelerated the transformation of the retail banking market (Colangelo, 2024; Polasik, 2024).[38]

The adoption of a unified GCC-wide approach to regulating banking and financial services could facilitate the placement of the GCC as a leader

[36] Qatar National Bank (2022, June 16*). QNB the first bank in Qatar to launch Open Banking platform for clients and FinTechs* [Press release] https://www.qnb.com/sites/qnb/qnbglobal/en/ennews16june-news.

[37] Qatar National Bank (2024, May 1). *QNB Unveils Qatar's First Open Banking API for Corporate Clients* [Press release] https://www.qnb.com/sites/qnb/qnbglobal/en/en1may2024news.

[38] Polasik, M et al. (2024). Evaluating the regulatory approach to Open Banking in Europe: An Empirical Study. *Financial Law Review*, 34(2), 59–90. https://doi.org/10.4467/22996834FLR.24.007.20612. Colangelo, G. (2024). Open Banking goes to Washington: Lessons from the EU on regulatory-driven data sharing regimes. *Computer Law & Security Review*, 54, 106–018.

in global financial innovation. However, the implementation of a supranational regulatory framework is not exempt from challenges, mainly due to the fact that the various countries are proceeding at a different pace in the establishment of their national frameworks and have adopted divergent strategies, regulation-led *versus* market-driven, to enable the provision of Open Banking products. Additional difficulties arise from the varying technological maturity and readiness of the incumbent banks in the region, which may make it difficult to ensure the required interoperability standards for the APIs that all incumbents and TPPs shall use to offer Open Banking services. Lastly, the existence of divergent laws in areas interlinked with the operation of Open Banking, such as privacy and cybersecurity, constitutes another obstacle to the establishment of a harmonized system for digitalized banking and finance in the Arabian Gulf.

The Role of the Various Entities Operating in the GCC Open Banking Ecosystem

The success of Open Banking in various countries across the globe is intertwined with the degree of participation of the banks in the transformation process triggered by allowing non-banking institutions to offer payment services and is also linked to the involvement of the banks in the regulatory process (Akyildirim et al., 2025).[39] In addition to the incumbent banks, other entities contribute to shaping the ecosystem, in particular Fintechs, BigTechs, and the regulators. One feature of the GCC Open Banking market is that it is significantly influenced by the Fintech industry

[39] Akyildirim, E. et al. (2025). Global perspectives on open banking: Regulatory impacts and market response. *Journal of International Financial Markets, Institutions & Money*, 101(6), 102–159. https://doi.org/10.1016/j.intfin.2025.102159.

(Khan et al., 2023),[40] whereas, unlike other jurisdictions where their presence is becoming concerning, Bigtech companies have not made their appearance yet (Casoria, 2023).[41]

The Gulf states have used national Fintech strategies and the establishment of Fintech regulatory sandboxes as the passepartout to open the market of payment services to non-traditional banking operators and facilitate innovation in the broader financial market, which might explain why some of these countries are shifting more rapidly than others outside the GCC towards the adoption of Open Finance frameworks. In fact, the Open Banking market and the Fintech industry are in a symbiotic relationship rather than in competition to offer innovative payment solutions, differing from what is witnessed in some states beyond the borders of the Arabian Gulf. Fintechs, particularly in the form of startups, are frontrunners in the race to offer advanced financial products and services, which range from sophisticated personal financial management applications to innovative digital payments and lending platforms alternative to the incumbents (Bi, 2025).[42] Their technological focus, combined with the APIs infrastructure provided by Open Banking, is seen as the key to enhance consumers' experience and lead transformation, with the Open Banking payments volume expected to reach over $930 billion by 2028 in the GCC.[43]

Regarding the banks, the Open Banking revolution is transforming them from custodians of customer data to facilitators of innovation in banking and finance. Since Open Banking paves the way to an increased level of competition in a market for a long time reserved for a selected few, the banks are compelled to rethink their traditional business approach

[40] Hussain Khan, H. et al. (2023). Fintech adoption, the regulatory environment and bank stability: An empirical investigation from GCC economies. *Borsa Istanbul Review* 23,1263–1281. https://doi.org/10.1016/j.bir.2023.10.010.

[41] Casoria, M. (2023). Untangling the Knots of Open Banking and Competition in the EU: BigTechs, Financial Intermediation, and Beyond. In A. Palmieri & G. Versaci (Eds.), *European Legal Strategies for payment systems in the Open Banking Age, Book series of the Department of Law of the University of Siena* (pp. 51–69). Edizioni Scientifiche Italiane.

[42] Bi, R. et al. (2025). Digital Transformation in the Gulf Cooperation Council Economies. *International Monetary Fund Departmental Papers*. https://doi.org/10.5089/9798400291449.087.

[43] Open Banking Fuels GCC Fintech Boom as UAE and Saudi Lead (2025, January 24). *Finance World*. https://thefinanceworld.com/open-banking-fuels-gcc-fintech-boom-as-uae-and-saudi-lead/.

and face an unprecedented scenario in the banking sector, namely, competition for the market between heterogeneous players (Camilleri, 2023).[44]

In order to reinvent themselves and stay competitive, one of the options is for the incumbents to invest heavily in research and development and leverage their access to broader customer data to offer digital payment solutions and personalized financial management applications that aggregate data from various accounts to provide users with comprehensive tools to see and manage their finances, refine credit-scoring models for more accurate risk assessment for clients with limited credit history, and develop new business models such as “Banking-as-a-Service” and “Banking-as-a-Product”, also referred to as “beyond banking strategy” (Martinez Resano, 2021).[45] An alternative tactic to retain customer base without considerable investments in technologically advanced infrastructures is for the banks to establish partnerships with Fintech companies due to their Artificial Intelligence (AI), machine learning, and analytics capabilities, partnerships which are beneficial not only for the incumbents but also for the Fintechs. Indeed, by working alongside banks, Fintech companies are able to remedy their lack of regulatory expertise, mitigate the burden of compliance with the banking regulations, and reduce the distrust towards not-banks circulating among the customers.

The reliance on the Fintech industry appears to be the preferred option of the banks in the GCC that, unlike banking institutions in more developed economies, are responding with minimal reservations to Open Banking initiatives seen as a way to enhance their services via the co-creation of cutting-edge solutions, such as digital wallets, buy-now-pay-later offerings, and products conceived specifically for corporate users—and maintain customer loyalty in an increasingly competitive market,

[44] Camilleri, E. (2023). "Banks as Platforms versus Platforms as Banks." In A. Palmieri & G. Versaci (Eds.), *European Legal Strategies for payment systems in the Open Banking Age, Book series of the Department of Law of the University of Siena* (pp. 31–50). Edizioni Scientifiche Italiane.

[45] Martinez Resano, J.R. (2021). Regulating for Competition with BigTechs: Banking as a Service and “Beyond Banking. *Financial Stability Review*, 41, 105–138.

while potentially expanding their revenue streams and reaching previously underserved customers through secured APIs (Khadige, 2024).[46]

Open Banking is praised by many due to its virtues for the entire banking and financial system, such as product innovation and diversification, increased digitalization, and enhanced competition in the retail banking market, and also because it benefits consumers and businesses by providing them with a wider range of offerings, such as more efficient and simplified payment services, usually at a lower cost, a more tailored banking experience, greater control over their financial data, real-time financial insights, and improved access to credit facilities, just to name a few. However, the adoption of Open Banking poses a series of challenges, mainly connected to data protection and cybersecurity concerns due to the sensitivity of financial data and the interoperability and standardization of the APIs required for accessing data, core input in Open Banking, and offering payment and related services (Frei, 2023).[47] Moreover, the presence of Fintechs in the banking and financial sectors has the potential to change how these markets function radically, and, thus, how to open the market to new entrants while ensuring financial stability has become a significant concern.

To overcome these challenges, the role of regulatory bodies, policymakers, and enforcement agencies is of paramount importance, since establishing sound legal frameworks and ensuring compliance appears to be the key strategy to mitigate risks, build user trust, facilitate data exchange, enable service integration, and boost the adoption of Open Banking services while preserving the resilience of the banking and financial system (Babina, 2025).[48]

As it can be inferred from the previous overview of the GCC Open Banking initiatives, in the region the central banks and other public authorities have played a pivotal role in establishing the Open Banking

[46] Khadige, A. et al. (2024, July 28). Open banking is a rich opportunity for GCC incumbent banks. *Finance Middle East*. https://www.financemiddleeast.com/banking-and-insurance/open-banking-is-a-rich-opportunity-for-gcc-incumbent-banks/.

[47] Frei, C. (2023). Open Banking: Opportunities and Risks. In T. Walker et al. (Eds.), *The Fintech Disruption: How Financial Innovation Is Transforming the Banking Industry* (pp. 167–189). Palgrave Macmillan.

[48] Babina, T. (2025). Customer data access and fintech entry: Early evidence from open banking. *Journal of financial economics*, 169. https://doi.org/10.1016/j.jfineco.2024.103950.

ecosystems, unlike other regional blocks, such as the European Union, where the driving force behind the implementation of Open Banking has been legislation. In particular, the GCC central banks have mandated the adoption of Open Banking services, usually after the creation of regulatory sandboxes where the banks and Fintechs have the opportunity to test their products and services in a controlled environment before launching them to the public to mitigate the risks related to threatening the financial stability of the GCC economies, have issued sectorial regulations facilitating data sharing to uphold innovation, and have set technical standards and guidelines to protect consumers and businesses in addition to performing monitoring and supervisory roles to ensure continuous compliance. Like in other jurisdictions where Open Banking has consolidated, the core issue the GCC regulators have to deal with is how to find an equilibrium between competing goals, since while it is undeniable that Open Banking contributes to enhancing competition and fostering innovation for the benefit of consumers and the well-functioning of the markets in line with the national economic visions, guaranteeing financial stability, ensuring data security, preventing cybersecurity threats, and maintaining compliance constitute critical aspects which require regulatory oversight and coordination between the legislators and the various competent authorities.

Open Banking Services as a Leverage for Financial Inclusion

A World Bank report published in 2020 found that Open Banking can produce potential advantages for people with low incomes around the world and those underserved by the existing financial providers; the report also stated that it was anticipated that by opening the retail banking market to new entrants, Open Banking would render the market more transparent and ensure that products best suited for the unbanked and poorer segments of the society would be developed (Plaitakis & Staschen, 2020).[49] From this perspective, Open Banking has the ability to promote the upgrade of the existing banking and financial offerings in both emerging and developed economies and, in doing so, promises to

[49] Plaitakis, A & Staschen, S. (2020). Open Banking: How to Design for Financial Inclusion. *World Bank—Consultative Group to Assist the Poor Working Paper.*

deliver greater financial inclusion, that is to say, allow everyone to receive formal financial services at affordable costs (Al Rifai & Albaker, 2025).[50]

Open Banking fosters financial inclusion by enabling every individual, also those who are unbanked or underbanked, and the micro, small and medium enterprises (MSMEs), to access a broader range of products and services, such as digital payments, customized financial management tools and similar solutions with the assurance of an enhanced and secure customer experience easily when sharing data, the user's most critical asset. In particular, for individuals, Open Banking simplifies the process of opening bank accounts, as it allows banking and financial institutions to use a wider set of data for identity verification and Know Your Customer procedures, moving away from sole reliance on traditional manual documentation. Another improved service concerns the access to borrowing for people with limited and no credit history since Open Banking helps develop credit scoring models that go beyond the traditional credit history, enabling banks and financial organizations to utilize alternative data to understand the individual's financial behavior, such as rent payments, utility payments, mobile top-ups, and spending habits. For the MSMEs, Open Banking is beneficial because it enables them to manage their finances more efficiently and gain better insights into their financial data and trends. Additionally, it simplifies the payment processing via direct account access, and it facilitates access to capital for growth and expansion since, through APIs, lenders can assess more easily the MSMEs' creditworthiness.[51]

A review of the statistics on financial inclusion across 22 Arab countries reveals that about 64 percent of the adult population lacked a bank or a similar financial account in 2021, with significant variation in such percentage between the different countries and with women being disproportionately disadvantaged in terms of holding a bank account or using mobile money services. People with disabilities face even more challenges and barriers due to physical and digital inaccessibility, limited

[50] Al Rifai, M. & Al Baker, Y. (2025). The Role of Financial Technology in Enhancing Financial Inclusion: A Regulatory Perspective on Current Industry Trends. *Corporate & Business Strategy Review*, 6(1), 43–52. https://doi.org/10.22495/cbsrv6i1art4.

[51] Tarabut (2023, May 17). *How Open Banking is a Key Driver of Financial Inclusion in MENA* [Press release]. https://www.tarabut.com/blogs/post/open-banking-key-driver-financial-inclusion-mena#:~:text=Thanks%20to%20open%20banking%2C%20bank s,right%20products%20for%20their%20needs.

financial literacy and the absence of appropriate support and regulatory frameworks. Similarly, small businesses encounter difficulties in receiving loans or lines of credit due to high borrowing costs, limited access to bank branches, prevalence of informal credit operations and the perception that small businesses are high-risk borrowers. In this context, Open Banking can become a catalyst for broader financial inclusion by enabling online services, such as digital wallets, to facilitate payments beyond traditional banking networks. Indeed, financial institutions in the whole Arab region, banks and non-banking operators alike have already undertaken a series of initiatives to expand financial inclusion beyond payments, such as developing mobile applications to facilitate access to banking services and tailoring credit, savings, and insurance offerings to the needs of underserved segments of the individuals and corporate entities.

Policymakers have also attempted to improve the situation, with some Arab countries taking the lead by implementing national financial inclusion strategies conceived to enhance access to financial products and services for underserved groups (Jales & Dimassi, 2025).[52] At the regional level, the Council of Arab Central Bank and Monetary Authorities Governors have launched the Financial Inclusion for the Arab Region Initiative (FIARI) which, with the support of the Arab Monetary Fund, the Deutsche Gesellschaft für Internationale Zusammenarbeit (GIZ) GmbH, the Alliance for Financial Inclusion, and the World Bank, seeks to empower policymakers and regulators to improve the accessibility, usage, and quality of responsible financial services for the unbanked and financially underserved Arab societies.[53]

In comparison to the persistent financial exclusion in the broader Arab region, the GCC countries are in a significantly better position, being high-income economies, and they are emerging as leaders in the digital finance sector, a driving force behind financial inclusion. Embracing digitalization in the banking sector has also allowed the banks in the region to remain resilient, improve operational efficiency, reduce transaction costs, expand their customer base, and drive innovation (Bi, 2025).[54]

[52] Jales, M & Sabbidin Dimassi, H. (2025). *Annual SDG Review 2025. Financial Inclusion in the Arab Region*, ESCWA.

[53] For more information, see the website of the Arab Monetary Fund https://www.amf.org.ae/en/fiari.

[54] Bi, R. et al. (2025). Digital Transformation in the Gulf Cooperation Council Economies. *International Monetary Fund Departmental Papers*.

As reported in the ESCWA Financial Inclusiveness Index dated 2023, among the Arabian Gulf states, Saudia Arabia is a frontrunner being the only country with relatively high scores for both access to and usage of financial services, although some observe that the degree of financial inclusion in the Kingdom is relatively low compared to other high-income economies for both individuals and SMEs (Khan & Alhadi, 2022).[55] Other statistics show that in the Arabian Gulf, the UAE is a frontrunner for digitalization and financial inclusion, with 84% of the adult population reportedly having a bank account and 48.5% using online banking[56]; these results have been facilitated by the FIT Program, which aims at accelerating the digital transformation process in financial services through nine key initiatives, one of which is represented by digital payment infrastructures and services. Once the Program is fully integrated, it will drive financial inclusion, promote payment innovation, security and efficiency, and achieve a cashless society.[57] The Omani government has implemented programs like "Sanad", to provide financial support to low-income families, and "Khazna" which makes available a microfinance scheme (Aggarwal et al., 2024).[58] Recent data on financial inclusion in Kuwait could not be found, since the most updated public information on the financial inclusion performance in the state are those contained in the World Bank Global Findex database dated 2017, which provides insight into how adults in more than 140 economies access accounts, make payments, save, borrow, and manage risk.[59]

[55] Khan, S. & Alhadi, F.A. (2022). Fintech and Financial Inclusion in Saudi Arabia. *Review of Economics and Finance*, 20(1), 857–866. https://doi.org/10.55365/1923.x2022.20.97.

[56] Arab Monetary Fund. (2023). *Guidelines for Effective Open Banking/Finance Adoptions*. https://www.amf.org.ae/sites/default/files/publications/2023-10/Guidelines%20for%20Effective%20Open%20Banking-Finance%20Adoption_0.pdf.

[57] Central Bank of the United Arab Emirates. (2023, February 12). *CBUAE launches a Financial Infrastructure Transformation Programme to accelerate the digital transformation of the financial services sector* [Press release]. https://www.centralbank.ae/en/news-and-publications/news-and-insights/press-release/cbuae-launches-a-financial-infrastructure-transformation-programme-to-accelerate-the-digital-transformation-of-the-financial-services-sector/.

[58] Aggarwal, G et al. (2024). Empowering Financial Inclusion in Oman: Leveraging FinTech for Future Economic Prosperity. *Global Scientific and Academic Research Journal of Economics, Business and Management*, 3(9), 19–25.

[59] Perez-Falcon, N. (2021). Financial Inclusion and Financial Literacy in Kuwait, *Institute of Banking Studies Kuwait Report*.

Despite these initiatives, some argue that simply extending access to digital payments is insufficient to enhance financial inclusion and that complementary financial inclusion policies regulating the usage dimension of digital payment solutions by end consumers, i.e., extending access to saving and borrowing, along with digital payroll practices for both private and public enterprises, are necessary to effectively boost inclusion within the GCC economy (Niankara, 2023).[60] In the region, Qatar is currently the only country to have implemented, since 2018, a National Financial Inclusion and Financial Literacy Strategy in line with Qatar National Vision 2030 and the objectives of the National Development Strategy,[61] which might constitute an additional reason to expedite the adoption of a comprehensive Open Banking framework.

In terms of implementation, banks in Saudi Arabia, Bahrain and Oman have been instructed by the respective central banks to specify in their strategic plans the percentage of loans reserved for small and medium-sized- enterprises, which are vital for the economic growth of these countries (Jales & Dimassi, 2025).[62] Moreover, Bahrain stands out for various initiatives undertaken by both banks and companies. Among such initiatives, the most commonly known and utilized is the application "Benefit Pay", which is a leading example of achieving financial inclusion for all since this app allows any organization in the Kingdom and any individual residing in Bahrain, both locals and foreigners, to perform a series of payment transactions, such as payments for purchases, peer-to-peer transfers, small instant payment, donations, payments to governmental and corporate entities, and equivalent transactions. Financial inclusion in the country is not limited to payments but expands to the larger fintech ecosystem, with several startups offering innovative financial services.[63]

Open Banking is widely seen as revolutionary for many reasons, and the provision of financial services to individuals and corporate entities in a vulnerable position because of age, income, geographical location,

[60] Niankara, I. (2023). The impact of financial inclusion on digital payment solution uptake within the Gulf Cooperation Council Economies. *International Journal of Innovation Studies*, 7, 1–17. https://doi.org/10.1016/j.ijis.2022.09.004.

[61] For more details, see the official website of the Qatar Financial Centre Regulatory Authority, https://www.qfcra.com/website-accessibility/.

[62] Jales, M & Sabbidin Dimassi, H. (2025). *Annual SDG Review 2025. Financial Inclusion in the Arab Region*, ESCWA.

[63] Bahrain FinTech Bay (2025). *Bahrain Fintech Ecosystem Report.*

gender, level of literacy, access to banking facilities, low or inexistent credit history is the most noble, but certainly not the immediate reason which triggers the vast amount of investments required for the development of APIs and the other innovative infrastructures needed to open the market of retail banking services. Open Banking contributes differently to enhancing financial inclusion in high-income economies, like the Arabian Gulf nations, in comparison with the wider Arab region. Indeed, while in the latter, the provision of digitalized banking solutions with less stringent requirements than those enforced by the banking institutions allows vulnerable individuals and corporate entities to access banking services they would already be deprived of, in the GCC nations, Open Banking constitutes an upgrade of the banking experience most individuals can already benefit from. In fact, although the GCC countries are progressing at different speeds to fill the gap between banked and unbanked individuals, most of them have implemented policy or industry-led initiatives to establish a more inclusive finance for all. Open Banking services represent only the first step towards a broader equal access to innovative payment services, savings and borrowing for all sections of the society; yet, considering that the Fintech industry is booming in most Gulf countries as a result of their economic diversification efforts, achieving more inclusivity in banking and finance is a realistic goal that can be reached through governmental policy interventions upholding the social benefits of the advancements in financial technology.

The Way Forward: Policy and Enforcement Developments in the GCC Open Banking Revolution

Riding the wave of the worldwide paradigm-shifting moment for the banking and financial sectors caused by the use of new technologies to offer digital payment services and bespoke innovative financial products, Open Banking is spreading across the Arabian Gulf countries largely because it is perceived as a means to enhance efficiency, consumer welfare and competitiveness, thereby generating new revenue streams in line with the national economic visions and boosting prosperity. The GCC countries have adopted somewhat divergent approaches towards the implementation of Open Banking solutions with Bahrain and Saudi Arabia preferring the implementation of a regulator-led comprehensive framework, Oman and Kuwait both at the early stages of regulating the provision of Open Banking services and the UAE and Qatar placed at the opposite pole, with the former being a regional frontrunner with its Open Finance Framework and the latter positioned as the final player due to the lag in the issuance of ad hoc regulations.

Despite the absence of a harmonized framework at the regional level, which has led each state to implement its recipe for Open Banking through regulations, guidelines, and market-led practices, all the stakeholders involved in shaping the ecosystem recognize that opening the banking and financial market to entities other than the incumbent banks is crucial for the implementation of their economic diversification strategies being leverage for captivating the interest of investors, both foreign and local. Indeed, the growth of the Fintech industry, fueled by the provision of Open Banking services, is attracting significant venture capital and private equity investments to the GCC, further accelerating the development of advanced financial solutions. Moreover, since the SMEs are the backbone of the GCC business landscape, the availability of more efficient services in support of capital growth and business endeavors represents a transformative opportunity for the regional economy.

Each of the economic operators involved in the Open Banking revolution in the Arabian Gulf has a different, but equally critical, role to play. The regulators shall endeavor to create a set of rules protective of the interests of all parties involved, while ensuring not to restrain innovation with overly demanding requirements; the banks are called to reinvent their business models to cope with the technological advancement and remain competitive, especially if they want to embark on cross-regional transactions; the fintechs, challenged by regulatory compliance requirements while having to develop innovative products to enter a market which has historically been very concentrated.

While the ongoing technological disruption has already changed the way banking institutions operate and serve their customers, the GCC Open Banking outlook is poised for further evolution due to emerging trends expected to impact the banking and financial markets. The first of these trends is the shift to Open Finance, which expands the principles of market openness underpinning Open Banking beyond traditional banking services to include products such as investments, pension funds, and insurance. Although, at the moment, the UAE is the only country in the Arabian Gulf block to have implemented regulations in the field, it is likely that in line with the domino effect which led the other governments to follow the Bahraini's lead on Open Banking, the other GCC policymakers will also embrace the movement towards a more holistic approach to financial services enabled by technology. A second critical development is the much-anticipated integration of AI with Open Banking to enhance customer service and improve operational efficiency by offering even more advanced products and services, such as AI-powered decision-making, better fraud detection and risk assessment against cybersecurity threats, enhanced data protection, real-time more tailored advisory services via chatbots and virtual assistants. The implications of developing AI-supported API frameworks will be the focus of future research on the topic.

To fully realize the capability of Open Banking, policymakers should focus on developing a comprehensive regulatory landscape that strikes a balance between fostering innovation in banking and finance and enhancing customers' welfare and financial inclusion. As more Gulf states adopt Open Banking regulations, regional cooperation in this field becomes desirable, despite its practical difficulties, to better align domestic regulatory approaches with international standards and facilitate maximized financial integration and interoperability within the GCC. This would lower the costs of cross-border payments, facilitate intra-regional transactions, and create a more interconnected ecosystem, thereby strengthening the GCC's position in the global arena and supporting its aspiration to emerge as a leader in the financial industry.

Regulatory initiatives alone might not be sufficient to fulfill the promises and the perils of Open Banking due to the competing goals which shape the inner nature of the ecosystem. Effective enforcement measures should also be implemented in cooperation among the various actors involved, namely central banks, data protection authorities, financial bodies, competition authorities, and industry operators, like banks and Fintechs, which should all proactively engage in this new era in banking and finance to bridge the gap between the economic interests behind investing in the necessary technological infrastructure to develop profitable and innovative Open Banking solutions and the need to protect consumers and businesses in the GCC market and meet their changing needs. Indeed, upholding the highest standards of security and compliance in all aspects of product and service deployment is crucial for building user trust in the system and encouraging wider adoption of reliable Open Banking services.

In conclusion, while the future of a technology-driven banking and finance framework that accommodates various economic operators is uncertain, Open Banking presents significant potential for the GCC to establish a more competitive, efficient, and inclusive financial landscape. By addressing current challenges and implementing strategic initiatives that align with international best practices, the Arabian Gulf can fully leverage Open Banking to stimulate economic growth, encourage innovation, and enhance the financial well-being of its citizens and businesses under the motto: "Let the user be in control" (Table 2.1).

Table 2.1 Open banking implementation timeline in the GCC

Country	*Key milestones with timeline*	*Implementation status*
Bahrain	**December 2018:** Central Bank of Bahrain (CBB) mandated Open Banking for all retail banks **October 2020:** Open Banking Framework launched **September 2021:** Rollout second phase of Open Banking **September 2024:** Expansion of the Open Banking framework with the introduction of implementation requirements	Pioneer in Open Banking/Fully operational framework
Saudi Arabia	**January 2021:** Saudi Central Bank (SAMA) released the Open Banking Policy **Early 2022:** Open Banking launched **January 2023:** SAMA launched the Open Banking Lab for testing **September 2024:** Updated Open Banking Framework released	Open Banking Framework Issued/ Advanced implementation
United Arab Emirates	**2021–2022:** Central Bank of the UAE (CBUAE) published sectorial regulations, while Open Banking is market-driven **February 2023:** Financial Infrastructure Transformation Program, including Open Finance, published **December 2023:** Open Finance Regulation (OFR) issued **April 2024:** OFR entered into force	Pioneer in Open Finance/ Framework under development

(continued)

Table 2.1 (continued)

Country	*Key milestones with timeline*	*Implementation status*
Oman	**December 2023:** Central Bank of Oman (CBO) issued Open Banking Data and Information Security Specifications rules **July 2024:** A draft Regulatory Framework for Open Banking (RFOB) released for public consultation **December 2024:** RFOB approved	Latest to issue an Open Banking Framework/ Implementation under development
Kuwait	**2023–2025:** The Central Bank of Kuwait (CBK) conducted studies on Open Banking and established an Open Banking Working Group **June 2025:** A draft of its Open Banking Regulatory Framework (OBRF) released for public consultation	Draft Open Banking Regulatory Framework issued/Early stage
Qatar	**2022:** Qatar National Bank (QNB) was the first to announce the launch of an Open Banking platform **May 2024:** QNB launched live Open Banking APIs for corporate clients **2026 (Expected):** QCB is scheduled to release a formal Open Banking Framework	Open Banking Framework not issued yet/Early stage

This table summarizes the key regulatory milestones in the implementation of Open Banking frameworks across the six GCC countries.

CHAPTER 3

Innovating Finance in the GCC: Open Banking, Metaverse, and Lessons from the Insha Case

Zhamal Nanaeva

Introduction

The Gulf Cooperation Council (GCC) has positioned itself as a leader in global digital transformation. Their strategic visions are closely aligned with the advancement in financial technology (fintech) and artificial intelligence (AI). National strategies across the region, such as Saudi Arabia's Vision 2030 and Qatar's Vision 2030, and the UAE Digital Economy Strategy, identify these technologies as crucial for long-term economic development, innovation, diversification, and advancement of sustainable digital landscapes. The increasing public and private investments in the fintech market, which is expected to surpass $3 billion by 2025, support the ambitious plans of regional governments (GCC Fintech Report 2024). Open banking emerges as one of the key components of financial sector transformation in the GCC.

Z. Nanaeva (✉)
Nordic Center for Islamic Economy and Finance, Tallinn, Estonia
e-mail: zhamal.nanaeva@ncief.org

K. Tsanis et al. (eds.), *Digital Finance and Transformation in the Gulf*,
https://doi.org/10.1007/978-981-92-1588-1_3

Over the last decade, open banking has gained increasing popularity, with the United Kingdom (UK) and the European Union (EU) serving as pioneers in its introduction. The UK reported reaching over 11.7 million active users of open banking and generating £4.1 billion in its growing ecosystem by May 2025 (International Banker 2025). This success confirms the potential of open banking to promote innovation, competition, and diversification of financial services.

The rapid advancement of fintech companies and digitalization of financial services have disrupted existing banking systems, providing more affordable, efficient, and customized services. Historically, traditional banks have maintained control over financial data of their customers, leveraging this dominance. Open banking grants customers ownership of their financial data, encouraging or requiring banks to share it with third-party financial service providers (TPPs) in a safe and secure manner. This data-sharing facilitates the advancement of fintech companies, enhancing the quality of financial services, improving operational efficiency, and accelerating the delivery of financial products.

The brief history of open banking demonstrates that success of such frameworks depends on appropriate regulatory support, secure technological infrastructure, and a clear understanding of possible risks. The presence of Islamic financial institutions within the conventional financial systems can add to the complexity of open banking regulation and management. Islamic finance is very relevant to the GCC, where Shariah-compliant financial products constitute a significant part of the banking sector and require a thorough understanding of religious principles with fintech advancements.

This paper, prepared for the Gulf Research Meeting workshop, aims to provide a practical understanding of the open banking model and offer recommendations for financial regulators and industry stakeholders in the GCC. Focusing on real-world applications, the study analyzes the existing open banking regulations and the case study of a fintech company. In contrast to conventional case studies, this paper investigates the case of *Insha*, a German Islamic fintech launched on the Solaris banking-as-a-service (BaaS) platform, which, despite a promising start, failed to maintain its operations. Insha and its experience provide a valuable case exhibiting challenges and risks of embedded models of open banking. Lessons derived from this case can be specifically valuable for the GCC stakeholders since the region remains at the early stages of open banking adoption.

The study attempts to answer the following research questions: How can insights from Insha's case assist the GCC's regulatory and institutional design for open banking and Islamic fintech integration? What implications do these insights hold for the future evolution of the GCC financial system toward open finance and the metaverse economy?

To answer these questions, the paper adopts a qualitative desk study of regulatory reports, fintech case studies and academic literature. It also includes insights from the interview conducted with the former manager of Insha. The rest of the paper is structured as follows. The first chapter defines open banking and surveys its global regulatory models. Chapter 2 analyzes the current state of open banking in the GCC. Chapter 3 presents the case study of Insha, identifying main challenges and institutional obstacles. Chapter 4 presents the policy recommendations for GCC regulators derived from the Insha case study. Chapter 5 discusses the future evolution of open banking toward open finance, open data economy and virtual economy.

Conceptualizing Open Banking: Regulations and Implications

Open banking is a regulatory and technological framework based on the sharing of financial data and account functionalities with third-party providers (TPPs), authorized by the customer, in a safe and secure manner. This sharing is facilitated through the opening of bank application programming interfaces (APIs). Interoperability of modular blocks within APIs allows TPPs to plug in without the specific knowledge of the provider's system (Nanaeva et al. 2021).

Open banking (OB) model carries significant benefits. Customers are expected to be the main beneficiaries of OB implementation. When the ownership of financial data is transferred to the customers, they authorize TPPs to access it. This enables the consolidation of customer financial activities, such as payables, receivables, cards, and accounts across multiple financial institutions, on a single screen, improving their control and management. Moreover, payments can be initiated directly through authorized platforms, without traditional bank intermediation, reducing transaction time and costs.

At the institutional level, easier access to financial data increases competition, encourages product innovation and improves risk management. Access to broader financial data enables a more accurate evaluation of risks, particularly credit risks (Goh 2024; Xie and Sijia 2024). Moreover, empirical studies demonstrate that OB reduces processing costs without increasing default rates (Fuster et al. 2019). Similarly, Babina et al. (2024) found that open banking expands customer access to financial services and provides broader borrowing opportunities for small and medium enterprises (SMEs).

Like any innovative system, open banking entails various risks and challenges. Since the OB model handles sensitive financial data, cybersecurity and data privacy are serious concerns. Additionally, limited customer financial literacy, insufficient staff training, investment requirements for new technologies, the need for a clear regulatory framework, and platform management are the primary challenges associated with OB implementation.

Globally, open banking implementation has emerged through two main approaches: regulation-driven initiatives and industry-driven initiatives. The United Kingdom (UK), the European Union (EU), and Australia are among the jurisdictions where regulators have initiated OB initiatives. Moreover, the EU has introduced open banking regulations in phases, culminating in the adoption of the revised Payment Services Directive (PSD2) in 2018 (European Payments Council 2021).

PSD2 defines two main types of third-party financial service providers: payment initiation service providers (PISPs) and account information service providers (AISPs). According to OB regulation in the EU, banks must allow immediate access to their APIs to PISPs free of charge upon customer request. Moreover, such access does not require any prior contractual agreement with the bank. PISPs, which must have a certain authorization, should request only data for the corresponding payment and cannot store it for future usage (Nanaeva et al. 2021). AISPs must be allowed to aggregate account data across banks and fintech companies on a single screen, but must comply with the General Data Protection Regulation (GDPR) and cannot store this data. To ensure data protection PSD2 requires the implementation of customer authentication (SCA) procedures based on multi-step identification.

Another successful example of a regulatory-driven OB ecosystem is the UK. The Competition and Markets Authority (CMA) launched its OB initiatives in 2018, ordering the nine largest UK banks (CMA9) to build standardized APIs and to allow licensed TTPs access to customer account and payment information. CMA9 include the following banks: AIB Group (UK) plc, trading as First Trust Bank in Northern Ireland, Bank of Ireland (UK) plc, Barclays Bank plc, HSBC Group, Lloyds Banking Group plc, Nationwide Building Society, Northern Bank Limited, trading as Danske Bank, NatWest Group plc, including The Royal Bank of Scotland, Santander UK plc. By September 2024, all nine banks had fully met the requirements by offering open banking payments and account information services and completing the final Open Banking Roadmap (International Banker 2025). In October 2024, the Data (Use and Access) Bill was introduced to the UK Parliament and is currently under consideration by the House of Lords. This new legislation ensures the expansion of the OB model into other sectors of the economy and enables account-to-account payments without the use of bank cards.

By contrast, in countries like the USA, India, or Japan, banks have initiated the opening of their APIs voluntarily, without pressure from regulators. Policymakers in these countries have promoted open banking initiatives without imposing regulatory force. In 2024, the US attempted to shift from an industry-driven to a regulatory-driven approach when the Consumer Financial Protection Bureau (CFPB) sought to mandate that financial institutions with assets exceeding $850 million facilitate the free and secure sharing of customer data with TPPs (McGlinchey Stafford PLLC 2025). However, the rule that took almost 14 years to finalize has been swiftly blocked by bank lobby groups. JPMorgan Chase & Co. has notably been the strongest opponent of this regulation, voicing the risks OB might pose to customers and payment systems in general (Bloomberg 2025). On the contrary, Financial Technology Association, an industry group, endorsed CFPB's Open Banking rule mentioning its ability to increase competition and customer satisfaction. By April 2025, 114 million customer connections had been established between US banks and fintech companies, up from 76 million in 2024, highlighting the growing demand for OB models.

Globally, the OB implementation combines regulatory and industry-driven approaches, and GCC members can gain valuable lessons from global open banking experience (see Table 3.1).

Open Banking in the GCC: Mapping the Trajectory

The Gulf Cooperation Council (GCC) consists of six countries, Bahrain, Kuwait, Oman, Qatar, Saudi Arabia, and the United Arab Emirates, located along the Persian Gulf and sharing similar cultural, religious, and political foundations (Encyclopedia Britannica 2025). All GCC members

Table 3.1 Overview of open banking initiatives across selected jurisdictions

Country/ Region	*Model type*	*Key regulatory body/ Initiative*	*Implementation features*	*Current stage/ Outcome*
European Union (EU)	Regulatory-driven	European Banking Authority (EBA) under PSD2 Directive	Mandatory open APIs, standardized technical and security frameworks, strong consumer protection	Mature implementation, foundation for move toward Open Finance
United Kingdom (UK)	Regulatory-driven	Financial Conduct Authority (FCA) and Competition and Markets Authority (CMA); Open Banking Implementation Entity (OBIE)	Uniform API standards; compulsory data-sharing for largest banks	Fully operational ecosystem, evolving toward Open Finance and Smart Data
Australia	Regulatory-driven	Australian Competition and Consumer Commission (ACCC); Consumer Data Right (CDR) framework	Cross-sectoral approach covering banking, energy, telecom, explicit consumer data rights	Advanced rollout; expanding into full economy data sharing
United States (US)	Industry-driven	No centralized regulator; led by Financial Data Exchange (FDX) consortium	Voluntary adoption of API standards, contractual data-sharing agreements between banks and fintechs	Rapid innovation, but fragmented ecosystem

(continued)

Table 3.1 (continued)

Country/ Region	*Model type*	*Key regulatory body/ Initiative*	*Implementation features*	*Current stage/ Outcome*
Singapore	Industry-driven → Hybrid	Monetary Authority of Singapore (MAS)	Initially voluntary API framework (APEX), later integrated into national fintech strategy, encourages self-regulation with regulatory guidance	Mature hybrid model combining innovation with oversight
Bahrain	Hybrid	Central Bank of Bahrain (CBB)	Mandated open banking API standards; industry sandbox for fintech partnerships	First GCC country with full open banking regulation (since 2020); expanding to Open Finance
Saudi Arabia (KSA)	Hybrid (Regulatory-led with industry input)	Saudi Central Bank (SAMA)	National Open Banking Framework (2022) with phased rollout; banks collaborate in implementation	Early implementation phase

(continued)

Table 3.1 (continued)

Country/ Region	*Model type*	*Key regulatory body/ Initiative*	*Implementation features*	*Current stage/ Outcome*
United Arab Emirates (UAE)	Industry-driven → Emerging hybrid	Central Bank of the UAE (CBUAE), DIFC, ADGM	No mandatory framework yet; several banks and fintechs using proprietary or consortium APIs	Fast-growing ecosystem; regulators moving toward open finance guidelines
Qatar	Regulatory-driven (nascent)	Qatar Central Bank (QCB)	Open Banking Framework (2024) establishing API standards and governance aligned with data privacy law	Pilot phase

have actively embraced digitalization across the industries, aiming to modernize their economies and reduce their longstanding reliance on hydrocarbon revenues.

One of the central components of GCC national strategic visions is the development of a strong fintech ecosystem and restructuring of traditional financial systems. These initiatives include fintech strategies, open banking frameworks, regulatory sandboxes, and accelerator programs (Licorne Gulf 2024). With a population of over 50 million, most of whom are young and tech-savvy, GCC countries offer a promising landscape for fintech advancement. Moreover, the adoption of open banking framework is mentioned as a crucial step in fintech progression in all the GCC strategic visions.

According to the recent IMF report on digital transformation in GCC economies, the region collectively achieved the following milestones in adopting fintech:

- Significantly expanded digital infrastructure that leads to increased digital access and connectivity;
- Enhanced financial inclusion due to the advancement of digital technologies;
- Maturity of government-led digital initiatives that improved efficiency of public services and accelerated fintech adoption;
- Economic growth positively correlated with the economic digitalization position, fintech as an important enabler of sustainable economic development.

Despite these promising milestones, open banking implementation remains in its nascent stages across the region. The forerunner in OB adoption has been Bahrain, which mandated standardization of retail banks' APIs in December 2018. In 2020, the Central Bank of Bahrain launched Open Banking Framework (Central Bank of Bahrain 2025), setting an example for other GCC members.

Saudi Arabia has since emerged as the leader of OB introduction and implementation. The Saudi Central Bank (SAMA) introduced its Open Banking Policy in 2022 with the implementation schedule, which began with account information services (AIS) before moving to payment initiation services (PIS) to build an open financial system (SAMA 2022). Its OB policy was followed by the initiation of the Open Banking Lab in 2023 (Open Banking Expo 2022). Contrasting the OB frameworks in the UK and the EU, the Saudi approach allows banks to charge the TPPs a premium for using their APIs. The rapidly growing number of fintech companies in the Kingdom provides strong incentives for the advancement of open banking. However, the fintech sector continues to face various challenges, including scarcity of local talents in fintech and open banking, limited technological capacity, low financial and digital literacy, and social constraints.

The Central Bank of the UAE has taken a slightly different approach, deciding to avoid limiting the ecosystem to open banking and moving directly to the Open Finance Regulation. The main modules of the proposed framework include an API Hub, Common Infrastructure Services, and a Trust Framework (FintEdu Admin 2024). Collectively, these components should enable licensed financial institutions to share consumer financial data, ensuring effortless transaction processing. Within one year, the UAE has started the implementation of the framework with the first UAE-based fintech, Pay10, achieving production status (Arabian

Business 2025). Open finance activities in the country are expected to be centralized under the watch of the recently introduced centralized platform, "Nebras Open Finance LLC".

The central banks of Oman and Kuwait followed the experiences of Bahrain, Saudi Arabia, and the UAE and introduced their respective Open Banking Frameworks in 2024 (Emanuel-Burns 2025; Tarabut 2024). Interestingly, the open banking initiative in Qatar was initiated by the industry when the country's largest commercial bank, Qatar National Bank, launched an OB platform in 2022 (Fintechnews Middle East 2025). The Qatar Central Bank announced plans to launch the Open Banking Framework by 2026.

Despite all the initiatives, OB adoption and implementation appear slow compared to fintech advancement in the region. This raises the question of whether open banking is a crucial condition for fintech advancement and whether OB frameworks should be industry or regulation-driven.

Case Study of Insha: Lessons from a Shariah-Compliant Fintech

The introduction of the revised Payment Service Directive (PSD2) catalyzed innovation within financial and banking sectors in the EU, specifically accelerating the development of banking-as-a-service (BaaS) platforms. BaaS, also known as an embedded finance platform, can be defined as an end-to-end model that enables non-banking businesses to offer digital banking services by integrating with the infrastructure of a licensed bank using open APIs (Hodges 2022). Solaris SE, launched in 2015, is one of the leading embedded finance platforms in Germany. The full banking license of Solaris enables embedded third-party financial service providers (TPPs) to deliver digital banking services as their offerings.

The TPPs can be onboarded onto Solaris' modular, structured platform in a specific module, depending on the company's functionality. As of 2025, over 90 companies have partnered with Solaris, including such firms as Samsung Pay, Coinbase, and American Express. In September 2024, more than 1.1 million credit cards of the Allgemeiner Deutscher Automobil-Club (ADAC), one of the largest automobile associations in Europe, migrated to the Solaris platform, highlighting Solaris' capacity to manage large-scale financial products (FinTech Futures 2024). The revenue of Solaris SE includes fees for using its APIs, transaction fees and revenues from loans offered on the platform.

In 2023 Solaris reported €137 million as net revenue. The same year the company encountered a net loss of €178 million due to the write-off of its Electronic Money Institution (EMI) activities (FinTech Futures 2024). Solaris acquired UK-based EMI in 2021 to gain easier access to UK and Lithuania markets. EMI was responsible for the provision of Visa debit cards, 2.5 million cards at the time of the acquisition, to the Binance customers in the European market. However, Binance terminated the agreement in 2023 causing the losses to Solaris SE. Additionally, in November 2023 EMI was fined €840,000 by the Bank of Lithuania for failing to comply with Anti-Money Laundering requirements. Moreover, in March 2024, BaFin (Federal Financial Supervisory Authority—the main financial regulatory body in Germany) fined Solaris €6.5 million for systematic late submission of anti-money laundering reports.

Insha, Germany's first Shariah-compliant fintech, has quickly become an example of how Islamic finance can operate within open banking framework in Europe. The case of Insha has been frequently cited in policy reports and media outlets as a case of values-based innovation in the European Islamic fintech landscape (Arab Monetary Fund 2022; Consultancy-me.com 2022; Dinç et al. 2021). Insha launched its operations in Germany in 2019. Initial investments in this start-up have been provided by Al Baraka Turk Participation Bank, followed by €2.5 million in seed funding from Param (Insha Ventures 2020). Embedded in the BaaS, Insha operated under its banking license while keeping its funds separately from the conventional financial platform of Solaris. PSD2 regulation and a BaaS model enabled Insha to offer a wide range of services—including interest-free accounts, ethical investment options, and digital money management—while ensuring that all financial transactions complied with Islamic principles. Its target customer base has been the German Muslim population, which reached approximately 5.5 million by 2023 (Deutsche Islam Konferenz 2023).

Insha experienced rapid early success, achieving 300 percent growth in the number of users (exceeding 40,000) and a transaction volume of $33 million by the beginning of 2020 (Loho 2020). OB regulation facilitated the growth of fintech companies like Insha by simplifying access to the market and enabling data aggregation. Obtaining a banking license is a cumbersome and lengthy process in Germany; thus, the open banking model offered by Solaris provides new opportunities for fintech start-ups. However, despite the promising start, Insha had to suspend operations in December 2023. Understanding the reasons behind the closure offers important lessons for regulators, policymakers, and practitioners.

The challenges faced by Insha that eventually led to its closure can be categorized into six broad categories: challenges associated with BaaS business model, licensing challenges, gaps in Islamic finance regulation, strategic challenges with the founding institution and low financial and technological literacy.

Firstly, BaaS model provides significant support for fintech start-ups when they enter the market and begin delivering their products. However, further expansion and scalability of the fintech within the platform can be challenging. The platform providers may be reluctant to support the introduction of new products due to the potential increase in risks and costs. This limits innovation and hinders the growth of the fintech company, challenging a sustainable long-term strategy for fintech on the platform. Thus, regulatory sandboxes and accelerators should consider supporting fintech start-ups not only at the beginning of their journey but also at later stages of expansion and operational growth.

Secondly, transitioning from the platform can be very challenging for the start-up. Embedded models help launch fintech services under the platform's banking license, while obtaining an independent banking license or an e-money license is a complex and lengthy process. Insha failed to obtain an e-money operating license, underscoring regulatory obstacles and challenges to achieving operational independence. National regulators should clarify, standardize and simplify the licensing process for fintech start-ups aiming to expand beyond BaaS platform.

Thirdly, Germany, like many other countries, lacks specific regulations for Islamic finance institutions. Islamic banks or fintech firms must operate under the standard banking law, while Shariah-compliance of offered products and services must be overseen internally (BaFin 2021). Insha observed such compliance under the supervision of the Shariah board of Al Baraka Turk Bank. However, if the fintech decides to leave the BaaS platform and operate independently, obtaining Shariah-compliance would have been difficult. Surprisingly, most GCC jurisdictions face the same issue of inconsistent Islamic finance regulation. Establishing standardized regulations for Islamic finance institutions can be crucial for advancing Islamic fintech and innovation.

Fourthly, Insha's initial funding has been provided by Al Baraka Turk bank, positioning it as the founding investor. However, with time, the involvement of the founder resulted in limiting innovation and reduction of company's profitability. Limited knowledge of the German market and reluctance to fund new projects created additional obstacles for Insha's advancement. Thus, it is crucial for fintech to have access to diversified funding sources and preserve operational independence. Access to venture capital or public–private partnership can help fintech companies to avoid excessive dependence on a single investor.

Fifthly, the scaling of Insha's operations was hindered by customers' low financial and technological literacy. The German financial market can be characterized as conservative, with many customers remaining loyal to traditional banks and preferring cash for everyday transactions. Financial technologies can still be viewed as highly risky, especially among the older German population. The median age in the country is 47.7 years, placing the majority of Germans in older demographics (PopulationPyramid.net 2024). Consequently, Germans often demonstrate caution toward digital financial products. Additionally, Islamic financial products are often faced with skepticism among German Muslims due to their limited understanding of Islamic finance principles. This highlights the importance of financial education for the general public and specific demographic groups.

In conclusion, despite its closure, the Insha case demonstrates that open banking provides benefits for fintech companies and customers. OB model enables fast customer onboarding, efficient payments, card issuance, and account aggregation. More importantly, it enables delivery of financial services to an underserved and unbanked segment of the population, including religious and ethically cautious customers.

Policy Recommendation for the GCC: Insights from Insha Case

First, regulators should reevaluate the conventional role of regulatory sandboxes and accelerators. Fintech start-ups usually receive support from these entities at the initial stages of testing and entering the market. However, fintech firms face new challenges as they grow beyond their early stage, when expanding their operations, adding new products, or scaling up their business. Therefore, regulators might continue backing start-ups, designing sandbox and accelerator programs that function as engagement platforms rather than trial environments. Delivering flexible regulatory guidance at various growth stages helps prevent market exits while building enduring fintech ecosystems.

Second, more thoughtful and customized assistance is needed for fintech companies that decide to shift from modules of BaaS platform into fully regulated financial institutions. In case the fintech start-up initially operating under the banking license of the platform decides to run independently later, regulators might consider supporting this transitional period. It will require clearly defining requirements, fees, timeframes, and available technical support for the fintech. Clear and transparent licensing procedures help to reduce regulatory uncertainty, enable fintech firms to develop long-term strategies, and build trust in regulatory frameworks.

Islamic banking regulatory frameworks remain underdeveloped or entirely absent in several GCC jurisdictions. The absence of transparent and standardized Islamic finance guidelines in the region might prevent Shariah-compliant fintech start-ups from operating beyond BaaS platforms in future. Regulators need to prioritize the development of Islamic banking guidelines to support digital business models. This might include clarifying and standardizing Shariah board requirements, defining permissible revenue models, and addressing the treatment of Islamic digital financial instruments. Moreover, the development of regulatory guidelines for Islamic finance in digital environments would increase trust and competitiveness of Islamic fintech companies.

Third, the scaling of open banking operations and their expansion across borders requires standardized regulatory frameworks across jurisdictions and sectors. Inconsistent API standards, along with varying data protection laws and customer authentication protocols across GCC states, create additional obstacles to the development of a unified fintech market. The adoption of common technical and legal standards in open banking by GCC countries would simplify compliance requirements and increase interoperability. The Gulf Cooperation Council Secretariat and the Arab Monetary Fund should collaborate to align these standards across GCC, drawing from the lessons of PSD2 implementation across EU countries.

Additionally, regulators and ecosystem builders should consider the sustainability of fintech start-ups as a priority. Regulators might collaborate with national development funds, innovation agencies, and international investment platforms to ensure capital access for promising fintech ventures. Seed funding and initial venture capital investments are a good initial provision for the start-ups, yet many fintech companies face long-term capital constraints that prevent them from expanding their operations or making essential market adaptations. Public policies that combine investment partnerships and innovation grants with preferential access to sovereign wealth funds can help address funding challenges. Financial independence and sufficient financial resources are the key drivers of innovation and market diversity.

Finally, open banking development continues to depend on the dynamic dialogue between regulators and practitioners as its fundamental component. Real market knowledge is necessary to guide both regulatory development and innovation planning processes. Regular feedback channels, in combination with working groups and formal consultations, allow regulatory entities to respond appropriately to new technological and business developments. Additionally, regulators should actively cooperate with Islamic fintech stakeholders to better understand operational challenges and opportunities, particularly those related to Shariah-compliance in digital environments.

The GCC can successfully adopt open banking by implementing adaptable and forward-thinking regulations that support inclusivity and accessibility. The case of Insha demonstrated that the long-term success of a fintech company depends on such components as support beyond their initial phases, clear protocols for migrating from BaaS platforms, Islamic banking regulations tailored for digital models, standardization across jurisdictions, and later funding opportunities. The GCC can become a global leader in financial innovation by strategically aligning such policies with national economic visions and goals in regional integration.

Looking Forward: From Open Banking to Metaverse Finance

The implementation of open banking is an important milestone in the transformation of the financial system. Several nations across the globe have advanced from the open banking framework to open finance—a broader framework in which customers own and share financial data across sectors. Australia, for example, is one of the leaders in open finance adoption. Australian Consumer Data Right framework extends sharing customer financial data beyond banking to energy and telecommunication sectors (Australian Treasury 2023). Moreover, the country aims to enable sharing of customer-control data across the industries, further shifting toward open data economy. The UK's Financial Conduct Authority has announced its plans to expand financial data-sharing to include mortgages, pensions, and insurance services (Financial Conduct Authority 2021). Meanwhile, Brazil has already included credit, insurance, investment, and pension services into data-sharing network, benefiting from establishment of centralized APIs frameworks (Banco Central do Brazil 2022). The European Union is also working on the implementation of PSD3 and the Open Finance Framework to expand financial data accessibility beyond PSD2 requirements and across member states (European Commission 2023).

These global advancements can have important implications for GCC countries. Regional policymakers and regulators must be ready to shift from open banking to open finance and open economy. Such a shift will allow customers to gain full ownership of their data, ensuring safe and seamless data-sharing across industries. While further improving financial inclusion and operational efficiency, such moves support the transition toward virtual finance in the Metaverse.

The Metaverse can be defined as a decentralized, immersive virtual environment where users, represented by their avatars, engage in social and economic activities (Aysan and Nanaeva 2024). Originally associated with gaming and entertainment, the Metaverse is advancing into commerce, communication, and finance. Bloomberg Intelligence report projected that Metaverse economy would reach $800 billion by 2024. Moreover, a survey commissioned by PayPal in 2022 revealed that over 37.5 million US users invested more than $28 billion in virtual economy, with 81% of respondents spending their time in gaming, 69%—in music and another 69%—in video entertainment, 50% in purchasing digital art works and 67%—virtual clothes and skin (Lau 2023). This data demonstrates that the Metaverse economy, based on principles of digital ownership and decentralized value creation, has emerged to stay and to continue expanding.

Blockchain technology and its derivatives have been behind the rapid Metaverse advancement. Cryptocurrencies, non-fungible tokens (NFTs), and decentralized autonomous organizations (DAOs) contribute to the establishment of secure and verifiable digital ownership and form the basic infrastructure of virtual economy. Advancement of AI further reinforces the virtual economy by improving data analytics, automation, and data security.

Financial institutions have begun to realize the necessity of a stable and secure financial system in the Metaverse. South Korean commercial banks, HSBC, and JP Morgan are among the first financial institutions that have already launched their virtual offices on platforms like Decentraland and Sandbox. According to a Strategy & report, the Metaverse can contribute more than $15 billion to GCC economies. Dubai, the regional leader in Metaverse adoption, has launched a Metaverse incubator and Metaverse strategy aiming for $4 billion toward its GDP from virtual activities. Consequently, GCC regulators and policymakers must include the transition toward virtual finance in their national digital transformation strategies.

The current stage of Metaverse development can be described as the digital twins phase, where companies, banks and even cities launch their virtual offices or copies on various platforms. This stage creates a strong demand for virtual land, property, and other digital assets. Following these activities, financial service providers in the Metaverse are expected to deliver a range of services, including virtual banking, digital asset management and decentralized finance solutions. The main service, at this phase, should be the facilitation of fast and effortless transactions between the virtual and real economies, as well as across different platforms within the Metaverse (Aysan et al. 2024).

To facilitate such interoperability, fintech companies need to provide hybrid accounts, operating both in fiat money and cryptocurrency and support payments for a digital asset with fiat money and for real-world goods in cryptocurrency. Digital wallets should be directly linked to conventional bank accounts, while virtual mortgages should be loaned against real-world assets, and vice versa. Financial institutions need to be capable of managing complex investment portfolios that may include crypto, NFTs, and other digital assets. Cases such as the BIS Project Dunbar and the IMF's 2024 CBDC Pilot Report demonstrate the need for regulatory and technical frameworks to enable traditional and digital finance systems to work in synergy (Bank for International Settlements 2022; International Monetary Fund 2024). Project Dunbar examines a shared multi-CBDC platform for cross-border payments, showing that technological interoperability must be matched by legal, governance, and supervisory frameworks. The IMF's 2024 CBDC Pilot Report summarizes lessons from national CBDC experiments, highlighting the need for coherent legal foundations and integration with existing payment and financial systems to safeguard stability and monetary sovereignty.

At the same time, Metaverse activities will require significant financial, technological, and human-related investments. Banks and fintech companies must start preparing now to remain competitive and be able to deal with complex virtual reality in the future.

The increasing adoption of virtual ownership and decentralized financial management creates challenges for regulatory bodies. The Metaverse requires new regulatory frameworks to address issues of digital identity, cross-platform interoperability, cybercrime, and consumer protection. Accordingly, financial regulators need to be capable of dealing with issues related to big data management, AI integration into financial systems and blockchain protocols.

The transition from open banking to open finance and then to virtual finance can be a fundamental transformation rather than a simple technological advancement. The GCC region should be ready to accept this transition as a strategic part of its economic diversification and innovation. Consequently, coordinated action between regulators, industry practitioners and civil society organizations is required to succeed in this transition.

Conclusion and Key Takeaways

The study highlights that GCC nations must take proactive steps to successfully adopt open banking, as a key driver of financial innovation and digital transformation. While the open banking landscape in Gulf countries is still developing, it offers the potential to increase financial inclusion, customer satisfaction, and competition in the financial sector. Analyzing the EU regulatory framework through the case of Insha, the study demonstrates that fintech success very much depends on regulatory clarity, operational autonomy, and alignment with technological and cultural norms. The eventual closure of Insha revealed structural weaknesses in BaaS dependencies and unique challenges of Shariah-compliant fintech operating within conventional financial systems.

The insights from Insha's case suggest the following major takeaways are essential for guiding GCC regulators and practitioners in open banking adoption and advancement.

First, the GCC needs to establish clear regulations that protect consumers and enable smooth data exchange between different jurisdictions. Gulf countries should draw from the lessons of EU, UK, and other countries to create interoperable regulatory systems, connecting traditional banks with fintech companies and digital asset platforms across all GCC nations.

Second, the regulatory sandbox system needs to expand beyond initial testing to provide ongoing support for fintech companies during their growth stages, both for compliance and for innovation development.

To boost Islamic fintech credibility and integration, the GCC needs to establish unified governance standards, standardized certification, and digital Shariah-compliance frameworks.

To ensure sustainable funding mechanisms for Islamic and conventional fintech companies, GCC members need to develop a blended financing tool, combining waqf, crowdfunding, and impact-driven funds.

Finally, open banking can be used as a starting point for future transition toward open finance, digital assets, and metaverse-based financial systems. GCC economies, with their young digitally native populations and extensive investments in AI and blockchain infrastructure, can position themselves as the leaders of such financial evolution.

When adopted properly, open banking enables the GCC to achieve more than just technological transformation; it supports the creation of a new financial framework in the region. Through its advancement in open banking, development of inclusive financial systems, and adoption of metaverse technologies, the GCC has significant opportunities to establish itself as a global leader in digitalized finance. However, a deeper understanding of emerging financial technologies and continuous engagement with global best practices are crucial to capture these opportunities.

It also defines the need for continued academic research and critical reflection. Careful, evidence-based studies can help identify what works best and effectively, and why certain models succeed in some contexts but fail in others. Additional research should be conducted to examine the social and ethical consequences of financial innovation, ensuring that open banking develops not just as a technical upgrade but as a foundation for a more inclusive, stable, and human-centered financial system in the GCC and beyond.

Acknowledgements The author acknowledges the use of ChatGPT to assist in creating the table and Grammarly to support spelling and language refinement; all ideas and analyses remain solely those of the author. The author also gratefully acknowledges insights gained from an interview with Mehmet Burak Dikmen, Insha's former Head of Growth, which informed the discussion of the Insha case.

References

Arab Monetary Fund. 2022. *Islamic Fintech in the Arab Region: Imperatives, Challenges and the Way Forward*. Abu Dhabi: Arab Monetary Fund. https://www.amf.org.ae/sites/default/files/publications/2022-02/Islamic%20Fintech_Final%20Draft_Final%20%20%281%29.pdf.

Arabian Business. "UAE Fintech Pay10 First to Launch on Central Bank's Open Finance Framework." *Arabian Business*, April 24, 2025. https://www.arabianbusiness.com/industries/banking-finance/uae-fintech-pay10-first-to-launch-on-central-banks-open-finance-framework.

Australian Treasury. 2023. *Consumer Data Right Strategic Assessment Report*. https://treasury.gov.au/publication/p2023-421483.

Aysan, Ahmet Faruk, and Zhamal Nanaeva. "Investigating Virtual Financial Ecosystem: Ascent of Metaverse Economics Research." *Efil Journal of Economic Research/Efil Ekonomi Araştırmaları Dergisi* 7, no. 3 (2024).

Aysan, Ahmet Faruk, Giray Gozgor, and Zhamal Nanaeva. "Technological perspectives of Metaverse for financial service providers." *Technological Forecasting and Social Change* 202 (2024): 123323.

Babina, Tanya, Saleem A. Bahaj, Greg Buchak, Filippo De Marco, Alexandra K. Foulis, William Gornall, Francesco Mazzola, and Tianyu Yu. 2024a. *Customer Data Access and Fintech Entry: Early Evidence from Open Banking*. https://doi.org/10.2139/ssrn.4716658.

BaFin (Federal Financial Supervisory Authority). 2021. *Islamic Finance in Germany: Supervisory Requirements and Challenges*. Accessed May 26, 2025. https://www.bafin.de/EN.

Banco Central do Brasil. 2022. *Open Finance in Brazil*. https://www.bcb.gov.br/en/financialstability/openfinance.

Bank for International Settlements Innovation Hub. (2022, September 2). *Project Dunbar: International settlements using multi-CBDCs*. https://www.bis.org/about/bisih/topics/cbdc/dunbar.htm.

Bloomberg Intelligence. 2021. *Metaverse May Be $800 Billion Market, Next Tech Platform*. December 1, 2021. https://www.bloomberg.com/professional/blog/metaverse-may-be-800-billion-market-next-tech-platform/.Central Bank of Bahrain. "CBB Launches the Bahrain Open Banking Framework." *Central Bank of Bahrain*, December 11, 2018. https://www.cbb.gov.bh/media-center/cbb-launches-the-bahrain-open-banking-framework/.

Bloomberg. "Banks, Fintechs Face Round Two of Fight over Data Sharing." *Mint*, May 14, 2025. https://www.livemint.com/companies/news/banks-fintechs-face-round-two-of-fight-over-data-sharing-11747166257938.html.

Central Bank of the United Arab Emirates. *Open Finance Regulation*. Accessed May 17, 2025. https://rulebook.centralbank.ae/en/rulebook/open-finance-regulation.

Consultancy-me.com. 2022. "The Global Islamic Fintech Banking Market: Trends and Outlook." *Consultancy-me.com*, January 17, 2022. https://www.consultancy-me.com/news/4595/the-global-islamic-fintech-banking-market-trends-and-outlook.

Deutsche Islam Konferenz. 2023. "Facts and Figures." Accessed May 19, 2025. https://www.deutsche-islam-konferenz.de/EN/DatenFakten/daten-fakten_node.html.

Dinç, Yusuf, Ruslan Nagayev, and Raqim Jahangir. 2021. "Analysis of Europe's First Fully-Fledged Islamic Digital Bank in the Arena of New Age Banking." *Journal of Islamic Economics* 2021/2: 35–53. https://www.researchgate.net/publication/353270636.

Emanuel-Burns, Cameron. "Central Bank of Oman Approves Regulatory Framework for Open Banking." *FinTech Futures*, January 2, 2025. https://www.fintechfutures.com/2025/01/central-bank-of-oman-approves-regulatory-framework-for-open-banking/.

Encyclopedia Britannica. 2025. "Gulf Cooperation Council." *Encyclopaedia Britannica*. Accessed May 26, 2025. https://www.britannica.com/topic/Gulf-Cooperation-Council.

European Commission. 2023. *Digital Finance Strategy and Retail Investment Strategy*. https://finance.ec.europa.eu/publications/digital-finance-strategy_en.

European Payments Council. 2021. *About SEPA*. https://www.europeanpaymentscouncil.eu/about-sepa/sepa-timeline.

Financial Conduct Authority. 2021. *Open Finance: Feedback Statement FS21/7*. https://www.fca.org.uk/publication/feedback/fs21-7.pdf.

FinTech Futures. 2024. "Embedded Finance Provider Solaris Embarks on 'New Chapter of Transformation', Says CEO." *FinTech Futures*, October 22, 2024. https://www.fintechfutures.com/embedded-finance/embedded-finance-provider-solaris-embarks-on-new-chapter-of-transformation-says-ceo.

Fintechnews Middle East. "Fintech on the Rise in Qatar Driven by Increased Adoption of Digital Payments and Strong Government Initiatives." *Fintechnews Middle East*, March 24, 2025. https://fintechnews.ae/25410/qatar/fintech-on-the-rise-in-qatar-driven-by-increased-adoption-of-digital-payments-and-strong-government-initiatives/.

FintEdu Admin. "CBUAE Introduces Open Finance Regulation to Boost Innovation and Competitiveness." *FintEdu*, June 28, 2024. https://fintedu.com/blog/index.php?entryid=1856.

Fuster, Andreas, Matthew Plosser, Philipp Schnabl, and James Vickery. 2019. "The Role of Technology in Mortgage Lending." *The Review of Financial Studies* 32 (5): 1854–1899. https://doi.org/10.1093/rfs/hhz018.

Goh, Rui Ying. 2024. *Unleashing the Potential of Open Banking: Three Use Cases for Risk Assessment*. Master's thesis, University of Edinburgh.

Gulf Cooperation Council Fintech Report. *GCC Fintech Landscape 2024: Trends, Opportunities, and Regulatory Outlook*. Manama: Bahrain FinTech Bay, 2024.

Hodges, Braeden. "Banking-as-a-Service: Fintechs Walking the Regulatory Perimeter." *Brook. J. Corp. Fin. & Com. L.* 17 (2022): 127.

Insha Ventures. 2020. "Fintech with principles raises €2.5m for European expansion." October 20, 2020. https://insha.ventures/newsroom-fintech.html.

International Banker. "Why 2025 Is Set to Be a Pivotal Year for Open Banking." *International Banker*, May 13, 2025. https://internationalbanker.com/banking/why-2025-is-set-to-be-a-pivotal-year-for-open-banking/.

International Monetary Fund. (2024). *CBDC pilot report: Cross-border interoperability and digital asset integration*. Washington, D.C.: International Monetary Fund. https://www.imf.org/en/Publications/Fintech-Notes.

Lau, I. K. 2023. *Metaverse and Money*. PayPal commissioned survey. https://newsroom.paypal-corp.com/2023-06-Metaverse-and-Money.

Licorne Gulf. 2024. "Navigating Fintech's Complex Future in the GCC." *Licorne Gulf*, May 28, 2024. https://www.licorne-gulf.com/post/navigating-fintech-s-complex-future-in-the-gcc.

Loho, P. 2020. "German Islamic Fintech Insha Releasing New App in July, Eyes Europe Expansion." *Salaam Gateway*, June 16, 2020. https://salaamgateway.com/story/german-islamic-fintech-insha-releasing-new-app-in-july-eyes-europe-expansion.

McGlinchey Stafford PLLC. 2025. "CFPB's Open Banking Rules: Dead on Arrival or Alive and Well?" *McGlinchey Stafford PLLC*, February 18, 2025. https://www.mcglinchey.com/insights/cfpbs-open-banking-rules-dead-on-arrival-or-alive-and-well/.

Nanaeva, Zhamal, Ahmet Faruk Aysan, and Nasim Shah Shirazi. "Open banking in Europe: the effect of the revised payment services directive on Solarisbank and Insha." *Journal of Payments Strategy & Systems* 15, no. 4 (2021): 432–444.

Open Banking Expo. "Saudi Central Bank Issues Second Release of Open Banking Framework." *Open Banking Expo*, November 7, 2022. https://www.openbankingexpo.com/news/saudi-central-bank-issues-second-release-of-open-banking-framework/.

PopulationPyramid.net. 2024. "Population of Germany 2024." Accessed May 27, 2025. https://www.populationpyramid.net/germany/2024/.

Saudi Central Bank. (2022). *Open Banking Policy* (English ed.). Riyadh: Saudi Central Bank. https://www.sama.gov.sa/en-US/Documents/Open_Banking_Policy-EN.pdf.

Tarabut. "2024—Navigating Open Banking in MENA's Financial Landscape." *Tarabut*, January 10, 2024. https://www.tarabut.com/blogs/post/2024-%E2%80%94-navigating-open-banking-in-mena-s-financial-landscape.

Xie, Chengbo, and Sijia Hu. "Open banking: an early review." *Journal of Internet and Digital Economics* 4, no. 2 (2024): 73–82.

CHAPTER 4

The Rise of Fintech in UAE and Saudi Arabia: Assessing Its Impact on Banking Performance and Identifying the Region's Fintech Leader

Saib Fakhar, Suha Bilquis, and Wajid Ali

Introduction

Banks have been the only global suppliers of financial services for many years. But developments in information technology and telecommunications changed the financial services industry. In an effort to lower the costs of financial intermediation, new providers of financial services have arisen (Dasilas and Karanović 2023). FinTech companies fall into two

S. Fakhar (✉)
New Delhi Institute of Management, New Delhi, India
e-mail: Saib.fakhar@ndimdelhi.org

S. Bilquis
Aligarh Muslim University, Aligarh, India

W. Ali
Fortune Institute of International Business, Delhi, India
e-mail: ali.10@iitj.ac.in

K. Tsanis et al. (eds.), *Digital Finance and Transformation in the Gulf*,
https://doi.org/10.1007/978-981-92-1588-1_4

categories: those that support bank operations by supplying technological tools, and those that offer financial services that banks typically provide (Romanova and Kudinska 2016). FinTech, or financial technology, has the capability to significantly improve the accessibility of financial services by eliminating information asymmetries in the credit market, permitting greater transparency, and cutting expenses (Gabor and Brooks 2017). One of the key components of financial services, lending services, has changed as a result of FinTech developments. FinTech enables lenders to provide borrowers with quick and easy credit solutions (Ali and Marisetty 2023). An estimated 795 billion USD was given to alternative financing through FinTech and Big Techs1 globally in 2019, of which about 223 billion USD came from FinTech and 572 billion USD from Big Tech. It is more well-established in nations with improved disclosures for investor protection, an effective legal system, and significant ease of doing business (Cornelli et al. 2022). FinTech contributes to greater financial stability for households by expanding access to credit and cushioning the impact of economic disruptions, thereby decreasing the need to delay consumption during periods of distress (Suri et al. 2021). Additionally, it improves credit assessments, reducing pressure on traditional banks and allowing more credit-constrained individuals to obtain financing (Balyuk 2023). Fintech is making financial services more convenient, accessible, and efficient. It also seeks to use innovation to upend the financial sector and question established banking (Aduba et al. 2023; Claessens et al. 2018; Thakor 2019; Vučinić 2020). The global health crisis (Covid'19) prompted a significant rise in the use of technology-driven lending platforms (Bao and Huang 2021). In the global framework, fintech helps maintain financial stability in 63 nations (Daud et al. 2022). Using the regulatory sandbox as a stand-in for fintech innovation, another study comes to the conclusion that it encourages stability (or instability) in both developed and emerging nations (Fung et al. 2020). On the contrary, multiple mechanisms exist through which fintech adoption can impact the stability of banks. Initially, fintech adoption entails the incorporation of innovative and frequently intricate technologies into banking processes. Integrating unfamiliar technology can provide hazards, including system failures, cyberattacks, and data breaches, which may jeopardise a bank's financial stability if not properly managed. Secondly, fintech can augment operational efficiency via automation and digitisation, potentially decreasing costs and enhancing profitability (Khan et al. 2023). The rapid rate of adoption and lagged regulatory measures have exposed the drawbacks of FinTech financing, in contrast to the benefits of these advances. The financial sector has experienced unknown and unanticipated effects as a result of the adoption of the FinTech lending model (Fu and Mishra 2022). There was a noticeable rise in suspicious lending applications in emerging nations, most likely as a result of consumers' extreme financial hardships and expulsion from the conventional credit market during the crisis (Ali and Marisetty 2023; Fu and Mishra 2022). In 2021, a working group of the Indian central bank found that among 1100 current loan applications in 81 app shops accessible to Indian Android users, 600 were fraudulent (Reserve Bank of India 2021). Innovative activities are influenced by the financial development of a country, as excessive financing may adversely impact growth (Xiao and Zhao 2012; Zhu et al. 2020). In response to the need for economic diversification and decreased reliance on oil, the GCC nations are fostering a conducive atmosphere for fintech adoption, which will ultimately promote economic growth and improve financial inclusion. Given that fintech possesses the capacity to transform the financial industry, its implications for financial stability have emerged as a critical worry for regulators and policymakers (Khan et al. 2023).

Research question:

To what degree has the expansion of fintech altered banking performance in the UAE and Saudi Arabia, and which nation exhibits greater fintech maturity and leadership within the GCC region?

Literature Review

Much of the existing literature on FinTech focuses on exploring its features and structure, with the term 'FinTech' first emerging in 1972 (Charnes et al. 1972), after which numerous studies have expanded research in this area. Zhu et al. (2025) FinTech as technological innovation in finance that can significantly alter the delivery and structure of financial services. Such innovation enhances banks' monitoring and governance capabilities, contributing to a disciplining mechanism within corporate entities. FinTech refers to the application of technology to deliver innovative and enhanced financial services. It can be succinctly stated as the amalgamation of finance and technology (Goldstein et al. 2019; Litimi et al. 2024; Thakor 2019). Notwithstanding the significant advancements in financial inclusion in recent years, the World Bank's 2017 Global Findex database indicated that 1.7 billion adults globally remain without access to formal financial services. The factors contributing to elevated financial exclusion encompass difficulties in meeting paperwork prerequisites, elevated service fees, and the proximity to the nearest financial institution (Demirguc-Kunt et al. 2018). FinTech enterprises are innovative entities involved in supply and settlement processes within the banking sector, encompassing lending, payments, personal finance management, crowdfunding, and cryptocurrencies (Phan et al. 2020). While FinTech lenders have significantly enhanced lending accessibility during the crisis, there are pervasive reservations about their services globally. During this period, predatory lending applications increased significantly, exploiting the financial hardships experienced by individuals (Ali and Marisetty 2023). This situation was not limited to developing nations, even in economically advanced countries such as the USA, predatory online lenders exploited vulnerable borrowers by imposing high interest rates, thereby entrenching them in cycles of debt. FinTech financing possesses both advantageous and disadvantageous aspects. The literature is nascent, and regulators are grappling with comprehending the welfare implications of swift technology progress in the financial services sector (Ali and Marisetty 2023). FinTech is regarded as a significant catalyst for financial inclusion, with mobile financial services representing the greatest potential for integrating the unbanked into the mainstream financial system. Empirical research from Kenya has confirmed that mobile money usage has elevated per capita consumption levels and lifted two percent of households out of poverty (Suri et al. 2021). The swift rise of digital finance companies prompted investors and market participants to partake in a significant trend of startup acquisitions (Das 2023). Thomas (2023) asserts that India ranks third globally in terms of FinTech activity and suggests fostering collaboration to advance the field. Zhou et al. (2015) highlighted how China's financial systems have undergone a digital transition in the last five years, positioning it as a frontrunner in the FinTech industry. Stern et al. (2017) detailed the evolution of financial technology in China, specifically highlighting how the proliferation of peer-to-peer lending platforms in the country's market has contributed to this sector's meteoric rise. Stern et al. (2017) examined the evolution of financial technology in China, specifically highlighting how the proliferation of peer-to-peer lending platforms in the country's market has contributed to this sector's meteoric rise. Li et al. (2017) analysed how investments in FinTech firms affected the stock prices of conventional banks in the US and discovered a favourable correlation.

Consumer theory and disruptive innovation theory provide an explanation for the impact of FinTech firms on banks (Phan et al. 2020). Aaker and Keller (1990) proposed under the consumer theory that new services, offered by companies like FinTech, can supplant old services, offered by institutions like traditional banks, by satisfying the same consumer need. Christensen (1990) highlighted the principle of disruptive innovation, new competitors can enter the market by using cutting-edge technology to make their products and services more accessible and affordable.

Problem Statement: The swift expansion of financial technology (fintech) is altering the global banking environment by redefining operational frameworks, client engagements, and income sources. In the GCC region, where conventional banking has traditionally been predominant, the emergence of fintech solutions, including digital payments, blockchain, peer-to-peer lending, and neobanks, is presenting unparalleled challenges and opportunities for financial institutions. Regardless of the burgeoning interest in technologically innovative solutions within the financial sector, there remains a notable deficiency in academic literature addressing FinTech industries in Gulf Cooperation Council (GCC) nations, where the determinants of FinTech development and banking performance have been examined in isolation. These nations have experienced an expanding FinTech ecosystem, propelled by factors such as governmental support, a youthful and technologically adept populace, and the ambition to diversify their economies beyond oil dependency (Litimi et al. 2024). For example, the Central Bank of the UAE has established a regulatory framework for digital payment services, while the Saudi Central Bank has implemented a regulatory sandbox to foster innovation in the financial sector.

This study enhances the existing literature on financial technology and banking performance in numerous significant aspects. This study is one of the few empirical analyses that concurrently examines the influence of fintech development on critical banking performance indicators—Return on Assets (ROA), Return on Equity (ROE), and Net Interest Margin (NIM) in the context of the Gulf Cooperation Council (GCC). This report examines the United Arab Emirates (UAE) and the Kingdom of Saudi Arabia (KSA), the two most vibrant fintech hubs in the region, highlighting differences in legislative frameworks, technical integration, and market development.

This research is methodologically distinct as it amalgamates data from various reliable sources like Bloomberg Terminal, Statista, and Crunchbase to create a comprehensive dataset spanning 2014 to 2024. This comprehensive data collection facilitates a deeper comprehension of banking basics and the dynamics of the fintech ecosystem, which prior GCC research has lacked due to dependence on secondary or descriptive information. The utilisation of both Ordinary Least Squares (OLS) and Quantile Regression enhances analytical rigour, enabling the investigation to reveal diverse impacts of fintech on varying levels of bank performance.

Third, in contrast to previous studies that predominantly highlight the beneficial impact of fintech on efficiency and competition, this research provides opposing empirical evidence: the expansion of fintech in the GCC, especially in the UAE and KSA, demonstrates a negative correlation with traditional bank profitability indicators. This discovery offers a new viewpoint in the current discussion on whether fintech serves as a complement or a disruptive influence to traditional banking. The advice for banks to form strategic alliances and invest stock in fintech firms offers a practical framework for risk mitigation and sustainable integration, enhancing the real-world relevance of the research beyond theoretical discussions.

This study expands comparative research by identifying the UAE and KSA as fintech leaders and demonstrating how regulatory proactivity and capital inflows influence unique innovation trajectories across the GCC. This not only updates the empirical evidence to 2025 but also offers a standard for future study on the long-term balance between technological disruption and financial stability in the Middle East.

Research Methodology

The conflicting findings about the influence of FinTech firms on bank profitability necessitate further academic inquiry, and this study seeks to enhance the discourse on the role of FinTech within banking research. The primary research objective of this study is to analyse the impact of growth of FinTech on bank performance utilising bank-level data from GCC countries. In what manner do the performance determinants of the banking industry influence the financial viability of banking institutions.

The research employs annual panel data from 2014 to 2024 for banks in the United Arab Emirates (UAE) and the Kingdom of Saudi Arabia (KSA). Data were downloaded in 2025, although the coverage period is restricted to observations from 2014 to 2024 to uphold uniformity among sources and guarantee data completeness. Consolidated bank-level financial data, encompassing ROA, ROE, NIM, CAP, LLP, and GD, were obtained from the Bloomberg Terminal to ensure consistency across institutions and eliminate redundancy from subsidiary-level reporting. Fintech-related metrics were sourced from Statista and Crunchbase, using datasets retrieved in 2025. Data from Statista were obtained from the reports titled "Fintech Market in the Middle East and North Africa" and "Digital Investment & Payments Segment Reports." Concurrently, Crunchbase data were refined by country (UAE and Saudi Arabia), industry category ("Fintech"), and organisation type ("Company/Startup") to ascertain the total number of active fintech firms and funding activities during the observation period. The baseline estimations utilise a fixed effects OLS model incorporating both bank fixed effects and year fixed effects to account for unobserved, time-invariant variation among banks and for common macroeconomic shocks across years. To mitigate potential serial correlation and heteroskedasticity among banks over time, standard errors are grouped at the bank-level. This guarantees strong inference by permitting arbitrary correlation of error terms within each bank while assuming independence among banks. A static fixed effects model An OLS model was utilised to ascertain the immediate impact of fintech activity on bank performance. Dynamic models like GMM were not utilised, as the study emphasises within-bank variation rather than persistence effects, and the primary fintech variable is predominantly exogenous to individual banks. The incorporation of both bank and year fixed effects, in conjunction with bank-level clustered standard errors, alleviates apprehensions regarding omitted variable bias and endogeneity. The variable FIN denotes the magnitude of fintech activity in each country and year, quantified as the total number of active fintech firms operating in the UAE and Saudi Arabia throughout the observation period. The data are compiled at the country-year level and subsequently assigned to each bank operating in that country for the corresponding year, ensuring uniform fintech exposure levels among all banks within a certain national market. This definition delineates the external technological and competitive pressures imposed by fintech expansion on traditional banks, as opposed to firm-specific adoption behaviours.

The prior repetition of the FIN variable in Table 4.1 constituted a formatting error; only the FIN variable (FIN) is utilised in the regression analysis, and this should supplant the redundant entry. The correction has been made in the table.

Table 4.1 Fixed effect regression

Variables	(1) Return on assets	(2) Return on equity	(3) Net interest margin
FIN	−0.351*	−0.271***	−0.472***
	(0.193)	(0.076)	(0.151)
TA	−0.509	0.062	−1.488***
	(0.451)	(0.185)	(0.385)
CAP	1.687***	0.313*	1.483***
	(0.411)	(0.182)	(0.334)
LLP	−0.672***	−0.178***	0.224**
	(0.123)	(0.051)	(0.097)
GROWTH	0.007	0.067**	0.075
	(0.085)	(0.033)	(0.067)
GDP	−0.143	2.813***	3.540*
	(2.556)	(1.017)	(1.986)
INF	0.054	0.014	0.015
	(0.046)	(0.018)	(0.036)
R-SQR	0.375	0.347	0.284
Observations	147	138	147
Number of id	17	17	17

Note Authors own compilation. Standard error in the parenthesis. *, **, *** Significant at 1, 5 and 10% levels (*** $p < 0.01$, ** $p < 0.05$, * $p < 0.1$). FIN—FinTech, TA—Total assets, CAP—EQUITY/TOTAL ASSET, LLP—Loan loss provisions, GD—Growth deposit, GDP—Economic growth, INF—Inflation

Variable Description

Variable	Definition	Source
ROA	Return on assets equals net income to total assets	Bloomberg Terminal
ROE	Return on equity equals net income to total equities	Bloomberg Terminal
NIM	Net interest margin equals net interest income to total assets	Bloomberg Terminal
FIN	Number of financial technology firms per annum	Statista/Crunchbase
CAP	Capital ratio equals equity over total assets	Bloomberg Terminal
LLP	Loan loss provisions equal loan loss provisions over total loans	Bloomberg Terminal
GD	Annualised growth of deposits	Bloomberg Terminal

(continued)

(continued)

Variable	*Definition*	*Source*
GDP	Gross domestic product growth (annual %)	World Development Indicators Database
INF	Inflation rate (annual %)	World Development Indicators Database

$PERF_{it} = \beta0 + \beta1 \cdot FINit + \beta2 \cdot TAit + \beta3 \cdot CAPit + \beta4 \cdot INFt + \beta5 \cdot GDit + \beta6 \cdot GDPit + \beta7 \cdot LLPit + \beta8 \cdot INFit + \epsilon it$

The aforementioned equation represents bank performance quantified by ROA, ROE, or NIM as a function of fintech activity and a series of control variables. The coefficient β1 illustrates the marginal impact of fintech advancement on banking performance, demonstrating how variations in fintech engagement affect profitability and efficiency. The coefficients β2 to β6 Illustrate the impact of the control variables capital adequacy (CAP), loan loss provisions (LLP), growth in deposits or credit (GD), GDP growth (GDP), and inflation (INF)—on performance. Bank fixed effects (μ_i) account for time-invariant disparities among banks, while year fixed effects (λt) control for macroeconomic or regulatory shocks that affect all banks within a specific year. The error term (εit) captures unseen elements influencing performance that are not elucidated by the listed variables.

Three regressions are conducted for the Kingdom of Saudi Arabia and three for the United Arab Emirates. The three bank performance metrics serve as proxies for the dependent variable $PERF_{it}$ for each nation.

Analysis and Interpretation

For UAE Panel

Fintech is financial progress, hence altering the interpretation of Table 4.1 considerably. The adverse coefficients for FIN (Fintech) in relation to Return on Assets (ROA), Return on Equity (ROE), and Net Interest Margin (NIM) indicate that Fintech advancement may be undermining the profitability of traditional banking in Dubai. Chen et al. (2019) fintech improves financial access and innovation but exerts competitive pressure on established banks, diminishing their profit margins. Vives (2017) asserts that Fintech newcomers diminish entry barriers in financial services, hence enhancing competition, especially in payments and loans, which may reduce interest margins and profits (Sabir et al. 2021). Frost (2020) indicates that Fintech diminishes banks' conventional advantages in client data and relationship banking, thereby undermining profitability in the short run. At the 10% level, the negative and statistically significant coefficient on FIN ($\beta = -0.351$, $p < 0.1$) indicates that there is a correlation between FinTech activity and a decrease in ROA. This could be a result of traditional banks' declining profitability due to rising competition from FinTech companies. The fact that FIN has a statistically significant negative coefficient for ROE ($\beta = -0.271$, $p < 0.01$) supports the idea that FinTech could be reducing the profitability of traditional banks. This effect appears to have a more noticeable influence on shareholder returns, as it is more significant compared to the ROA regression. The expansion of FinTech is linked to net interest margins, possibly as a result of increased pricing competition and disintermediation in lending and deposit-taking functions, as indicated by the large and statistically significant negative coefficient ($\beta = -0.472$, $p < 0.01$) for FIN in the NIM regression.

Boot and Marinc (2010) large incumbent banks face challenges in swiftly adapting to Fintech disruptions due to their legacy systems and intricate organisational structures. Major banks in Dubai may encounter margin compression due to nimble Fintech competitors providing more cost-effective and expedited services.

In Table 4.2, Panel Quantile Regression results offer a detailed perspective on the influence of Fintech (FIN) and other variables on Return on Assets (ROA) across various segments of the profitability distribution, ranging from underperforming to high-performing institutions. Let us analyse this in the context of Fintech literature and pertinent empirical research. Fintech poses a greater disruption to established, profitable institutions. High-performing banks predominantly depend on interest-based revenue and traditional business models, rendering them more susceptible to digital disintermediation (Thomas Philippon 2016). At the 25th percentile (poor performers) Fintech exerts a considerable adverse impact. The impact intensifies in the 75th (−0.470) and 90th (−0.956) percentiles. At the median (50th percentile), the effect is negative, however, not statistically significant.

In Table 4.3, the adverse and substantial effect of fintech is particularly evident at elevated quantiles of ROE, suggesting that more profitable enterprises are disproportionately influenced by fintech participation. This may indicate competitive disruption or efficiency pressures caused by

Table 4.2 Panel quantile regression (return on assets)

ROA	*(1)* *q25*	*(2)* *q50*	*(3)* *q75*	*(4)* *q90*
FIN	−0.311**	−0.218	−0.470***	−0.956***
	(0.141)	(0.133)	(0.163)	(0.343)
TA	−1.611***	−1.542***	−1.487***	−1.753**
	(0.305)	(0.244)	(0.300)	(0.675)
CAP	2.041***	1.816***	1.783***	1.985***
	(0.371)	(0.256)	(0.279)	(0.665)
LLP	−0.168*	−0.092	−0.064	−0.178
	(0.093)	(0.137)	(0.121)	(0.251)
GROWTH	0.010	0.003	0.053	0.093
	(0.065)	(0.065)	(0.083)	(0.105)
GDP	2.250	3.819**	6.900***	12.624***
	(2.272)	(1.831)	(2.577)	(4.060)
INF	0.061	0.090*	0.015	−0.040
	(0.042)	(0.047)	(0.046)	(0.067)
Constant	−60.316	−103.572**	−188.961***	−344.985***
	(63.030)	(51.110)	(71.609)	(112.047)
Observations	147	147	147	147

Note Authors own compilation. Standard error in the parenthesis. *, **, *** Significant at 1, 5 and 10% levels (***$p < 0.01$, **$p < 0.05$, *$p < 0.1$). FIN—FinTech, TA—Total assets, CAP—EQUITY/ TOTAL ASSET, LLP—Loan loss provisions, GD—Growth deposit, GDP—Economic growth, and INF—Inflation

fintech developments. The panel quantile regression analysis indicates that Fintech (FIN) exerts a significant and progressively detrimental effect on ROE, especially at elevated quantiles. Koenker and Bassett (1978) quantile regression estimator is utilised to analyse the disparate impacts of FinTech expansion on the distribution of bank performance metrics. The estimator minimises an asymmetric loss function, enabling the conditional effects of FinTech activity on bank profitability to vary across quantiles of performance metrics such as ROA, ROE, and NIM. Standard errors are calculated using a bootstrapping method (500 replications) to achieve robust inference in the presence of non-normal residuals and possible heteroskedasticity.

The quantile analysis indicates that the influence of FinTech (FIN) on bank performance varies across different profitability levels. In the panels for both the UAE and Saudi Arabia, the q75 and q90 quantiles exhibit statistically significant and economically substantial negative coefficients

Table 4.3 Panel Quantile regression (Return on Equity)

ROE	*(1)* *q25*	*(2)* *q50*	*(3)* *q75*	*(4)* *q90*
FIN	−0.264***	−0.162	−0.311***	−0.472***
	(0.076)	(0.101)	(0.096)	(0.113)
TA	−0.014	0.052	−0.240	0.076
	(0.117)	(0.160)	(0.285)	(0.476)
CAP	0.262*	0.175	0.485*	0.183
	(0.133)	(0.154)	(0.279)	(0.495)
LLP	−0.050	0.001	−0.073	−0.062
	(0.047)	(0.062)	(0.076)	(0.052)
GROWTH	0.032	0.061	0.052	0.042
	(0.058)	(0.049)	(0.064)	(0.054)
GDP	2.505***	2.546	3.863**	5.660***
	(0.906)	(1.999)	(1.639)	(1.307)
INF	0.001	0.033	−0.009	−0.011
	(0.019)	(0.034)	(0.015)	(0.018)
Constant	−68.866***	−70.594	−105.600**	−155.911***
	(25.124)	(55.632)	(45.350)	(36.388)
Observations	138	138	138	138

Note Authors own compilation. Standard error in the parenthesis. *, **, *** Significant at 1, 5 and 10% levels (***$p < 0.01$, **$p < 0.05$, *$p < 0.1$). FIN—Financial development, TA—Total assets, CAP—EQUITY/TOTAL ASSET, LLP—Loan loss provisions, GD—Growth deposit, GDP—Economic growth, INF—Inflation

for ROA and ROE, indicating that high-performing banks are disproportionately impacted by FinTech competition. This corresponds with the research (e.g., Philippon 2016; Frost 2020) suggesting that FinTech entrants diminish the margins of established, lucrative banks via digital disintermediation and pricing competition.

In Table 4.4 FinTech demonstrates a negative and statistically significant impact on NIM at the 25th ($\beta = -0.305$, $p < 0.05$) and 90th quantiles ($\beta = -1.728$, $p < 0.01$). This indicates that in banks with both low and high net interest margins, more financial development generally narrows interest margins, perhaps as a result of heightened competition and more effective financial intermediation (Demirguc and Huizinga 1998). The effect is statistically insignificant at the median and 75th quantile, indicating that its influence is more evident at the extremes of the NIM distribution. Quantile regression reveals that the factors influencing NIM vary among banks. Financial development, bank size,

Table 4.4 Panel quantile regression (net interest margin)

NIM	*(1)* *q25*	*(2)* *q50*	*(3)* *q75*	*(4)* *q90*
FIN	−0.305**	−0.206	−0.692	−1.728***
	(0.117)	(0.271)	(0.423)	(0.649)
TA	−2.085***	−2.514***	−2.488***	−2.445*
	(0.338)	(0.401)	(0.597)	(1.308)
CAP	1.795***	2.010***	1.771***	1.713
	(0.326)	(0.224)	(0.394)	(1.234)
LLP	0.396**	0.583***	0.793***	1.031**
	(0.164)	(0.202)	(0.253)	(0.441)
GROWTH	0.045	0.013	−0.152	−0.219
	(0.089)	(0.099)	(0.098)	(0.234)
GDP	2.677	3.271	8.902	20.883***
	(2.300)	(3.932)	(6.188)	(7.273)
INF	0.048	0.089	0.051	−0.076
	(0.040)	(0.062)	(0.060)	(0.112)
Constant	−66.681	−81.648	−235.650	−567.222***
	(63.715)	(108.843)	(171.685)	(202.079)
Observations	147	147	147	147

Note Authors own compilation. Standard error in the parenthesis. *, **, *** Significant at 1, 5 and 10% levels (***$p < 0.01$, **$p < 0.05$, *$p < 0.1$). FIN—FinTech, TA—Total assets, CAP—EQUITY/TOTAL ASSET, LLP—Loan loss provisions, GD—Growth deposit, GDP—Economic growth, INF—Inflation

and capitalisation exert varying influences throughout the NIM distribution, highlighting the significance of variation in banking behaviour. This sophisticated comprehension can assist policymakers in directing reforms and bank managers in customising plans according to respective NIM profiles.

For Saudi Arabian Panel

For Table 4.5 FinTech correlates with a marginal decrease in ROA, either attributable to heightened competition or diminished interest spreads in more advanced financial markets. This corroborates the findings of (Demirguc and Huizinga 1998), who determined that more profound financial systems impose downward pressure on bank profitability. Nonetheless, the little impact on ROE and NIM indicates that this effect is less pronounced on equity returns and margins within this model. At the 10% level, the negative and statistically significant coefficient on FIN ($\beta = -0.225$, $p < 0.1$) indicates that there is a slight decrease in bank profitability as assessed by ROA when there is more FinTech activity. This could be a sign of the more cutthroat market conditions brought about by FinTech innovations, where margins are getting squeezed. The ROE model does not definitively state that FinTech has an influence on equity returns because the coefficient on FIN is negative ($\beta = -1.585$), but it is not statistically significant. Unlike ROA and ROE, FIN has a small positive effect on NIM ($\beta = 0.036$), which means there is no clear association between FinTech activity and banks' net interest spread in the simple regression.

In Table 4.6 the model indicates that financial technology may exert intricate consequences, particularly on highly lucrative enterprises. Quantile regression uncovers variability in the factors influencing profitability

Table 4.5 Simple regression

Variables	*(1) ROA*	*(2) ROE*	*(3) NIM*
FIN	−0.225*	−1.585	0.036
	(0.136)	(1.031)	(0.205)
TA	0.641**	17.153***	0.186
	(0.280)	(2.118)	(0.350)
CAP	0.034	−11.680***	−0.197
	(0.247)	(1.866)	(0.307)
LLP	−0.134**	−1.001**	0.349***
	(0.065)	(0.495)	(0.082)
GROWTH	−0.004	−0.018	0.027
	(0.031)	(0.237)	(0.040)
GDP	0.483	6.614	0.160
	(1.778)	(13.451)	(2.712)
INF	−0.029	−0.169	−0.064
	(0.028)	(0.215)	(0.045)
Constant	−18.540	−254.456	−4.010
	(50.721)	(383.658)	(77.391)
R-SQR	0.487	0.553	0.321
Observations	93	93	93
Number of id	11	11	11

Note Authors own compilation. Standard error in the parenthesis. *, **, *** Significant at 1, 5 and 10% levels (***$p < 0.01$, **$p < 0.05$, *$p < 0.1$). FIN—FinTech, TA—Total asset, CAP—EQUITY/TOTAL ASSET, LLP—Loan loss provisions, GD—Growth deposit, GDP—Economic growth, INF—Inflation that ordinary least squares may overlook. The output exhibits a negative and marginally significant effect solely at the 90th percentile. This suggests that in high-performing enterprises (upper ROA quantile), enhanced financial technology may somewhat diminish ROA, possibly due to heightened financialisation risks or inefficiencies. Total asset becomes statistically significant at the 75th and 90th quantiles, indicating that larger enterprises experience economies of scale and exhibit more profitability in higher ROA distributions.

In Table 4.7 fintech becomes significant and adverse alone at the 90th quantile, suggesting that for the most profitable enterprises regarding ROE, heightened adoption or exposure to financial technology may somewhat diminish profitability potentially due to integration expenses or technology-related inefficiencies in the short term.

In Table 4.8 has no statistically significant impact on NIM at any quantile, however the coefficient rises with increasing quantiles. This indicates a possibly beneficial, although weak and non-robust, link for more

Table 4.6 Panel quantile regression for return on assets

ROA	*(1)* *25*	*(2)* *50*	*(3)* *75*	*(4)* *90*
FIN	−0.184	−0.195	−0.125	−0.201*
	(0.144)	(0.161)	(0.172)	(0.118)
TA	0.345	0.465	0.871***	0.790**
	(0.408)	(0.387)	(0.263)	(0.318)
CAP	0.321	0.188	−0.243	−0.127
	(0.373)	(0.350)	(0.212)	(0.235)
LLP	−0.112	−0.085	−0.082	−0.058
	(0.153)	(0.086)	(0.078)	(0.098)
GROWTH	−0.002	0.049	−0.001	0.004
	(0.045)	(0.034)	(0.042)	(0.075)
GDP	−0.876	0.339	−0.950	0.557
	(1.910)	(1.924)	(2.371)	(1.805)
INF	−0.040	−0.058*	−0.019	−0.031
	(0.071)	(0.031)	(0.029)	(0.028)
Constant	20.778	−14.257	22.306	−21.031
	(54.591)	(54.435)	(66.735)	(50.876)
Observations	93	93	93	93

Note Authors own compilation. Standard error in the parenthesis. *, **, *** Significant at 1, 5 and 10% levels (***$p < 0.01$, **$p < 0.05$, *$p < 0.1$). FIN—FinTech, TA—Total assets, CAP—EQUITY/TOTAL ASSET, LLP—Loan loss provisions, GD—Growth deposit, GDP—Economic growth, INF—Inflation

Table 4.7 Panel quantile regression for return on equity

ROE	*(1)* *25*	*(2)* *50*	*(3)* *75*	*(4)* *90*
FIN	−0.150	−0.142	−0.134	−0.142**
	(0.091)	(0.133)	(0.102)	(0.062)
TA	1.269***	1.234***	1.324***	1.190***
	(0.347)	(0.284)	(0.111)	(0.195)
CAP	−0.737**	−0.880***	−1.002***	−0.902***
	(0.357)	(0.243)	(0.103)	(0.164)
LLP	−0.117	−0.033	−0.034	−0.015
	(0.108)	(0.060)	(0.038)	(0.033)
GROWTH	−0.022	0.011	−0.018	−0.010
	(0.024)	(0.016)	(0.027)	(0.022)
GDP	−0.275	0.941	0.984	1.156
	(1.331)	(1.694)	(1.243)	(1.023)
INF	−0.016	−0.019	−0.001	−0.002
	(0.035)	(0.021)	(0.011)	(0.009)
Constant	3.742	−29.828	−30.801	−35.180
	(38.158)	(48.574)	(35.761)	(29.072)
Observations	93	93	93	93

Note Authors own compilation. Standard error in the parenthesis. *, **, *** Significant at 1, 5 and 10% levels (***$p < 0.01$, **$p < 0.05$, *$p < 0.1$). FIN—FinTech, TA—Total assets, CAP—EQUITY/TOTAL ASSET, LLP—Loan loss provisions, GD—Growth deposit, GDP—Economic growth, INF—Inflation

profitable enterprises, yet it lacks the reliability to establish a definitive relationship.

Findings and Discussion

It appears from the data that fintech is linked to a small drop in ROA, which means that banks' bottom lines might take a hit as technology becomes more integrated. Demirgüç-Kunt and Huizinga (1998) provided theoretical explanations and empirical evidence that show how deeper and more sophisticated financial systems impair profitability due to heightened competitive pressures and narrower interest spreads. This finding is in line with their findings. These findings imply that, according to the general model, advances in fintech may influence operational efficiency and asset returns, but they do not always result in decreased returns for shareholders or interest-based income. Still, a different panel quantile regression analysis shows that the fintech-profitability association varies

Table 4.8 Panel quantile regression for net interest margin

NIM	*(1)* *25*	*(2)* *50*	*(3)* *75*	*(4)* *90*
FIN	0.011	−0.018	0.075	0.340
	(0.267)	(0.210)	(0.224)	(0.403)
TA	−0.342	0.091	0.212	0.263
	(0.420)	(0.566)	(0.534)	(0.716)
CAP	0.270	−0.253	−0.346	−0.265
	(0.431)	(0.509)	(0.404)	(0.520)
LLP	0.351***	0.359***	0.357***	0.268**
	(0.130)	(0.132)	(0.133)	(0.126)
GROWTH	0.013	0.001	0.036	−0.036
	(0.067)	(0.050)	(0.066)	(0.097)
GDP	1.140	2.136	−0.616	−5.100
	(3.099)	(2.649)	(3.016)	(4.372)
INF	−0.046	−0.059	−0.066	−0.073
	(0.062)	(0.053)	(0.072)	(0.069)
Constant	−30.860	−59.019	19.613	147.277
	(88.289)	(74.920)	(86.774)	(127.089)
Observations	93	93	93	93

Note Authors own compilation. Standard error in the parenthesis. *, **, *** Significant at 1, 5 and 10 percent levels (***$p < 0.01$, **$p < 0.05$, *$p < 0.1$). FIN—FinTech, TA—Total assets, CAP—EQUITY/TOTAL ASSET, LLP—Loan loss provisions, GD—Growth deposit, GDP—Economic growth, INF—Inflation

among performance quartiles. There appears to be a preponderance of negative effects in high-performing firms, as Table shows that the impact of fintech on ROA becomes statistically significant at the 90th percentile. This can be because of the growing expense of integration, the difficulties of adopting new technologies, or the financialisation risks that hit very lucrative businesses the hardest. In a study conducted by Cecchetti and Kharroubi (2019), it was shown that financial development can start to have a detrimental effect on economic performance beyond a certain point, owing to inefficiencies and misallocation of resources.

The report offers an extensive examination of the influence of financial technology (Fintech) on banking performance indicators Return on Assets (ROA), Return on Equity (ROE), and Net Interest Margin (NIM) specifically within Dubai's banking sector. Findings from econometric methods, such as Panel Quantile Regression, indicate that Fintech, rather than general financial development, significantly influences the transformation of traditional banking profitability. The report offers a thorough examination of the influence of financial technology (Fintech) on banking performance indicators Return on Assets (ROA), Return on Equity (ROE), and Net Interest Margin. The baseline study (Table 4.1) indicates that Fintech developments are associated with a reduction in all three profitability metrics (ROA, ROE, and NIM), suggesting that the incorporation of Fintech may be undermining the conventional profit models of established banks. This aligns with existing literature that highlights Fintech's disruptive capabilities. Chen et al. (2019) contend that although Fintech improves financial accessibility and fosters innovation, it imposes competitive strain on traditional institutions, hence diminishing profit margins. Vives (2017) and Sabir et al. (2021) observe that Fintech diminishes entry barriers in loans and payments, hence heightening rivalry and constricting profit margins. Frost (2020) emphasises that digital advances undermine banks' conventional advantages, including relationship banking and exclusive client data, but Boot and Marinc (2010) argue that large banks face challenges in rapid adaptation due to outdated infrastructures.

Conclusion and Implications

The results of this study are in line with previous research on the revolutionary impact of Fintech on the financial markets. Demirgüç-Kunt and Huizinga (1998), Chen et al. (2019), and Vives (2017) are among the researchers who have highlighted how agile Fintech firms' entrance and rising financial sophistication pose a threat to the profitability of incumbent banks. This is because these firms reduce market share and narrow interest spreads. The fact that conventional financial institutions are sluggish to respond to technology developments is making the problem worse (Boot and Marinc 2010; Frost 2020). In conclusion, Fintech is great for innovation and accessibility, but it changes the dynamics of competition, which can hurt profits, particularly for long-standing institutions. It is imperative that policymakers and bank executives have a level head when dealing with Fintech integration, taking full use of its potential while simultaneously minimising the fundamental threats it may cause to the profitability of conventional banking. Research in the future might go more into the ways in which various Fintech applications (such as payments, lending, and AI-driven credit rating) affect different parts of a bank's performance. As of 2025, the two most prominent GCC fintech hubs are the Kingdom of Saudi Arabia (KSA) and the United

Arab Emirates (UAE). Both countries have achieved remarkable strides in developing robust fintech ecosystems, thanks to their aggressive regulatory frameworks, substantial investments, and an increase in innovative entrepreneurs.

The study presents robust empirical evidence indicating that the emergence of FinTech has adversely affected the performance of traditional banking, specifically regarding return on assets (ROA), return on equity (ROE), and net interest margin (NIM), among banks in the United Arab Emirates (UAE) and Saudi Arabia from 2014 to 2024. The quantile regression analysis indicates that this negative effect is especially significant among high-performing banks, suggesting that digital entrants are increasingly competing with established entities that possess substantial profitability and market presence. These findings highlight the necessity for regulators to reconcile innovation, competition, and systemic stability from a policy perspective. Central banks and financial regulators in the UAE and Saudi Arabia have implemented advanced measures via FinTech sandboxes, open banking initiatives, and digital licensing frameworks (Saudi Central Bank [SAMA] 2023; Central Bank of the UAE 2022).

In conclusion, the evidence given suggests that FinTech's disruptive growth in the GCC is fundamentally transforming the competitive and regulatory landscape of banking. An anticipatory strategy rooted in inclusive regulation, strategic partnerships, and focused investment in innovation will ascertain whether FinTech becomes a destabilising disruptor or a transformative catalyst for financial modernisation in the region's swiftly digitising economy.

Appendix

For UAE Panel

First Abu Dhabi Bank PJSC (FAB UH)
Emirates NBD Bank PJSC (EMIRATES UH)
Emirates Islamic Bank PJSC (EIB UH)
Abu Dhabi Commercial Bank PJSC (ADCB UH)
Dubai Islamic Bank PJSC (DIB UH)
Abu Dhabi Islamic Bank PJSC (ADIB UH)
Mashreqbank PSC (MASQ UH)
Commercial Bank of Dubai PSC (CBD UH)
National Bank of Fujairah PJSC (NBF UH)

(continued)

(continued)

National Bank of Ras Al-Khaimah PSC/The (RAKBANK UH)
National Bank of Umm Al-Qaiwain PSC (NBQ UH)
Sharjah Islamic Bank (SIB UH)
United Arab Bank PJSC (UAB UH)
Ajman Bank PJSC (AJMANBAN UH)
Invest bank PSC (INVESTB UH)
Commercial Bank International PJSC (CBI UH)
Bank of Sharjah (BOS UH)

For Saudi Panel

Al Rajhi Bank (RJHI AB)
Alinma Bank (ALINMA AB)
Arab National Bank (ARNB AB)
Bank AlBilad (ALBI AB)
Bank Al-Jazira (BJAZ AB)
Banque Saudi Fransi (BSF AB)
Riyad Bank (RIBL AB)
Samba Financial Group (SAMBA AB)
Saudi Awwal Bank (SABB AB)
Saudi Investment Bank/The (SIBC AB)
Saudi National Bank

References

Aaker, D.A., Keller, K.L., 1990. Consumer Evaluations of Brand Extensions. J. Mark. 54, 27. https://doi.org/10.2307/1252171.

Aduba, J.J., Asgari, B., Izawa, H., 2023. Does FinTech penetration drive financial development? Evidence from panel analysis of emerging and developing economies. Borsa Istanbul Rev. 23, 1078–1097. https://doi.org/10.1016/j.bir.2023.06.001.

Ali, A., Marisetty, V.B., 2023. Are FinTech lending apps harmful? Evidence from user experience in the Indian market. Br. Account. Rev. 101269. https://doi.org/10.1016/j.bar.2023.101269.

Arner, D. W., Buckley, R. P., Zetzsche, D. A., & Veidt, R. (2020). FinTech, regtech, and the reconceptualization of financial regulation. Northwestern Journal of International Law & Business, 40(3), 1–54.

Balyuk, T., 2023. FinTech Lending and Bank Credit Access for Consumers. Manage. Sci. 69, 555–575. https://doi.org/10.1287/mnsc.2022.4319.

Bao, Z., Huang, D., 2021. Shadow Banking in a Crisis: Evidence from Fintech During COVID-19. J. Financ. Quant. Anal. 56, 2320–2355. https://doi.org/10.1017/S0022109021000430.

Boot, A.W.A., Marinc, M., 2010. Financial innovation : Economic growth versus instability in bank-based versus financial market driven economies. Present. Bank. Light Glob. Cris. Bank. Light Glob. Cris. Conf. 1–31.

Cecchetti, S. G., Kharroubi, E., 2019. Why does credit growth crowd out real economic growth? Manch. Sch. 87, 1–28.

Central Bank of the UAE. (2022). UAE FinTech Strategy and Open Banking Framework. Abu Dhabi: Central Bank Publications.

Charnes, A., Raike, W.M., Bettinger, C.O., 1972. An extremal and information-theoretic characterization of some interzonal transfer models. Socioecon. Plann. Sci. 6, 531–537. https://doi.org/10.1016/0038-0121(72)90020-1.

Chen, M.A., Wu, Q., Yang, B., 2019. How Valuable Is FinTech Innovation? Rev. Financ. Stud. 32, 2062–2106. https://doi.org/10.1093/rfs/hhy130.

Christensen, C.M., 1990. The Innovator's Dilemma. Entomol. Exp. Appl. 57, 191–200. https://doi.org/10.1111/j.1570-7458.1990.tb01430.x.

Claessens, S., Frost, J., Turner, G., Zhu, F., 2018. Fintech credit markets around the world: size, drivers. BIS Q. Rev. 1, 29–49.

Cornelli, G., Frost, J., Gambacorta, L., 2022. Fintech and Big Tech As the New Credit Provider 82–91. https://doi.org/10.53465/edamba.2021.9788022549301.82-91.

Cornelli, G., Frost, J., Gambacorta, L., Rau, P. R., & Wardrop, R. (2023). Fintech and banking: Unbundling the financial services industry. BIS Quarterly Review, Bank for International Settlements.

Das, K.C., 2023. What Affects Startup Acquisition in Emerging Economy? Evidence from India. J. Emerg. Mark. Financ. 22, 111–134. https://doi.org/10.1177/09726527221141787.

Dasilas, A., Karanović, G., 2023. The impact of FinTech firms on bank performance: evidence from the UK. EuroMed J. Bus. https://doi.org/10.1108/EMJB-04-2023-0099.

Daud, S.N.M., Ahmad, A.H., Khalid, A., Azman-Saini, W.N.W., 2022. FinTech and financial stability: Threat or opportunity? Financ. Res. Lett. 47, 102667. https://doi.org/10.1016/j.frl.2021.102667.

Demirguc-Kunt, A., Klapper, L., Hess, J., 2018. The Global Findex Database 2017. World Bank.

Demirguc, A., Huizinga, H., 1998. Determinants of commercial bank interest margins and profitability: some international evidence 43, 1–9.

Frost, J., 2020. The economic forces driving fintech adoption across countries. Technol. Revolut. Financ. Serv. How Banks, FinTechs, Cust. Win Together 70–89. https://doi.org/10.2139/ssrn.3515326.

Fu, J., Mishra, M., 2022. Combatting fraudulent and predatory fintech apps with machine learning.

Fung, D.W.H., Lee, W.Y., Yeh, J.J.H., Yuen, F.L., 2020. Friend or foe: The divergent effects of FinTech on financial stability. Emerg. Mark. Rev. 45, 100727. https://doi.org/10.1016/j.ememar.2020.100727.

Gabor, D., Brooks, S., 2017. The digital revolution in financial inclusion: international development in the fintech era. New Polit. Econ. 22, 423–436. https://doi.org/10.1080/13563467.2017.1259298.

Goldstein, I., Jiang, W., Karolyi, G.A., 2019. To FinTech and beyond. Rev. Financ. Stud. 32, 1647–1661. https://doi.org/10.1093/rfs/hhz025.

Khan, H.H., Khan, S., Ghafoor, A., 2023. Fintech adoption, the regulatory environment and bank stability: An empirical investigation from GCC economies. Borsa Istanbul Rev. 23, 1263–1281. https://doi.org/10.1016/j.bir.2023.10.010.

Koenker, R., & Bassett Jr, G. (1978). Regression quantiles. Econometrica: journal of the Econometric Society, 33–50.

Li, Y., Spigt, R., Swinkels, L., 2017. The impact of FinTech start-ups on incumbent retail banks' share prices. Financ. Innov. 3. https://doi.org/10.1186/s40854-017-0076-7.

Litimi, H., BenSaïda, A., Raheem, M.M., 2024. Impact of FinTech Growth on Bank Performance in GCC Region. J. Emerg. Mark. Financ. 23, 227–245. https://doi.org/10.1177/09726527231218423.

Phan, D.H.B., Narayan, P.K., Rahman, R.E., Hutabarat, A.R., 2020. Do financial technology firms influence bank performance? Pacific Basin Financ. J. 62, 101210. https://doi.org/10.1016/j.pacfin.2019.101210.

Philippon, T. (2016). The FinTech opportunity. NBER Working Paper No. 22476, National Bureau of Economic Research.

https://rbi.org.in/.

Romanova, I., Kudinska, M., 2016. Banking and fintech: A challenge or opportunity? Contemp. Stud. Econ. Financ. Anal. 98, 21–35. https://doi.org/10.1108/S1569-375920160000098002.

Sabir, S.A., Javed, T., Khan, S.A.L.I., Javed, M.Z., 2021. Investment Behaviour of Individual Investors of Pakistan Stock Market with Moderating Role of Financial Literacy. J. Contemp. Issues Bus. Gov. 27. https://doi.org/10.47750/cibg.2021.27.02.134.

Saudi Central Bank (SAMA). (2023). Annual FinTech Report 2023. Riyadh: SAMA Publication.

Stern, C., Makinen, M., Qian, Z., 2017. FinTechs in China—with a special focus on peer to peer lending. J. Chinese Econ. Foreign Trade Stud. 10, 215–228. https://doi.org/10.1108/JCEFTS-06-2017-0015.

Suri, T., Bharadwaj, P., Jack, W., 2021. Fintech and household resilience to shocks: Evidence from digital loans in Kenya. J. Dev. Econ. 153, 102697. https://doi.org/10.1016/j.jdeveco.2021.102697.

Thakor, A. V., 2019. FinTech and banking: What Do We Know? 1–23.

Thomas, N.M., 2023. Modeling key enablers influencing FinTechs offering SME credit services: A multi-stakeholder perspective. Electron. Mark. 33. https://doi.org/10.1007/s12525-023-00627-6.

Thomas Philippon, 2016. The FinTech opportunity 4, 2016.

Vives, X., 2017. FinTech and banking. Friends or foes? Eur. Econ.

Vučinić, M., 2020. Fintech and Financial Stability Potential Influence of FinTech on Financial Stability, Risks and Benefits. J. Cent. Bank. Theory Pract. 9, 43–66. https://doi.org/10.2478/jcbtp-2020-0013.

Xiao, S., Zhao, S., 2012. Financial development, government ownership of banks and firm innovation. J. Int. Money Financ. 31, 880–906. https://doi.org/10.1016/j.jimonfin.2012.01.006.

Zhou, W., DouglasArner, D.W., Buckley, R.P., 2015. Regulation of digital financial services in China: last mover advantage?

Zhu, R., Tan, K., Xin, X., Wang, Q., 2025. Jo u a of. J. Behav. Exp. Financ. 124046. https://doi.org/10.1016/j.jbef.2025.101055.

Zhu, X., Asimakopoulos, S., Kim, J., 2020. Financial development and innovation-led growth: Is too much finance better? J. Int. Money Financ. 100, 102083. https://doi.org/10.1016/j.jimonfin.2019.102083.

PART II

Fintech, Islamic Finance, and Regulatory Innovation

CHAPTER 5

From Silos to Systems: Leveraging the X-Tech Perspective for Shari'ah Compliance and Integration

Ali Polat

Introduction

Emerging technologies need their own paradigm and require changes in conventional understanding of the businesses. Such a dynamic landscape is the reason why business and technological siloed systems need to be converted into X-Tech perspectives. A system approach to technological developments will help for such conversion. Kronblad and Jensen (2023) state in their interviews with legal professionals working in the field of LegalTech that these changes lead to differences even in how individuals

Throughout this paper, *digital maturity* refers to the institutional capacity to adopt, integrate, and scale technological systems—both human and infrastructural.

A. Polat (✉)
Faculty of Political Science, Department of Economics, Ankara Yildirim Beyazit University, Ankara, Turkey
e-mail: alipolat@aybu.edu.tr

K. Tsanis et al. (eds.), *Digital Finance and Transformation in the Gulf*,
https://doi.org/10.1007/978-981-92-1588-1_5

define themselves in the workplace and construct a professional identity. Meaning that it is not only the way tasks are carried out and the prevalence of intense technology that are changing; the perspective of the human resources performing these tasks toward their profession, their working environment, and their understanding of professionalism are also transforming. In this paper, X-Tech is defined as a transversal, system-level technological paradigm that connects multiple technology-enabled verticals—FinTech, RegTech, LegalTech, InsurTech, SupTech, TaxTech, ESG-Tech—through shared architectures, semantic interoperability, and unified governance layers. Unlike domain-specific "Tech" verticals, which optimize isolated functions, X-Tech treats technologies as interconnected components of a broader socio-technical fabric shaped jointly by regulatory, ethical, and sectoral logics (Tanaka 2019, 2021; Cao 2024). Thus, X-Tech is not a new acronym among many but an integrative logic for orchestrating cross-sector capabilities under a common design philosophy rooted in Shari'ah governance and systemic digital maturity.

The main argument of this study is that the integration of traditional service methods with emerging technologies such as artificial intelligence (AI), blockchain, the Internet of Things (IoT), cloud computing, big data analytics, distributed ledger technology, and others brings about radical changes of all scales for all institutions with horizontal and vertical interconnections (public-private-semi-public), as well as individuals. To be prepared for this transformation, we must align our relationship with technology and our perspective accordingly. While part of this preparation concerns digital literacy and digital infrastructure, another part involves the necessity for digital transformation strategies to possess a holistic and forward-looking perspective geared toward integration.

To have a Shari'ah Governance and compliance consistent with the different technologies mentioned above, one should understand the evolving landscape of the technology. The letter "X," in the first part of X-tech term, is almost a buzzword that business environments like. There were no words in the dictionary beginning with the letter as late as 1806. The letter X has long functioned as a symbol for something more meaningful and the need for abstraction set the stage for X's popularity across the tech world (Burton 2018). Even more specific use of X is introduced by the era of AI, like X-AI, which refers to the new age of AI and the emerging AI ecosystem (Cao 2024). Even the literature on X-tech is not mature and still developing. Tanaka (2019) and (2021) are the papers where X-tech is used as a term in the title and both articles analyze how life insurance companies in Japan must transform their organizational structures to adapt to and thrive in the era of X-Tech—a term that encompasses technologies like FinTech, InsurTech, HealthTech, and MedTech. The term in that sense is defined as "X-Tech can be described as a phenomenon involving the separation and integration of value chain elements across various industries including Information and Communication Technologies (ICT)."

In this article the contribution to discussion is more on the interconnectedness and interdependence of these acronyms and X-tech can be understood and defined as follow: The X-Tech perspective is not merely about applying technology within a single domain (such as FinTech or LegalTech), but about systematically interlinking multiple technology-enabled verticals. It connects specialized tech domains (e.g., FinTech, LegalTech, SupTech) through cross-functional architectures and shared infrastructure, and further integrates macro-level clusters (e.g., tax tech with economic tech, or ESG tech with finance tech) into a dynamic, semantic ecosystem. This transversal logic transforms isolated silos into an interconnected network of technologies—enabling systemic innovation, regulatory intelligence, and governance agility across sectors.

There is no single term or theory that directly captures the concept that overly specialized technological silos targeting highly specific domains may later lead to integration problems. However, the concepts of siloed systems (technical debt[1] also) emerge as useful frameworks to help define and understand this issue.

In business management and IT, the concept of a "silo" refers to systems, processes, or departments that operate in isolation from others. Risks associated with siloed systems include inefficiency, unnecessary duplication, and lack of communication or integration between systems (McHugh 2022). A similar branch exists in public administration literature. A "silo" in the public sector, which can be described as a hierarchical

[1] Technical debt is a software engineering concept that refers to the additional rework cost incurred when developers choose an easy, quick solution instead of a more robust one (Tom et al. 2013). If each "tech" is developed in isolation without considering integration with others, there is a risk of accumulating technical debt. This technical debt can lead to significant costs, both in terms of software development and opportunity costs. If the interoperability of information systems or software is not designed with the interaction of all these technologies in mind, integrating them in the future may pose a serious challenge.

organization, aims to maximize vertical coordination at the expense of horizontal coordination. These are structures that focus more on their own internal performance and narrow objectives. Since completely dismantling such structures would entail political and administrative costs, a perspective must be developed that enables silos to function in effective coordination with one another. The Hong Kong case demonstrates that significant increases in efficiency can be achieved even in silo-dominant systems when coordination is enhanced (Scott and Gong 2021).

Although the X-Tech paradigm overlaps with several adjacent ideas in the digital transformation literature, it is conceptually distinct in scope and purpose. First, platformization focuses on creating multisided digital platforms that facilitate interactions and transactions (Gawer 2022), whereas X-Tech emphasizes governance-centric interoperability across heterogeneous technologies and sectors rather than platform economics. Second, ecosystem integration describes coordination among interconnected actors within a sector (Jacobides et al. 2018); X-Tech, by contrast, extends beyond sectoral ecosystems to integrate macro-level regulatory, ethical, legal, and technological infrastructures into one unified governance fabric. Third, FinTech/RegTech convergence concerns the merging of financial innovation with regulatory automation (von Solms 2021), but remains domain-specific. X-Tech subsumes such convergence as only one subset of a larger architecture in which technological, regulatory, legal, and ethical components are semantically linked to enable systemic Shari'ah-driven intelligence across industries. In this sense, X-Tech provides a higher-order conceptual frame that explains how vertical technologies evolve from isolated optimizers into interdependent components of an integrated compliance ecosystem.

This paper consists of five sections. After the Introduction, the literature is discussed, and the conceptual framework of X-Tech is established. This is followed by an analysis of digital transformation as a prerequisite for integrated governance. The fourth section explores how Shari'ah compliance can be embedded into technological architecture, and the final section presents the challenges, policy tools, and future research agenda.

Literature Review

Digital transformation has emerged as a key force reshaping industries, governments, and societies. As countries strive to address the challenges and opportunities of the digital era, they are integrating conventional services with emerging technologies under a variety of acronyms such as fintech, LegalTech, RegTech, Edutech, and more. Digital transformation is not merely about adopting new technologies; it is fundamentally about rethinking how organizations deliver value to their stakeholders. According to Xue et al. (2022), "*digital transformation can significantly promote green technology innovation in ways that alleviate financial constraints and attract government subsidies.*" Furthermore, the combination of different technologies can lead to the development of critical capabilities that enhance sustainable performance and enable the formulation of sustainable strategies (Stroumpoulis and Kopanaki 2022).

Since the subject we are addressing involves an interdisciplinary approach, the connections will be discussed through other relevant literature and specific studies. The intersection of Shari'ah Compliance and use of AI and different technologies in this study is defined as X-tech. Therefore, such interconnectedness will be discussed and a developed Shari'ah Governance Framework through X-tech will be discussed.

While this study situates the relationship between technological developments and Shari'ah governance within an interdisciplinary X-Tech perspective, it must be recognized that such framing remains, to a degree, constrained by legacy domain boundaries embedded in the mental models of researchers, developers, and practitioners (Bento et al. 2020; Scott and Gong 2021). Overcoming these departmental and silo-oriented paradigms are inherently difficult, as technological implementations of this magnitude correspond to a broader, emergent future of cross-sectoral integration rather than present-day institutional realities (OECD 2022; WEF 2025). This wider systemic dimension—namely, the fact that all technological, regulatory, and ethical layers ultimately interrelate—should therefore not be overlooked when interpreting the discussions that follow (Asian Development Bank 2022; Tanaka 2021).

Usually, the literature discusses how specific domains merge with specific technologies. For example, Solms (2021) emphasizes that to comply with complex financial regulations, banks should integrate Regulatory Technologies (RegTech) into their treasury operations. This would enable digital platforms to manage both strategic operations and advanced regulatory processes. From this perspective, numerous domains with interconnected bilateral relationships will emerge, all of which will later need to be addressed through a holistic perspective.

Beyond sector-specific integrations, understanding the organizational and human factors that influence digital transformation is equally critical. Crusoe et al. (2023) conducted an empirical study on the antecedents of successful digital transformation, examining 91 municipalities in Sweden. They found that the antecedents of digital transformation were largely unknown and explored the dimensions of this issue. The study revealed that many individuals did not fully understand what needed to be done and often left the responsibility to IT departments. However, this lack of knowledge is not a viable solution for achieving successful digital transformation; therefore, it is essential for everyone to learn what their role and responsibilities are in the process.

This highlights a broader governance challenge—how fragmented institutional structures and siloed operations can further complicate digital transformation efforts. Scott and Gong (2021) emphasize the necessity of coordination among silo-type organizations in public institutions, stating that in the case of Hong Kong, high-level bureaucrats were able to address these issues through three types of coordination: informal, semi-formal, and formal.

Grassi and Lanfranchi (2022) discuss the relationship between data, technology, and regulation in the public and private sector use of RegTech. While stakeholders benefit from advantages such as high efficiency and effectiveness, accurate operations, transparency, and lower compliance costs, the authors also highlight risks such as cyber threats, algorithmic biases, and dehumanization. When these issues are viewed from a siloed perspective, the advantages tend to diminish, while disadvantages and additional risks are likely to increase.

In fact, these risks also require examination from a distinct perspective. Li et al. (2023) explore whether there is a potential gap in the design of information systems when applying technologies currently used in the financial sector to other industries within a legal framework. For example, regulatory integration in the financial sector may be considered relatively mature.

However, such maturity has not yet been achieved in non-financial sectors, and the technological maturity of Shariah governance remains even more limited and fragmented by comparison.

Bento et al. (2020) reviewed the literature on organizational silos and, upon examining 40 studies—20 of which were empirical—identified structures that fall under the definition of silos based on their objectives, variables, and methods. The study concludes that the silo approach poses a barrier to achieving organizational goals, as it constitutes a threat to internal collaboration within institutions.

The study by Pivavarava and Koop (2023) aims to bring together two emerging areas related to economic regulation. These areas include the digital practices of National Regulatory Authorities (NRAs) and the digital initiatives developed by these NRAs to enhance consumer participation in the regulatory process. To reconnect the regulatory state with its citizens, the authors propose a new framework that comprehensively captures the digital capacities of NRAs and distinguishes the multiple channels through which consumers interact digitally with NRAs in key regulatory procedures such as information provision, communication, education, and decision-making. To measure the degree of digitalization of regulatory functions, they created a composite index on digital adoption for 236 individual NRAs using a cross-sectional dataset covering 42 geographically diverse EU and OECD countries. In addition to offering recommendations for enhancing the effectiveness of regulatory procedures through consumer-centered digital transformation, the study also provides suggestions for government initiatives aimed at increasing digital trust among consumers and fostering e-participation in economic regulation.

Certainly, conducting case studies on "silo systems" and "technical debt" is also essential. However, organizations that operate with a silo mentality may be reluctant to disclose details about their weaknesses or strengths. There is often a negative perception associated with silo-style management. As noted by Scott and Gong (2021)., the lack of information sharing, unresolved legal disputes with other public institutions, and ineffective coordination—combined with an inward-focused mindset and narrow perspective—can significantly hinder organizational performance. Bezes et al. (2013) further argue that such perspectives can transform institutions into "single-purpose organizations."

As a result, delays in decision-making processes, duplication of resource usage, poor service quality, failure to resolve critical issues, and difficulties in collaborating with non-governmental actors emerge as key consequences of these structural problems.

In a comprehensive report by Millard (2023) on the impact of digital transformation on public administration, the need to define potential future scenarios for new governance models that support the delivery of innovative, human-centered, and inclusive public services in the EU is emphasized.

By analyzing the highest-level documents from 290 Swedish municipalities during the years 2021–2022, Carlsson et al. (2023) found that there has been a noticeable shift in digital transformation strategies—specifically in terms of resource allocation and goal-setting—toward greater emphasis on external value and innovation activities.

The OECD's (2023a) benchmarking study highlights that there are strong foundational efforts to enhance digital maturity. Digital maturity, which has gained increasing attention in the post-pandemic period, reflects the transformation of services into digital formats by both the public and private sectors. Through various digital maturity assessment models, attempts have been made to understand the scope and quality of digital transformation more effectively.

Taken together, the reviewed literature reveals three structural gaps that the X-Tech paradigm seeks to address: silo fragmentation, maturity asymmetries, and governance incoherence. The organizational silos and technical debt literature (Bento et al. 2020; Scott and Gong 2021; Tom et al. 2013) highlights how isolated technical systems and inward-looking bureaucratic units obstruct interoperability—directly motivating X-Tech's emphasis on shared infrastructures and cross-sector architectures. Research on digital maturity and public sector transformation (Carlsson et al. 2023; Crusoe et al. 2023; OECD 2023b) demonstrates that uneven digital maturity slows systemic integration, informing our argument that X-Tech requires coordinated advancement across institutions, not isolated innovation. Finally, the Shari'ah governance literature (Li et al. 2023; Malik 2020; Soualhi 2023) shows that compliance mechanisms remain fragmented and reactive, reinforcing the need for a transversal governance fabric where jurisprudential rigor and technological optimization evolve in tandem. These strands collectively form the conceptual foundation for the X-Tech framework developed in the following sections.

Shari'ah Compliance Framework

The convergence of digital transformation and Islamic finance has reached a critical juncture where traditional Shariah governance frameworks must evolve beyond their current siloed structure to embrace a systematic, technology-integrated approach. This research examines how the X-Tech perspective—a transversal methodology that connects disparate technological solutions under unified governance principles—can revolutionize Shariah compliance from reactive oversight to proactive, intelligent monitoring systems that preserve the maqāṣid al-Sharīʿah while enabling operational excellence.

Current Framework Architecture

Shariah governance frameworks (SGFs) in Islamic financial institutions (IFI) operate through multi-layered oversight mechanisms designed to ensure comprehensive compliance with Islamic law principles (Soualhi 2023). These frameworks typically encompass Board of Directors oversight, Shariah Supervisory Boards, Shariah Compliance Departments, Internal Shariah Audit Units, and Product Development departments, each functioning with distinct roles and responsibilities. The State Bank of Pakistan's regulatory framework, for instance, mandates that Islamic banking institutions establish effective mechanisms for Board oversight, accountability of management and staff, independent Shariah Boards with Resident Shariah Board Members, and comprehensive compliance review mechanisms (State Bank of Pakistan 2025).

The traditional governance model centers on a stakeholder-oriented system that balances the interests of shareholders, customers, creditors, suppliers, and governments while maintaining religious obligations. This approach recognizes that Islamic financial institutions serve stakeholders who specifically seek Shariah-compliant financial services, creating unique fiduciary responsibilities that extend beyond conventional corporate governance.

However, the current structure often results in fragmented oversight where different governance organs operate in relative isolation, creating potential gaps in real-time compliance monitoring and systemic risk assessment (Faizol bin Ismail 2018).

The regulatory landscape varies significantly across jurisdictions, with some countries like Malaysia implementing two-tier Shariah board models that address both institutional and national-level Shariah matters (Faizol bin Ismail 2018). The Islamic Financial Services Board (IFSB) has attempted to harmonize these approaches through exposure drafts that seek industry feedback on comprehensive SGF requirements, including establishment of Central Shariah Boards, mandatory external Shariah audits, and specific governance considerations for Islamic windows (State Bank of Pakistan 2025).

Despite their structured oversight mechanisms, current Shari'ah governance frameworks face several systemic limitations. The literature consistently shows that SGFs suffer from fragmented lines of accountability, inconsistent documentation practices, and slow, manual fatwā validation cycles that are ill-suited to real-time financial operations (Malik 2020; Soualhi 2023). Cross-jurisdictional variability in Shari'ah standards further produces interpretive divergence, complicating compliance for institutions operating across borders (Li et al. 2023). Additionally, SGFs often lack the digital infrastructure needed for automated monitoring—resulting in reactive rather than preventive compliance systems (Mohamed et al. 2024). These constraints underscore the need for a unified architectural approach capable of integrating jurisprudential oversight with technological scalability.

Digital Integration Challenges

The integration of digital technologies into existing Shariah governance structures reveals significant asymmetries in technological maturity across the Islamic finance ecosystem (Afdawaiza et al. 2024). While some institutions embrace blockchain applications and AI for compliance monitoring, others continue to rely on manual fatwā registers and paper-based documentation systems.

This digital divide creates operational inefficiencies and compounds compliance risks as institutions struggle to maintain consistent standards across heterogeneous technological environments (Al Nabhany 2024).

Islamic financial institutions face particular challenges in implementing Shariah-compliant digital solutions due to the need for continuous scholarly oversight and validation. The lack of universal Shariah compliance standards across jurisdictions creates additional complexity for fintech companies operating in multiple markets, highlighting the need for harmonized regulatory approaches that balance innovation with religious compliance. Furthermore, technical challenges arise when integrating

Shariah compliance into automated systems like AI and smart contracts, requiring close collaboration between Islamic scholars and technology developers to ensure compliance without compromising efficiency and scalability (Mohamed et al. 2024).

X-Tech Paradigm for Shariah Governance

The X-Tech approach to Shariah governance, a technological convergence framework, represents a fundamental shift from vertical technology silos to horizontal integration platforms that treat jurisprudential rigor and digital optimization as complementary rather than competing priorities. (NLP technologies can analyze vast amounts of legal documents and contracts, flagging clauses or terms that may be non-compliant with Shariah principles while cross-referencing established guidelines to ensure terms related to interest, speculation, gambling, and prohibited industries are properly identified (Al Nabhany, 2024).

The X-Tech architecture is designed to be modular, allowing both coordinated and unilateral implementation. Some components—such as standardized Shari'ah taxonomies, interoperable fatwā registries, and unified API protocols—require jurisdictional harmonization to achieve their full network effects, especially in cross-border Islamic finance (Baan 2022; State Bank of Pakistan 2025). However, other elements can be adopted independently by single institutions without regulatory alignment, including AI-assisted contract screening, blockchain-based audit trails, internal knowledge graphs, and automated Shari'ah compliance dashboards. This dual structure ensures that X-Tech can deliver immediate value at the institutional level while progressively moving the industry toward a coordinated, multi-jurisdictional compliance ecosystem.

Machine-learning algorithms enable real-time transaction monitoring by assigning risk scores based on likelihood of non-compliance, allowing compliance officers to prioritize high-risk areas and improve overall efficiency. These systems can recognize patterns and anomalies in financial transactions, immediately identifying potentially problematic activities such as interest-based lending or investments in haram industries. The continuous learning capability of AI systems allows them to improve over time, reducing the need for manual intervention while enhancing accuracy in compliance detection (Al Nabhany 2024).

Blockchain technology offers promise for Shariah governance through its immutable record-keeping capabilities and transparency features. The technology is considered Shariah-compliant as it functions as a neutral database tool that stores records transparently and securely, aligning with Islamic finance rules that emphasize transparency and authenticity in financial transactions (Mohamed et al. 2024). Smart contracts running on blockchain platforms can automate contractual processes for Islamic institutions while enforcing Shariah parameters directly within contract terms (Labuan 2024).

Integrated Compliance Architecture

The implementation of X-Tech solutions in Shariah governance requires sophisticated integration architectures that connect multiple stakeholder systems while maintaining data sovereignty and privacy protection. Islamic RegTech solutions can provide real-time Shariah reporting through cloud-based analytics, detect compliance and regulatory risks, assess halal/haram risk exposure, and facilitate counterparty due diligence across the Islamic world. These systems enable real-time transaction monitoring and automated auditing processes, particularly valuable when trading across parties from different schools of Islamic thought, madhāhib (Baan 2022).

AI applications in Shariah compliance extend beyond simple transaction screening to encompass comprehensive document analysis and regulatory reporting. AI-powered systems can sift through vast amounts of documentation in fractions of the time required for manual review, highlighting potential issues for further examination by Shariah scholars while reducing human error and ensuring consistent application of Shariah principles.

However, the implementation of AI in Shariah compliance requires careful attention to interpretability and transparency, as decision-making processes must be explainable to Shariah scholars and other stakeholders (Al Nabhany 2024).

Governance Model Evolution and Discussion

Digital Transformation: A Pre-requisite for X-Tech

The digital age presents both challenges and opportunities for countries aiming to leverage the power of technology to achieve sustainable societal progress. By integrating X-tech perspectives, countries can bridge the divide between the public and private sectors, promoting collaboration and innovation. As Furr et al. (2022) point out, digital transformation is a strategic choice for global enterprises, emphasizing the importance of communication between products and platforms, firms and ecosystems, and people and tools. By adopting a holistic approach to digital transformation, countries can secure sustainable growth, enhanced citizen services, and a competitive advantage in the global digital economy. Nations must remain agile, continuously updating their strategies in response to emerging X-tech trends, and ensure that their digital transformation journeys are inclusive, sustainable, and forward-looking.

There is a growing body of literature on the prerequisites for effective digital transformation. It is crucial to leverage robust and cost-effective digital infrastructures capable of transforming not only companies but entire industries (Gurbaxani and Dunkle 2019). Therefore, continuous investment in digital infrastructure is essential. Digital transformation strategies based on digital platforms can offer comprehensive solutions, such as opening markets for e-services, strengthening local infrastructures, and enhancing digital skills. Komninos et al. (2021) highlighted the importance of digital transformation strategies in shaping urban ecosystems. Siloed development within public and private sectors can lead to inefficiencies and missed opportunities for synergy. Gao et al. (2022) found that the impact of digital transformation is more pronounced in private firms and businesses lacking high technology, suggesting a growing need for more integrated strategies. For SMEs, key factors in digital transformation include investment in digital technologies, the digital skills of employees, and comprehensive digital transformation strategies (Teng et al. 2022). Hence, the human dimension of digital transformation must be approached more realistically, shifting the focus from consumers to producers. These insights point to the necessity of approaching digital transformation not just as a technical upgrade, but as a strategic, organizational, and regulatory realignment effort—especially in the context of X-tech convergence.

If X-tech technologies are developed separately by the public or private sectors and managed within siloed structures—focusing on short-term, institution-centric goals rather than the broader picture—they may lead to multidimensional problems. These potential issues can be summarized as follows:

- Siloed Development: Leads to systems that are difficult to integrate. When technologies from different sectors need to interact, this can cause inefficiencies. In larger organizations and expanding software environments, lack of integration may result in irreversible problems. Siloed systems are the result and perspective of siloed development and Siloed systems generate three predictable problems documented across digital transformation literature: technical fragmentation, duplication of processes, and missed opportunities for cross-sector integration (Bento et al. 2020; Scott and Gong 2021).
- Missed Opportunities for Synergy: When sectors concentrate solely on short-term, internal objectives, they may overlook collaborative opportunities that could yield innovative, cross-sectoral solutions. Focusing on immediate gains can hinder long-term progress. For instance, technology may benefit one sector in the short run but cause long-term adverse effects in another.
- Duplication of Efforts: Without a broader perspective and intersectoral communication, there is a risk of redundant efforts, leading to wasted resources. Excessive efforts without a change in communication and vision amount to nothing more than inefficiency.
- Suboptimal User Experience: For end-users interacting with multiple X-tech platforms, the absence of unity and integration may result in a fragmented and frustrating experience.
- Regulatory and Compliance Challenges: In sectors like fintech, legaltech, and regtech, siloed development may lead to blind spots in regulation or inconsistencies in compliance standards. These issues can translate into significant security risks—especially in interconnected domains. Vulnerabilities in one sector may expose others to increased risk.

These limitations reinforce the need for an X-Tech architecture grounded in integrated design principles. As mentioned by Fong et al. (2021) Seven technologies shaping the future of fintech and among these are AI, blockchain, cloud computing, IOT, open source-SaaS, no-code, low-code, and hyper automation. To efficiently benefit from these future technologies, X-tech perspective is needed together with a mature digital environment in each and every dimensions (Fig. 5.1).

Ali et al. (2025) discuss the AI in Finance and how IFI will adapt to such changes. Table 5.2 provides the use of AI in different areas and in different potential. However, there are additional innovative use cases

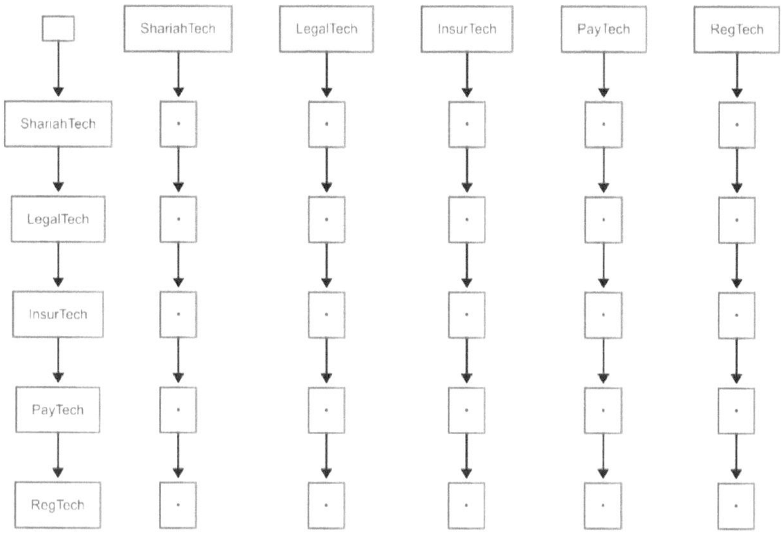

Fig. 5.1 Matrix of connectedness for X-tech perspectives (*Source* Created by author by using mermaid code)

of AI: Automated Sharia Compliance Audits, smart contracts, a finance expert, education, zakat calculation, waqf management, robo advisory, etc.

However, interpreting these use cases solely within the boundaries of financial operations risks narrowing the conceptual scope of AI and limiting its relevance to the broader X-Tech paradigm. AI-driven capabilities—such as automated Shari'ah compliance audits, semantic rule-based engines, cross-sectoral knowledge graphs, integrated regulatory reporting modules, and ESG-aligned risk analytics—operate across multiple verticals simultaneously, not only within finance. Therefore, rather than viewing Table 5.1 as a static classification of financial tasks, it should be understood as an indicative framework showing how AI reshapes office-layered functions across interconnected X-Tech domains including RegTech, LegalTech, SupTech, TaxTech, and ESG-Tech. This transversal interpretation aligns the table with the systemic and cross-domain nature of the X-Tech architecture.

In summary, developing and managing X-tech technologies through a holistic, integrated approach that considers the broader ecosystem

Table 5.1 Literature foundations informing the X-Tech framework

Literature stream	*Literature*	*Core insights from literature*	*Direct implications for the X-Tech paradigm*
Organizational Silos & Technical Debt	Bento et al. (2020) and Scott and Gong (2021)	• Fragmentation of systems and decision-making • Duplication of processes and resources • Weak horizontal coordination across units	• Necessity of unified API layers • Integration-first architecture • Cross-sector interoperability protocols
Digital Transformation & Digital Maturity	Carlsson et al. (2023) and Crusoe et al. (2023) and OECD (2023a)	• Uneven technological readiness across institutions • Limited digital skills in public and private sectors • Slow adaptation to emerging technologies	• Importance of coordinated maturity-mapping • Capability building across institutions • Harmonized infrastructure for X-Tech rollout
Public Governance & Regulatory Integration	Grassi and Lanfranchi (2022) and Pivavarava and Koop (2023)	• Fragmented regulatory structures • Inconsistent adoption of digital tools by regulators • Gaps in consumer/market participation	• Need for federated governance layers • Real-time regulatory intelligence systems • Shared data standards across sectors
Shari'ah Governance & Islamic Finance Regulation	Malik (2020), Mohamed et al. (2024) and Soualhi (2023)	• Reactive and manual compliance processes • Heterogeneity in Shari'ah rulings and standards • Absence of automated jurisprudential workflows	• Embedding Shari'ah logic into digital architecture • AI-assisted fatwā review and compliance checks • Integrated audit trails and jurisprudential APIs

Source Compiled by the author based on reviewed literature

Table 5.2 Use of AI in finance

Front office	Chatbots and Robo Advisors Credit Scoring Biometrics
Middle office	Fraud Management Compliance with Legal Requirements
Back office	ChatBot in different time efficiency tasks

Source Ali et al. (2025)

and long-term impacts is critical to maximizing benefits and minimizing challenges.

Stakeholder Integration Mechanisms

The X-Tech paradigm necessitates evolution in traditional Shariah governance models to accommodate increased stakeholder participation and real-time decision-making processes. Contemporary Shariah governance faces key challenges including changing stakeholder mindsets regarding differences between conventional and Islamic governance models, understanding conceptual implications of these differences, addressing "people risk" in governance organs, and establishing infrastructure without making Islamic finance prohibitively expensive (Malik 2020).

Effective Shariah governance requires robust organizational arrangements that ensure oversight, responsibility, and accountability across boards of directors, management, and Shariah committees. The governance framework must balance interests of shareholders, stakeholders, and society while fulfilling religious obligations, creating legitimacy for Islamic banks, and enhancing public confidence while reducing reputational risk. This stakeholder-oriented approach aligns with Islamic principles of property rights and commitment to contractual obligations that govern economic and social behavior (Malik 2020).

The integration of technology into governance structures demands new forms of collaboration between technologists, Shariah scholars, and regulatory bodies. Successful digital transformation in Islamic banks often depends on close partnerships between these stakeholders to ensure technological advancements are implemented without compromising Shariah principles. This collaborative approach creates balanced frameworks that support both innovation and ethical integrity while maintaining the authority and accountability of traditional Shariah oversight mechanisms.

Conclusion

The siloed development of technologies—fintech, regtech, paytech, insurtech, legaltech—has created sector-specific efficiencies but also new forms of fragmentation. This presents a significant governance risk in Islamic finance, where ethical compliance, transparency, and holistic oversight are foundational. As individual domains evolve, the risk is not just technological redundancy, but systemic incoherence: disconnected APIs, overlapping audits, inconsistent Shariah interpretations, and underleveraged compliance automation.

The proposed X-Tech framework emerges not just as a convergence of tools, but as a unified philosophy: a multidisciplinary ecosystem where Shariah principles are embedded at the design level of every module—smart contracts, AI audits, legal workflows, and payment mechanisms. This holistic architecture shifts Islamic financial governance away from reactive, document-based oversight toward integrated, real-time compliance engines aligned with both regulatory requirements and the maqāṣid al-Sharīʿah (objectives of Islamic law).

In practice, this means leveraging AI not only to automate due diligence but also to flag Riba and Gharar in live contracts. It means deploying blockchain not just for transparency, but for embedding fatwas directly into smart contracts. It means creating shared infrastructure—fatwa APIs, tokenized Shariah validation, cross-border sandboxes—that encourages global standardization and reduces "fatwa shopping" and local fragmentation. The use case of IoT-based Sukuk for trade finance is just one early proof of concept that reflects the power of embedded Shariah controls in decentralized financial architecture.

However, realizing this paradigm is not without challenges. Regulatory fragmentation, legacy banking architecture, and the lack of standardized digital Shariah modules still stand in the way. Therefore, stakeholder collaboration is critical: banks, central regulators, technologists, and Shariah scholars must co-develop operational standards and shared frameworks. Institutional readiness must include modular design thinking, agent-based simulation for risk modeling, and integration of legaltech automation for standardized documentation and dispute resolution.

The X-Tech paradigm has direct implications for regulators, Islamic financial institutions, and Shari'ah supervisory bodies. For regulators, X-Tech highlights the need for harmonized digital standards—particularly shared taxonomies, interoperable APIs, and cross-jurisdictional fatwā registries—that reduce interpretive fragmentation and enhance supervisory visibility (Soualhi 2023; State Bank of Pakistan 2025). Financial institutions can adopt modular components such as AI-assisted screening, blockchain-based audit trails, and maturity-mapping tools to accelerate compliance transformation without waiting for sector-wide reforms (Mohamed et al. 2024). Shari'ah bodies, meanwhile, benefit from digital infrastructures that operationalize jurisprudential reasoning, shorten review cycles, and support consistent rulings across products and markets. Together, these policy directions signal a shift from reactive compliance management toward coordinated, technology-enabled ethical governance.

A promising direction for future scholarship lies in developing standards for agentic AI systems that participate in Shari'ah-sensitive financial workflows. As Islamic finance moves toward real-time, machine-executed compliance, rigorous research is needed to define accountability structures, model validation protocols, and juristic boundaries for autonomous agents. Another important avenue is the design of cross-border Shari'ah compliance APIs—shared digital interfaces through which institutions and regulators can access harmonized fatwā data, risk scores, and machine-readable jurisprudential logic. Finally, comparative digital maturity benchmarking across OIC and non-OIC jurisdictions would enable policymakers to identify asymmetries in readiness and prioritize coordinated investment in infrastructure. These research pathways would extend the X-Tech framework from conceptual blueprint to implementable global standards.

In conclusion, the X-Tech model presents an opportunity for the Islamic finance industry to lead not just in compliance, but in design—engineering systems that are ethically native, technically scalable, and globally interoperable. Nations and institutions that champion this convergence will not only fulfill religious and regulatory obligations more efficiently but will redefine trust in digital financial systems for a new generation.

References

Afdawaiza, Mas'ud, R., & Q. Manulandon, S. (2024). Islamic Banks in the Digital Age: Balancing Innovation with Sharia Principles. *IKONOMIKA: Jurnal Ekonomi Dan Bisnis Islam*, *9*(1). https://ejournal.radenintan.ac.id/index.php/ikonomika

Al Nabhany, M. A. (2024, August 23). *Artificial Intelligence (AI): A tool for Shari'ah Compliance Audit and Reviews in Islamic Financial Institutions*. https://www.linkedin.com/pulse/artificial-intelligence-ai-tool-shariah-compliance-audit-alidini-krevf/

Ali, H., Aysan, A. F., & Mesroua, M. (2025). *AI in Finance: Applications for Global Finance Institutions and Adaptations for Islamic Finance* (pp. 139–154). https://doi.org/10.1007/978-3-031-70355-3_11

Asian Development Bank. (2022). *Building Regulatory and Supervisory Technology Ecosystems*. https://doi.org/10.22617/TCS220330-2

Baan, H. (2022, February 5). *Shariah Compliant Regtech Beyond Self-Regulated Ecosystems*. https://iaif.ir/index.php/en/news-archive-en/item/4494-shariah-compliant-regtech-beyond-self-regulated-ecosystems

Bento, F., Tagliabue, M., & Lorenzo, F. (2020). Organizational Silos: A Scoping Review Informed by a Behavioral Perspective on Systems and Networks. *Societies*, *10*(3), 56. https://doi.org/10.3390/soc10030056

Bezes, P., Fimreite, A. L., Lidec, P. Le, & Lægreid, P. (2013). Understanding Organizational Reforms in the Modern State: Specialization and Integration in Norway and France. *Governance*, *26*(1). https://doi.org/10.1111/j.1468-0491.2012.01608.x

Burton, A. (2018, July 13). *Why does tech love the letter X? | The Outline*. https://theoutline.com/post/4919/x-why-does-tech-love-the-letter-x

Cao, L. (2024). Ai4tech: X-AI enabling X-Tech with human-like, generative, decentralized, humanoid and metaverse AI. *International Journal of Data Science and Analytics*, *18*(3), 219–238. https://doi.org/10.1007/s41060-024-00615-9

Carlsson, F., Matteby, M., & Magnusson, J. (2023). Digital Transformation Drift. *Proceedings of the 24th Annual International Conference on Digital Government Research*, 318–326. https://doi.org/10.1145/3598469.3598504

Crusoe, J., Magnusson, J., & Torell, J. (2023). Ignorance in public sector digital transformation. *Proceedings of the 24th Annual International Conference on Digital Government Research*, 338–348. https://doi.org/10.1145/3598469.3598507

Faizol bin Ismail, A. (2018). *The Principles of Shariah Governance as Practiced by Islamic Financial Institutions*.

Fong, D., Han, F., Liu, L., Qu, J., & Shek, A. (2021, November 9). *Seven technologies shaping the future of fintech | McKinsey*. McKinsey &

Company. https://www.mckinsey.com/cn/our-insights/our-insights/seven-technologies-shaping-the-future-of-fintech

Furr, N., Ozcan, P., & Eisenhardt, K. M. (2022). What is digital transformation? Core tensions facing established companies on the global stage. *Global Strategy Journal*, *12*(4), 595–618. https://doi.org/10.1002/gsj.1442

Gao, F., Lin, C., & Zhai, H. (2022). Digital Transformation, Corporate Innovation, and International Strategy: Empirical Evidence from Listed Companies in China. *Sustainability (Switzerland)*, *14*(13). https://doi.org/10.3390/su14138137

Gawer, A. (2022). Digital platforms and ecosystems: remarks on the dominant organizational forms of the digital age. *Innovation: Organization and Management*, *24*(1). https://doi.org/10.1080/14479338.2021.1965888

Grassi, L., & Lanfranchi, D. (2022). RegTech in public and private sectors: the nexus between data, technology and regulation. *Journal of Industrial and Business Economics*, *49*(3). https://doi.org/10.1007/s40812-022-00226-0

Gurbaxani, V., & Dunkle, D. (2019). Gearing up for successful digital transformation. *MIS Quarterly Executive*, *18*(3). https://doi.org/10.17705/2msqe.00017

Jacobides, M. G., Cennamo, C., & Gawer, A. (2018). Towards a theory of ecosystems. *Strategic Management Journal*, *39*(8). https://doi.org/10.1002/smj.2904

Komninos, N., Kakderi, C., Collado, A., Papadaki, I., & Panori, A. (2021). Digital Transformation of City Ecosystems: Platforms Shaping Engagement and Externalities across Vertical Markets. *Journal of Urban Technology*, *28*(1–2). https://doi.org/10.1080/10630732.2020.1805712

Kronblad, C., & Jensen, S. H. (2023). ' Being a professional is not the same as acting professionally '—How digital technologies have empowered the creation and enactment of a new professional identity in law. *Journal of Professions and Organization*. https://doi.org/10.1093/jpo/joad005

Labuan. (2024). *Labuan Shariah-Compliant Blockchain Hub "World's First shariah-Compliant BlockChain Hub."* https://www.labuanibfc.com/clients/asset_52E835CC-1342-4701-B6FA-E2CD03AD74B4/contentms/img/publications/brochures/2024/FINAL-VER.-Labuan-Shariah-Compliant-Blockchain-Hub-Booklet_26052024.pdf

Li, J., Maiti, A., & Fei, J. (2023). Features and Scope of Regulatory Technologies: Challenges and Opportunities with Industrial Internet of Things. *Future Internet*, *15*(8), 256. https://doi.org/10.3390/fi15080256

Malik, R. (2020). *Shari'ah Governance Framework and AAOIFI*.

McHugh, B. (2022, November 8). *How to Identify and Break Down Tech Silos in IT*. ActiveBatch. https://www.advsyscon.com/blog/break-down-silos-in-it/#:~:text=A%20silo%20is%20a%20team,cloud%2C%20SAP%20and%20so%20on.

Millard, J. (2023). *Exploring the impact of digital transformation on public governance Prevailing (public) governance models throughout Europe.*

Mohamed, S., Alfzari, A. A., Rosman, A. S., Bayoumi, K., Basit, A., & Darawi, S. @. (2024). *Shariah Compliance in Fintech App Solutions: An Islamic Legal Perspective.* https://doi.org/10.6007/IJARBSS/v14-i11/23169

OECD. (2022). *Digital Transformation Maturity Model.*

OECD. (2023a). *Digital Government Review of Türkiye.* OECD. https://doi.org/10.1787/3958d102-en

OECD. (2023b). *Initial Policy Consideration for Generative Artificial Intelligence.* https://www.oecd.org/content/dam/oecd/en/publications/reports/2023/09/initial-policy-considerations-for-generative-artificial-intelligence_1a9ab450/fae2d1e6-en.pdf

Pivavarava, A. V., & Koop, C. (2023). *The adoption of digital practices by economic regulators: mapping digital pathways for consumer e-participation* (ISSN 1471-0498).

Scott, I., & Gong, T. (2021). Coordinating government silos: challenges and opportunities. *Global Public Policy and Governance, 1*(1). https://doi.org/10.1007/s43508-021-00004-z

Soualhi, Y. (2023). *Shariah governance practices in the global Islamic finance industry - INCEIF University.* https://inceif.edu.my/shariah-governance-practices-in-the-global-islamic-finance-industry/

State Bank of Pakistan. (2025). *Shariah Governance Framework for Islamic Financial Institutions.* https://www.sbp.org.pk/ifpd/2024/C8-Annex.pdf

Stroumpoulis, A., & Kopanaki, E. (2022). Theoretical Perspectives on Sustainable Supply Chain Management and Digital Transformation: A Literature Review and a Conceptual Framework. *Sustainability (Switzerland), 14*(8). https://doi.org/10.3390/su14084862

Tanaka, T. (2019). The life insurance business and its potential under the influence of X-Tech. *Seimei Hoken Ronshū, 208*(Suppl.), 177–213.

Tanaka, T. (2021). Corporate organization of life insurance companies under X-Tech: Building an organization for innovation X-Tech における生命保険企業の企業組織 - イノベーション創出に向けた組織の構築 -. *Seimei Hoken Ronshū, 217*, 33–55.

Teng, X., Wu, Z., & Yang, F. (2022). Research on the Relationship between Digital Transformation and Performance of SMEs. *Sustainability (Switzerland), 14*(10). https://doi.org/10.3390/su14106012

Tom, E., Aurum, A., & Vidgen, R. (2013a). An exploration of technical debt. *Journal of Systems and Software, 86*(6), 1498–1516. https://doi.org/10.1016/j.jss.2012.12.052

von Solms, J. (2021). Integrating Regulatory Technology (RegTech) into the digital transformation of a bank Treasury. *Journal of Banking Regulation, 22*(2), 152–168. https://doi.org/10.1057/s41261-020-00134-0

WEF. (2025). *Technology Convergence Report*.
Xue, L., Zhang, Q., Zhang, X., & Li, C. (2022). Can Digital Transformation Promote Green Technology Innovation? *Sustainability (Switzerland)*, *14*(12). https://doi.org/10.3390/su14127497

CHAPTER 6

Assessing the GCC Regulatory Landscape for FinTech

Hamoudah S. Al-Zaini and Khalid I. Ahmad

Introduction

Financial technology, or FinTech, is considered one of the most significant innovations in the financial services sector over the last few decades (Gulamhuseinwala and Kotecha 2016; Fülöp et al. 2016). FinTech refers to the use of technology to deliver new financial solutions (Cai 2018), and it includes a broad range of financial solutions, including mobile banking, online payments, peer-to-peer lending, robo-advisory, blockchain-based transactions, smart contracts, and artificial intelligence-powered customer interfaces.

FinTech firms are challenging the status quo and offering customers alternatives to the traditional channels to access financial services (World Bank 2021a). FinTech solutions offer numerous opportunities to improve

H. S. Al-Zaini (✉) · K. I. Ahmad
College of Law, Hamad Bin Khalifa University (HBKU), Doha, Qatar
e-mail: halzaini@hbku.edu.qa

K. I. Ahmad
e-mail: kahmed@hbku.edu.qa

K. Tsanis et al. (eds.), *Digital Finance and Transformation in the Gulf*,
https://doi.org/10.1007/978-981-92-1588-1_6

efficiency, accessibility, reduce costs, and enhance customers' experience. Nonetheless, FinTech introduces new challenges, such as regulatory compliance, systemic risks, and cybersecurity threats (Khan et al. 2023).

The FinTech ecosystem usually comprises three major participants, which include governments, financial institutions, and entrepreneurs. Furthermore, well-established and startup FinTech firms are important components of the ecosystem. Governments play an important role by introducing domestic policies and regulations to support the development of the FinTech ecosystem. While financial institutions contribute expertise, entrepreneurs support innovation. Though the three participants usually function independently, they collaborate to stimulate technological innovation and create growth opportunities for the different sub-segments of the financial industry (Diemers et al. 2015).

In line with the significant global transformation enabled by FinTech innovations, the FinTech landscape in the GCC has seen major growth in recent years. The GCC FinTech market is expected to grow from $250 million in 2022 to approximately $2 billion by 2030 (Roland Berger 2024). The six GCC countries share the goal of diversifying their economies and reducing oil dependence. Therefore, these countries are fostering a favorable environment for FinTech adoption, which will ultimately stimulate economic growth and enhance financial inclusion. Accordingly, the six countries have formulated their diversification plans and named them National Visions. Since all GCC members are considered high-income States with well-developed technological infrastructure and adoption, the six countries are deemed well-developed for digital adoption. In addition, all regional economies have easy access to the Internet and mobile subscriptions (World Bank 2021b).

Since FinTech has the potential to disrupt the financial sector, its impact on financial stability has become a significant concern for the GCC regulators and policymakers. The GCC governments have introduced different regulatory sandboxes,[1] which are designed to facilitate FinTech experimentation in a controlled environment to address these

[1] A regulatory sandbox is a formal regulatory programme within a regulatory authority that allows market participants to test new financial services or models with live customers, subject to certain safeguards and oversight (see Cambridge Centre for Alternative Finance—CCAF [2021]. See also FinTech Regulation in the Middle East and North Africa, Cambridge Centre for Alternative Finance at the University of Cambridge, Judge Business School, Cambridge, 10).

concerns and strike a balance between innovation and stability. Establishing regulatory sandboxes reflects the GCC countries' commitment to encouraging FinTech innovation while safeguarding financial stability.

Despite rapid regulatory progress across all six countries, the current GCC FinTech ecosystems remain fragmented, creating barriers for most firms' scaling and regional integration. The GCC FinTech sector still requires additional regulations to address cross-border compliance, financial stability, technology adoption, and competition issues (IMF 2025). To underscore the importance of introducing a regional, or cross-border, FinTech sandbox, this paper discusses the domestic regulations applied by each of the GCC countries. The multifaceted realm of FinTech includes new digital products such as cryptocurrencies, digital assets, innovative digital banks (DB), buy-now-pay-later (BNPL) services, open banking (OB), and payment service providers (PSPs).

Establishing GCC as a Regional Economic Bloc

The heads of the Arabian Gulf states, Bahrain, Kuwait, Oma, Qatar, Saudi Arabia, and the United Arab Emirates, met on 25 May 1981 and agreed on a regional framework to establish effective coordination, integration, and inter-connection among the six members in different fields to achieve economic unity among the six States. According to Article 1 of the GCC Charter, the Cooperation Council for the Arab States of the Gulf (GCC) was established (GCC Charter 1981). Article 4 of the GCC Charter stipulates that one of the main objectives of the regional bloc is to formulate similar regulations in different fields, including economic and financial affairs (GCC Charter 1981). The same Article emphasizes stimulating scientific and technological progress by establishing scientific research and joint ventures, and by encouraging private sector cooperation for the good of the GCC peoples (GCC Charter 1981).

After more than four decades, the GCC is now considered a success story of regional economic integration and has become a major economic player in the Middle East and global markets (Al-Zaini et al. 2025). The GCC has achieved numerous milestones throughout its long journey and has effectively strengthened its position at both regional and global levels. The GCC's role in establishing regional economic integration among its members can be summarized in four stages (Fig. 6.1).

The first stage of the GCC economic integration was achieved through the establishment of the Free Trade Area (FTA). The GCC-FTA entered

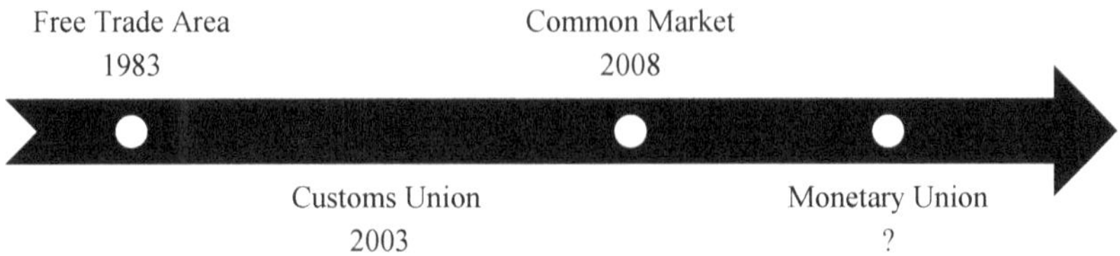

Fig. 6.1 Stages of economic integration in the GCC

into force in March 1983 and lasted for twenty years. One of the main objectives of the GCC-FTA is to facilitate the importation and exportation of national products among GCC members by exempting industrial and agricultural goods and natural resources from customs duties. Additionally, the regional FTA removed the requirement for a local agent and simplified domestic procedures by mandating only a certificate of origin and an export manifest (GCC: The Process and Achievements 2014). Two decades later, in 2003, the heads of the GCC States agreed to move to the next stage and establish the Customs Union (GCC CU). All six members agreed to apply a common external tariff of five percent, and to implement a unified customs procedure (Al-Dardari et al. 2014). In addition, GCC CU stipulated that customs duties on foreign goods should be collected only once at the first entry point, and foreign goods are allowed to move freely across GCC countries without additional fees (GCC—The Process and Achievements 2014).

In 2008, all GCC members agreed to accelerate their economic integration plan and decided to move to the third stage by launching the GCC Common Market. The main objective of the GCC Common Market is to increase production efficiency and optimize the use of national resources across the GCC by promoting the free movement of capital, goods, services, and labor (Malkawi 2011). In addition, the Common Market has helped to improve the GCC's negotiating position in international economic forums (Low and Salazar 2011). As part of the Common Market, all members agreed to eliminate their customs duties, adopt common trade policies, and move toward greater harmonization of their domestic policies (Malkawi 2011).

In 2008, all members signed the Monetary Union Agreement (MUA). The Monetary Union is considered the final stage for achieving full economic integration among the six countries. This goal is provided in Article 4 of the GCC Economic Agreement (GCC Economic Agreement

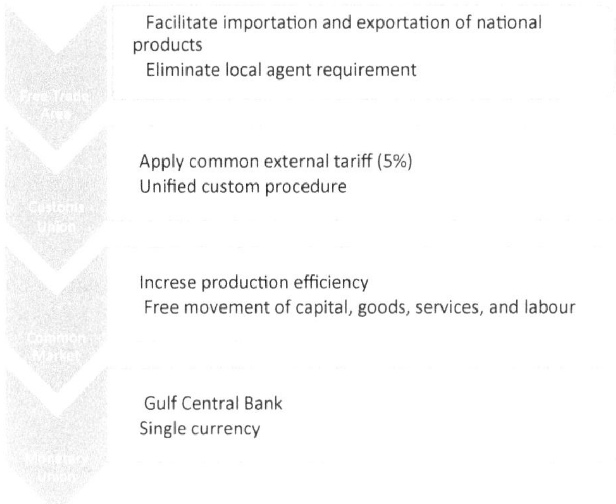

Fig. 6.2 Achievements of economic integration in the GCC

2001). The Economic Agreement mandated that all members should harmonize their economic policies, especially fiscal and monetary policies, and banking regulations. However, the monetary union has not been achieved since Oman, and the United Arab Emirates (UAE) have deferred the full implementation of the Agreement for various reasons (Pinto 2018). The main achievements of the GCC economic integration process are summarized below (Fig. 6.2).

The next section focuses on the GCC countries' national plans to diversify their domestic economies through the implementation of their national visions.

National Visions of the GCC Countries

All GCC countries have launched their National Visions. Bahrain and Qatar were the first two members to launch their national visions in 2008. Bahrain named its plan 'Bahrain Economic Vision 2030,' while Qatar named its plan 'Qatar National Vision 2030.' Two years later, in 2010, the UAE launched its short-term plan under the name 'UAE Vision 2021.' The UAE national vision was linked to the country's Golden Jubilee in 2021. Then, in 2022, the UAE enacted its new plan, 'We The UAE

2031.' Saudi Arabia launched its ambitious national vision, 'Saudi Vision 2030,' in 2016. One year later, in 2017, Kuwait introduced its national plan titled 'Kuwait Vision 2035 – New Kuwait.' Lastly, 'Oman Vision 2040' was introduced by Oman in 2020.

Almost all GCC national visions share similar economic goals, aiming to achieve economic diversification and sustainable development by 2030 or later. The shared goal arises from the fact that almost all six countries have been heavily reliant on revenues from oil and natural gas exports. In addition, by analyzing the six national visions, it becomes clear that all plans aim to achieve similar, and even identical, goals. These similar goals would drive competition among the six GCC members. For example, all plans include appealing strategies and policies that offer different incentive structures to attract foreign direct investment.

- **Bahrain Economic Vision 2030**

Bahrain's economic vision aims to shift the national economy from one built on oil wealth to a productive, globally competitive one. Bahrain's strategy considers the national financial sector as the major economic engine for growth. The national vision focuses on supporting the financial sector through steady growth in other high-potential sectors. The government aims to create an environment highly conducive to entrepreneurship and innovation. In addition, the Vision improves access to capital, including venture capital, for small and medium enterprises (SMEs). Moreover, it provides for establishing a platform to advance innovations toward market readiness, which supports the country's tapping into the global knowledge economy (Bahrain Economic Vision 2008).

- **Kuwait Vision 2035—New Kuwait**

Kuwait Vision aims to restore the regional leadership role as a financial and commercial hub. The 'New Kuwait' is designed to transform Kuwait into a regional and international financial and trade hub (Kuwait Vision 2017). One of the Kuwaiti government's objectives is to make Kuwait more attractive to foreign investors, and to increase direct foreign investment by 300% and attract more than KWD 400 million, equivalent to USD 1.3 billion, to invest in information technology, services and renewable energy in the short and medium terms (Kuwait National Development Plan 2022).

- **Oman Vision 2040**

Oman's vision aims to establish a diversified and sustainable economy built on technology, knowledge, and innovation. According to the government strategy, the economy should operate within integrated frameworks to ensure competitiveness and embrace industrial revolutions. The objectives for economic diversification do not focus on specific sectors. Instead, it provides the government with the flexibility to identify every five years the sectors that drive economic diversification and other competent sectors. In addition, the strategy is designed to focus on the research and development ecosystem, covering the different sectors and institutions (Oman Vision 2020).

- **Qatar National Vision 2030**

Qatar National Vision (QNV) 2030 is underpinned by four interconnected pillars: economic, social, human, and environmental development. The Economic Development pillar aims to achieve sustainable economic prosperity through responsible resource management, economic diversification, and private sector growth. In addition, the economic development strategy aims to balance hydrocarbon reserves and production, develop a vibrant non-oil economy, maintain financial stability, promote open markets, and create a business environment that attracts both domestic and foreign investment (Qatar National Vision 2008).

The primary objective of QNV is to allow the country to sustain its development while enhancing the quality of life for its populace. The economic development framework is based on three fundamental principles: sound economic management, responsible resource exploitation, and commitment to economic diversification. The concept of 'suitable economic diversification' within Qatar's vision involves gradually reducing dependence on hydrocarbon industries and enhancing the private sector's role to maintain competitiveness. Qatar National Development Strategy also focuses on achieving economic diversification by bolstering entrepreneurship, improving the business climate, strengthening regional integration, and reforming the labor market. The third national development strategy (NDS3) includes an explicit objective of attracting USD 100 billion as foreign direct investment, and to launch 35 FinTech firms (Third Qatar National Development Strategy 2024).

- **Saudi Vision 2030**

Saudi Arabia's Vision 2030 is a transformative blueprint aimed at reducing the Kingdom's dependence on oil and diversifying its economy for long-term sustainability. Saudi Vision is anchored in three key pillars: a vibrant society, a thriving economy, and an ambitious nation. Central to this vision is the pursuit of economic diversification, representing a fundamental shift in Saudi Arabia's outlook. By increasing the contributions of non-oil industries, the country seeks to build a more resilient and sustainable economic framework that can withstand global oil price fluctuations. To achieve its economic diversification plan, the government targets growth in sectors such as tourism, mining, logistics, and technology. The vision underscores the importance of privatization and encourages private sector participation in economic activities. In addition, the strategy supported by plans to establish special economic zones to attract foreign direct investment and promote entrepreneurship among citizens (Saudi Vision 2016). The National Investment Strategy aims to enhance the inflow of FDI to reach 5.7% of GDP and position the Kingdom among the top ten economies in the Global Competitiveness Index by 2030 (Ministry of Economy and Planning 2023).

- **We the UAE 2031—Toward New Peaks**

The UAE Vision 2031 focuses on fast-paced economic growth in partnership with the private sector, achieved by focusing on key national sectors, which include advanced industries, the digital economy, information and communication technology (ICT), communication, services, financial technology, logistical services and tourism (We The UAE 2030 2022).

While all national visions of the GCC states emphasize economic diversification and encourage innovation, overlapping incentives have resulted in intra-regional competition rather than promoting and supporting regional economic integration. A key challenge for the GCC Council is to harmonize the different national visions and create a unified regional strategy that promotes a single market for the GCC digital economy and FinTech initiatives.

GCC FinTech Hubs with Varying Regulatory Requirements

This section discusses the several FinTech hubs established in the GCC, and examines the domestic regulatory requirements established by the GCC Central Banks and Financial Markets Authorities for four FinTech products and services. The four FinTech products and services discussed are: buy-now-pay-later (BNPL), digital banking (DB), open banking (OB), and payment service provider (PSP).

GCC FinTech Hubs

FinTech adoption in the financial sector is critical, as it plays an important role in developing various sectors of the economy (Khan et al. 2021). International FinTech Hubs have adopted various approaches to support FinTech innovation, regulate the development environment, and address financial and technological challenges. One of these approaches, used by the majority of international hubs, is the regulatory sandboxes, which support and promote innovation in financial technology. Regulatory sandboxes enable effective risk management and control while fostering innovation.

As all GCC countries aim to diversify their economies, promoting and investing in financial innovation is seen as a key source and driver of economic diversification (Dahdal et al. 2022). To encourage innovation in FinTech, all GCC countries have introduced regulatory sandboxes to support FinTech and startup firms to test their products and services in a controlled environment under the regulators' guidance (IMF 2025). For example, Central Banks of Bahrain, Kuwait, Oman, Qatar, Saudi Arabia, and the UAE have all introduced their FinTech strategies and set up government-sponsored accelerators and incubators (IMF 2025). Moreover, some of the GCC FinTech Hubs are now large enough to rank among the top global FinTech hubs (Strategy& 2022).

For example, Abu Dhabi Global Markets (ADGM), a common law and free economic jurisdiction in the UAE, launched its 'FinTech RegLab' in 2016, and it is ranked 23rd globally (The Global Financial Centres 2025). Dubai International Financial Centre (DIFC), another common law and free economic jurisdiction in the UAE, launched its FinTech Hive in 2017 and is now ranked 9th globally (The Global Financial Centres 2025). The Hive is the first and largest financial technology accelerator in MENA and South Asia (Di Maggio and Gamze 2020). Both ADGM and DIFC attract international founders, enabling them to benefit from key features, including access to significant markets in financial services. Both platforms also have investors willing to fund FinTech firms. Additionally, ADGM and DIFC offer various forms of early-stage support, including financial and non-financial assistance. Early-stage funding is managed through the Abu Dhabi Investment Office (ADIO) and through the Ghadan 21 Fund[2] (Zarrouk et al. 2021).

Saudi Arabia launched its 'FinTech Saudi' in 2018, and it is ranked 58th globally (The Global Financial Centres 2025). 'FinTech Saudi' was launched by the Saudi Central Bank in partnership with the Capital Market Authority to act as a catalyst to transform Saudi Arabia into an innovative FinTech hub with a thriving and responsible FinTech ecosystem.

Qatar launched its FinTech Hub in 2018, and it is ranked 66th globally (The Global Financial Centres 2025). According to Qatar's FinTech strategy, the Qatar Central Bank serves as the orchestrator and regulator of the FinTech ecosystem, while both the Qatar Financial Centre (QFC) and Qatar Development Bank (QDB) function as sector developers (Refinitiv 2021). The QFC, a common law and free economic jurisdiction in Qatar, provides various incentives and benefits tailored specifically for FinTech firms looking to establish their business within the QFC (QFC 2021). On the other hand, QDB supports local entrepreneurs and SMEs in scaling and participating in international markets (Cochrane and Al-Habani 2023).

Bahrain also launched 'FinTech Bay' in 2018 and is ranked 69th globally (The Global Financial Centres 2025). FinTech Bay is also one of the largest FinTech centers in the Middle East, and one of Bahrain's most important initiatives that focuses on investing in innovation such as advanced laboratories, business accelerators, and educational opportunities.

[2] 'Ghadan 21' is an AED 50 billion accelerator programme launched by Abu Dhabi in 2019. The Programme supports the transformation of the emirate's economy, knowledge ecosystem, and communities.

In 2020, Oman launched its FinTech hub to establish a dynamic digital financial ecosystem. This program aims to support financial development through innovation and provide sustainable assistance to competitive and diverse sectors in Oman.

The Central Bank of the UAE also established its FinTech Office in 2020. The FinTech Office aims to develop a robust FinTech ecosystem in the UAE and position the country as a leading FinTech hub both regionally and internationally. The UAE's FinTech ecosystem is built on five key pillars: demand, capital, policy, talent, and infrastructure.

Finally, Kuwait launched its 'Wolooj Innovation Hub' in 2024, and it is ranked 71st globally (The Global Financial Centres 2025). Wolooj hub is an initiative accelerator program designed to foster creativity, innovation, and entrepreneurship within the local FinTech ecosystem. It provides participants with the necessary support, resources, and mentorship needed to transform their ideas into successful ventures based on pre-defined themes.

Most FinTech hubs in the GCC (Fig. 6.3) offer similar and competitive support services (Strategy& 2022).

- **Domestic FinTech Regulations**

The concept of the regulatory sandbox was first introduced by the UK's Financial Conduct Authority (FCA) to provide greater room for innovation (Guo and Liang 2016). The UK regulator introduced its regulatory sandbox to provide a testing ground for FinTech firms to test new products under supervision and gain access to finance without the costs and restrictions of standard regulatory requirements (Truby 2020). The use of a regulatory sandbox allows the testing of digital services with customers in a safe and supervised environment where such testing does not result in regulatory consequences (Ibrahim and Truby 2022). As of 2020, 73 regulatory sandboxes for FinTech operated in 57 countries (World Bank 2020a).

The regulatory landscape for FinTech in the GCC is also evolving rapidly, demonstrating the region's ambition to become a global hub for FinTech. Each GCC country has made important progress in establishing a regulatory environment that supports innovation (Alessio and Petratos 2024).

Fig. 6.3 Ranking and services of the GCC FinTech Hubs

The following section outlines key regulatory frameworks and initiatives in the GCC, emphasizing each country's strategies to promote FinTech growth while ensuring effective oversight.

- **Central Bank of Bahrain—CBB**

Bahrain has established itself as a pioneer in FinTech regulation within the GCC (Alessio and Petratos 2024). The CBB has introduced its Regulatory Sandbox to allow startups and FinTech firms to provide innovative banking and financial solutions. Additionally, the CBB has issued specific regulations for crowdfunding, digital financial advice, and cryptocurrency exchanges, positioning Bahrain as a forward-thinking jurisdiction in the Fintech space (Alessio and Petratos 2024).

The CBB has also established a dedicated FinTech Innovation Unit to support individual and corporate customers in the financial services sector by encouraging an agile regulatory framework that fosters FinTech and innovations. The FinTech Innovation Unit is responsible for approving applications from FinTech firms wishing to participate in the regulatory sandbox. It supervises the testing progress of authorized sandbox participants and monitors technical and regulatory developments in the FinTech sector, both regionally and internationally. The Unit also leads all strategic FinTech initiatives and collaborates closely with stakeholders within the Bahraini FinTech ecosystem (CBB—FinTech and Innovation).

- **Central Bank of Kuwait—CBK**

The CBK and the Communication and Information Technology Regulatory Authority (CITRA) have collaborated to establish a regulatory sandbox designed to foster FinTech growth and enable banking systems to test new technologies (Alessio and Petratos 2024). Additionally, CBK has prioritized digital payments and cybersecurity by issuing guidelines that promote secure and efficient digital transactions. To modernize the financial sector, the CBK has implemented several key initiatives and created a dedicated FinTech unit, recognizing that FinTech is a major driver of change in the local banking sector (CBK).

- **Central Bank of Oman—CBO**

The CBO, in collaboration with the Capital Market Authority (CMA), has launched the FinTech Regulatory Sandbox (FRS). This initiative supports electronic payments, mobile banking, and blockchain technology. The FRS provides FinTech firms with the opportunity to experiment and test new digital financial products and services in a controlled regulatory environment. Regulators may, or may not, grant certain regulatory relaxations of regulations for the purpose of testing these innovations.

Furthermore, the FRS allows regulators, financial institutions, FinTech firms, and customers to conduct live tests and evaluate the benefits, limitations, and risks associated with new innovative products and services. This testing environment is monitored by the regulatory authority, the CBO. The CMA has also been proactive in regulating digital assets and crowdfunding platforms, promoting a secure and innovative financial ecosystem (Alessio and Petratos 2024).

- **Qatar Central Bank—QCB**

QCB has made significant strides in developing the FinTech Regulatory environment in Qatar and issued its regulations to govern electronic payments, digital wallets, and cybersecurity to ensure a robust infrastructure for digital finance. In addition, QCB has established the FinTech Supervision Department (FSD) and introduced the Policy and Regulation Section (PRS) as part of the FSD to ensure that sound regulatory requirements are in place for FinTech firms that prevent harm, reduce risks, and foster innovation in the market. PRS focuses on issuing the policies and regulations required to regulate the conduct of FinTech firms and their activities. In addition, PRS is mandated to set better regulatory standards and promote competition and innovations (QCB).

On the other hand, Qatar Financial Centre (QFC) offers a legal and regulatory framework that supports a diverse range of financial services, including FinTech (Alessio and Petratos 2024). In 2020, QFC established its Tech Circle, and in 2023, it introduced its Digital Assets Lab. Additionally, in 2024, QFC enacted its FinTech Rules as part of its Non-regulated Activities (QFC Rules).

- **Saudi Central Bank—SAMA**

In coordination with the Saudi Capital Markets Authority (CMA), SAMA[3] launched FinTech Saudi. FinTech Saudi is designed to act as a catalyst for the development of the FinTech industry in Saudi Arabia and aims to transform the Kingdom into an innovative FinTech hub with a thriving and responsible FinTech ecosystem. The CMA has also issued digital financial services, crowdfunding, and cryptocurrency guidelines, promoting a diverse and secure financial sector (Alessio and Petratos 2024).

- **Central Bank of the UAE—CBUAE**

CBUAE has developed regulations for digital payments, stored value facilities, and electronic KYC processes. In addition, CBUAE established the FinTech Office to build a mature FinTech ecosystem in the country and position the UAE as the foremost FinTech hub regionally and globally. The FinTech Office is mandated to work closely with key stakeholders to develop a FinTech ecosystem with five pillars. These pillars include demand, capital, policy, talent, and infrastructure (CBUAE).

Abu Dhabi Global Market (ADGM) launched the Regulatory Laboratory (RegLab) in 2016 (Arab Monetary Fund 2020). The RegLab is a FinTech regulatory sandbox designed to enable the development and controlled live testing of innovative technologies, fostering innovation in the UAE financial services market for both new market entrants and existing financial institutions (Arab Monetary Fund 2020). In 2018, ADGM introduced a comprehensive crypto-asset regime, and in 2019, launched its regulatory frameworks for digital banking, digital securities, robo-advisory, and the use of API's (Arab Monetary Fund 2020).

On the other hand, Dubai International Financial Centre (DIFC), together with the Dubai Financial Services Authority (DFSA), introduced its regulatory sandbox to permit a bespoke, firm-specific regime for a limited testing period for new, innovative technologies (Arab Monetary Fund 2020).

[3] The Saudi Central Bank, previously known as the Saudi Arabian Monetary Authority (SAMA). In 2020, SAMA was renamed the Saudi Central Bank. However, it has continued to use the 'SAMA' acronym.

GCC FinTech Regulations of Selected FinTech Products

1. Buy-Now-Pay-Later (BNPL)

Alternative payment methods (APMs), such as BNPL, enable consumers to make purchases and pay for them over time. APMs usually offer short-term financing options with no interest. While the concept of BNPL, which essentially involves buying on credit, dates to the 1840s, modern FinTech solutions have emerged since the 2010s to address challenges related to financing, such as complexity, high fees, and annual percentage rates (APRs). BNPL has become one of the favored payment methods for both online and in-store transactions. The forecast for global BNPL gross merchandise value (GMV) is expected to grow from USD 433 billion in 2022 to USD 960 billion by 2028 (Deloitte 2023).

GCC countries are experiencing a significant shift in the regulation of BNPL services. This transformation reflects the collective commitment to creating a secure, consumer-focused financial landscape, particularly as new financial technologies emerge. The growth in e-commerce is driving the demand for BNPL services in the Gulf. As more consumers shop online, they increasingly seek convenient and flexible payment methods like BNPL.

BNPL is a useful payment method for consumers looking to spread the cost of large purchases over time. In addition, the evolving regulatory environment in the GCC presents attractive opportunities for BNPL providers. For that reason, the GCC regulations emphasize the importance of educating consumers and exercising caution regarding the risks associated with BNPL services. Well-structured GCC regulations have the potential to enhance consumer confidence, promote healthy competition, and foster an environment where BNPL providers prioritize ethical conduct.

- **Bahrain**

CBB does not have specific regulations for BNPL providers. However, the CBB has amended the existing rules related to financing companies (Type 3) included in the CBB Rulebook volume 5. The amended rules are designed to cater to financing companies with a limited scope of short-term installment credit activities, such as BNPL and other business models. According to the amended rules, BNPL providers must comply with the existing capital requirements provided under the Capital Adequacy Module (CAM), which provides that a licensee must always maintain a minimum paid-up capital of BHD 5 million (CBB Capital Adequacy Module 2019). However, the CBB is authorized to permit BNPL providers to maintain a lower capital based on the nature, scale, and size of operation. BNPL providers are also required to comply with consumer protection measures. They should implement a rigorous risk assessment and compliance framework to ensure transparency in fees and terms. Additionally, BNPL companies must take steps to protect consumers from over-indebtedness (CBB Rulebook).

- **Kuwait**

In 2023, the CBK issued new instructions for regulating the electronic payment of funds. According to these regulations, BNPL providers must comply with the requirements applicable to large electronic money service providers (EMSPs). For instance, they are required to maintain a minimum paid-up capital of KWD 1,000,000 as ongoing capital. Additionally, the total credit extended to a single consumer, across all e-money accounts, must not exceed KWD 5,000, and the total monthly transactions processed through e-money for any customer must not exceed KWD 5,000 (CBK Instructions for Regulating the Electronic Payment of Funds 2023).

- **Oman**

In 2024, the CBO issued a consultation paper outlining a draft licensing and regulatory framework for BNPL services. The draft framework includes several key requirements. For example, BNPL companies must always maintain a minimum capital of OMR 250,000, and they must provide a performance guarantee of either OMR 10,000 or 2% of their paid-up capital, whichever amount is higher, with a maximum limit of OMR 100,000. To mitigate the risk of over-indebtedness, the CBO has set a cap of OMR 1,500 on the total credit that can be extended to a customer across all BNPL providers. In addition, BNPL companies are not permitted to disburse cash or extend credit for investment products, virtual assets, items prohibited in Oman, or any other products or services banned by the CBO. The draft framework stipulates that BNPL providers must maintain a debt burden ratio (DBR) of 60% for credit limits exceeding OMR 200, and the maximum repayment period is capped at 12 months. To ensure robust control, all credit facilities extended by BNPL providers must be reported to the Oman Credit and Financial Information Centre (Mala'a) within one working day from the date the credit facility is granted.

The draft framework allows for both conventional and Sharia-compliant BNPL business models. BNPL companies that offer Islamic products are required to meet additional governance requirements and provide disclosures to assure stakeholders that they comply with Sharia principles. Additionally, BNPL providers offering Sharia-compliant products must appoint a qualified Sharia Advisor. The proposed regulations and restrictions from the CBO aim to ensure the safe operation of BNPL services while protecting consumers from over-indebtedness (CBO Consultation Paper 2024).

- **Qatar**

QCB issued regulations for licensing and regulating BNPL in 2023. According to the new regulations, BNPL providers must maintain a minimum initial paid-up capital of QAR 5 million or 15% of their outstanding loans, whichever amount is higher. Additionally, all licensed BNPL providers are required to submit a performance guarantee of at least 2% of the capital requirement or QAR 200,000, whichever is higher. The maximum credit amount that can be extended to each customer by all BNPL providers cannot exceed QAR 25,000 at any time. BNPL providers must also regularly report all lending facilities to the Qatar Credit Bureau. Moreover, the regulations stipulate that the debt burden ratio (DBR) for Qatari nationals is capped at 75% of the customer's monthly salary, including any social allowance, while for expatriates residing in Qatar, the DBR is limited to 50%.

The QCB regulations permit both conventional and Sharia-compliant BNPL business models. BNPL providers offering Islamic products must adhere to additional governance requirements. This includes providing disclosures to ensure compliance with Sharia principles. Furthermore,

BNPL providers that offer Sharia-compliant products must obtain QCB approval to appoint a qualified Sharia Advisor (QCB Regulations for Licensing and Regulating BNPL 2023).

- **Saudi Arabia**

In 2023, SAMA published the 'Rules for Regulating BNPL Companies.' According to these new regulations, BNPL providers are required to obtain a license and comply with specific requirements. For example, BNPL providers must maintain a minimum capital of SAR 5 million, which may be increased or decreased by SAMA as it deems appropriate. In addition, the total outstanding financing for each consumer must not exceed SAR 5,000, though this limit may also increase or decrease by SAMA as it deems appropriate. Additionally, the total number of installments for repayment is capped at 12. Furthermore, collection methods must be conducted through electronic channels, and cash requests are prohibited. The regulations also address anti-money laundering (AML) and counter-terrorist financing (CTF) compliance, as well as data privacy requirements as outlined in the Saudi Personal Data Protection Law (PDPL) (SAMA Rules for Regulating Buy-Now-Pay-Later Companies 2023).

- **UAE**

In 2023, CBUAE introduced a framework to regulate short-term credit facilities. According to the updated Finance Companies Regulation, BNPL providers, defined as restricted licensed finance companies (RLFCs), must operate either as agents or be licensed as finance companies or banks, all under the supervision of CBUAE. Additionally, RLFCs are required to maintain aggregate funds of AED 20 million, or an amount equivalent to 5% of their outstanding lending volume, whichever is higher. These capital funds include paid-up capital, reserve (excluding revaluation reserve), and retained earnings.

The CBUAE mandates that the maximum total short-term credit extended to a consumer at any given time must not exceed AED 20,000, or the equivalent of three months verified net income of the consumer, whichever is lower, subject to any restrictions established by the relevant

UAE laws. Moreover, the total fees—including late payment fees—charged on any short-term credit must not exceed 30% of the original credit amount. The repayment for these loans must not exceed twelve months from the date of the original lending agreement. Furthermore, RLFCs and Agents are required to establish approved principles and policies for corporate governance. They must also implement appropriate risk management frameworks, adequate internal controls, and ensure proper segregation of duties within their organizational structure (UAE Finance Companies Regulation 2023).

Without considering the other requirements and restrictions, the minimum capital thresholds established by the GCC countries indicate that Oman, Saudi Arabia, and Qatar would be more favorable destinations for BNPL providers, given their lower capital requirements (Table 6.1). In contrast, Bahrain, the UAE, and Kuwait have stricter regulations regarding these capital requirements.

2. Digital Banking

Digital banking service is an advanced financial solution that utilizes technology to offer a comprehensive range of services. It goes beyond basic functions such as checking account balances or transferring funds. Digital banking services include online banking, mobile banking, virtual assistance, and more. Online and mobile banking are essential components of the broader digital banking ecosystem.

The digital banking transformation in GCC is rapidly changing the way banks operate and how customers interact with financial services. Several only-digital banks, also known as neobanks, have received licenses across the GCC, particularly in Bahrain, Saudi Arabia, and the UAE. The

Table 6.1 Minimum capital requirements for BNPL providers

Bahrain	*Kuwait*	*Oman*	*Qatar*	*Saudi Arabia*	*UAE*
BHD 5,000,000 USD 13,297,872	KWD 1,000,000 USD 3,258,551	OMR 250,000 USD 649,349	QAR 5,000,000 USD 1,373,626	SAR 5,000,000 USD 1,333,333	AED 20,000,000 USD 5,445,881

capital requirements[4] for obtaining digital banking licenses vary across GCC countries, reflecting the region's unique financial landscape.

- **Bahrain**

CBB has not set a minimum capital requirement specifically for digital or electronic banking licenses. According to Rule CA-1.1.1, a licensee must always maintain a minimum paid-up capital of BHD 2 million. The CBB may require a higher amount of capital on a case-by-case basis. Additionally, all establishments supervised by the CBB are required to maintain a minimum liquidity coverage ratio of 100% and undergo credible stress tests to assess their capital and liquidity positions (CBB Rulebook). Furthermore, the CBB implements additional measures to establish an environment that supports both financial growth and stability.

- **Kuwait**

In 2022, CBK issued guidelines outlining the requirements for establishing digital banks. These banks can operate under three different business models. They may operate as a unit within a traditional bank, or as a partnership between a traditional bank and a digital institution, where the bank manages core banking operations and the digital institution handles customer relations, branding, and other aspects of operations and services. The third business model is the establishment of a standalone digital bank. According to CBK instruction for regulating the electronic payment of funds, Article 5 stipulates that the minimum capital requirement for small e-money service providers is KWD 100,000 in paid-up equity, while for large e-money service providers, the minimum capital is set at KWD 1 million. Additionally, CBK emphasizes the need for a robust risk management framework and a comprehensive compliance program (CBK Press Release 2022).

- **Oman**

[4] Capital requirements refer to the minimum amount of capital that digital banking entities are mandated to hold.

In 2025, CBO issued the regulatory framework for digital banks. According to the new regulatory framework, there are two types of digital banking licenses. The first type is a Category 1 Digital Banking License, which allows a digital bank to carry out banking business without limitations. This license requires a minimum paid-up share capital of OMR 30 million for a locally incorporated joint stock company or a branch of a foreign bank. The Governor of the CBO is authorized to determine such a capital requirement. The second type is Category 2 Digital Banking License, which can carry out banking business with restrictions such as (i) the maximum deposit from a single customer and their related parties not exceeding 1% of the deposit portfolio, (ii) credit facilities to large corporates not exceeding 40% of the bank's overall lending portfolio, and (iii) not to carry out any proprietary trading activities). Restrictions (i) and (ii) do not apply for the first two years from the commencement of the digital bank's business. This license requires a minimum paid-up share capital of OMR 10 million for a locally incorporated joint stock company or a branch of a foreign bank. The CBO's Governor is empowered to determine capital requirements.

- **Qatar**

In December 2024, the QCB issued the Regulatory Framework for Digital Banks, aligned with the Third Financial Sector Strategy and the FinTech Strategy. This framework introduces a two-phase licensing process for digital banks. Phase One serves as the foundational phase, during which certain restrictions apply. This phase represents the default entry point for a QCB-licensed digital bank. In Phase Two, the licensed digital bank becomes a full-fledged entity, and all restrictions from Phase One are lifted. As part of Phase One, QCB mandates that digital banks must have a minimum initial paid-up capital of QAR 100 million, as well as ongoing capital requirements. For Phase Two, the QCB will assess the minimum capital requirement on a case-by-case basis, considering the scale and complexity of the digital bank's operation as outlined in its business plan and in line with ICAAP considerations. Additionally, the QCB may increase or decrease the minimum paid-up capital requirements based on the prevailing market conditions or if it determines that the digital bank's proposed business model, activities, or operational scale and size warrant changes (QCB Regulatory Framework for Digital Banks 2024).

- **Saudi Arabia**

SAMA does not require specific capital requirements for setting up digital banks. In 2020, SAMA issued the additional licensing guidelines and criteria for digital-only banks in Saudi Arabia. According to the guidelines, applicants are required to submit an Internal Capital Adequacy Assessment Plan (ICAAP), and an Internal Liquidity Adequacy Assessment Plan (ILAAP) along with the applications, and SAMA will assess the adequacy of capital of applicants on a case-by-case basis considering the scale, nature, and complexity if the operations as proposed in the Business Plan, ICAAP and ILAAP of the applicants. Furthermore, licensing conditions include additional mandatory requirements. For example, digital-only banks must be set up as locally incorporated joint stock companies. Promoters for digital-only banks must have experience and knowledge in the financial industry; appropriate technology-related experience and knowledge; and financial capacity to support setting up digital-only banks.

- **UAE**

According to Article 156 of the Federal Decree Law No. 6 of 2025, pertaining to the Central Bank and the regulation of financial institutions and insurance business, CBUAE has the exclusive authority to issue regulations, rules, and procedures related to digital banking operations, digital money, payment tokenization, and stored value facilities. Additionally, the CBUAE is responsible for regulating wholesale and retail payment systems, including cross-border payment systems and associates digital banking and financial services (CBUAE Law 2025). Currently, the CBUAE regulations do not specify capital requirements for digital banks. These requirements are anticipated to be included in the UAE's Digital Bank License Framework (Table 6.2).

3. **Open Banking**

Bahrain, Saudi Arabia, and the UAE have emerged as leaders in implementing Open Banking (OB).[5] The three countries have taken both

[5] Open banking refers to sharing customers' data and information among financial services providers to deliver various online financial services.

Table 6.2 Minimum capital requirements for digital banking

Bahrain	BHD 2,000,000	USD 5,319,149
Kuwait	KWD 1,000,000	USD 3,258,551
Oman		
Category 1	OMR 30,000,000	USD 77,921,916
Category 2	OMR 10,000,000	USD 25,973,972
Qatar	QAR 100,000,000	USD 27,472,527
Saudi Arabia	Not determined	
UAE	Not determined	

regulatory-driven and industry-led approaches to ensure a smooth transition to Open Banking. Central Banks in these countries have adopted a phased approach, focusing on principles as they draft frameworks and issue licenses to data aggregation firms. Open Banking is viewed as a key driver of FinTech innovation in these countries.

On the other hand, Kuwait, Oman, and Qatar are considered fast followers. The three countries have established regulatory sandboxes to test and develop Open Banking-related products and services. Qatar Central Bank has taken a significant step by launching an Open Banking platform in July 2022. Kuwait and Oman have joined the Open Banking trend by unveiling initiatives to create related products and services within their regulatory sandboxes. All three countries have structured FinTech strategies in place, and the growth of digital banks is expected to be pivotal in developing Open Banking ecosystems.

- **Bahrain**

CBB pioneered OB regulations in the GCC in 2017. It was the first to establish a sandbox for OB and issued the first fully licensed OB firm, Tarabut Gateway, in partnership with CBB in 2019. Additionally, in 2022, FinTech Galaxy became the first Open Finance (OF) platform to be licensed in the GCC (Roland Berger 2024).

- **Kuwait**

In June 2025, CBK issued a draft regulatory framework for open banking. The framework aims to create a supportive infrastructure for the Kuwaiti banking and financial sector by enhancing collaboration between banks and FinTech firms. The goal is to develop the sector, improve services, promote the national economy, and support digitization in alignment with the 'New Kuwait 2035' vision. CBK also stated that once the regulatory framework is finalized, open banking services will be launched in phases, following thorough testing to ensure their safety.

- **Oman**

In June 2025, the CBO issued the open banking regulatory framework. This framework mainly consolidated earlier versions of the API specifications and technology requirements, and it became effective immediately from the date of issuance. According to Article 2.3.4, open banking service providers are required to maintain a minimum capital of OMR 100,000. Additionally, existing payment service providers (PSPs) with a Category 1 license must have an additional OMR 100,000. Existing PSP Category 2 licensees are also required to hold a base capital of OMR 100,000, on top of their existing base capital of OMR 200,000. However, existing PSP Category 3 licensees are not obligated to hold additional capital beyond their existing base capital of OMR 300,000.

The framework allows third-party service providers, such as FinTech companies, to access customers' banking data with their consent, enabling the development of new products and services. This approach increases competition, encourages innovation, and expands the range of financial services available to consumers.

- **Qatar**

Initially, the adoption of OB was driven by the private sector. In 2023, Qatar National Bank (QNB), the largest bank in the country, began developing mobile applications for the Application Programming Interface (API). The recent strategy from QCB for FinTech emphasizes OB (Roland Berger 2024).

- **Saudi Arabia**

SAMA published the OB framework in 2022, and in 2023, it established an OB Lab. SAMA's framework allows banks and FinTech firms to test their new solutions. According to SAMA's website, there are currently 12 firms that have been approved for the production of Account Information Service Providers (AISPs) (Roland Berger 2024).

- **UAE**

Although ADMG (for Abu Dhabi Global Market) and DIFC have issued their OB FinTech Regulations, CBUAE has not issued its OB regulations. In 2022, the DFSA granted Tarabut Gateway its first OB license. In the same year, DIFC also, in partnership with Tarabut, launched the first Open Finance Lab (OFLab) (Roland Berger 2024).

4. **Payment Service Provider (PSP) Framework**

Kuwait, Qatar, Saudi Arabia, and the UAE have varying capital requirements for different types of PSP licenses. This approach aims to balance the promotion of FinTech innovation while maintaining financial stability. In contrast, Bahrain has applied the lowest capital requirements for PSPs, which is designed to foster FinTech growth by providing an easier entry point for FinTech startups while still ensuring financial stability through stringent measures. Oman, on the other hand, imposes minimal capital requirements across all types of PSPs.

- **Bahrain**

A PSP is required to provide a bank guarantee of BHD 100,000 issued by a retail bank licensed in Bahrain.

- **Kuwait**

CBK implements varying capital requirements for different types of PSP licenses to encourage FinTech innovation while ensuring financial stability. For electronic payment institutions (EPI), the capital requirement is KWD 1 million. Meanwhile, for electronic payment agents (EPA), the capital requirement is KWD 20,000.

- **Oman**

CBO has established a single, minimal capital requirement for all types of PSPs to attract FinTech investments and foster a vibrant FinTech community. This initiative aims to encourage more innovators to explore and experiment within the FinTech sector. The minimal capital requirement is set at OMR 500,000.

- **Qatar**

QCB establishes varying capital requirements for different types of PSP licenses. This strategy aims to balance the promotion of FinTech innovation with the need to maintain financial stability. Specifically, a small PSP must have a capital of QAR 2 million, a medium PSP needs to maintain a capital of QAR 5 million, and a large PSP is required to have a capital of QAR 10 million.

- **Saudi Arabia**

SAMA requires different capital requirements for PSPs: a micro-PSP must have a minimum capital of SAR 1 million, while a major PSP needs to have a capital of SAR 3 million.

- **UAE**

CBUAE has established specific capital requirements for PSPs, which are categorized as follows:

- Category 1: this includes Category 2 services plus Payment Token Services, with capital requirements ranging from AED 1.5 million to AED 3 million.
- Category 2: this encompasses Category 3 services along with Cross-border Fund Transfer Services, requiring capital between AED 1 million and AED 2 million.
- Category 3: this category includes Payment Account Issuance, Payment Instrument Issuance, Merchant Acquiring Services, Payment Aggregation, and Domestic Fund Transfer Services, with capital requirements ranging from AED 500,000 to AED 1 million.
- Category 4: this includes Payment Initiation and Payment Account Information Services, which require a capital of AED 100,000.

Based on the varying regulatory requirements set by the central banks in the GCC (Table 6.3), foreign investors looking to enter the region should carefully assess the different capital requirements, in addition to other requirements, when considering opportunities with payment service providers. Additionally, financial institutions need to understand that the distinct capital requirements in each GCC country reflect the unique FinTech landscapes present in those countries. To succeed, investors should tailor their strategies to align with the regulatory environment of the specific country they plan to operate in or enter.

To describe the complexity within a single jurisdiction, such as in the UAE, FinTech firms established in the ADGM or the DIFC must still obtain licenses in the other emirates, where they wish to offer their digital products and services. Currently, neither of these free zones provides a licensing passport to operate in other emirates, including the 'onshore' UAE. Consequently, FinTech entrepreneurs who set up their businesses in these free zones must navigate various regulations set by different authorities in the 'onshore' UAE. This includes regulations from the CBUAE for traditional baking and financing activities, the SCA for securities and investment activities, and the UAE Insurance Authority for insurance

Table 6.3 Minimum capital requirements for PSPs

Bahrain	BHD 100,000	USD 265,957
Kuwait		
EPI	KWD 1,000,000	USD 3,258,551
EPA	KWD 100,000	USD 325,855
Oman	OMR 500,000	USD 1,298,699
Qatar		
Small	QAR 2,000,000	USD 549,451
Medium	QAR 5,000,000	USD 1,373,626
Large	QAR 10,000,000	USD 2,747,253
Saudi Arabia		
Micro	SAR 1,000,000	USD 266,667
Major	SAR 3,000,000	USD 800,000
UAE		
Category 1	AED 1,500,000–3,000,001	USD 408,441–816,882
Category 2	AED 1,000,000–2,000,000	USD 272,294–544,588
Category 3	AED 500,000–1,000,000	USD 136,147–272,294
Category 4	AED 100,000	USD 27,229

products, including investment contracts sold by independent financial advisors (IFAs) in the UAE (Clifford Chance 2019).

The Need for GCC Regional Sandbox

Given the different regulatory requirements across GCC countries, foreign investors and FinTech firms often struggle to identify the most suitable sandbox for participation. Additionally, the number of applications that each national sandbox can accept may be limited. Therefore, the introduction of GCC Regional Sandboxes, backed by strategic resource allocation, would enhance opportunities for FinTech firms.

Article 4 of the GCC Charter provides for establishing effective coordination, integration, and inter-connection among the six GCC member states across various fields to achieve economic unity. To promote uniform regulations across various fields, the article identifies six key areas, one of which includes economic and financial affairs. Moreover, Article 4 emphasizes that all members should work toward stimulating scientific and technological progress in several fields, including industry. This can be achieved by creating scientific research centers, undertaking joint projects, and encouraging cooperation in the private sector for the benefit of their people (GCC Charter 1981).

Chapter III of the GCC Economic Agreement focuses on financial and monetary cooperation. Under the same chapter, Article Four emphasizes that all member states should coordinate their financial, monetary, and banking policies. It also encourages cooperation between monetary agencies and central banks, with the aim of establishing a single currency to support their economic goals. In addition, Article Five stipulates that member states should work toward unifying investment rules and regulations to create a joint investment policy. This policy should guide both domestic and foreign investments to align with their interests and promote the development and progress of their rules. Lastly, Article Twenty-Five mandates that all GGC members take necessary actions to facilitate banking and trade exchange through electronic means of communication. They should also work to unify their electronic commerce legislation (GCC Economic Agreement 2001).

Given the diverse national visions and competing FinTech hubs across the GCC countries, policymakers should consider the creation of a regional FinTech regulatory framework. The multijurisdictional framework will promote the growth of the FinTech sector across the GCC and support FinTech and startup firms as they scale both regionally and globally.

The fragmented markets and varying levels of FinTech regulatory infrastructure across the GCC pose significant challenges for FinTech companies, as there is no standardized ecosystem. For instance, the Central Banks in the GCC have implemented different regulations for similar FinTech products, such as cryptocurrencies and digital assets. The Central Bank of Bahrain and the Central Bank of the UAE have allowed trading in these assets. Meanwhile, the Central Bank of Oman and the Saudi Central Bank have adopted a more cautious approach. While neither of these central banks bans trading in digital assets, they restrict banks from engaging in cryptocurrency and digital asset trading. Conversely, the Central Bank of Kuwait and the Qatar Central Bank have implemented a clear, yet conservative stance, with the Qatar Central Bank permitting only the trading of tokenized securities under specific conditions.

GCC policymakers also need to address the challenges faced by FinTech companies and work toward harmonizing domestic policies across the GCC. The current fragmented FinTech regulations create a complex environment for companies trying to operate in different GCC countries. Secondly, the GCC should establish a cross-border legal framework for data sharing, particularly in a financial context, among its member states. Thirdly, scaling is essential for FinTech companies; however, it is difficult in the GCC region due to the fragmented nature of regional markets. Fourth, FinTech and startup firms require easier access to capital, including increased venture capital (VC) funding. At present, GCC governments are the primary source of funding. The private sector in GCC countries needs to play a larger role by supporting the development of a deeper market to enable FinTech companies to scale up and achieve sustainable growth (Strategy& 2022).

Recently, several GCC countries have introduced new immigration regulations and visa processes to attract foreign investors and experienced professionals who can enhance the sophistication and delivery of FinTech systems and related support services.

Multijurisdictional Regulatory Sandboxes

This section presents various multijurisdictional regulatory sandboxes across Africa, Asia, and the EU. It also highlights the benefits of establishing multijurisdictional regulatory sandboxes for FinTech products and services.

1. Africa

The African Continental Free Trade Area (AfCFTA) is a key component of the overarching plan called 'Agenda 2063: The Africa We Want.' This agenda was launched during the Golden Jubilee celebration of the Solemn Declaration of the Organization of African Unity (OAU) in May 2013. It serves as the continent's strategic framework for achieving the Pan-African Vision over a period of 50 years, from 2013 to 2063.

The AfCFTA agreement is recognized as the world's largest free trade area, encompassing 55 member states of the African Union (AU) and eight Regional Economic Communities. According to Article 3 of the agreement, one of the key objectives of the AfCFTA is to 'create a single market for goods and services, facilitated by movement of people, to deepen the economic integration of the African continent' (AfCFTA Agreement 2019).

One of the primary goals of the digital transformation strategy for Africa is to leverage digital technologies and innovation to transform African societies and economies. This transformation aims to promote integration across the continent, generate inclusive economic growth, stimulate job creation, bridge digital divides, and eradicate poverty. To create an enabling ecosystem that addresses all interrelated barriers and needs, the strategy will enhance advisory services to encourage digital entrepreneurship for digital enterprises. This includes developing a comprehensive continental mapping of ecosystems and building on existing initiatives to identify and support the scaling up of innovative models and financing platforms (African Union 2020). Furthermore, Africa aims to establish a conducive environment for the development and adoption of digital financial services. To achieve this objective, the continent plans to implement a supportive regulatory framework that facilitates the integration of various FinTech solutions and, where feasible, conventional banking services. The goal is to target the remittance payments market, further extend services to the unbanked population, and increase their access to financial services (African Union 2020).

Africa has two notable Pan-African sandboxes. The first one is the Ecobank Group FinTech sandbox, which aims to promote financial inclusion across the region by providing a secure environment for innovators (Ecobank 2021). It allows access to Ecobank's application programming interfaces (APIs), enabling the development of innovative solutions. As part of its open banking strategy, Ecobank's FinTech sandbox has delivered significant benefits for both the bank and the public. For example, it has facilitated cash access for the underbanked in Togo and supported youth banking initiatives in Kenya.

The second regional sandbox is the Digital Earth Africa (DEA) sandbox. DEA sandbox operates as a cloud-based platform designed for analysis and computation. It offers limited, free computing resources for technical users and data scientists, allowing them to explore data and products available from Digital Earth Africa.

Similar to the GCC region, many FinTech regulatory sandboxes in Arica are specific to individual countries. As of October 2024, about 25 regulatory sandboxes are operating across 15 African countries, spanning FinTech, data governance, and artificial intelligence (Datasphere Initiative 2025). These African regulatory sandboxes are supervised by national central banks and financial market authorities. They focus on promoting inclusive financial innovation, enhancing digital payments, facilitating cross-border remittances, and developing alternative lending models.

2. **Asia**

In 2017, the International Finance Corporation (IFC), a member of the World Bank Group, the Monetary Authority of Singapore (MAS), and the ASEAN Bankers Association (ABA) agreed to establish an industry FinTech sandbox for financial institutions and FinTech firms as part of the ASEAN Financial Innovation Network (AFIN). The multijurisdictional sandbox aims to support financial services innovation and inclusion in less developed markets within the ASEAN region, providing a platform for collaboration and innovation among financial institutions and FinTech companies.

Additionally, AFIN offers an integrated platform for collaboration between ASEAN banks, microfinance institutions, non-banking financial institutions (NBFIs), and regional FinTech centers. AFIN, along with MAS and other regulators, cooperate to create a practical environment where banks and regulators can gain better insight into the evolving impact of FinTech. This collaboration also addresses key challenges such as security, data privacy, and consumer protection (AFIN 2017).

3. **Europe**

In 2019, the European Commission (EC) and the European Supervisory Authorities (ESAs) established the European Forum for Innovation Facilitators (EFIF) to enhance cooperation and coordination in technology within the EU financial sector. The EFIF serves as a dedicated point of contact for companies and startups to address FinTech-related inquiries with competent authorities.

According to its Terms of Reference, the primary objective of the EFIF is to promote coordination and cooperation among national innovation facilitators and to support the scaling of innovation in the financial sector. EFIF provides a platform for the EU financial supervisors to meet regularly and share experiences gained from their interactions with firms through an initiative known as 'innovation facilitators,' which include regulatory sandboxes and innovation hubs.

The goals of the regular meetings among EU financial supervisors are to exchange technological expertise, reach common views on the regulatory treatment of innovative products, services, and business models, and foster bilateral and multilateral coordination on sandbox testing, where appropriate.

In September 2020, the EC adopted the Digital Finance Strategy to promote a more competitive and innovative financial sector in Europe. One of the key initiatives of this strategy is the Digital Finance Platform, which aims to support innovation in finance and establish a true single market for digital financial services. The EU digital platform includes a new data hub, cross-border services, FinTech mapping, and provides an overview of the latest policy updates, calls to action, and upcoming events.

Given the strategies adopted by the three other regions, the GCC Council may consider establishing a regional FinTech regulatory sandbox modeled after either the Asian or EU framework, or a blend of both.

Advantages of GCC Multijurisdictional FinTech Sandbox

In early 2018, the UK's Financial Conduct Authority (FCA) proposed the establishment of a global sandbox that would allow firms to test innovative products, services, or business models across multiple jurisdictions. This idea culminated in the formal launch of the Global Financial Innovation Network (GFIN) in January 2019, initiated by a coalition of international financial regulators and organizations, including the World Bank Group. The aim of GFIN is to create a platform for shared knowledge and experiences in financial innovation.

Currently, GFIN has a network of over 60 members and observers dedicated to fostering financial innovation. The GFIN Board includes representatives from the Central Bank of Bahrain and the Dubai Financial Services Authority. Additionally, several GCC regulators are part of the GFIN, including the Central Bank of the UAE, Abu Dhabi Global Market, the UAE Securities and Commodities Authority, the Kuwait Capital Markets Authority, and the Qatar Financial Centre Regulatory Authority. Furthermore, Qatar Development Bank is affiliated with GFIN.

The GCC Council can benefit from the experience of the various GCC regulators involved in GFIN. The Council can play a significant role in coordinating and encouraging its member states to establish a multijurisdictional FinTech regulatory sandbox. This regional sandbox would grant successful FinTech firms cross-border passports or licenses to operate within the GCC, provided they meet any specific requirements.

When effectively implemented, a multijurisdictional FinTech sandbox can enable companies and startups to benefit from streamlined licensing and reciprocal licensing arrangements (World Bank 2020a). Additionally, such a sandbox would facilitate and support the movement and operation of FinTech firms across the GCC while fostering cooperation among regulators. This collaborative approach allows FinTech companies to scale more rapidly on a regional and global level (World Bank 2020b). Moreover, participating in multijurisdictional regulatory sandboxes can lead to a 30–50% reduction in time-to-market for FinTech and startup firms. This acceleration is often coupled with increased investor confidence due to lower regulatory risks (World Bank 2020b). Coordination among GCC regulators also helps minimize the risks associated with regulatory arbitrage, ensuring that FinTech firms denied licensing in one country cannot gain access through another jurisdiction (World Bank 2020a).

Establishing a regional FinTech regulatory framework would facilitate the harmonization of rules and regulations across all Central Banks and other regulatory authorities, enabling the acceptance of regional GCC license, or passport. The implementation of the GCC passport would eliminate some redundant local requirements, such as obtaining a separate domestic license from each local regulator. Additionally, concluding an agreement on a cross-border data framework within the GCC would help FinTech firms scale and expand across the region by enabling access to consumer data across GCC countries. More importantly, this regional data-sharing framework would unify efforts within the GCC and position the region as a global hub for FinTech services.

While some constructive tension among various domestic sandboxes, such as those in the UAE, can spur innovation, careful coordination at both local and regional levels is essential. This is particularly important since FinTech innovations frequently intersect established regulatory boundaries (World Bank 2020a). The GCC sandbox should be designed to enhance the appeal of the GCC as a cohesive regional economic bloc and provide unified access to a single digital market. This multijurisdictional regulatory sandbox would also serve as a common platform for GCC central banks and financial centers, enabling them to harmonize their local policies and regulatory requirements.

The GCC sandbox would facilitate both local and international applicants in testing their financial solutions in an accessible, efficient, and cost-effective manner, ensuring that customers' risks and the stability of the financial systems in the GCC countries remain protected. By presenting all GCC members as a single regional bloc instead of as separate markets, the sandbox would offer FinTech and startup firms an attractive business opportunity. It would provide a larger and more diverse market along with a clearly defined multijurisdictional regulatory framework.

It is critical to emphasize that the multijurisdictional regulatory sandbox will not replace local regulators or domestic policies. Instead, it will standardize the licensing process, address uncertainties, eliminate duplication, and reduce overall costs for FinTech and startup firms. Additionally, the GCC sandbox will offer applicants better opportunities to engage effectively with GCC regulators. Firms that successfully complete experiments and exit the GCC sandbox will have a clearer understanding of due diligence and compliance requirements for their proposed financial solutions. Local authorities can also interact with applicants and provide guidance on the commercial deployment process in alignment with their country's national regulations. Furthermore, having a regional platform will facilitate information sharing among all relevant competent authorities, including central banks and financial market regulators.

Despite the many advantages of multijurisdictional FinTech sandboxes, achieving the necessary harmonization across different jurisdictions has proven to be challenging (World Bank 2020a).

Conclusion

FinTech has emerged as one of the most significant, innovative, and transformative developments in the financial services sector over the past decade. All GCC countries should seize this opportunity by implementing multijurisdictional regulatory sandboxes. These initiatives would promote economic integration among the GCC countries and foster the growth of the region's FinTech sector.

Policymakers in the GCC must address various obstacles that hinder the expansion of FinTech firms across the region. The current disjointed approach limits the scalability of innovation. By achieving regional harmonization, where the results of regulatory sandboxes are mutually recognized across different GCC markets, cross-border products can be rolled out more quickly, enhancing investment flows (World Bank 2020b). Furthermore, regulatory harmonization would enable FinTech firms to expand into new markets more efficiently.

While startups will still need to obtain licenses, increased regulatory transparency and public engagement would facilitate geographic expansion (Ahmad 2023). Finally, the GCC Council should establish a cross-border data regulatory framework to facilitate data sharing, particularly in the financial context, among the GCC countries.

References

Abdallah Al-Dardari and others, Arab Integration, A 21st Century Development Imperative (United Nations Economic and Social Commission for Western Asia - ESCWA 2014).

Abu Dhabi Global Markets (ADGM).

African Development Bank Group, 'Understanding the Importance of Regulatory Sandbox Environments and Encouraging their Adoption' (2022).
African Union, 'The Digital Transformation Strategy for Africa' (2020).
Ahmad, Amjad, 'Unleashing Mideast Fintech' (2023) Finance & Development Magazine – International Monetary Fund.
Alessio, Faccia, and Pythagoras Petratos, 'Enhancing Security in GCC Fintech: Framework, Policies and Industry Standards' (2024) ICISE 24: Proceedings of the 2024 9th International Conference on Information Systems Engineering.
Arab Monetary Fund, and Council of Arab Central Banks and Monetary Authorities Governors, 'FinTech Strategy Guidelines for the Arab Region' (2020) Arab Regional FinTech Working Group, Report No 140.
ASEAN Financial Innovation Network – AFIN (2017).
Bahrain Economic Vision 2030 (2008).
Bashar H Malkawi, 'Legal Architecture and Design for Gulf Cooperation Council Economic Integration' (2011) Journal for Juridical Science.
Cai, Cynthia Weiyi, 'Disruption of financial intermediation by FinTech: A review on crowdfunding and blockchain' (2018) Accounting & Finance.
CBK Instructions for Regulating the Electronic Payment of Funds (2023).
CBO Consultation Paper on draft licensing and regulatory framework for BNPL (2024).
CCB Capital Adequacy Module (2019) For Microfinance Institutions Capital Adequacy and Liquidity Requirements Module.
Central Bank of Bahrain (CBB).
Central Bank of Kuwait (CBK).
Central Bank of Kuwait Press Announcing Digital Banks Guidelines (2022).
Central Bank of Oman (CBO).
Central Bank of the UAE (CBUAE).
Central Bank of the UAE, Federal Decree-Law No. (6) of 2025 Regarding the Central Bank, Regulation of Financial Institutions and Activities, and Insurance Business.
Central Bank of the UAE, Finance Companies Regulation (2023).
Central Bank Qatar (QCB).
Clifford Chance, 'FinTech in the Middle East – Developments Across MENA' (2019)
Dahdal, Andrew M., Jon M. Truby, and Imad Antoine Ibrahim. 'Sandboxes in the Desert: Is a Cross-Border 'Gulf-Box' Feasible?' (2022) 14 Law, Innovation and Technology 02.
Datasphere Initiative, 'Africa Sandboxes Outlook' (2025).
Deloitte, Buy Now Pay Later: The Future of BNPL in the Middle East (2023)
Di Maggio, Marco, and Gamze Yucaoglu, 'FinTech Hive at DIFC: Creating a FinTech Ecosystem in Dubai' (2020) Harvard Business School case 220–066.

Diemers D, Lamaa A, Salamat J, Steffens T. 'Developing a FinTech Ecosystem in the GCC: Let's Get Ready for Takeoff' (2015) Strategy&, PwC.
Dubai International Financial Centre (DIFC).
Ecobank FinTech Sandbox 2021).
Economic Agreement between the Gulf Cooperation Council States (adopted 31 December 2001).
Fülöp A, Lachowski A, Martyniuk D, Stasczak S, Spionek A, Bartosiak A. 'FinTech in CEE: Chartering the Course for Innovation in Financial Services Technology' (2016) Deloitte, UK Department for International Trade.
Gulamhuseinwala I, Kotecha V., 'UK FinTech on the Cutting Edge: An Evaluation of the International FinTech Sector' (2016) Ernst & Young.
Gulf Council Cooperation Charter, Adopted 25 May 1981.
Guo, Ye, and Chen Liang, 'Blockchain Application and Outlook in the Banking Industry' (2016) Financial Innovation Journal.
Habib Hussain Khan, Shoaib Khan, Abdul Ghafoor, 'FinTech adoption, the regulatory environment and bank stability: An empirical investigation from GCC economies' (2023).
Hamoudah Al-Zaini, Aisha Al-Nama, and Georgios Dimitropoulos, 'The Gulf Cooperation Council' in Julien Chaisse and Christoph Herrmann (eds), *The International Law of Economic Integration* (Oxford University Press 2025).
Imad Antoine Ibrahim; Jon Truby, 'Governance in the Era of Blockchain Technology in Qatar: A Roadmap and a Manual for Trade Finance' (2022) Journal of Banking Regulation.
IMF, 'Digital Transformation in the Gulf Cooperation Council Economies' (2025) Middle East and Central Asia Department – Departmental Paper.
Khan, S., Bashir, U., & Islam, M. S., 'Determinants of capital structure of banks: Evidence from the Kingdom of Saudi Arabia' (2021) International Journal of Islamic and Middle Eastern Finance and Management.
Kuwait National Development Plan (2022).
Kuwait Vision 2035 – New Kuwait (2017).
Linda Low and Lorraine Carlos Salazar, 'The Gulf Cooperation Council: A Rising Power Lessons for ASEAN' (2011) Asean Studies Centre, Report No. 12.
Logan Cochrane and Reem Al-Habani, 'Sustainable Qatar: Social, Political, and Environmental Perspectives' (2023) Springer – Gulf Studies, Volume 9.
Luiz Pinto, 'Sustaining the GCC Currency Pegs: The Need for Collaboration' (Brookings' Doha Centre, 19 February 2018).
Ministry of Economy and Planning, 'Accelerating the Economic Transformation of Saudi Arabia through Investments' (2023).
Oman Vision 2040 (2020).
Qatar Financial Centre (QFC) Rules.
Qatar Financial Centre (QFC).
Qatar National Vision 2030 (2008).

Qatar Third National Development Strategy 2024–2030 (2024).
QCB BNPL Regulation: Licensing and Regulating BNPL Providers (2023).
QCB Regulatory Framework for Digital Banks 2024.
Refinitiv, Invest Qatar, and Qatar Financial Centre, 'Qatari FinTech Landscape & Commercial Opportunities' (2021).
Report – International Monetary Fund, 'Digital Transformation in the Gulf Cooperation Council Economies' (2025) Middle East and Central Asia Department.
Richie Santosdiaz, 'Overview of Key Fintech Hubs Across the Middle East and Africa' (2021) The Fintech Times.
Roland Berger, Embedded FinTech in GCC: A USD 2 bn Opportunity Revolutionizing the Financial Services sector.' (2024).
SAMA additional licensing guidelines and criteria for digital-only banks in Saudi Arabia (2020)
SAMA Rules for Regulating Buy-Now-Pay-Later (BNPL) Companies (2023).
Saudi Central Bank – National FinTech Strategy 2023 (2022).
Saudi Central Bank (SAMA).
Saudi Vision 2030 (2016).
Secretariate General – Cooperation Council for the Arab States of the Gulf (GCC), 'GCC: The Process and Achievements' (2014) Division of Information Affairs - 8th Edition.
Strategy&, 'Fintech in the Middle East: Building on the Momentum' (2022).
The African Continental Free Trade Area (AfCFTA), entered into force on 30 May 2019.
The Global Financial Centres Index 38 (2025).
Truby, Jon, 'FinTech and the City: Sandbox 2.0 Policy and Regulatory Reform Proposals' (2020) International Review of Law, Computers and Technology.
United Arab Emirates National Vision 2031 'We The UAE 2031' (2022).
World Bank Group, 'Fintech and the Future of Finance – Overview Paper' (2022).
World Bank, 'Global Experience from Regulatory Sandboxes: Finance, Competitiveness & Innovation Global Practice' (2020a) FinTech Note No. 8.
World Bank, 'How Regulators Respond to FinTech: Evaluating the Different Approaches – Sandboxes and Beyond' (2020b) FinTech Note No. 5.
World Bank, 'Developing Digital Payment Services in the Middle East and North Africa: a Strategic Approach' (2021a).
World Bank, World Development Indicators, (2021b).
Zarrouk, Hajer, Teheni El Ghak, and Abderazak Bakhouche, 'Exploring Economic and Technological Determinants of FinTech Startups' Success and Growth in the United Arab Emirates' (2021) Journal of Open Innovation: Technology, Market, and Complexity.

CHAPTER 7

Generative AI and IP Law—Incorporating the Information Delta Theory to advance AI Regulation in the Gulf States

Stefan Papastefanou

Introduction

OpenAI's *DALL·E 3* has been one of the most complex and successful text-to-image and text-to-video models that are able to create digital artworks that are essentially indistinguishable from conventional digital artworks (Betker et al. 2023, pp. 1 et seq.). The central feature of such models is their ability to take as input a natural language description and produce an image matching that description.

With the advent of such advanced generative AI systems, new questions arise regarding authorship, copyright, and intellectual property (IP)

S. Papastefanou (✉)
Applied Research Center for Intellectual Assets and the Law in Asia (ARCIALA), Germany and Singapore Management University, Bras Basah, Singapore
e-mail: stefan.papastefanou@whitecase.com

Center for Transnational IP, Media and Technology Law and Policy, Bucerius Law School, Hamburg, Germany

K. Tsanis et al. (eds.), *Digital Finance and Transformation in the Gulf*,
https://doi.org/10.1007/978-981-92-1588-1_7

rights. AI tools like DALL·E 3 can autonomously generate high-quality images based on user-inputted text, raising the issue of whether the human user or the AI system or no one should be considered the "author" of the resulting works.

While there have been a myriad of legal opinions and even a fair amount of jurisprudence on this topic, those opinions usually focus on an approach of legal and philosophical principles. Core elements such as "control" (Leiman 2020, p. 252), "foreseeability" (Kowert 2017, pp. 181 et seq.) and "tool-character" (Murray 2024, pp. 78 et seq.) are usually identified and then applied generally to the collective term of "Generative AI". While useful, this approach has two shortcomings. First, it is difficult to define "control" and "foreseeability" when applying Generative AI programs in a practical sense. Secondly, most recent approaches suffer from "over-inclusivity": Generative AI applications use a wide variety of fundamentally different technological approaches, which makes defining an abstract legal standard very difficult, if not impossible.

This paper describes how the "Information Delta Theory" as a novel analytical framework is designed to address these issues. The Information Delta Theory is a framework that measures the quantifiable difference in informational content between a user's input and an AI system's output. By assessing how much additional complexity, structure, or detail the AI introduces beyond what the human provides, the theory offers an objective method for determining the respective creative contributions of humans and generative AI systems. By quantifying the informational transformation that occurs between user input and AI output, the theory provides an objective basis for assessing the creative contributions of both human users and AI systems. This approach has significant implications for copyright law and offers a foundation for developing more tailored AI regulations, particularly in innovation-forward contexts like the Gulf States.

Unlike existing approaches that rely on abstract notions such as control, foreseeability, or the tool-character of AI systems, the Information Delta Theory avoids subjective criteria altogether by providing a quantifiable measurement of the informational transformation between input and output. By grounding authorship analysis in measurable informational change rather than inferred human control and abstract concepts, this approach offers a more objective and technologically neutral basis for evaluating AI-generated works.

The Concept of the Information Delta Theory

To understand the difference and novelty of the Information Delta Theory, it is first necessary to outline the current status quo of the discussion of so-called "generative AI" (Dornis and Stober 2024, p. 298) in relation to authorship, in particular copyright law. Without a clear definition of terms and criteria, a legal analysis quickly meanders into non-applicable generality.[1]

Current Discussion re. Authorship and Generative AI

"Generative AI" has not yet been explicitly regulated by the most relevant copyright law jurisdictions. Rather, the general principles of copyright law and creativity are employed to address the arising questions about authorship.

For example., the U.S. Copyright Act includes specific provisions regarding the requirements for protection (*Zarya of the Dawn* 2024, p. 3). In order to be protected by copyright a work must "*possess more than a de minimis quantum of creativity*" *(Feist Publications, Inc. v. Rural Tel. Serv. Company Inc.* 1991, p. 363). Besides a modicum of creativity that the work has to express, it must be the product of an independent creation of the author *(Zarya of the Dawn* 2024, p. 3).

The U.S. jurisdiction uniformly interprets the term "*work[...] of an author*[2]" in such a way that the work must have been created by a human being (*Zarya of the Dawn* 2024, p. 3). The U.S. Court of Appeals ruled that a book made of words "*'authored' by non-human spiritual beings*" (*Burrow-Giles Lithographic Company v. Sarony* 1884, pp. 56–58) can only be protected by copyright law if a "*human selection and arrangement of the revelations*" was made (*Urantia Foundation v. Kristen Maaheera,* Ninth Circuit 1997, pp. 957–959). This approach was further confirmed by the U.S. Copyright Office. According to its Compendium the key question in order to determine whether a work created with the assistance of technology is protected by copyright is "*whether the 'work' is basically one of human authorship, with the computer [or other device] merely being an* ***assisting instrument****, or whether the traditional elements in the work*

[1] Serving as a suboptimal example: Käde (2024, p. 174).

[2] Emphasis added by the author.

(literary, artistic, or musical expression or elements of selection, arrangement, etc.*) were actually conceived and executed not by man but by a machine*".[3] The decisive factor in this context is whether the human had control over the creative decisions during the creative process and created the "traditional elements of authorship" by himself.[4]

In the latest edition of its Compendium of Copyright Office Practices, it is stated that the Office "*will not register works produced by a machine or mere mechanical process that operates randomly or automatically without any creative input or intervention from a human author*" (U.S. Copyright Office 2021, para. 313).

Similarly, under EU law a work must be the result of a direct and purposeful intellectual creative or design process (Ahlberg 2022, para. 2 marginal no. 54) and must have already taken on a perceptible form (Olbrich et al. 2022, p. 870). A result that is based on an action but is accidental is therefore meaningless under copyright law due to the lack of an intellectual creative process (Ahlberg 2022, para. 2 marginal no. 54), as are mere ideas or creative intentions (Olbrich et al. 2022, p. 870).

Ultimately, what matters in most jurisdictions is whether the work, despite the use of technology, is a product of human creativity. This is not the case if the essential creative decisions were made by the **technological tool** that has been used (Lauber-Rönsberg 2019, p.248), and the human had no creative control during the creative process (U.S. Copyright Office 2024, p. 4).

The legal discourse seems to focus on essentially two factors: *foreseeability* (von Welser 2024, p. 1411) and *control* (Käde 2024). Without particularly detailed prompts or considerable creative reworking an AI may not be qualified as a tool of a human creator and the output be eligible for copyright protection (Raue 2024). The general standard, however, is abstract and refers to the question of "*human*" creation (Kraetzig 2024, p. 700). While strict foreseeability may not be necessarily present in a conventional creation, some authors argue that a narrow "*attribution context*" between individual and AI system is required for

[3] *U.S. Copyright Office*, Compendium of U.S. Copyright Office Practices sec. 313.2 (3d ed. 2021) (quoting *U.S. Copyright Office*, Sixty-Eight Annual Report of the Register of Copyrights for the Fiscal Year Ending June 30, 1965, p. 5 (1966).

[4] *U.S. Copyright Office*, Copyright Registration Guidance: Works Containing Material Generated by Artificial Intelligence, 16.03.2023, p. 4 (quoting *Burrow-Giles Lithographic Company v. Sarony*, 111 U.S. 53, 61 (1884)).

the tool qualification (Schneider 2024, p. 727). Others define the same abstract term with different wording, such as "*setting such an individual framework [for the AI] that it is reflected in the concrete result of the creative process*" (Kaesling 2024), the ability of the user to control the output of the AI system "*very accurately*" (Zönnchen 2024, p. 8) or whether an AI system functions in a "*substantially autonomous manner*" (Novelli et al. 2024, p. 20).

It is evident that at the core of the entire discussion is the search for a standard of foreseeability and control. However, none of the current approaches allow for a practical applicability but instead chose to utilize a variety of different but similar abstract terms.

Legal and Policy Implications for the Gulf States

The foreseeability and control frameworks that dominate current legal discourse around AI-generated works are fraught with limitations. These frameworks often lead to inconsistent outcomes because they rely on abstract concepts that are difficult to define and measure.

By offering objective criteria for evaluating creative contributions, the Information Delta Theory can guide the development of policies that promote both AI adoption and legal certainty. Legal certainty is the most significant factor that current copyright law frameworks lack. Hence, this approach has the potential to be unique in its novelty as well as practicability. The framework aligns with national strategies like the UAE National AI Strategy 2031 and Saudi Arabia's Vision 2030,[5] which focus on promoting both innovation and responsible AI governance.

The Information Delta Theory

The *Information Delta Theory* proposes a framework for understanding the role of AI systems in creative processes by quantifying the difference between the input provided by a user and the output produced by the AI. This theory attempts to assess the "*delta*" or change in informational content.

[5] https://www.vision2030.gov.sa/en

Conceptual Framework of Information Delta Theory

In essence, the theory analyzes the disparity between the information present in the input (e.g., a user's text prompt) and the significantly expanded or altered information in the AI-generated output (e.g., an image or text).

The core of the theory revolves around the measurable difference in informational content between what is input into a generative AI tool and what is output by the tool (Raue 2024).

The input information includes the user's prompt, which may be simple or complex. The input is typically defined by a relatively low level of detail or creativity compared to the final product, especially when working with sophisticated AI models like DALL·E 3.

Output Information: The output produced by the AI system is often far richer and more detailed, consisting of visual, stylistic, and compositional elements that may not be explicitly present in the input. Therefore, the AI generates a significant expansion in the informational complexity of the content.

Said difference or "delta" between the input and output can be analyzed in terms of **quantitative difference**. To ensure a truly objective approach data complexity metrics will be employed.

Mathematical Background

To ensure a rigorous approach, advanced principles from **information theory**, **combinatorics**, and **complexity theory** are, albeit in a simplified version appropriate and practical for the issue at hand.

The core difficulty in assessing authorship in generative AI lies in quantifying the informational transformation between input and output, the problem is fundamentally mathematical in nature. Mathematical problems require mathematical solutions; accordingly, measures such as Shannon entropy and Kolmogorov complexity offer a level of precision and replicability that current doctrinal tests—built on inherently subjective notions like control, foreseeability, or the "tool vs. agent" characterization—cannot provide. By grounding authorship analysis in quantifiable informational metrics rather than interpretive legal criteria, the Information Delta Theory reduces ambiguity, enhances consistency across cases, and enables courts and regulators to apply standards that are transparent, objective, and technologically neutral.

Several branches of mathematics offer formal methods to measure and quantify the "information" present in any given data set, be it textual input or visual output.

The key theories include:

1. **Shannon Entropy** (measuring uncertainty in data) (Lin et al. 2024, pp. 141 et seq.; Bromiley et al. 2010, pp. 1 et seq.),
2. **Kolmogorov Complexity** (quantifying the complexity of an object by the shortest description) (Lin and Vitanyi 2019, pp. 15 et seq.),
3. **Combinatorics** (measuring possible configurations of elements) (Roberts and Tesmann 2024, pp. 19 et seq.).

Shannon entropy provides a measure of uncertainty or unpredictability in a system (Lin et al. 2024, pp. 141 et seq.; Bromiley et al. 2010, pp. 1 et seq.). It quantifies the amount of "surprise" present in a message by calculating the average information content of the possible outcomes in a random variable (Lin et al. 2024, pp. 141 et seq.; Bromiley et al. 2010, pp. 1 et seq.). The entropy $H(X)$ of a random variable X with possible outcomes $\{x_1, x_1, \ldots, x_n\}$ and associated probabilities $p(x_1), p(x_1), \ldots, p(x_n)$ is defined as:

$$H(X) = -\sum_{i=1}^{n} p(x_i) log_2 p(x_i)$$

This formula expresses the expected value of the information content of a message. Intuitively, entropy increases as the probability distribution becomes more uniform (i.e., when all outcomes are equally likely) (Bromiley et al. 2010, pp. 6 et seq.) and decreases when one outcome is much more probable than others (Lin et al. 2024, p. 143).

For a simple input like a text prompt (e.g., the word "house"), the entropy can be calculated based on the probability distribution of letters or words in the given language. For instance, in English, the letter "e" is far more common than "q," which affects the entropy calculation.

For an AI-generated image, the entropy increases dramatically because each pixel has a range of values, and the probability distribution of the arrangement of colors and shapes is far more complex than the letter distribution in a text input.

Step-by-Step Example

For an input prompt with n characters chosen from an alphabet of size k, if the distribution of letters is uniform (i.e., each letter has an equal probability $p = \frac{1}{k}$) the entropy H_{input} of the input can be calculated as:

$$H_{input} = -n \cdot log_2 \frac{1}{k} = nlog_2 k$$

For a word like "house" (5 letters from an alphabet of 26 letters), the entropy is:

$$H_{input} = 5 \cdot log_2(26) \approx 5 \cdot 4,7 = 23.5bits$$

For the output, assuming a digital image with $m \times n$ pixels, where each pixel can have one of 256^3 possible RGB color values, the entropy H_{output} becomes:

$$H_{output} = m \times n \times 3 \cdot log_2(256) = m \times n \times 24bits$$

For a 1000×1000 pixel image, this yields:

$$H_{output} = 1,000 \times 1,000 \times 24 = 24,000,000bits$$

Clearly, the output entropy is vastly higher than the input entropy, reflecting the complexity added by the AI system.

In essence, entropy illustrates how unpredictable or information-rich a piece of data is. A short text prompt contains only limited information, while a fully generated image contains millions of possible color and pixel combinations. Entropy therefore helps show in an objectively measurable way that the AI introduces far more informational content than the user provides.

This quantitative expansion is legally significant because it highlights when the AI, rather than the human user, is contributing the majority of the creative information. Entropy therefore provides the first building block for understanding how authorship should be allocated in generative systems.

Kolmogorov complexity (or algorithmic complexity) measures the complexity of an object based on the length of the shortest program (in some fixed programming language) (Lin and Vitanyi 2019, pp. 15 et seq.) that can generate the object. Formally, the Kolmogorov complexity K (x) of a string x is defined as:

$$K(x) = min\{|p| : U(p) = x\}$$

where:

- $U(p)$ is a universal Turing machine that takes a program p and outputs x,
- $|p|$ is the length of the program in bits.

This concept provides a way of thinking about complexity in terms of compressibility (Lin and Vitanyi 2019, pp. 19 et seq.). A highly structured object (such as a simple repetitive pattern) has low Kolmogorov complexity because it can be described with a short program (Lin and Vitanyi 2019, p. 21). In contrast, a random or highly detailed object has high complexity because the shortest program that generates it will be nearly as long as the object itself (Lin and Vitanyi 2019, p. 23 et seq.).

For a simple word prompt like "house," the Kolmogorov complexity is quite low, as it requires only a few bits to describe. A generated image, however, has much higher Kolmogorov complexity because the visual content (with textures, lighting, shapes, etc.) is difficult to compress into a short description.

Step-by-Step Example

- **Input Complexity**: For the word "house," the program that generates it might simply be a list of characters or an ASCII string, which can be stored in roughly 5 bytes (40 bits), implying a Kolmogorov complexity of approximately $K(House) \approx 40bits$.
- **Output Complexity**: The AI-generated image, being visually complex, would require far more bits to describe. Even advanced compression techniques (like JPEG) would result in a file size of, say, 500 kilobytes, implying K $(Image) \approx 500 \times 8 = 4,000,000bits$.

Thus, the **Kolmogorov delta** between the input and output reflects the degree to which the AI has added complexity:

$$\Delta K = K_{output} - K_{input} = 4,000,000 - 40 = 3,999,960bits.$$

This shows that the AI is responsible for generating the majority of the complexity in the output, highlighting its significant role.

Kolmogorov complexity focuses on how difficult it is to describe something in the shortest possible form. A simple word or prompt can be described in a few characters, but a detailed image requires a large amount of data even in compressed form. This demonstrates that the AI is generating new, non-derivative content that cannot be reduced to the user's brief prompt.

This shift in descriptive complexity maps directly onto legal questions of creative contribution. If the shortest possible description of the output is orders of magnitude larger than the input, this supports the claim that the AI is adding legally relevant creative content rather than merely implementing the user's instructions.

Finally, combinatorics helps quantify the number of possible configurations for a given set of elements (Roberts and Tesmann 2024, pp. 24 et seq.). In the context of AI-generated content, combinatorial methods can be used to measure the possible combinations of letters in an input, or the potential arrangements of pixels in an image output (Roberts and Tesman 2024, p. 27).

For a text prompt of length n composed of characters from an alphabet of size k, the total number of possible combinations C_{input} is given by:

$$C_{input} = k^n$$

For the word "house" (5 letters, 26 letters in the alphabet):

$$C_{input} = 26^5 = 11,881,376$$

For a digital image with $m \times n$ pixels, where each pixel can take one of 256^3 color values, the total number of possible configurations C_{output} is:

$$C_{output} = \left(256^3\right)^{m \times n} = 256^{3 \times m \times n}$$

For a 1000×1000 pixel image:

$$C_{output} = 256^{3,000,000} \approx 10^{7,207,520}$$

The **combinatorial delta** between input and output is astronomically large, further highlighting the informational explosion introduced by the AI.

Combinatorics shows how explosively the number of possible outputs increases when moving from text to images. Even a simple image has an astronomically large number of possible configurations, underscoring that the AI's output cannot reasonably be predicted or controlled by the user.

This further distinguishes AI-generated outputs from traditional tools and reinforces why a quantitative framework is essential.

Such a combinatorial explosion further reinforces that human control and foreseeability, which are key elements in existing legal tests, are inherently limited in generative systems. Legally, this supports replacing subjective control-based standards with objective measures of informational contribution.

The **Information Delta** Δ represents the difference in informational content between the AI's output and the user's input. Mathematically, it can be framed as the difference between the informational complexity of the output and that of the input. Using entropy as the measure, the delta can be expressed as:

$$\Delta = H_{output} - H_{input}$$

For the examples discussed:

$$\Delta = 24,000,000 bits - 23.5 bits = 23,999,976.5 bits$$

In perspective, the use of the **Kolmogorov complexity** provides the following results:

$$\Delta K = K_{output} - K_{input} = 4,000,000 - 40 = 3,999,960 bits$$

In simpler terms, the mathematical tools discussed (entropy, Kolmogorov complexity, and combinatorics) all show the same thing: generative AI greatly expands the amount of information contained in a user's input. These tools differ in how they measure complexity, but they consistently demonstrate that even a short prompt produces an output with vastly more informational content. This provides a solid quantitative foundation for determining when an AI system is contributing original material rather than merely reproducing what the user specified.

Concepts of Positive, Negative, and Neutral Information Delta

After an information delta has been identified, the concepts of **positive information delta** and **negative information delta** are introduced.

A **positive information delta** occurs when the informational content of the output is greater than that of the input. This is the most common scenario in generative AI processes, where the system takes a relatively simple input and produces a highly complex output.

Let:

- H_{input} represent the Shannon entropy or informational content of the input,
- H_{output} represent the entropy or informational content of the output.

The **information delta** Δ is defined as:

$$\Delta = H_{output} - H_{input}$$

A **positive delta** occurs when:

$$\Delta > 0 or equivalently H_{output} > H_{input}$$

In terms of **Kolmogorov complexity**, a positive delta signifies that the shortest description of the output (in terms of the smallest algorithm that can generate it) is longer than the description of the input.

If:

- K_{input} is the Kolmogorov complexity of the input,
- K_{output} is the Kolmogorov complexity of the output,

A positive delta in Kolmogorov complexity is observed when:

$$\Delta K = K_{output} - K_{input} > 0$$

This means the AI introduces more complexity during the generation process than was present in the original input.

In cases of a positive delta, the legal question centers around the origin of the information and whether a human individual provides the additional information. Without respective involvement, the use of the AI system may not be considered a tool. In addition, this approach finally allows to provide a more accurate definition of "generative" AI, as it is unambiguous that the process "generates" more information than initially provided.

A **negative information delta** occurs when the output contains less informational content than the input. This could happen when the output is a simplification, abstraction, or filtering of the input, such that the complexity is reduced rather than expanded. *Generally*, such a negative information delta does not affect the determination of authorship since no additional information is added (Betker et al. 2023, pp. 1 et seq.). In cases of a negative delta, the user's input plays a more significant role in shaping the final output, as the AI system is essentially simplifying or condensing the input rather than expanding on it. This could imply that the user should retain more control over the final product, as their original input is more heavily represented in the final output.

While the focus is on **positive** and **negative deltas**, it is theoretically possible for the information delta to be **neutral**, where the input and output have nearly identical informational content.

Application and Limitations of the Information Delta Theory

Following the general description of the concept, the capabilities of the Information Delta Theory can best be analyzed through a practical application. For the purposes of this paper, this showcase will focus on the technology of DALL E 3, which is one of the most sophisticated and advanced AI system with regards to image creation (Betker et al. 2023, p. 4). The complexity provides the appropriate challenge, since most other legal approaches describe AI systems as a "black box".

Technical Overview of DALL E 3: From Prompt to Image

Given the complexity of the DALL E 3 model and the different steps involved, it is helpful to initially provide an overview of the different steps and how they relate to the Information Delta approach before explaining them in more technical detail (Table 7.1).

Natural Language Processing and Prompt Interpretation

The first stage of the DALL E 3 process is the understanding and breakdown of the user's prompt. This stage is critical in establishing the nature of human input in the creative process. DALL E 3 relies on OpenAI's GPT (Generative Pre-trained Transformer) (Lin et al. 2024, pp. 7 et seq.; Lomas et al. 2024, p. 10) architecture, which is also the backbone of advanced language models like GPT-4 (Betker et al. 2023, pp. 5 et seq.). The model's ability to parse and interpret human language determines the extent to which a user can influence the outcome of the generated image.

Table 7.1 Summary of the AI image generation pipeline

Stage	*Description*	*Information delta*	*Notes*
User Prompt	The user provides a short text description (e.g., "a house on a hill at sunset")	Minimal; basic semantic direction only	Serves as the baseline input with low informational content
NLP Interpretation	The model parses the text, identifies objects, relationships, and meaning	Small; semantic structure and inferred relationships	Begins transforming the input but adds little net complexity
Latent Space Representation	The AI maps concepts (house, hill, sunset) into multidimensional abstract features	Moderate; possible styles, shapes, textures, spatial relations	Large jump in informational complexity; AI introduces variations not specified by user
Diffusion Image Generation	Starting from random noise, the AI iteratively "denoises" until a complete image emerges	Very large; colors, lighting, textures, object details, pixel-level composition	This is where the major positive information delta occurs; the AI adds most of the final complexity
Post-Processing & Output	The system refines color balance, sharpness, and coherence; applies safety filters	Small; quality adjustments and corrections	Finalizes output; does not significantly affect the overall delta

The model breaks down the sentence into core components (subject, action, setting), analyzing each word's contribution to the scene (Lin et al. 2024, pp. 8 et seq.). In this stage, the user's creative input is clearly present, as they define the broad elements of the image. However, this input remains somewhat abstract, as the user does not control the specifics of how each element will appear in the final image (Lin et al. 2024, p. 9).

Latent Space Representation and Image Conceptualization
Once the text prompt is understood and categorized, DALL·E 3 moves to the next phase: converting the semantic meaning of the prompt into a "latent representation." This step is highly abstract and involves mapping the linguistic input onto a high-dimensional mathematical space, known as latent space. In this space, the various elements of the image—such

as shapes, textures, and colors—are encoded as numerical values (Betker et al. 2023, pp. 6 et seq.; Lin et al. 2024, p. 8; Lomas et al. 2024, p. 9).

Latent space can be understood as a conceptual blueprint for the final image. When DALL·E 3 generates a latent representation, it does not create an image directly. Rather, it generates a compressed version of all the visual features that the image will contain, including object shapes, textures, colors, and the spatial relationship of the objects (Lin et al. 2024, pp. 7 et seq.).

The system's vast training data allows it to generate plausible representations, even for highly imaginative prompts (Betker et al. 2023, pp. 9 et seq.), but the precise appearance of the final image is not under the user's direct control.

Image Generation via Diffusion Process

The actual generation of the image takes place through a method known as a **diffusion model**, which involves a step-by-step refinement of a random noise pattern into a fully formed image (Betker et al. 2023, pp. 7 et seq.). This process reflects the gradual transformation of latent space information into visual form.

Diffusion models begin with a random noise field, which is progressively refined over multiple iterations (Lomas et al. 2024, p. 12; Lin et al. 2024, pp. 7 et seq.). In each step, the noise is reduced, and the latent space representation guides the model toward generating the shapes, textures, and colors that match the user's prompt. This iterative process allows the model to gradually "denoise" the image, turning abstract mathematical representations into concrete visual elements (Betker et al. 2023, pp. 8 et seq.).

While the user has influenced the direction of the image through the prompt, the specific decisions about how the image is formed — such as how textures are rendered or how colors are blended — are determined by the AI's internal algorithms (Betker et al. 2023, pp. 10 et seq.). The user cannot intervene in this process, further complicating the attribution of authorship.

During this phase, the AI makes numerous adjustments to specify the general input, e.g., the **color palette** (while a user may provide a broad description of colors, the exact shades, gradients, and combinations are determined by the AI system) (Lin et al. 2024, pp. 7 et seq.; Lomas et al., 2024, p. 13) and **object details** (the AI determines how detailed to make certain elements of the image) (Lomas et al., 2024, pp. 14 et seq.).

Post-Processing and Output Rendering
Once the diffusion model has fully generated the image, DALL·E 3 engages in a final round of post-processing to ensure that the image is polished and visually coherent.

The AI system automatically adjusts certain aspects of the image to enhance quality. This includes refining color balance, correcting any visual artifacts, and sharpening edges. These technical adjustments are critical to ensuring that the image meets the user's expectations, especially in terms of clarity and aesthetic appeal. Although a user can provide feedback and request new images by adjusting the prompt, they do not have direct control over the final output.

In addition to enhancing visual quality, DALL·E 3 includes ethical safeguards to prevent the generation of harmful or inappropriate content. The system is designed to filter out requests that involve violence, nudity, or other objectionable material.[6]

Application of Information Delta Theory to the DALL·E 3 Process

To apply the Information Delta Theory, this paper will examine each phase of the algorithm and quantify the difference in informational content between the input and output at that step.

User Text Prompt to Natural Language Processing (NLP) and Semantic Understanding
The process begins with the user providing a text prompt. This text prompt is relatively simple and represents a **low amount of informational content** compared to the final image.

- **Input Example**: Consider the text prompt "a house on a hill at sunset."

[6] This content moderation step underscores the fact that the developers and operators of DALL·E 3 maintain a degree of oversight over the output, which could be relevant when considering questions of legal liability or responsibility for the generated content.

- The prompt contains 28 characters (assuming spaces are ignored). If we assume the input consists of characters from the English alphabet (26 letters) and spaces, the total number of possible combinations is:

$$C_{input} = (26 + 1)^{28} \approx 5.5 \times 10^{40}$$

- **Entropy Calculation**: Using Shannon entropy, assuming an equal probability for each character:

$$H_{input} = 28 \times log_2(27) \approx 28 \times 4.75 = 133 bits$$

- The informational content of the input is small, just 133 bits, representing the user's narrow creative direction.

Once the user provides the text prompt, DALL·E 3 employs **natural language processing (NLP)** algorithms to interpret and understand the prompt. This stage involves breaking down the input into semantically meaningful components (e.g., identifying objects, actions, and relationships).

At this stage, a small information delta at this stage by extracting deeper meanings and relationships between the words in the prompt. However, the informational content added here is mainly **structural** rather than **additive**. It doesn't add much new complexity but begins to organize the user's input into a more detailed understanding.

For instance, from the input "house on a hill at sunset," the AI will infer the relationships between "house," "hill," and "sunset," preparing it for the image generation phase. This is akin to a slight reorganization of the input information, contributing minimally to the overall delta.

Latent Space Representation—Transition from Text to Abstract Features

At this stage, DALL·E 3 converts the understood text into a **latent space representation**, the high-dimensional mathematical space where abstract concepts are encoded. The AI maps each semantic component (house, hill, sunset) into this latent space, which encodes information such as shape, texture, color, and spatial relationships.

This is the first major point where DALL·E 3 starts to introduce significant new information. The AI is tasked with converting simple textual descriptions into complex abstract concepts that contain more detail than the original input. For example, "house" as a word becomes a multidimensional concept in latent space that could represent various possible architectural styles, materials, sizes, and positions.

The complexity of representing these abstract visual elements is much higher than the simplicity of the text input. While the word "house" might be low in complexity, the latent space must account for all possible variations of houses (modern, traditional, etc.). The AI introduces new possibilities that were not explicitly present in the input.

If the textual description could be encoded in a few dozen bits, the latent space requires many more to account for these new possibilities. This increase in complexity is where a significant information delta begins to emerge.

Image Generation via Diffusion Model

The **diffusion model** is the heart of DALL·E 3's image generation process. Consequently, the most significant delta occurs here. The process of transforming random noise into a coherent image involves introducing a vast amount of **new informational content**. The image must account for the following:

Pixel Information: Each pixel in a generated image has color information (RGB values), and for a high-resolution image with m × nm \times nm × n pixels, the total number of possible pixel configurations is:

$$C_{output} = \left(256^3\right)^{m\times n} = 256^{3\times m\times n}$$

As discussed earlier, for a 1000 × 1000 pixel image, this gives approximately $10^{7,207,520}$ possible configurations, representing an enormous increase in informational content compared to the text input.

Entropy of the Output: The Shannon entropy for this output, given that each pixel can take on 2563256^32563 possible values, is:

$$H_{output} = m \times n \times 3 \cdot log_2(256) = m \times n \times 24bits$$

For a 1000 × 1000 image:

$$H_{output} = 1,000 \times 1,000 \times 24 = 24,000,000 bits$$

The output's complexity far exceeds that of the input, showing that the AI is responsible for adding the majority of the new information. This stage is where the **Information Delta** reaches its peak, as the relatively simple input is expanded into a highly complex image.

According to the Kolmogorov Complexity of Output, the shortest description of a complex image is nearly as long as the image itself, especially if the image contains intricate textures and lighting effects. While the text input was simple, describing the generated image would require millions of bits, contributing to a large Kolmogorov delta.

Post-Processing and Final Output Rendering
After the image has been generated, DALL·E 3 applies a final stage of **post-processing** to enhance visual quality. The refinements added during this stage are minor. Hence, the delta introduced here is smaller than during the diffusion process but still non-trivial, as the post-processing ensures that the image is polished and aesthetically pleasing as well as complies with OpenAI's content guidelines.

These technical findings feed directly into the subsequent legal analysis: once we can quantify how much information the AI, rather than the human, introduces, we can anchor authorship, ownership, and regulatory decisions in objective measures rather than abstract doctrinal criteria.

Total Information Delta Calculation and Conclusion
By the end of the DALL·E 3 process, the **Information Delta** is enormous. The input, which consisted of just a few characters with limited entropy, has been transformed into a highly detailed image with millions of possible pixel configurations. The bulk of the delta occurs during the diffusion model stage, where the AI system introduces new information that vastly expands upon the user's original input. For the purposes of this paper, we will use the Shannon entropy approach, since the size of the numbers of the other approaches is difficult to meaningfully display in a legal research paper:

- **Input**: $H_{input} = 133 bits$
- **Output**: $H_{output} \approx 24,000,000 bits$

Thus, the total **Information Delta** is:

$$\Delta = 24,000,000\ bits\ -\ 133\ bits = 23,999,867\ bits$$

This massive delta demonstrates that the AI is primarily responsible for introducing new informational content. On the other hand, the user's input, while crucial for direction, provides only a small fraction of the total informational content of the final output.

This quantifiable delta offers an objective basis for whether an AI system may be considered "generative" as opposed to non-generative AI systems.

More importantly, to answer this initial question of authorship with regard to AI-generated content, it can be observed that during the process, the most prominent positive information delta is achieved by the diffusion model, which in turn uses the training data in a specific algorithmic way.

The step-by-step analysis of DALL·E 3 shows that the largest increases in informational content occur within the AI model itself, not in the user's input. While the user provides direction, the AI generates the vast majority of informational complexity. This measurable expansion of information is precisely what makes generative AI distinct from traditional creative tools and why Information Delta Theory offers a clearer foundation for authorship analysis.

Limitations of the Information Delta Theory

While the Information Delta theory offers a novel framework for quantifying the informational difference between input and output in AI-generated works, it also faces several limitations. These challenges arise from both the mathematical foundations of the theory and its application in legal contexts, particularly regarding copyright law. Some key limitations and possible ways to mitigate them are outlined below.

Difficulty in Accurately Measuring Information Content

One of the primary challenges of the Information Delta theory is the difficulty in accurately quantifying the informational content of both inputs and outputs. While Shannon entropy, Kolmogorov complexity, and combinatorics provide robust mathematical tools for this purpose, applying these tools to complex, real-world data (such as text or images) is not always straightforward.

Kolmogorov complexity, for instance, is an abstract mathematical concept that is often impractical to calculate for complex real-world objects like images or highly structured text (Li and Vitanyi 2019, pp. 42 et seq.). Additionally, Shannon entropy assumes knowledge of the probability distribution of the system, which can be difficult to determine in real-world scenarios (Li and Vitanyi 2019, pp. 44 et seq.).

In addition, artistic or creative works may have elements of subjectivity that are not easily captured by mathematical measures. For example, two images of similar pixel complexity might differ vastly in terms of their aesthetic or emotional value, which is difficult to quantify purely mathematically.

One way to address this issue is to rely on approximations of Kolmogorov complexity and entropy using practical algorithms, such as file compression techniques (Li and Vitanyi 2019, pp. 46 et seq.). For instance, by compressing a generated image and measuring the size of the compressed file, we can get a rough estimate of its complexity. While not exact, this approach provides a practical alternative for calculating complexity.

Another potential solution could involve combining **quantitative** and **qualitative** metrics. For instance, mathematical measures like entropy could be supplemented with expert opinions on aesthetic or artistic value. Courts and legal scholars could develop hybrid tests that balance informational complexity with the subjective creative value of the input and output.

Information Does Not Always Equate to Creativity

A second limitation of the theory is that **information content** does not necessarily equate to **creativity** or **artistic merit**. A highly detailed and complex output may contain a large amount of information, but this does not always mean the work is creative or novel. Conversely, a simple output may be highly creative despite containing less informational content.

The theory's reliance on quantitative measures like entropy and complexity may lead to the erroneous conclusion that more complex outputs are inherently more creative. However, this is not always the case, as creativity often involves the novelty and originality of ideas rather than their sheer informational content.

One way to address this limitation is by incorporating a test for novelty or originality in addition to informational content. Courts could require that outputs demonstrate some level of novelty beyond the mere increase in complexity to qualify as creative contributions. This approach would ensure that an AI's ability to generate large amounts of data doesn't automatically translate into products being public domain.

Attribution of Information Delta to the AI vs. the User
Another challenge lies in attributing the information delta to the appropriate party. While the theory quantifies the difference between input and output, it doesn't directly address whether this delta should be attributed to the AI system to the user who initiated the process.

The theory's reliance on the mathematical difference between input and output does not inherently capture the extent of the user's contribution. A user's prompt may seem simple, but if it requires deep creative thought or involves extensive knowledge, their contribution could be undervalued by focusing solely on the informational content.

One potential solution is to introduce a method for weighting the user's input based on its complexity or significance. This could involve creating a legal framework that takes into account not just the informational content but also the creative intent and effort behind the input. For instance, more detailed or carefully crafted prompts could receive a higher weight in determining authorship.

Another way to address this issue is to develop models of shared authorship that recognize both the user's contribution (through the prompt) and other human individuals such as the programmer or data analyst who contributed through generating new information.

Dynamic Nature of AI Models and Iterative Improvements
AI models like DALL·E 3 are dynamic systems that continually improve over time through retraining and optimization (Lomas et al. 2024, pp. 1 et seq.). This presents a challenge for the Information Delta theory, which assumes a static relationship between input and output. As models evolve and produce better outputs with the same inputs, the information delta may change over time.

The theory may struggle to account for changes in the delta over time. For example, if the same input is processed by a more advanced version of the AI system, the delta might increase as the model produces better, more detailed outputs. This dynamic quality raises questions about how to assess authorship when the delta is constantly shifting.

One solution could be to adopt a snapshot approach, where the delta is calculated based on the model's current capabilities at the time the input is processed. This allows the delta to be assessed in a specific moment in time, providing a fixed basis for legal decisions.

Another potential solution is to create versioning systems for AI models, where the delta is calculated relative to the version of the AI used at the time. This would allow legal disputes over authorship or ownership to be tied to specific AI capabilities and ensure that future improvements in the model do not retroactively affect previous outputs.

Verification and Auditability of Delta Calculations

A further practical limitation concerns the verification and auditability of delta measurements. For IDT to function as a reliable legal and regulatory tool, stakeholders must be able to reproduce or independently confirm the informational delta between input and output. However, this presents several challenges. Developers may be reluctant to disclose internal model operations, and raw access to latent space representations or diffusion-stage data may reveal proprietary information. Users typically lack the technical capability to conduct independent measurements, while regulators require verifiable yet non-intrusive methods to ensure compliance.

These challenges can be mitigated by adopting standardized approximation techniques, such as entropy estimation, compression-based complexity measures, and hashed intermediate logs. Such methods allow delta calculations to be verified without exposing sensitive model parameters. Cryptographic provenance mechanisms can further ensure the integrity of logged transformations. Nevertheless, the requirement for transparent verification introduces an additional layer of technical and administrative complexity. Ensuring consistent, trustworthy audits across jurisdictions will depend on cooperation between developers, users, and regulators, as well as the establishment of shared standards governing how delta values are recorded, reported, and reviewed.

Information Delta Theory as the Core of Regulatory Framework Design

In sum, the Information Delta Theory provides a structured basis for distinguishing human creativity from autonomous machine contribution, offering courts a more objective standard than existing control- or foreseeability-based tests. By quantifying informational transformation, IDT supports clearer authorship determinations, more consistent allocation of rights and responsibilities, and improved legal certainty across jurisdictions. For regulators, the theory also enables the development of transparent, scalable governance mechanisms that align AI accountability with measurable system behavior rather than subjective doctrinal judgments.

Theoretical Approach and Key Elements

By embedding the Information Delta Theory into the core of regulatory frameworks, the Gulf States can create a model that both protects intellectual property and promotes AI development. This theory-driven approach provides a clear foundation for legal certainty, balancing creative innovation with responsible regulation.

Regulatory frameworks for generative AI should incorporate mechanisms to monitor and assess the transformation of information throughout the creative process. To achieve this, Generative AI models must be required to log and quantify informational changes at each stage, creating a robust foundation for determining the extent of machine versus human contribution. These metrics will serve as essential tools to evaluate whether the output significantly surpasses the input in complexity. Such assessments can guide decisions regarding joint or collaborative authorship, ensuring a fair allocation of rights based on measurable contributions.

A scalable authorship system should be implemented, allowing for rights adjustments according to the degree of input influence. For instance, when a user's prompt plays a substantial role in shaping the final output, the user would be entitled to a greater share of ownership.

Additionally, delta-based benchmarks should be established to assess the innovative potential of generative AI outputs. These benchmarks can be tied to incentives that reward high-delta outputs contributing to technological advancement, thereby motivating developers to create AI systems capable of expanding creative boundaries.

Transparency must also be a cornerstone of this framework. AI developers should be mandated to disclose the AI's role in producing informational deltas, ensuring that users are fully aware of the extent and nature of AI-generated transformations.

Gulf States should actively pursue international partnerships to develop unified standards for measuring and regulating informational deltas. Through collaboration with global counterparts, these nations can harmonize their policies with international best practices, fostering both innovation and regulatory consistency in the rapidly evolving field of generative AI.

In particular, the adoption of the Information Delta Theory offers particular advantages for Gulf States whose copyright regimes still rely on traditional notions of authorship while simultaneously pursuing ambitious national AI strategies. Although jurisdictions such as the UAE, Saudi Arabia, Qatar, and Bahrain differ in the maturity of their AI regulatory ecosystems, they share two common features: (1) copyright laws that presuppose human authorship, and (2) emerging AI governance frameworks that seek to ensure responsible development and deployment of advanced systems. In this environment, IDT provides a coherent bridge between long-standing IP doctrines and the rapidly evolving realities of generative AI.

United Arab Emirates (UAE)

Under the UAE Copyright Law (Federal Decree-Law No. 38 of 2021), authorship is understood as a human-directed creative act, yet the law also protects software-generated works without defining how to allocate creative responsibility when an AI system plays a dominant role. Because the UAE's wider AI strategy emphasizes innovation and high-value digital transformation, IDT can help resolve this ambiguity by offering a measurable standard for determining when the human user contributes sufficiently to qualify as the author. Where the information delta is small—meaning the AI operates more as a conventional tool—the user's claim to authorship is strengthened. Where the delta is large, the output may fall outside classical conceptions of human authorship, enabling regulators to develop clearer rules for system accountability.

Saudi Arabia

Following Vision 2030, Saudi Arabia has issued AI ethics principles (through SDAIA) and copyright guidelines for AI-related works. These guidelines acknowledge the difficulties in attributing authorship when AI systems make substantial creative contributions, but they do not specify how such contributions should be measured. IDT provides a practical method for implementing these guidelines by quantifying the extent to which generative systems introduce new informational content. Courts and administrative bodies could therefore use delta measurements to determine whether the human input meets the threshold of creative authorship under Saudi copyright law, while regulators can use the same metrics to assess system autonomy and accountability.

Qatar

Qatar's ethical AI principles and sector-specific guidelines emphasize human oversight and IP compliance, yet the country lacks detailed statutory rules governing AI-generated creative works. IDT offers a workable framework for institutions that must evaluate whether a generated output reflects genuine human creativity or whether the AI system has added substantial independent content. As Qatar continues to refine its AI governance initiatives, delta-based assessments can facilitate clearer delineation of rights and responsibilities, particularly in media, finance, and government applications where generative AI is increasingly used.

Bahrain

Bahrain's existing copyright statute assumes human originality, while its emerging AI Regulation Law moves toward a licensing and accountability model for AI developers and operators. IDT can help reconcile these two frameworks by providing a methodology that simultaneously informs ownership questions (under the Copyright Law) and responsibility questions (under the AI regulatory framework). If the information delta demonstrates that the AI is responsible for most of the novel informational content, the system's developer or operator may bear greater governance obligations even when no traditional human author exists.

Across all four jurisdictions, IDT creates a shared analytic foundation that supports both IP protection and AI governance. By quantifying creative transformation instead of relying on abstract concepts of control, foreseeability, or tool-character, the theory enables courts, policymakers, and practitioners to evaluate authorship and system accountability in a more transparent and consistent manner. This not only supports legal certainty, which is an explicit priority in regional innovation strategies, but also positions Gulf States to lead in crafting clear, technologically informed AI frameworks. Therefore, this approach may be applied unilaterally or could be used across the GCC to further strengthen the region in its entirety.

To further showcase the suitability of the Information Delta Theory, the following comparison table provides a comprehensive and comparative overview (Table 7.2):

Example of a Legislative Approach

Article 1—Definitions

For the purposes of this Act

(1) "Information Delta" refers to the measurable increase or decrease in informational complexity between the input provided and the output generated by an algorithmic system. The method of calculating the "Information Delta" is specified in Appendix 1.[7]
(2) "Positive Information Delta" refers to an increase of complexity re. the Information Delta.
(3) "Generative AI System" refers to any algorithmic system capable of introducing a "Positive Information Delta".
(4) "Attribution Threshold" refers to the quantitative measure at which creative contributions are attributed to a human user or the AI system based on the delta. The method for considering the Information Delta is specified in Appendix 2.[8]

[7] Including a dynamic Appendix in the legislation allows to adjust the calculation method to further developments in AI systems.

[8] A second Appendix can be utilized to include qualitative measurements to counter the limitations of a purely quantitative approach.

Table 7.2 Comparative overview of gulf states

Jurisdiction	*Current copyright framework*	*AI governance status*	*Key legal ambiguity for generative AI*	*How IDT addresses the gap*
UAE	Copyright Law requires human authorship but protects computer-generated works without clarifying authorship thresholds	National AI Strategy 2031; ethics principles; no binding generative-AI specific statute	Lack of criteria for distinguishing human authorship from AI-generated creativity	Provides quantifiable threshold for human contribution; helps determine when AI acts as a tool vs an autonomous creator
Saudi Arabia	Copyright requires human creativity; SAIP guidelines address AI but do not define how to measure contribution	SDAIA AI ethics principles; soft-law guidance for AI-related works	Unclear whether human prompts constitute "creative input" sufficient for authorship	Offers metrics to apply SAIP guidance consistently; delta size shows whether human input is legally meaningful
Qatar	No explicit statute for AI-generated works; traditional copyright doctrine presumes human authorship	Ethical AI Principles (MCIT); sector regulations in finance and media	Certainty issues when AI outputs exceed human direction; compliance duties unclear	Delta measurement helps organizations assess authorship, ownership, and IP compliance obligations
Bahrain	Copyright Law requires human originality; no dedicated copyright rules for AI outputs	Draft AI Regulation Law includes licensing, accountability, transparency	Tension between traditional copyright and emerging AI regulation responsibilities	Delta analysis links authorship (copyright) with accountability (AI law); clarifies responsibility when AI contributes most

(5) "Developers" refers to (...)[9]

Article 2—Logging and Reporting

(1) Developers of Generative AI systems shall implement mechanisms to record Information Deltas at each stage of processing within each specific algorithm.
(2) Periodic reports on delta-based transformations shall be submitted to the Regulatory Authority to assess compliance with authorship and ownership criteria.

Article 3—Collaborative Authorship

(1) Authorship rights shall be allocated in accordance with the measured Information Delta and the relevant Attribution Threshold.
(2) Where the Positive Information Delta and Attribution Threshold indicate substantial non-human contribution, the output shall be treated as a collaborative work unless otherwise agreed upon by relevant parties.[10]

Article 4—Transparency Requirements

(1) Generative AI Systems must adhere to transparency standards, including disclosure of training data and algorithmic decision-making processes to the Regulatory Authority.
(2) Users of Generative AI Systems shall have the right to access records of the delta transformations related to their generated outputs.
(3) The right according to (2) is limited to a quantitative demonstration of the Information Delta and may not lead to the disclosure of the specific algorithm.

[9] In order to focus on the novel approach, this example is not going to include general and already established definitions.

[10] As an alternative, the output might be considered public domain; however, the intention is to further innovation which arguably is best incentivized by providing rights to the parties involved.

Article 5— International Cooperation

(1) The Regulatory Authority shall engage with international counterparts to harmonize standards for delta-based evaluation and authorship determination.
(2) Mutual recognition agreements may be established to promote cross-border consistency in AI governance.
(3) For the purposes of (1) and (2), the Regulatory Authority shall publish its methods outlined in Appendix 1 and Appendix 2 and regularly adjust said methods with experts as well as representatives from affected parties and industries.

Illustrative Cases Demonstrating How Information Delta Theory Resolves Real-World Disputes

1. **China Internet Court: Iterative Prompting as Creative Contribution**

In one of the earliest judicial decisions addressing generative-AI authorship, the Bejing Chinese Internet Court held that a creator who produced an image through multiple rounds of iterative prompting exercised sufficient human involvement to qualify for copyright protection. The court found that the user's repeated refinements and adjustments demonstrated "intellectual investment" and "personalized expression," even though the final image was rendered by an AI system. The case was recently upheld on September 16, 2025.[11]

IDT Application

Under IDT, each iteration in the prompting process would generate a measurable *delta—a* shift in informational content from the previous prompt to the next output. The cumulative deltas produced by successive refinements would quantify the user's creative contribution over time. If the aggregated human-driven deltas exceed a legally defined

[11] https://www.chinaiplawupdate.com/2025/09/beijing-internet-court-requires-evidence-of-creative-effort-to-claim-copyright-protection-in-ai-generated-images/

threshold, the system would classify the work as having substantial human authorship.

This offers several advantages over the court's qualitative reasoning:

- It avoids subjective speculation about the "degree" of user involvement.
- It tracks creative contribution numerically, iteration by iteration.
- It creates a repeatable test for future cases involving iterative prompting.

In short, IDT would confirm that the outcome in the Chinese case was correct, but would ground the analysis in a transparent, measurable framework rather than judicial intuition.

2. **U.S. Copyright Office: The "Zarya of the Dawn" Comic Case (*Zarya of the Dawn*, 2023)**

In the U.S. Copyright Office's decision regarding *Zarya of the Dawn*, the Office recognized copyright in the text and overall compilation but denied protection for the Midjourney-generated images, holding that they were not created by a human author. The Office reasoned that the user's prompt was too general to constitute traditional elements of authorship, and that the AI introduced unpredictable visual elements that could not be meaningfully controlled by the human creator.

IDT Application

Under IDT, a comparison between the informational content of a short textual prompt (low-entropy, low-complexity input) and a fully rendered image (high-entropy, high-complexity output) would reveal a large positive information delta. This quantifiable delta demonstrates that the AI and not the human creator generated the majority of the informational content in each image.

Thus

- The theory supports the Copyright Office's conclusion but
- provides a mathematically grounded explanation for why the images lack sufficient human authorship.

Conversely, IDT would also show that the selection, arrangement, and narrative integration of the images into the comic create additional informational deltas attributable to the human author. These smaller, but legally meaningful, deltas justify protection for the compilation and textual narrative while denying it for the AI-generated images.

Conclusion

The rapid development of generative AI technologies like DALL·E 3 has brought new and complex challenges to the field of intellectual property law, particularly in determining authorship and ownership of AI-generated works. Traditional legal frameworks, which often rely on abstract concepts such as **foreseeability, control,** and the extent to which an AI system is a mere **tool** in the hands of the user, are increasingly inadequate in addressing the unique characteristics of AI creativity. These older approaches tend to focus on qualitative and subjective elements that are difficult to quantify, leading to inconsistencies in legal interpretation and uncertainty for creators and AI developers alike.

The Information Delta theory utilizes a mathematical basis for assessing creative contributions by measuring the difference in informational content between the user's input and the AI's output. This quantifiable approach is rooted in well-established mathematical principles, such as Shannon entropy, Kolmogorov complexity, and combinatorics, which allow for precise measurements of complexity and informational change.

Adopting the Information Delta theory could help resolve key issues surrounding authorship, ownership, and copyright in AI-generated works by:

1. **Providing clarity** in legal disputes over authorship, by offering a method to objectively measure contributions.
2. **Reducing ambiguity** in intellectual property law by moving away from subjective concepts like control and foreseeability.
3. **Encouraging innovation** by establishing a legal framework that fairly recognizes both human and AI contributions.

The Gulf States are uniquely positioned to become global leaders in mathematically grounded AI regulation. Their existing innovation strategies and ambitions in digital transformation create a political and economic environment that is unusually receptive to technically sophisticated regulatory concepts. By incorporating a formal framework such as the Information Delta Theory into their copyright and AI-governance regimes, Gulf legislators can move beyond the largely qualitative standards that currently dominate in the US, EU, and China, and instead anchor key legal questions—authorship, ownership, and accountability—in transparent, quantifiable metrics.

If Gulf regulators adopt delta-based thresholds for determining when AI systems are "generative," when human authorship remains predominant, or when enhanced oversight obligations are triggered, they would set a global benchmark for technically robust, innovation-friendly AI law. Such an approach would not only offer greater legal certainty for domestic stakeholders but would also attract international developers and investors seeking jurisdictions where the allocation of rights and responsibilities follows predictable, mathematically defined criteria. In doing so, the Gulf States could help shape emerging international standards, positioning themselves not merely as regulatory followers but as norm entrepreneurs in the design of next-generation AI regulation.

Further work is needed to refine and operationalize the Information Delta Theory in legal and policy contexts. First, empirical studies should test delta thresholds across different generative models and modalities to determine when informational expansion becomes legally significant for authorship or liability purposes. Second, research is required on evidentiary standards and court admissibility, including how delta calculations can be presented as expert evidence without revealing proprietary model details. Third, developing standardized benchmarks and technical protocols (analogous to model cards or AI provenance frameworks) would allow regulators, developers, and independent auditors to measure deltas consistently across jurisdictions. Finally, comparative legal analysis should explore how IDT integrates with divergent copyright doctrines and AI governance regimes globally, helping to harmonize emerging regulatory approaches.

References

Ahlberg, H., & Götting, H.-P. (2022). BeckOK Urheberrecht (34. ed.). C. H. BECK.

Betker J., Goh G., Jing L., Brooks T. & OpenAI (2023). Improving Image Generation with Better Captions.

Bromiley P., Thacker N., Manjon J., Statistical interpretation of non-local means (2010), IET Computer Vision, 162–172.

Burrow-Giles Lithographic Company v. Sarony. 1884. 111 U.S. 53.

Dornis T. W. & Stober S. (2024). Urheberrecht und Training generativer KI-Modelle. *Digitization and the Law.* https://doi.org/10.5771/9783748949558

Feist Publications, Inc. v. Rural Tel. Serv. Co.. 1991. 499 U.S. 340.

Kaesling, K. (2024). Malerei mit KI: Urheberrechtliche Zuordnung bei Schöpfung mit Text-to-Image LLMs. *Zeitschrift für Urheber- und Medienrecht (ZUM) 7/2024*: 493–501.

Käde, L. Dr. (2024). Do You Remember?—Enthalten KI-Modelle Vervielfältigungen von Trainingsdaten, lassen sich diese gezielt rekonstruieren und welche Implikationen hat das für das Urheberrecht?. *Zeitschrift für Urheber- und Medienrecht (ZUM) 3/2024*, 174–183.

Kowert W. (2017). The Foreseeability of Human–Artificial Intelligence Interactions. *Texas Law Review 96 (1)*: 181–204.

Kraetzig, V. Dr. (2024). KI-Kunst als schöpferische Zerstörung. *Neue Juristische Wochenzeitschrift (NJW) 2024:* 697–702.

Lauber-Rönsberg, A. (2019). Autonome „Schöpfung“—Urheberschaft und Schutzfähigkeit. *Gewerblicher Rechtsschutz und Urheberrecht (GRUR) 3/2019*: 244–253.

Leiman, T. (2020). Law and tech collide: foreseeability, reasonableness and advanced driver assistance systems. *Policy and Society, Vol. 40, Issue 2, 2021:* 250–271.

Li, M. & Vitányi, P. (2019). An Introduction to Kolmogorov Complexity and Its Applications (4. ed.). Springer. https://doi.org/10.1007/978-3-030-11298-1

Lin, Z., Cheng, M., He, R., Ubul, K., Silamu, W., Zha, H., Zhou, J., Liu, C. (2024). Pattern Recognition and Computer Vision.

Lomas, D., Heckert P., Maden, W., Developing and evaluating a design method for positive artificial intelligence (2024).

Murray, M. D. (2024). Tools Do Not Create: Human Authorship in the Use of Generative Artificial Intelligence. *Case W. Res. J.L. Tech. & Internet Vol. 15, Issue 1, 2024:* 76–105.

Novelli, C., Casolari, F., Hacker, P., Spedicato, G. & Floridi, L. (2024). Generative AI in EU law: Liability, privacy, intellectual property, and cybersecurity. *Computer Law & Security Review Vol. 55, 2024.* https://doi.org/10.1016/j.clsr.2024.106066

Olbrich, M., von Bongers, C. & Pampel, J. (2022). Urheberrechtsschutz für Kunstwerke künstlicher Intelligenz?. *Gewerblicher Rechtsschutz und Urheberrecht (GRUR) 12/2022*: 870–876.

Raue, B. Prof. Dr. (2024). Kreativität im Zeitalter ihrer technischen Reproduzierbarkeit: Generative KI als Totengräberin des Urheberrechts? Eine Gedankenskizze. *Zeitschrift für Urheber- und Medienrecht (ZUM) 3/2024*, 157–166.

Roberts, F. S. & Tesmann, B. (2024). Applied Combinatorics (3. ed.). CRC Press, Taylor & Francis Group.

Schneider, A. (2024). KI-unterstütztes Coding in der Spieleentwicklung: Urheberrechtliche Folgen für die Spieleindustrie. *Multimedia und Recht (MMR) Heft MMR-Beilage 9/2024:* 724–728

Urantia Foundation v. Kristen Maaherra. 9th Cir. 1997. 114 F. 3d 955.

U.S. Copyright Office (2021). Compendium of U.S. Copyright Office Practices (3. ed.). Retrieved from: https://www.copyright.gov/comp3/docs/compendium.pdf

U.S. Copyright Office (2024). Cancellation Decision re: Zarya of the Dawn (VAu001480196) at 2 (Feb. 21, 2023), Retrieved from: https://www.copyright.gov/docs/zarya-of-the-dawn.pdf

Von Welser, M. (2024). Die KI-Verordnung—ein Überblick über das weltweit erste Regelwerk für künstliche Intelligenz. *Gewerblicher Rechtsschutz und Urheberrecht in der Praxis (GRUR-Prax) 15/2024:* 485–488.

Zönnchen, B. (2024). Generative KI: Zwischen Werkzeug und Kommunikationspartner. Retrieved from: https://mediapool.hm.edu/media/mucdai/mucdai_research/Beitrag_Artifical_Communic-ation

CHAPTER 8

Smart Contracts: Code, Normativity and Legal Change in Saudi Arabia

Jonathan G. Ercanbrack

Introduction

As blockchain is integrated into the economy, smart contracts will cause significant changes to contracts and contract law. Written in code, smart contracts are machine readable programs that will self-execute when a set of pre-determined terms are met.[1] These programmable contracts can encode an agreement between two or more parties and self-execute when specified criteria are met. Beyond satisfying common contractual terms, smart contracts minimise breaches of contract, both accidental and malicious, and lower transaction costs related to fraud loss, arbitration and

[1] K. Lauslahti, J. Mattila & T. Seppala, 'Smart contracts–how will blockchain technology affect contractual practices? ETLA Reports, No. 68', ETLA Reports, online at: https://papers.ssrn.com/sol3/papers.cfm?abstract_id=3154043, accessed 9 January 2017.

J. G. Ercanbrack (✉)
Reader in Transnational Financial Law, SOAS College of Law, University of London, London, England
e-mail: je6@soas.ac.uk

K. Tsanis et al. (eds.), *Digital Finance and Transformation in the Gulf*,
https://doi.org/10.1007/978-981-92-1588-1_8

enforcement.[2] They are based on the idea that many types of contractual clauses can be embedded in hardware and software in a way that makes breach of contract expensive or even prohibitive.[3]

The use of code to give effect to contractual terms and conditions is a radical departure from law that is deliberated in parliaments and courts. Smart contracts use code as the vehicle of contracts, which avoids the abstraction and vagueness of human language contracts. To send Bitcoin or to conclude a smart contract is to trust the network of computers known as nodes but not to trust a specific human being or a central authority such as the state. There is no trusted party, whether it be developers of the code, miners or users.[4]

The contract law of contemporary states is framed around human relationships in which natural language is the medium of contracting. Contract law helps parties to coordinate their economic and personal interests by providing a framework of rules and principles that allow parties to form, enforce and resolve disputes. The application of these principles relies on the exercise of human judgement, discretion and equity in heterogeneous socio-economic interactions and transactions. If smart contracts are designed to extricate contracts from the problems that arise in these relationships, then the human interest in contracting will have to make way for the logic of machines. This embodies a shift from language to code, reorienting the nature and meaning of legal principles and rules since smart contract code is deterministic and automatic whereas language is abstract and vague. The conduct or execution of smart contract code becomes the interpretive focal point by which legal principles will need to be assessed, reoriented, modified or extended to facilitate this mode of code-based contracting.

The magnitude of these changes may be particularly significant in relational contract cultures such as Saudi Arabia whose traditional contracting rules and principles offer a markedly different theory of contract than the classical theory of contract in western legal traditions. Saudi law and legal culture are oriented toward relational contracting since Islamic law, which governs this jurisdiction, is based on a social structure of shared meanings,

[2] N. Szabo, 'Formalizing and securing relationships on public networks', *First Monday* 2(9) (1997). doi:10.5210/fm.v2i9.548.

[3] Ibid.

[4] K. Werbach, *The Blockchain and the New Architecture of Trust* (Massachusetts: The MIT Press, 2018).

language and normativity within which all social action is framed.[5] Islamic contracts are theoretically and historically embedded in identifiable relationships, e.g., investment partnerships, which are based on trust. In these types of contracts, the norms of ongoing relations can modify, supplement or even supplant contractual obligations.[6] This relational-societal approach to contract emphasises the cooperative aspects of present and future relations. The breakdown of cooperation is framed around 'what is necessary or desirable to restore present and future cooperation'.[7] Rather than providing only money remedies or in some cases, specific performance, in traditional Saudi law, negotiation, mediation and some forms of arbitration are seen as the primary means to restore cooperation and harmony.

Using a comparative law methodology, this study assesses how Saudi contract law might deal with smart contracts, focusing on bedrock principles such as consent and mandatory terms like good faith, capacity and certainty. Saudi Arabia has recently issued a Civil Transactions Law (hereinafter, 'Civil Code') that integrates Islamic principles into modern legal concepts, transforming this legal system for the purpose of facilitating and regulating technological innovation in the Kingdom.[8] The assessment of smart contracts in Saudi law illustrates the technology focused legal development that is necessary to develop the law and institutions which ensure the equitable and remedial nature of Saudi contract law in the machine economy. To do so requires legal rules and principles derived in human relationships to be expressible to inanimate code, lending these same principles a more technically oriented application and circumscribed meaning.

The study is organised in the following manner. In section "Blockchain Technology and Smart Contracts", the characteristics of smart contracts

[5] D. Campbell, *Ian Macneil and the Relational Theory of Contract. CDAMS Discussion Paper 04/1E* (Kobe: Kobe University, 2004), 10; A.H. El-Zein, 'Beyond ideology and theology: the search for the anthropology of Islam', *Annual Review of Anthropology* 6(1) (1977): 227–254, 251. doi:10.1146/annurev.an.06.100177.001303.

[6] G.K. Hadfield, 'Problematic relations: franchising and the law of incomplete contracts', *Stanford Law Review* 42(4) (1990): 927, 929. doi:10.2307/1228908.

[7] I.R. MacNeil, 'Restatement (second) of contracts and presentiation', *Virginia Law Review* 60(4) (1974): 589, 741. doi:10.2307/1072414.

[8] The Civil Transactions Law of the Kingdom of Saudi Arabia, Royal Decree M/191 dated 15/12/2023.

and the legal relationships involved in different types of smart contracts are considered. Section "The Sharia as a Source of the Saudi Civil Code" considers the Sharia (Islamic law) as a source of the Saudi Civil Code. The discussion seeks to understand its role in contemporary Saudi contract law. In section "Smart Contracts and Saudi Contract Law", two fundamental parameters of contract formation are considered in relation to two distinct smart contract scenarios. The section grapples with whether a computable programme's actions can show intention and whether the direct expression of human will is necessary to show consent in Saudi law. In section "Mandatory Requirements" the Civil Code's mandatory principles are considered, beginning with good faith. The analysis addresses the concept, whether it embodies human behaviour and the ways in which it may be relevant when smart contracts autonomously enter into contracts. Saudi law's requirements regarding capacity, certainty and the avoidance of uncertainty (*gharar*) are considered in relation to the smart contract scenarios introduced in section "Smart Contracts and Saudi Contract Law". Finally, concluding remarks are offered.

Blockchain Technology and Smart Contracts

Nick Szabo, a technologist and lawyer, who coined the term 'smart contract', defined it as:

> a computerized transaction protocol that executes the terms of a contract. The general objectives of smart contract design are to satisfy common contractual conditions (such as payment terms, liens, confidentiality, and even enforcement), minimize exceptions both malicious and accidental, and minimize the need for trusted intermediaries. Related economic goals include lowering fraud loss, arbitration and enforcement costs, and other transaction costs.[9]

Modern smart contracts are machine-readable programmes that will self-execute when a set of pre-determined terms are met.[10] The

[9] A. Sanitt & S. Green, 'Smart contracts' *online at:* https://www.nortonrosefulbright.com/en/knowledge/publications/1bcdc200/smart-contracts, *accessed 3 March 2024.*

[10] Lauslahti, *supra* note 1.

autonomous performance of smart contracts is perhaps their most distinctive and controversial feature.[11] As digital programs based on a decentralised blockchain architecture, once preconditions have been, smart contracts automatically self-execute their encoded terms. The blockchain executes and records smart contracts in the blockchain, making it difficult, if not impossible, to revoke or modify smart contracts ex post.

Blockchains, which on a basic level, are historical records of transactions organised using a Merkel tree data structure, are very difficult to edit or modify. Making a change requires a new transaction that automatically initiates a new 'fork' to prevent duplication.[12] This 'immutable' quality of blockchains is what makes it a trustworthy architecture for transferring value. Value is attributed to cryptocurrencies because there is no way to tamper with a cryptocurrency's recorded information on the blockchain.[13]

Nick Szabo identified a primitive ancestor of smart contracts, which is the vending machine. A vending machine requires coins via a simple mechanism for dispensing a product according to a displayed price. This is a unilateral offer that can be accepted by anyone who inserts coins that match the displayed price. The vending machine's lockbox and other security mechanisms protect the machine and its contents from attackers. The designers of the machine have ensured that the amount the machine takes in coins is less than the cost of breaking the machine,[14] which highlights the designers' attention to disincentivising opportunistic economic behaviour.

In contrast to the vending machine, traditional, natural language contracts are intended to be read by human beings and later adjudicated by a judge if a dispute arises. Digital or 'electronic' contracts—on the other hand—are often understood as natural language agreements, albeit ones that are given effect on electronic platforms (e.g., 'browse-wrap' website agreements or even agreements agreed via e-mail). These types of digital agreements are designed to be read and understood by humans and not by computers. Further, these are intermediated contracts that can

[11] T. Xu, 'Smart contracts: the limits of autonomous performance', in J. Allen & P. Hunn (eds.), *Smart Legal Contracts: Computable Law in Theory and Practice* (Oxford: Oxford University Press, 2022) 225–245, 227.

[12] Werbach, *supra* note 4.

[13] Ibid.

[14] Szabo, *supra* note 2.

easily be revoked and rectified. By contrast, smart contracts are not merely electronic in form but also purposely designed to be understood and read by computers, raising distinct contract law issues.[15]

The technical grammar of smart contracts maximises parties' capacity to increase the *ex ante* legal certainty of their automated assessments and in so doing architect the degree to which courts might entertain ex post corrections.[16] The prima facie assessments made possible by smart contracts should reduce uncertainty, fostering foreseeability and confidence in contract. However, because smart contracts are recorded on the blockchain, the ex post remedial flexibility provided by courts may not be available if such assessments are occasionally incorrect.

The UK Law Commission on Smart Contracts suggests that smart contracts should be seen on a spectrum in which three different types of agreements are envisioned.[17] On one end of the spectrum are natural language contracts that include a short section of code. Further along the spectrum are hybrid contracts in which an agreement consists of both a written, natural language contract and a smart contract. Known as the 'Ricardian contract', a piece of code embedded in a DLT contains a hashed reference to a natural language contract.[18] Ricardian contracts are generally used to supplement smart contracts by adding natural language terms such as governing law and jurisdiction clauses as well as dispute resolution mechanisms.[19] Courts will not have difficulties in determining whether an agreement has been reached in the first two types of agreements as the issues do not depart from well-rehearsed case law. At present, businesses may prefer these types of smart contracts because the risks and costs of code-only smart contracts are too high.[20]

Only smart contracts based entirely on code raise novel legal questions. This is the type of smart contract that parties engineer to rely entirely on the DLT to carry out their intentions and to avoid the intervention of the

[15] H. Surden, 'Computable contracts', *University of California Davis Law Review* 4 (2012–2013): 629.

[16] Ibid.

[17] Law Commission, *Smart Legal Contracts: Advice to Government* (London: Law Commission, 2021).

[18] Sanitt, *supra* note 9.

[19] Ibid.

[20] For example, the supply chain business uses natural language contracts to give effect to smart contract program.

legal system to reverse immutable transactions.[21] However, attempts to stay outside of the regulatory perimeter are often unsuccessful particularly when self-executing software seeks to implement contractual terms on an immutable basis so that the law has little recourse.[22]

The Sharia as a Source of the Saudi Civil Code

The Sharia's uncodified plurality and absence of precedence created legal uncertainty for foreign investors in Saudi Arabia. The Civil Code seeks to provide greater clarity, encourage consistency of interpretation and to limit the range of jurisprudence that can be brought to bear in legal decisions.[23] These legal parameters—clarity, certainty and consistency—are the institutions or rules of game of the global economy.[24] Civil Codes, which are largely of western inspiration, have historically displaced the Sharia 'almost in its entirety' from a wide range of legal subjects including commercial and criminal law.[25] By contrast, the Saudi Civil Code embeds traditional Saudi contract law in a formal, hierarchical structure and adds substantive foreign provisions.

However, the codification of Islamic law, which is necessary to facilitate technological innovation in the global economy, is incentivised by market forces and the demands of modern legal systems that prioritise uniformity,

[21] Sanitt, *supra* note 9.

[22] A. Ferreira, 'Regulating smart contracts: legal revolution or simply evolution?', *Telecommunications Policy* 45(2) (2021): 102,081. doi:10.1016/j.telpol.2020.102081.

[23] A&O Shearman, 'KSA civil code: forming a contract', online at: https://www.lexology.com/library/detail.aspx?g=807d0f6f-0ae1-4c9a-971a-fe3443a292b1, accessed 16 October 2023; A&O Shearman, 'Introducing the new KSA civil code', online at: https://www.aoshearman.com/en/insights/introducing-the-new-ksa-civil-code, accessed 26 August 2025.

[24] J.G. Ercanbrack & A. Ali, 'The new legalities of Islamic contractual interpretation: institutional frameworks and the displacement of intention', *International Journal of Islamic and Middle Eastern Finance and Management* 17(6) (2024): 1196–1212. doi:10.1108/imefm-03-2024-0156.

[25] J.N.D. Anderson, *Islamic Law in the Modern World* (New York: New York University Press, 1959), 8.

hierarchy, clarity, and certainty.[26] It represents a transformation of traditional Saudi law that creates a formal, hierarchical and organised structure of law in contrast to Islamic law's intrinsic diversity and casuistic application. A Muslim jurist extracts his interpretation of Islamic law from the sources of law (*uṣūl al-fiqh*) to the best of his ability (*ijtihād*). His interpretation is only probable and hence a fallible interpretation of God's law, producing a diversity of views (*fiqh*) concerning any legal issue.[27] Indeed, the legal meaning of sources is frequently unclear, and their interpretation is widely debated, so that one cannot speak of a single Islamic legal system.[28]

The contract-related elements of the Civil Code are framed in the manner of western contract law so that a breach or other problem brings to bear the contract rules and principles that ensure parties' consent is safeguarded.[29] Remedies compensate the injured party with money as if the contractual bargain had been performed. By contrast, traditional Saudi law does not award expectation interests since these losses are considered speculative and thus contravene the Islamic prohibition of *gharar* (uncertainty).[30] This rule has now been changed in the new Civil Code, paving the way for contractual practices that lend themselves to the global technological transformation that is underway.

While there are a limited number of mandatory provisions in the Civil Code, there is still no conclusive information as to how these will be interpreted. Since the Sharia remains the ultimate authority in Saudi Arabia and the Civil Code does not alter the position regarding judicial precedent, it is likely that the Sharia will continue to play an important role in the interpretation of the Civil Code. In fact, the Civil Code lists forty-one Sharia principles which serve as guiding principles for transactions and

[26] J. Ercanbrack, 'The standardization of Islamic financial law: lawmaking in modern financial markets', *The American Journal of Comparative Law* 67(4) (2019): 825–860. doi:10.1093/ajcl/avz010.

[27] B. Weiss, 'Interpretation in Islamic law: the theory of Ijtihad', *American Journal of Comparative Law* 26 (1977–1978): 199–212, 199.

[28] Grasshoff argues that there are as many Islamic legal systems as there are Muslim jurists: "Daher giebt es im Islam so viele originale Rechtssysteme als es originale Juristen giebt". R. Grasshoff, *Die Suftaga und Ḥawāla Der Araber: Ein Beitrag Zur Geschichte Des Wechsels*, PhD Thesis, Albertus-Universität, Prussia, 1899, 12.

[29] MacNeil, *supra* note 7, p. 737.

[30] K. Bälz & F. Fawzy, 'Saudi Arabia—the new civil transactions law', *Arab Law Quarterly* 1 (2024): 1–14, 7. doi:10.1163/15730255-bja10162.

are to be applied to the extent that other provisions do not address the matter. If none of the Civil Code's provisions, including the listed Sharia principles, apply to a particular matter, the Sharia is to be consulted.[31] Other sources of interpretation, such as the civil codes enacted in other GCC countries, may offer some insight into how courts will interpret the Civil Code to the extent that these countries' civil codes contain similar provisions.[32]

Smart Contracts and Saudi Contract Law

In 2013, when Vitalik Buterin introduced the Ethereum blockchain, he did not conceive of smart contracts as contracts in the legal sense of the word. Quite the opposite, he defined smart contracts as 'systems which automatically move digital assets according to arbitrary pre-specified rules'. Smart contracts 'should not be seen as something that should be 'fulfilled' or 'complied with'.[33] However, the question as to whether the language of 'contracts' is a poor fit has been widely debated.[34]

Every jurisdiction has its own contract formation rules, but there is considerable overlap in legal systems' requirements. In Arab legal systems, these conditions require consent, lawful cause, and the subject matter of the contract must be possible and defined or capable of being defined.[35] These characteristics originate or are compatible with the Sharia, which lays particular emphasis on transparency and certainty in contract as well as lawfulness of the subject matter according to Islamic principles. Like

[31] Abuhimed AlSheikh Almagbani & Clifford Chance, 'Civil transactions law of Saudi Arabia', online at: https://www.cliffordchance.com/content/dam/cliffordchance/briefings/2024/02/ashcc-civil-transactions-law.pdf, accessed 26 August 2025.

[32] A&O Shearman, *supra* note 23.

[33] V. Buterin, 'Ethereum white paper: a next generation smart contract & decentralised application platform', online at: https://blockchainlab.com/pdf/Ethereum_white_paper-a_next_generation_smart_contract_and_decentralized_application_platform-vitalik-buterin.pdf, accessed 28 August 2025.

[34] E. Mik, 'Smart contracts: terminology, technical limitations and real world complexity', online at: https://ssrn.com/abstract=3038406 or http://dx.doi.org/10.2139/ssrn.3038406, accessed 17 August 2024; M. Raskin, 'The law and legality of smart contracts', *Georgetown Law Technology Review* 1(2) (2017): 305.

[35] Arab Regional Fintech Working Group, *Guidance Note on Adopting Smart Contracts and Smart Legal Enforceability in Arab Countries. Council of Arab Central Banks and Monetary Authorities Governors, No. 185* (Abu Dhabi: Arab Monetary Fund, 2022).

smart contracts, emphasis on ex ante enforcement characterises Islamic law's approach to contract. Islamic law lays stress on the pre-contractual filtering of religiously prohibited subject matters (pork, alcohol, pornography, etc.) as well as the prohibition of certain contractual practices (the use of interest (*ribā*), excessive uncertainty (*gharar*) and speculation (*maysīr*) that invalidate a contract.[36] Muslim jurists believe that these principles foster equitable exchange and maintain social harmony. Contracts containing these elements are neither valid nor binding.

The Saudi Civil Code provides that a valid contract requires mutual consent and intention to create legal relations (Art. 31–32). Mutual consent is found in the meeting of the minds or the exchange of a matching offer and acceptance (Art. 32). An offer (*ījāb*) is a contracting party's declaration or statement to contract with one or more persons on certain terms, which is meant to elicit and receive an acceptance.[37] Acceptance (*qabūl*) must match the exact terms of the offer whereas anything else is a counteroffer and thus not capable of accepting the offer. Furthermore, an intention to be contractually bound can be expressed orally, in writing, via exchange or other understandable indicators that establish liability (Art. 33(2)).

The Civil Code's contract interpretation principles resemble the interpretational approach of other Arab Gulf states. The parties' intentions will be construed according to the plain meaning of words in the Civil Code's objective approach to contractual interpretation (Art 104). Only ambiguous contractual language should be construed and then only by considering customary practice, the circumstances of the conclusion of the contract, the nature of the transaction and in view of the interests of the party who bears the burden of the obligation.[38] When the language of a contract is clear it is binding, regardless of the intentions of the parties. However, the Civil Code's contextual approach to construction does not employ the reasonable person approach in English common law, which

[36] The Hanafis consider invalid subject matters or contractual practices as suspending a contract's validity. Once the invalidating element has been removed, the contract becomes valid and binding.

[37] I. Bantekas, et al., *Islamic Contract Law* (Oxford: Oxford University Press, 2024), 2.05.

[38] N. Ikram & G. Parlascino, 'Saudi Arabia's civil transactions law', International Bar Association, online at: https://www.ibanet.org/clint-june-2024-feature-3#:~:text=Article%2068%20of%20the%20Code,weakness')%20of%20the%20other, accessed 25 July 2024.

provides a third-party interpretation of the intentions of the parties in any particular transaction. By contrast, the invisible will of the parties matters, which Al-Sanhuri regarded as the 'reality of the contract'.[39] The modern approach to interpretation in Arab Civil Codes is closer to traditional Maliki and Hanbali perspectives which lend weight to the underlying motives or intentions of the contract even when these are not immediately apparent. However, these traditional approaches apply a subjective approach that invalidates a contract whose cause (*qaṣd*) or *niyya* (intention) is prohibited on the condition that the opposing party knows about this intention or has strong evidence of it.[40]

Two scenarios arise in relation to solely code smart contracts that produce novel legal questions. From a technical perspective, smart contracts are placed on the blockchain by a single user, representing unilateral promises to provide a determinate computation. The smart contract is technically valid as soon as the miner has integrated it into a block, which is stored at a particular address. When an event (transactions initiated or information received via so-called oracles) proscribed in the smart contract takes place, a transaction comprising this data is sent to the address and the blockchain executes and records the smart contract's codes or clauses.[41] The first scenario is where parties have deployed a smart contract on a DLT or other smart contract platform and interact with the code while not otherwise engaging in natural language communications. The question is whether the contracting parties' interactions with the code constitute consent. The second scenario describes a situation where the parties deploy smart contracts on a DLT, and those programs interact and execute transactions autonomously. In the second scenario, the question is whether the parties can be held to be legally bound due to their deployment of the programs.[42]

[39] Lexis Middle East, 'Legacy in law: an introduction to the monumental life & work of Abdel Razzaq Al Sanhouri', Lexis Nexis, online at: https://www.lexismiddleeast.com/book/AlSanhouriBooklet/Legacy_in_Law_An_Introduction_to_the_Monumental_Life__Work_of_Abdel_Razzaq_Al_Sanhouri, accessed 30 July 2019.

[40] A.A.W.I. Rushd, *Bidāyat Al-Mujtahid wa Nihāyat Al-Muqtaṣid* (Beirut: Dār Al-Maᶜrifa, 1982).

[41] BBVA Research, 'Digital economy outlook', BBVA, online at: https://www.bbvaresearch.com/wp-content/uploads/2015/10/Digital_Economy_Outlook_Oct15.pdf, accessed October 2015.

[42] Law Commission, *supra* note 17, p. 40.

Consent can be challenging to determine as it relies on the court discerning an exchange of offer and acceptance or the meeting of the minds. To determine consent courts will seek to discern parties' intentions to be contractually bound, which, when expressed in code, is not easily determined.[43] However, placing a smart contract on the blockchain may be construed as a unilateral offer, which is capable of acceptance via conduct. Smart contracts have certain, well-defined and fixed conditions embedded in their code, which self-execute when preconditions (such as the transfer of a cryptocurrency) are fulfilled. Courts are therefore likely to see them as offers[44] that are not able to be revoked due to blockchain's immutable character, which Saudi law normally allows (Art 35).

According to Islamic law, a valid offer can be based on mere conduct. Although Ibn Taymiyya, a classical Hanbali jurist whose jurisprudence is influential in Saudi Arabia, argued that conduct should be recognised in custom, presumably because the use of such conduct implies that the offeror is aware of the practice.[45] By contrast, if the smart contract is viewed as an invitation to treat or negotiate, it will not be viewed as an offer. Advertisements or 'offers to the world' are normally viewed as mere declarations to enter negotiations unless, according to Saudi law, a clear price is shown, and no other evidence indicates that an offer is not in the offing (Art 34). If a precondition of the smart contract is a transfer of cryptocurrency, Saudi law will likely construe this price as indicative of an offer that is capable of being accepted.

Recall the vending machine example which by interacting with it exhibits an intention to purchase items from the machine. The proprietor, for his part, wants to sell items via the vending machine and has purchased and stocked these items within the machine for a customer's purchase. This tacit agreement reflects a similar transaction-based interpretation of smart contracts.[46] Muslim jurists view tacit agreements known as the *bayʿ al-taʿatī* or *muʿāṭāt* as validly concluded through

[43] M.O.M. Alhejaili, 'Integrating smart contracts into the legal framework of Saudi Arabia', *International Journal of Law and Management* 67(2) (2024): 230–248. doi:10.1108/ijlma-03-2024-0086.

[44] T. Schrepel, *Smart Contracts and the Digital Single Market through the Lens of a Law & Technology Approach* (Brussels: European Commission, 2021).

[45] Bantekas, *supra* note 37.

[46] R. Koulu, 'Blockchains and online dispute resolution: smart contracts as an alternative to enforcement', *SCRIPTed* 13(1) (2016): 40–69. doi:10.2966/scrip.130116.40.

the taking and giving of the subject matter without written or verbal exchange. Traditional Hanbali law, like contemporary Saudi law, permits the formation of contract by nearly any means which convey mutual assent including behavioural implications such as gestures or silent exchanges of the countervalues.[47] The general rule in communicating offer and acceptance is based on an Islamic maxim which provides that 'contracts are formed from intentions'. If parties' intentions are manifest, the medium for conveying those intentions will be considered valid.[48] In every case, the facts determine whether the actions of the parties demonstrate characteristics that satisfy the requirements of a legally binding contract.[49]

However, the programming language used to structure smart contracts (e.g., Solidity, C + +) may raise doubts as to whether the parties understood the obligations and thus intended to be bound.[50] There can be no consent if the parties have not understood their reciprocal rights and obligations. Given the difficulty of enforcing smart contracts ex post, and the challenge of interpreting parties' intentions when no human language communication is used, disclosure may have a role to play. Reference to smart contracts' immutable nature and the availability of technical solutions to stop contractual performance such as so-called kill switches may be warranted.[51] Natural language translations of consumer contracts in easily readable and understandable language may be appropriate.[52]

In many jurisdictions, consumer contracts are subject to mandatory statutory and regulatory law that seeks to protect consumers against unfair terms and trade practices. Particularly in relation to the boilerplate contractual terms of so-called 'take-it-or-leave-it' contracts, statutory law provides an effective means of regulating unfair terms that private law enforcement is not capable of providing.[53] The Saudi civil code regulates

[47] F.E. Vogel, *Saudi Business Law in Practice* (New York: Bloomsbury Publishing, 2019), 119.

[48] Bantekas, *supra* note 37, 2.41.

[49] Lauslahti, *supra* note 1.

[50] Schrepel, *supra* note 44.

[51] Ibid.

[52] Ferreira, *supra* note 22, p. 5.

[53] S. Bright, 'Winning the battle against unfair contract terms', *Legal Studies* 20(3) (2000): 331–352, 331. doi:10.1111/j.1748-121x.2000.tb00147.x.

consumer contracts in contracts of adhesion in which consumers have little if any bargaining power (Art 96). However, the Civil Code does not provide general rules on the incorporation of terms which makes it uncertain as to whether certain terms will be held to be incorporated into the contract. Article 68 does strengthen the position of weaker parties or consumers as it deals with 'unjust contracts' and provides the court with the discretion to reduce or increase the extent of the obligations under the contract. The court may invalidate the contract if one of the contracting parties takes advantage or 'exploits an apparent weakness' of the other party.[54] However, the Civil Code does not provide an 'unfairness test' that provides guidelines or parameters the court could use to determine the substance of this provision. However, given smart contracts' design which seeks to reduce the transaction costs associated with intermediaries including courts, special attention should be given to statutory requirements to provide a high degree of clarity and certainty to protect consumers when they use smart contracts.

An example of one of the more comprehensive laws on blockchain technology is the US state of Illinois' Blockchain Technology Act (BTA). The Act provides a high degree of legal clarity on the legal status of smart contracts and their legal effects. Notably, section 10 provides that[55]:

(a) A smart contract, record or signature may not be denied legal effect or enforceability solely because a blockchain was used to create, store, or verify the smart contract, record or signature
(b) In a proceeding evidence of a smart contract, record or signature must not be excluded solely because a blockchain was used to create, store or verify the smart contract, record or signature.
(c) If a law requires a record to be in writing, submission of a blockchain which electronically contains the record satisfies the law.
(d) If a law requires a signature, submission of a blockchain which electronically contains the signature or verifies the intent of a person to provide the signature satisfies the law.

[54] Ikram, *supra* note 38.

[55] Blockchain Technology Act, *Illinois Blockchain Technology Act HB3575* (State of Illinois, United States of America: Blockchain Technology Act, 2020).

The BTA's approach to recording contracts on a blockchain does not displace the mandatory rules of traditional, natural language contracts. Instead, the Act relies on Illinois state law or the Uniform Commercial Code to regulate unfair contractual terms. However, the BTA requires a notice to be in writing in relation to a range of issues which are meant to protect weaker parties including: the cancellation of a public utility service; default, acceleration, repossession, foreclosure, or eviction, or the right to cure, under a credit agreement secured by or a rental agreement for a primary residence of a natural person; as well as notifications of product recalls and the cancellation of health insurance policies and/or benefits.[56]

In the second scenario, smart contracts are deployed on a distributed ledger and those programs interact and undertake a transaction with one another. Can the parties be said to have formed an agreement based on the smart contracts which they deployed on a distributed ledger? In principle, Saudi law is sufficiently broad and general to facilitate this type of contracting. We have observed that in Saudi law, offer and acceptance can be expressed in any way that shows consent, whether it be directly or through implication (Art 33(1)-(2)). However, the parties may not be aware that a contract has been formed, nor will they know of the specific terms of the concluded contract, which raises novel considerations such as whether consent must involve the direct coming together of two human wills, which Al-Sanhuri regarded as the backbone of the contract.[57]

International case law may offer a helpful precedent. In *Quoine Pte Ltd v B2C2*, the Singapore Court of Appeal ruled that an agreement formed through the operation of algorithms can amount to a valid contract.[58] The court based this decision on an automated electronic contracting process found in the insurance industry. Insurance brokers received quotations based on a software's automatic calculations of a set of pre-programmed criteria and agreed contracts on behalf of their customers. In *R (Software Solutions Partners Ltd) v HM Customs & Excise* (hereinafter, 'Software Solutions'), the software automatically generated an offer of insurance if its conditions were met. The insurance broker could accept the quotation on behalf of the customer, which would then

[56] Ibid, S 15 (d)(1)–(4).

[57] Lexis Middle East, *supra* note 39.

[58] *Quoine Pte Ltd v B2C2 Ltd* [2020] SGCA(I) 2.

lead to the conclusion of an insurance contract. The judge in *Software Solutions* could not find any reason why, in principle, a contract could not be formed on that basis. The well-known English case, *Thornton v Shoe Lane Parking Ltd,* provided an important precedent for his decision. In that case, a customer, driving up to the barrier of an automatic car park, inserts money into the machine and is issued a ticket. Assessing this fact pattern, Lord Denning said: 'It can be translated into offer and acceptance in this way: the offer is made when the proprietor of the machine holds it out as being ready to receive the money. The acceptance takes place when the customer puts his money into the slot'.[59] Applying this principle in *Software Solutions*, the judge held that insurers held out the software as the automatic medium for forming the contract. The broker's input of the necessary information into the software constituted a valid acceptance and no further human intervention was necessary for the formation of a binding contract.[60]

The Court of Appeal in *Quoine* was prepared to accept that the terms of the offer were sufficiently clear if they were within the ambit of the algorithm's programmed parameters and these parameters were sufficiently 'held out' by the parties. The UK Law Commission on Smart Contracts suggests that the question as to whether the parties held out smart contracts for the purposes of reaching an agreement might be determined through an examination of the operation of the smart contract's code.[61] For example, if the smart contract's programmed conditions are set up to indicate an offer and acceptance once certain criteria are met, one might conclude that the parties have held out their smart contracts for purposes of entering into these types of agreements. Ultimately, determining whether the parties have entered into an agreement on specified terms is a question of fact that will be decided based on various factors. If it cannot be determined that the parties 'held out' smart contracts for the purposes of entering into an agreement, then no agreement can be said to have been consented to.[62]

[59] *Thornton v Shoe Lane Parking Ltd* [1971] QB 163, [169].

[60] *R (Software Solutions Partners Ltd) v HM Customs & Excise* [2007] EWHC 971 (Admin), [67].

[61] Law Commission, *supra* note 17.

[62] Ibid.

However, the Civil Code emphasises that a contract depends on the meeting of the contractors' wills, who have legal capacity to express will (Art 32), which may prevent the court from finding consent in this scenario. The law expressly refers to human contractors (*mutʿāqadīn*) with legal capacity (*ahlīya*) which requires an act of human will that is capable of objectively showing consent through offer and acceptance.

While the Civil Code emphasises that consent is based on legal persons agreeing to a contract, the Electronic Transactions Regulation (ETR) which regulates electronic agents, provides that:

> The electronic record is considered to be issued by the originator if it is sent by him or by another person on his behalf or sent by an automated system programmed by the originator to automatically act on behalf of the originator [...].[63]

Section 12 of the ETR is construed as permitting an electronic agent to form a legally valid contract despite the absence of human intervention in agreeing the contract. A person using an electronic agent for making a contract is legally bound.[64] High frequency trading (HFT) or algorithmic trading is an example of an electronic agent that can form a legally valid contract. HFTs are automated systems that buy and sell on electronic exchange platforms in which IT-enabled trading infrastructure known as straight-through processing allows the entire trading process, from initiation to payments and clearing, to be carried out as a seamless electronic flow of transaction-processing steps with no need for human intervention.[65] Trading positions or the decision to trade might be held for only a few seconds or less. The machine may decide to go long and buy a quantity of shares or some other financial instrument for several seconds and then sell these to a buyer in an entirely automated process that can create a steady stream of revenue twenty-four hours per day.[66] According to the

[63] Electronic Transactions Regulation, *Electronic Transactions Regulation (Saudi Arabia), Issued by Royal Decree No. M/18 dated 8.3.1428 AH* (2007), S 12.

[64] W. Almajid, *The Legal Enforceability of Contracts made by Electronic Agents under Islamic Law: A Critical Analysis of the Effectiveness of Legal Reform in Saudi Arabia*, PhD Thesis, University of Central Lancashire, United Kingdom, 2010, 118.

[65] D. Cliff & P. Treleaven, *Technology Trends in the Financial Markets: A 2020 Vision* (London: Government Office for Science, 2010).

[66] Ibid.

ETR, these trades, which are now common in Saudi Arabia,[67] are valid and binding contracts in Saudi law. If that is the case, it may be contrary to market expectations, practice and law to prohibit a smart contract from being enforced as a legally binding contract under Saudi law.

However, the ETR assumes that automated programs work automatically rather than autonomously. Electronic agents such as smart contracts are therefore regarded as tools used by individuals to transact contracts rather than autonomously formed contracts which legal persons have no knowledge of.[68] When the contracting parties are not even aware that an offer or acceptance has been made, it seems unlikely that courts will find that consent has been given. However, as discussed, the issue for the courts may centre on whether the parameters of the smart contract have been held out by the originators of the code for the purpose of concluding a contract. When these parameters can objectively be said to have been 'held out', attributing the actions of a smart contract to the will of a legal person may be less of a stretch for the court.

Mandatory Requirements

Good Faith

Mandatory good faith requirements strengthen the Civil Code's regulation of contracts involving weaker parties in that Article 95 requires that contracts are 'executed in accordance with its terms and in a manner consistent with the requirements of good faith'. Based on an Islamic law maxim that stipulates 'there shall be neither harming nor reciprocation of harm',[69] Article 41 extends the principle to pre-contractual negotiations. A party will be acting in bad faith if the party knowingly withholds key information or if a party negotiated without the genuine intent of reaching an agreement.[70] Saudi courts view all stages of a contract

[67] C. Preece, 'Saudi exchange makes push into algo and high frequency trading', The Trade News, online at: https://www.thetradenews.com/saudi-exchange-makes-push-into-algo-and-high-frequency-trading/, accessed 26 August 2025.

[68] Almajid, *supra* note 63, p. 119.

[69] A. Khalifa, et al., 'The doctrines of good faith and abuse of right under Saudi law', Freshfields, online at: https://riskandcompliance.freshfields.com/post/102hhog/the-doctrines-of-good-faith-and-abuse-of-right-under-saudi-law, accessed 1 February 2022.

[70] Ikram, *supra* note 38.

including negotiation, formation, performance and termination as subject to this broad duty, having attached great importance to ensuring that contractual obligations are kept.[71] Although the concept of good faith is not specifically discussed in *fiqh* (Islamic jurisprudence), it is widely accepted that Islamic law recognises the principle. For example, the good faith principle is evident in the class of contracts known as trust-based sales (*buyu' al-amanah*) which require that the seller reveal the cost price, the purchase price paid by the seller and the profit or discount to the prospective buyer.[72] Furthermore, the duty to act in good faith is expressly required in many Civil Codes in the Middle East such as the UAE Civil Code which, while not specifically defined, is construed as requiring honesty, fairness and avoiding taking unfair advantage or exploiting others (UAE Civil Code, art 246).[73]

However, smart contract code may not be capable of giving effect to vague, open-textured principles such as good faith since these human behaviour centred principles are simply too ambiguous and context-dependent to be translated into code.[74] Open norms such as good faith do not produce rules with specific requirements but rather their content takes shape in the way in which the norm is applied. For example, if one considers terms such as 'honesty', 'fairness' or 'faithfulness' which reflect the parameters of good faith in civil law countries, it is immediately evident that these concepts relate to the internal state of mind of the parties that are not easily known.[75] As autonomous agents, smart contracts can react autonomously in their environment and solve tasks without any intervention of the user.[76] They are capable of making

[71] Khalifa, *supra* note 68.

[72] Although good faith is not expressly discussed in Islamic *fiqh* (jurisprudence), one could easily argue that fundamental principles of Islamic commercial law are based on good faith. E. Shoarian & M. Jafari, 'Good faith principle in contract law: a comparative study under Sharīʿah, Islamic law jurisdictions with emphasis on Iranian law', *Arab Law Quarterly* 37(4) (2023): 391–417, 398. doi:10.1163/15730255-bja10089.

[73] Federal Law No. 5 of 1985 Concerning the Issuance of the Civil Transactions Law of the United Arab Emirates.

[74] Xu, *supra* note 11, p. 234.

[75] E.M. Weitzenbock, 'Good faith and fair dealing in contracts formed and performed by electronic agents', *Artificial Intelligence and Law* 12(1–2) (2004): 83–110, 89. doi:10.1007/s10506-004-1908-0.

[76] S. Wettig & E. Zehender, 'A legal analysis of human and electronic agents', *Artificial Intelligence and Law* 12(1–2) (2004): 111–135, 112. doi:10.1007/s10506-004-0815-8.

determinations which are appropriate to their objectives and can act on those determinations.[77] However, they function as 'cryptographic boxes' containing information that can only be unlocked when certain predefined conditions are met which makes these agents deterministic rather than smart.[78] One can look at the execution of a smart contract to determine the goals and determinations of a smart contract. If the objective element of the good faith principle is taken into consideration, the observed conduct of autonomous agents can be used as a means of assessment.[79]

The 'trustless' characteristic of smart contracts that run on the blockchain is intrinsically designed to avoid the opportunistic behaviour that the good faith principle seeks to regulate in many civil law legal systems. This may place a burden on the developers of smart contracts to 'maintain conditions in which good faith is no longer necessary'.[80] Disclosure of a smart contract's terms and capacity for self-execution as well as the difficulty of rescission will be a necessary means of meeting the good faith requirement.

Legal Capacity

The Civil Code regulates legal capacity (Art 47) in much the same way that Islamic law does. Minors, mentally deficient or ill persons as well as spendthrifts (*safīh*) are deemed to be interdicted by law (*hajr*). Al-Sanhuri distinguishes between the capacity that one is born with, which relates to age and mental competence and the capacity that is based on the responsibility of a person's actions.[81] The former type of legal capacity is *ahlīya*

[77] Weitzenbck, *supra* note 73, p. 90.

[78] L.E. Jehl & B. Bartish, 'Blockchain 'smart contracts'–a new transactional framework', Bloomberg Law, online at: https://www.bloomberglaw.com/external/document/X4SGO17O000000/tech-telecom-professional-perspective-blockchain-smart-contracts, accessed May 2018.

[79] Weitzenbock, *supra* note 73, p. 104.

[80] R. Herian, 'Techno-legal supertoys: smart contracts and the fetishization of legal certainty', in J. Allen & P. Hunn (eds.), *Smart Legal Contracts: Computable Law in Theory and Practice* (Oxford: Oxford University Press, 2022) 246–268, 265.

[81] Lexis Middle East, *supra* note 39.

al-wujūb which is an individual's capacity to acquire rights and obligations and therefore can be termed the capacity for acquisition.[82] The second type of legal capacity is *ahlīya al-adāʾ*, which is the capacity to act or the 'capability of a human being to issue statements and perform acts to which the Lawgiver has assigned certain legal effects'.[83] Interdiction (*ḥajr*) of the *safīh* or other 'imprudent persons' blocks or denies the non-discerning person to dispose freely of their wealth,[84] which, according to Article 48 of the Civil Code, requires a court ruling. However, article 55 limits the liability of contractual parties affected by their counterpart's imperfect capacity. Should such a person have employed deceptive means to conceal their incapacity, they alone bear liability for any damage inflicted on the other party.

An essential element of consent is possessing the capacity to enter into contracts which reflects a person's cognisance and awareness and their 'capacity' to fully understand the rights and duties of the contractual bargain. Parties who transact smart contracts may lack the legal capacity to enter into legally binding agreements since DLT systems do not check for legal capacity and anyone can open an account even if in law they would be regarded as having insufficient legal capacity to do so. Legal capacity to enter a contract is only problematic where smart contracts are embedded in public, permissionless blockchains, which allow pseudonymous individuals to interact with smart contracts without having had their identities verified. One way of dealing with this problem is to impose legal limits on who can gain access to a private cryptographic key or is allowed to sign a transaction.[85]

Certainty

The Civil Code requires that the object of a contract must be achievable and clearly defined.[86] According to Saudi law, certainty in the object

[82] I.A.K. Nyazee, *Islamic Jurisprudence: Usul al-Fiqh* (Virginia: The Other Press, The International Institute of Islamic, 2000), 111.

[83] M.I.A. Al-Sarakhsī, *Usūl al-Sarakhsi[ed.* Abu al-Wafaʾ al-Afghāni, *Lajnat Iḥyaʾ al-Maʿārif al-Nuʿmāniyya]* (n.d.).

[84] Bantekas, *supra* note 37.

[85] Law Commission, *supra* note 17.

[86] A&O Shearman, *supra* note 23.

of contract (*maḥal al-ᶜaqd*) is clarified in terms of considering the non-existence of the subject matter. A contract will be valid if there is certainty that a non-existent subject matter will come into existence in the future. A contract is only void when a contract is tainted by *gharar* but this may occur in cases in which subject matters exist or are not yet in existence.[87] The term *gharar,* defined as 'uncertainty', is based on an interpretation of the Qur'an which prohibits gambling and speculation as well as several *ḥadīths*. The *ḥadīths*widen the range of meaning of the prohibition significantly.[88] Several requirements are considered relevant in relation to *gharar*, which according to Ibn Rushd, a Maliki scholar, causes the buyer to suffer damage because of a want of knowledge (*jahl*) related to the price or the object of purchase including: (1) both the price and the subject matter must be in existence; (2) the characteristics of these must be known; (3) their amount must be determined; (4) the parties must have control over these factors so as to ensure that the transaction can take place; (5) and, finally, the date of future performance, if any, must be defined.[89] According to the principle, such knowledge is needed to achieve consent, which cannot be found for the transfer of what does not exist or about which the parties have no knowledge unless risk itself is included as the object of sale.[90]

Article 43 provides further guidance. It deals with bilateral executory contracts in which parties agree to contract in the future. The essential terms of that contract and the period within which the contract is to be entered into must be agreed in advance alongside any conditions the law requires that contract to have, including formality conditions. The essential terms include the subject matter of the contract, the rights, obligations and responsibilities of the parties, the parties involved and the duration and any other essential elements of the contract. The article does not clarify whether the subject matter of the contract must be in existence at

[87] Bantekas, *supra* note 37, [5.25].

[88] The Quran warns believers accordingly: 'You who believe, intoxicants and gambling [*maysīr*], idolatrous practices, and [divining with] arrows are repugnant acts – Satan's doing – shun them so that you may prosper. With intoxicants and gambling, Satan seeks only to incite enmity and hatred among you, and to stop you remembering God and prayer. Will you not give them up?' (Quran: 5:90–91).

[89] I. Rushd, *The Distinguished Jurist's Primer, a Translation of Al-Bidayat Al-Mujtahid* (England: Garnet Publishing Limited, 1996) 148 and 172.

[90] Vogel, *supra* note 47.

the time of contract, but in view of Hanbali law, if it is certain that the subject matter will come into existence, the *gharar* prohibition may not apply. Similarly, the article does not clarify whether a fixed price must be determined at the outset. Presumably, however, the ETR's regulation of electronic agents' transactions (discussed above)—is applicable to smart contracts and the absence of a fixed price will not invalidate contracts formed by electronic agents.

The article overturns a longstanding principle in Islamic law that prohibits exchanges in which both countervalues are delayed since deferment to the future involves gambling.[91] Known as the *bayᶜ al-kāli bi-al-kāli* or with no performance occurring at once, this type of transaction is the forbidden sale of one debt for another.[92] However, the Civil Code's facilitation of bilateral executory transactions underscores the Saudi legislator's recognition that this class of contract, which includes futures and forward sales, is essential in modern commerce and finance.[93] However, smart contracts will test how far the courts are willing to go. Whether smart contracts' programmed conditions satisfy the article's 'essential terms' requirement, or the time requirement, will depend on how courts interpret the programmed but autonomous nature of this type of smart contract, which agree a contract only when pre-programmed conditions are satisfied.

Importantly, these conditions are frequently based on off-chain events over which the parties exercise no control, since oracles feed information into smart contracts. Oracles are third-party intermediaries that can collect, validate and transmit data from external sources.[94] They act as bridges between the blockchain and the outside world and can

[91] W. Al-Zuḥaylī, M.A. El-Gamal, & M.S. Eissa, *Financial Transactions in Islamic Jurisprudence* (Saudi Arabia: Dar Al-Fikr, 2007), 109.

[92] Ibid, p. 79.

[93] M.H. Kamali, 'Commodity futures: an Islamic legal analysis', *Thunderbird International Business Review* 49(3) (2007): 309–339, 314. doi:10.1002/tie.20146.

[94] K. Mammadzada et al., 'Blockchain oracles: a framework for blockchain-based applications', in A. Asatiani et al. (eds.), *Business Process Management: Blockchain and Robotic Process Automation Forum* (Cham: Springer International Publishing, 2020) 19–34.

transmit both inbound and outbound data.[95] Courts will need to determine whether that risk constitutes only minor *gharar* (*al-gharar al-yasīr*), which does not necessarily render transactions void.[96]

In any case, it will be important to consider the nature of code. A code expressed in vague or inconsistent instructions or one which omits essential instructions would not be performed by a computer.[97] Code that is certain and contains correct syntax and all essential instructions including the price (or the parameters in which the price and other essential elements are to be determined) and the subject matter will be performed by the computer. The certainty of code, therefore, may persuade the court that smart contracts are achievable and are clearly defined contracts.

Concluding Remarks

The medium of code as the vehicle for smart contracts is designed to extract contracts from the opportunistic and uncertain behaviours involved in natural language contracting. The law will need to reframe its traditional, language-based focus to provide the same remedial flexibility when dealing with code-based contracts. In Saudi Arabia, this reorientation appears to be relatively unproblematic. The law can deal with issues involving consent or even mandatory requirements such as good faith, capacity and certainty but some adaptations and statutory modifications may be warranted, particularly in relation to unfair terms and other consumer protections. Moreover, new modes of interpreting these requirements will be necessary. This change may necessitate a marked reorientation of contractual interpretation principles and a demand for judicial expertise in relation to adjudicating code-based contracts.

Code as a contractual language shifts the interpretive locus from the intentions expressed in human language relationships to the conduct of code. However, code does what it has been programmed to do. Understanding code and the intentions of coders as opposed to those of the contracting parties represents a fundamental shift in this type of

[95] A. Beniiche, 'A study of blockchain oracles', arXiv preprint arXiv:2004.07140 (2004).

[96] A. Al-Saati, 'The permissible gharar (risk) in classical Islamic jurisprudence', *Journal of King Abdulaziz University-Islamic Economics* 16(2) (2003): 3–19. doi:10.4197/islec.16-2.1.

[97] Law Commission, *supra* note 17.

contracting and, one, which represents a revolution in terms of how contract is understood and framed around human relationships.

The Saudi Civil Code lays an important foundation for facilitating and regulating smart contracts. The Sharia's prominent role in the Civil Code has been adapted in form and substance, but these legal changes do not reflect an full-scale abandonment of Saudi Arabia's rich jurisprudential tradition. Rather, the Civil Code provides a new structure and principles that are capable of giving effect to technological innovation while seeking to preserve traditional norms. Although the locus of interpretation shifts towards code, the traditional concepts of contract, supplemented by technology-specific regulation such as the ETR, can regulate the innovation of the machine economy in a way that preserves the normative structure of Islamic law whilst providing parties with remedial flexibility. However, the use of code as a vehicle of contracting will likely alter the norms of contractual practices over time because contracting via algorithms extracts contracts from the social relations of human-language contracting.

CHAPTER 9

Consumer Protection Regulations for Crowdfunding in the GCC: An Overview and Comparison

Habib Ahmed

Enhancing financial inclusion is a key tool to promote inclusive development. However, micro, small and medium enterprises (MSMEs) face a huge financing gap, which is estimated to be USD 5.3 trillion in emerging and developing economies (World Bank and IFC, 2017, p. 27). The corresponding equity financing gap is valued at US$3.92 trillion (World Bank, 2020b, p. 73). Fintechs have the potential to close this gap by providing financing to unserved and underserved clients. In particular, crowdfunding platforms (CFPs) provide alternative sources of financing for small and medium enterprises (SMEs) that cannot access financing from traditional sources such as banks. CFPs also provide opportunities to investors who are not able to invest in capital markets.

H. Ahmed (✉)
Durham University Business School, Durham University, Durham, UK
e-mail: habib.ahmed@durham.ac.uk

Department of Islamic Banking, University of Jordan, Amman, Jordan

K. Tsanis et al. (eds.), *Digital Finance and Transformation in the Gulf*,
https://doi.org/10.1007/978-981-92-1588-1_9

In their role as intermediaries, CFPs facilitate the exchange of information and funds between prospective firms/entrepreneurs and investors. While CFPs can contribute to financial inclusion, their development would require a sound ecosystem and an enabling legal and regulatory regime. The ecosystem includes technological infrastructures, availability of internet services, efficient payment infrastructure and access to social media platforms (Jenik et al., 2017; World Bank, 2013). Furthermore, the development of any financial system, including crowdfunding, depends on a sound and enabling regulatory framework. While the objectives of regulators include financial inclusion, competition and efficiency, they are also concerned about financial stability, consumer protection and financial integrity.

CFPs act as an intermediary and perform the brokerage function in financial intermediation by matching the lenders/investors and borrowers/issuers (Havrylchyk, 2021; Pekmezovic and Walker, 2016). Since CFPs are not involved with maturity and liquidity transformation, their business models do not pose micro-prudential risks that can lead to financial instability. However, as the success of crowdfunding depends on raising funds from retail and institutional financiers/investors, its success depends on building trust in the system. The law and finance literature maintains that investors' protection is essential for promoting investments in capital markets (La Porta et al., 1997, 1998). Thus, a key role of an enabling legal and regulatory framework is to protect the interests of lenders/investors so that they can provide the necessary funds, and crowdfunding can thrive.

The paper aims to identify the key elements of a regulatory framework for CFPs that can protect the lenders/investors and apply this to assess the CFP regulations in four GCC countries (Bahrain, Oman, Saudi Arabia and UAE). After identifying the features of different types of CFPs (debt-based, investment-based, donation-based and rewards-based), the regulatory concerns arising from them are outlined. The paper focuses on how regulations are framed for crowdfunding platforms to accomplish the regulatory objective of protecting lenders/investors. While there is a growing literature examining various aspects of fintechs in general, including crowdfunding in the GCC region, research examining the regulatory frameworks and approaches is scant. For example, in a structured literature review of 89 studies on crowdfunding in GCC from 1981 to 2021, none of the studies covers regulatory issues (Thottoli, 2022).

Since the paper will examine the regulatory regimes for CFPs, it uses a qualitative method of content analysis of relevant laws and regulations of different countries, along with the relevant literature. The paper also uses leximetrics to assess the status of regulatory regimes of select GCC countries (Bahrain, Oman, Saudi Arabia, and UAE). Leximetrics enables comparative analysis and the identification of the strengths and gaps of crowdfunding regulations in these jurisdictions. The assessment enables suggesting policy recommendations to strengthen the regulatory frameworks, which can help promote the crowdfunding industry to enhance financial inclusion.

Crowdfunding: Features and Role

Crowdfunding is defined as 'the practice of obtaining needed funding (as for a new business) by soliciting contributions from a large number of people, especially from the online community'[1] or 'an umbrella term describing the use of small amounts of money, obtained from a large number of individuals or organisations, to fund a project, a business or personal loan, and other needs through an online web-based platform' (Kirby and Worner, 2014, p. 4). Crowdfunding can be categorised as donation-based crowdfunding, reward-based crowdfunding, equity-based crowdfunding (ECF) and debt-based crowdfunding (DCF) (Cicchiello, 2020; Jenik et al., 2017; Kirby and Worner, 2014; Meadows, 2018; World Bank, 2013). In donation-based crowdfunding, donations are made by philanthropic funders without any expectation of returns. Reward-based models provide funders with a token gift or enable them to pre-purchase a product or service. ECF investments are considered long-term investments in the form of equity and investors face business and liquidity risks.[2] In DCF, funding is in the form of time-bound loans from multiple lenders who face credit risk. DCF can be consumer-to-business (C2B) or consumer-to-consumer (C2C). The focus of this paper is the former two market-based financing mechanisms (ECF and DCF) that operate to provide financial returns to creditors and investors.

[1] https://www.merriam-webster.com/dictionary/crowdfunding.

[2] Liquidity of crowdfunding investments will depend on the opportunities of selling equities or debt in secondary markets or through bulletin boards.

The functions of a financial intermediary can be understood in terms of their role in resolving the frictions of intermediation. The key frictions arising in financial intermediation relate to information, communication and coordination problems, implementing incomplete contracts and market-related problems (Aaron et al., 2017; Boot et al., 2021; Havrylchyk, 2021). Resolving these frictions requires developing business models and operational structures that can minimise the risks and transaction costs. The information problems include adverse selection and moral hazard problems which, if acute, will prevent investors from participating in crowdfunding. The information problems may be acute for firms using the CFPs, as they are usually small and cannot get financing from traditional sources such as banks due to opaque information and higher risks. A key role of the crowdfunding platforms (CFP) is to provide accurate and relevant information on the projects. Thus, CFPs perform the function of delegated monitor and have to do due diligence and come up with appropriate credit scores for the projects.

Communication frictions arise in difficulties in establishing relationships and delivering services to customers through different distributional channels (Boot et al., 2021). A related problem of coordination arises in matching the parties (buyers and sellers) and can exist at the investment stage and also when the investors want to sell their investments. For example, entrepreneurs seeking funds are unable to communicate with the investors, and exchanges provide opportunities for matchmaking between investors and seekers of funds. Furthermore, to increase the liquidity of investments, some CFPs provide secondary markets or have bulletin boards to facilitate the trading of debt and equity investments (Havrylchyk, 2021). The market-related frictions relate to barriers to entry that can arise due to various factors. Other than competing with existing financial institutions providing similar services that have an information advantage and enjoy economies of scale, onerous regulations can also hinder the growth of CFPs (Havrylchyk, 2021).

Regulatory Objectives and Crowdfunding

Regulations must fulfil the broader public policy objectives of enhancing overall public welfare and mitigating societal risks and concerns on the other hand. The specific regulatory objectives of enhancing public welfare are innovation and market development, financial inclusion, competition and efficiency. Financial inclusion is welfare-enhancing as it has the potential to reduce poverty and positively impact economic growth (World Bank, 2020b). Increasing competition is a regulatory objective as it increases the number of firms providing products giving consumers more product choices at lower costs (Arner et al., 2016; Feyen et al., 2023b; FSB, 2017; Didenko, 2018). The use of digital technology also increases efficiency as it decreases the fixed and marginal costs of production and enables the provision of services faster and at lower costs (World Bank, 2022). Promoting crowdfunding helps achieve these regulatory objectives as it facilitates innovation and market development that make financial services available to all segments of the population efficiently and at competitive prices.

While crowdfunding can promote the welfare-enhancing objectives of market development, financial inclusion, competition and efficiency, regulators have to consider the societal risks and concerns that can arise in the financial sector, which includes financial stability, financial integrity and consumer protection. Financial stability is maintained by mitigating the prudential risks at the micro or firm level and the macro or systems level (Amstad, 2019; Arner et al., 2016; Feyen et al., 2023; Didenko, 2018). Since CFPs are not engaged with maturity and liquidity transformation and act as intermediaries between providers and users of funds, the micro-prudential stability-related risks are relatively small.

The integrity of the financial system is maintained to protect individuals and markets against crime and illicit activities that include money laundering and terrorism financing (Amstad, 2019; Brummer and Yadav, 2019, p. 242; Chatain et al., 2022; Feyen et al., 2023; FSB, 2017). Financial integrity is maintained by imposing anti-money laundering (AML) and counter-terrorism financing (CTF) regulations. AML/CTF-related regulations will apply to CFPs as risks of money laundering and terrorism financing will be similar to other investment systems (World Bank, 2013). CFPs have to abide by the financial integrity regulations as required for other financial institutions and brokerage firms, and have to carry out consumer due diligence (CDD) and know-your-client (KYC) procedures to ensure that investors fulfil the AML/CTF regulations.

A key aim of regulators is to protect consumers by using conduct regulations to promote fair business practices and prohibit practices that are unfair, abusive or deceptive. In the case of crowdfunding, this objective becomes important as many investors come from the bottom of the pyramid (Jenik et al., 2017). Key aspects of consumer protection regulations need to address the risks that investors face. Other than the default risk and liquidity risk, investors using CFPs also face risks of fraud, cyber-risks, lack of transparency and risk disclosure, fair handling of complaints and risk of platform closure or failure (Kirby and Worner, 2014; Pekmezovic and Walker, 2016; World Bank, 2013). Regulations related to consumer protection become very important as they build trust among investors to invest and make crowdfunding thrive (World Bank, 2013). The key principles guiding the protection of financial consumers and elements of consumer protection regulations are discussed next.

Consumer Protection Regulations: Principles and Framework for Assessment

G20/OECD High-Level Principles on Financial Consumer Protection (HLPFCP) identifies principles for protecting financial consumers (G20/OECD, 2022). The 12 principles cover the following broad categories of topics: laws, regulations and supervision, financial access and literacy, information and data, fair practices and protecting consumers' interests and appropriate products. Some issues related to consumer protection are also covered under Banking Core Principle 25 (Operational risk) which calls for having necessary controls to prevent internal and external fraud, issues related to execution, delivery, and process management particularly when using agents, inappropriate products and business practices, disruption and system failures and protection of consumers' personal and financial information (BCBS, 2016, pp. 27–28).

The HLPFCP Principle 3 (Access and Inclusion) and Principle 5 (Competition) relate to the welfare-enhancing objectives of the regulations discussed above. Furthermore, Principle 9 (Responsible Business Conduct and Culture of Financial Services Providers and Intermediaries) stipulates that financial service providers should work in the best interest of the consumers and uphold consumer protection. The specific elements of consumer protection regulations that are relevant to CFPs are presented below.

Fair Practice and Protection from Fraud and Deception: Principle 6 (Equitable and Fair Treatment of Consumers) of HLPFCP stipulates that consumers must be treated 'equitably, honestly and fairly at all stages of the relationship with the financial services providers' (G20/OECD, 2022, p. 7). Furthermore, Principle 10 (Protection of Consumer Assets against Fraud, Scams and Misuse) calls for developing control and protection mechanisms to protect consumers' assets. These mechanisms should protect consumers using digital products from online scams, fraud, misuse and other digital security risks (G20/OECD, 2022, pp. 7, 9). CFPs should carry out due diligence on projects listed on the platform and take adequate steps to minimise cyberattacks and the risks of fraud.

Transparency and Information Disclosure: Customers should be provided information on the material aspects of all stages of a product, including the benefits, risks and terms and conditions (Principle 7 Disclosure and Transparency) (G20/OECD, 2022, p. 7). There are additional issues to be considered when products are sold through digital means. There is a need to ensure that advice and information provided to clients through digital means are adequate and match the customers' objectives, profile, financial literacy and experience and disclosures to consumers can be made proportionate and more targeted (OECD 2019, pp. 36–37). CFPs should be required to provide adequate, truthful and relevant information to the investors related to different aspects of projects listed on the platform.

Data Protection and Privacy: Principle 11 (Protection of Consumer Data and Privacy) stipulates that 'Consumers' financial and personal information should be protected through appropriate control and protection mechanisms' which 'should acknowledge the rights of consumers regarding consenting to data-sharing, accessing their data, being informed about breaches impacting their data, and seeking redress such as the prompt correction and/or deletion of inaccurate, or unlawfully collected or processed data' (G20/OECD, 2022, p. 9).

Suitability of Products and Appropriateness of Investors: Principle 8 (Quality Financial Products) calls for products that 'are designed to meet the interests and objectives of the target consumers and to contribute to their financial well-being' (G20/OECD, 2022, p. 7). In doing so, the digital skills of different customers need to be considered (G20/OECD, 2022, p. 6). To protect retail consumers from investment risks, the regulators can identify limits on the amounts that can be invested by retail investors and tie the investment amounts to their income or net wealth. In some cases, only high-net-worth individuals or accredited investors are allowed to invest (World Bank, 2013).

Setting up Disputes/Complaints Handling Mechanism: Principle 12 (Complaints Handling and Redress) of HLPFCP requires having 'accessible, affordable, independent, fair, accountable, timely and efficient' complaints handling and redress mechanisms (G20/OECD, 2022, p. 9).

CFPs should design effective mechanisms to deal with complaints and to protect the rights of investors by leveraging technology.

Consumer Protection Regulations for CFPs: A Framework for Assessment

Given the regulatory objectives and the principles of consumer protection, elements of a sound regulatory framework to assess the status of consumer protection regulations for crowdfunding can be identified under two broad categories, as shown below.

A. Overall Regulatory Regimes for Crowdfunding

  A.1. Regulatory Authorities and Specific Laws and Regulations.
  A.2. *Regulatory perimeters and activities:* Types of activities that CFPs are permitted to offer.

B. Specific Regulatory Issues Related to Consumer/Investor Protection

  B.1. *Fair practice and protection from fraud and deception:* Regulations should ensure that the platforms are fair and provide protection against fraud and deception.
  B.2. *Disclosure, transparency, clear and truthful communications:* Since investors make decisions to invest in different projects based on the information provided on the platform, it is important to ensure that the platform is transparent and provides clear and truthful information about itself and the projects hosted.
  B.3. *Suitability and appropriateness of investors:* Assess the suitability of lenders/investors and classify them according to their economic status, knowledge, etc. and impose limits accordingly.
  B.4. *Data protection:* Clients engaging with CFPs provide sensitive personal and financial data to the platforms. Regulations should ensure that the data collected on individuals and companies is secure and not misused.

B.5. *Setting up disputes/complaints handling mechanisms:* Require having a mechanism where customers can raise complaints about products or errors in execution, and a process for their resolution.

Assessment of the financial consumer protection regime in any jurisdiction would require evaluating the legal and regulatory framework. One way to evaluate the legal and regulatory framework is to use leximetrics, which is a 'systematic quantitative methodology' (Cooter and Ginsburg, 2003: 2) and includes a 'quantitative measurement of law' (Buchanan et al., 2014: 5; Lele and Siems, 2007: 18). Leximetrics involves deriving indices by first selecting relevant variables that serve as the benchmark and then coding the laws and regulations and evaluating them in light of the former. A simple way to quantify the laws would be to use a binary coding method in terms of the presence or absence of the variables in the relevant laws and assign a score of '1' for the former and '0' for the latter. The index is estimated by adding the scores, and it provides an assessment of the overall status of legal institutions. While most of the empirical 'law and finance' literature uses binary classifications, legal scholars such as Armour et al. (2009), Lele and Siems (2007) and Siems (2008) also suggest using non-binary coding.

To come up with an objective way to assess the regulatory framework for consumer protection of crowdfunding lenders/investors, this paper classifies the status of regulatory rules for elements identified under consumer protection (Category B) above into three types: 'Not covered' (score of 0), 'Briefly covered' (score of 1), and 'Widely covered' (score of 2). While 'Briefly covered' implies indicating the issue in general terms without providing details, 'Widely covered' means that specific, detailed rules are provided. For example, in the case of *Fair Practice and Protection from Fraud and Deception,* Saudi Arabia is scored 'Briefly covered' as the regulations indicate that the DCF platform should comply with the relevant requirements and instructions of SAMA on financial crimes and fraud (Article 18, No. 2, SAMA, 2021) without specifying the specific types of financial crimes or fraud that can occur in crowdfunding. Oman is scored 'Broadly covered' as it specifies different steps that need to be taken by the CF platform such as the operator must ensure that the fees paid by the users are fair, reasonable and transparent and must not engage in any business practices that appear to be deceitful, improper or oppressive (Article 19, No. 14, 15, CMAO, 2021). A related aspect to the classifications is that 'Briefly covered' usually has a few (one to three) sentences on the subject matter, while 'Broadly covered' has many sentences covering the issue.

Regulatory Status for Crowdfunding: Country Case Studies

Given the regulatory objectives, countries have adopted different regulatory approaches for CF regulations, which include prohibited, unregulated and regulated. When regulated, the regulations can take different forms: regulated under existing regulations, regulated under existing regulations with adjustments and regulated under a new regulatory framework (World Bank and CCAF 2019). Furthermore, regulatory regimes for CFPs usually distinguish between ECF and DCF. For example, while some jurisdictions allow both equity and debt-based platforms (Austria, Belgium, Finland, Mexico, Portugal), in some other countries, either DCF or ECF platforms are permitted, such as Italy, which has regulations on the latter only. In countries that do not have CF regulations, CFPs adapt to the relevant existing regulations of securities trading, payment institutions or banks. For example, in Sweden and Denmark DCF platforms are considered payment institutions, in Norway they are registered as loan intermediaries and in the Netherlands consumer to business platforms get a licence from the Dutch Financial Markets Authority to carry out brokerage activities (Havrylchyk 2021: 19). In this paper, we examine the crowdfunding regulations focussing on consumer protection for four GCC countries (Bahrain, Oman, Saudi Arabia and United Arab Emirates UAE) using the framework developed in the previous section.

A. Overall Regulatory Regimes for Crowdfunding

A.1. Regulatory Authorities and Specific Laws and Regulations

Bahrain: CFP falls under specialised licences and is regulated by the 'Crowdfunding Platform Operators Module' issued by the Central Bank of Bahrain (CBB) in April 2022 under its Rulebook Volume 5, Type 7 Ancillary Service Provider (hereafter referred to as Rulebook) (CBB, 2022a). The module is divided into the following chapters: Introduction (CFP-A), Operating Requirements (CFP-1) and Obligations of the borrower/issuer (CFP-2).[3] Beyond the rules of the Crowdfunding Platform Operations Module, the CF operators must also abide by some other modules that include the Authorisation Module (CBB, 2022b), Principles of Business Module, Auditors and Accounting Standards Module, Financial Crime Module, Enforcement Module, CBB Reporting Requirements Module and the High-level Controls Module (CFP-A.1.1) (CBB, 2020).

Oman: Crowdfunding operations were declared to be a regulated activity by the Capital Markets Authority of Oman (CMAO) in its Decision No. 151/2021 and identified CFPs as companies operating in the field of securities (Petrou and Al Hinai 2022). Subsequently, CMA issued Decision No. E/153/2021 'Rules for Crowdfunding Platforms' (hereafter referred to as Rules) in November 2021 detailing the regulatory rules guiding CFPs (CMAO 2021). Furthermore, the requirements of Part Four of the Executive Regulation of Capital Market Law also apply to crowdfunding activity (Article 2, CMAO, 2021).

Saudi Arabia: Saudi Central Bank (SAMA) issued 'Rules for Engaging in Debt-Based Crowdfunding' in December 2020 and later published 'The Updated Rules for Engaging in Debt-Based Crowdfunding' in December 2021 (SAMA, 2021). Furthermore, SAMA also published 'Licensing Requirements for Crowd Lending Activity' outlining the licensing requirements and procedures for crowdfunding platforms. The discussions below are based on the latter regulatory document (hereafter referred to as Rules).

UAE: UAE has separate laws/regulations related to debt-based and equity-based CFPs. The Central Bank of the UAE (CBUAE) published the 'Loan-based Crowdfunding Activities Regulation' (CBUAE, 2020) in 2020 and the government of the UAE issued the 'Cabinet Resolution No. (36) of 2022 Concerning Regulating Activity of the Crowdfunding Platform Operator' (UAE Government, 2022) in 2022. The latter law applies to equity-based crowdfunding and is regulated by the Securities and Commodities Authority (SCA).[4] The SCA should take all required

[3] The Articles refer to CBB (2022a), Crowdfunding Platform Operators Module under Rulebook Volume 5, Type 7 Ancillary Service Provider.

[4] The law defines crowdfunding as a means to 'obtaining funds from investors for the purpose of financing its project through the platform in exchange for shares in the capital of a company that will be established or a company established to execute this project' (Article 1).

procedures to supervise, control and inspect the ECF platform according to the regulations and resolutions (Article 9.1, UAE Government, 2022).

A.2. Regulatory Perimeters and Activities

Bahrain: Crowdfunding activities fall under 'regulated specialised activities' and require a specialised licence (UG-A.1.4 in CBB, 2022a). The regulations apply to both financing-based and equity-based CFPs and do not apply to rewards-based and donation-based platforms (CFP-A.1.1, CBB, 2022a). While financing-based models are debt-based, equity-based models can issue different types of equity shares. CFPs can operate either financing/equity-based models or both models on the same platform (CFP-A.1.3, CBB, 2022a). CFPs are allowed to carry out person-to-business (P2B) and business-to-business activities only (CFP-A.1.2, CBB, 2022a). Furthermore, income-generating residential and commercial real estate can also be hosted on the platforms. Commercial entities incorporated in Bahrain or overseas can be hosted by CFPs (CFP-1.1.12, CBB, 2022a).[5]

Oman: Article (3) of the CMAO (2021) Rules recognises donation, reward, equity and peer-to-peer crowding activities. Peer-to-peer crowding includes invoice financing and debt-based investment notes that can be converted to equity (Article 4, No. 4, CMAO, 2021). CFPs can be used to raise funds by commercial companies and enterprises, not by individuals (Article 4). Furthermore, public joint stock companies, companies and enterprises with no specific business plans and non-profit organisations are not allowed to use CFPs to raise funds (Article 5, CMAO, 2021). Investors/donors and companies seeking funds can be from both within and outside Oman (Article 6, CMAO, 2021).

Saudi Arabia: The SAMA (2021) Rules apply to companies licenced to engage in debt-based crowdfunding (Article 2). Debt-based crowdfunding (DCF) can be carried out after obtaining a licence from SAMA and guided by the Finance Companies Control Law and instructions issued by SAMA (Article 4, SAMA, 2021). Approval of the licence is done in phases with an initial approval (Article 10, SAMA, 2021) and final approval of the licence after all SAMA makes onsite visits, meets the company's executives and reviews its regulations, procedures and records

[5] Overseas companies that are UN sanctioned, non-cooperative or from high-risk jurisdictions are not allowed to be hosted by CFPs (CFP-1.1.12).

(Article 12, SAMA, 2021). A licenced DCF operator is not allowed to engage in any other activity unless approval for it is taken from SAMA (Article 12, SAMA, 2021). The licence term is valid for five years and can be renewed after that (Article 13, SAMA, 2021). The fee for licence issuance is SAR 5000 and SAR 2000 for licence renewal (Article 16, SAMA, 2021). The financing from CFP must be for commercial purposes only and not for consumer purposes (Article 28, No. 2, SAMA, 2021).

UAE Loan-based CF: As indicated above, loan-based CF (LCF) is regulated by CBUAE. CBUAE (2020) identifies the purpose of regulating loan-based crowdfunding platforms as safeguarding the financial system from the risks posed by LCF and protecting the interests of consumers (CBUAE, 2020). A borrower eligible to use LCF to raise funds must be a registered UAE company (Article 1.1, CBUAE, 2020). A company intending to carry out LCF activities must apply to CBUAE for a Loan-based crowdfunding licence and indicate if they are applying for Category 1 or Category 2 (Article 2.3, 3.3, CBUAE, 2020). Category 1 (large) LCF includes cumulative loans over a calendar year equal to or more than AED 5 million, and in Category 2 (small), the cumulative loans over the year are less than AED 5 million (Article 2.1, CBUAE, 2020). A platform with a Category 2 licence can upgrade to Category 1 by providing evidence of meeting all regulatory requirements of the latter (Article 2.4, CBUAE, 2020). A CF company licensed as Category 1 cannot be deemed as Category 2 without written approval from CBUAE (Article 2.5, CBUAE, 2020).

UAE Equity-based CF: ECF platforms must have a licence from SCA and pay the prescribed fees (Article 4A & C, UAE Government, 2022). Some entities, such as joint stock companies, investment funds, entities operating within the securities, insurance and banking services, companies intending to grant loans or invest in other companies and companies with paid-up capital of 6 million UAE dirhams, are not allowed to raise funds on the ECF platforms (Article 3, UAE Government, 2022).

Table 9.1 provides an overview of the regulatory regimes for CFPs in the sample countries.

B. Specific Regulatory Issues Related to Consumer/Investor Protection

B.1. Fair Practice and Protection from Fraud and Deception

Table 9.1 Regulatory authorities, relevant laws and regulations and regulatory perimeters for CFPs

Countries	Regulatory authorities	Relevant laws and regulations	Regulatory perimeters and activities
Bahrain	Central Bank of Bahrain (CBB)	'Crowdfunding Platform Operators Module' under its Rulebook Volume 5, Type 7 Ancillary Service Provider (CBB, 2022a)	Financing (debt)-based and equity-based
Oman	Capital Markets Authority of Oman (CMA)	CMA Decision No. E/153/2021 'Rules for Crowdfunding Platforms' (CMAO, 2021)	Donation, reward, equity and peer-to-peer (invoice financing and debt-based investments notes) crowdfunding
Saudi Arabia	Saudi Central Bank (SAMA)	'The Updated Rules for Engaging in Debt-Based Crowdfunding', (SAMA, 2021)	Debt-based
UAE	Central Bank of the UAE (CBUAE) Securities and Commodities Authority (SCA)	'Loan-based Crowdfunding Activities Regulation' (CBUAE, 2020) 'Cabinet Resolution No. (36) of 2022 'Concerning Regulating Activity of the Crowdfunding Platform Operator' (UAE Government, 2022)	Debt-based and equity-based

Bahrain: A CFP is required to withdraw an offer from a borrower/issuer if the platform is aware of any information on the offer that is misleading, deceptive or fraudulent (CFP-1.1.3, CBB, 2022a). Furthermore, the clients' funds are segregated from those of CFP and fraud risks must be adequately controlled and mitigated (CFP-1.4.2, CBB, 2022a).

Oman: Article 18 of the CMAO (2021) Rules requires the policies, processes and operating systems of CFPs to have sufficient provisions for the proper functioning of the platform and protection of investors and public interest. The CFP must ensure that its directors, CEO and persons responsible for operations and financial management are fit and proper in terms of their qualifications, and free of crime, deceitful practices or disciplinary action (Article 15, CMAO, 2021). The CFP licence must be able to operate an orderly, fair and transparent platform (Article 15) and observe the principles of honesty, integrity, fairness and equality when carrying out business (Article 22, No.1). The policies, processes and operating systems of the platform should promote fairness and transparency and promote fair treatment for any person who is applying to be hosted or is hosted (Article 18, Nos. 3, 5, CMAO, 2021). The operator must ensure that the fees paid by the users are fair, reasonable and transparent and must not engage in any business practices that appear to be deceitful, improper or oppressive (Article 19, No. 14, 15, CMAO, 2021).

Saudi Arabia: The DCF platform should comply with the relevant requirements and instructions of SAMA on financial crimes and fraud (Article 18, No. 2, SAMA, 2021) and adhere to the Code of Conduct and Work Ethics in Financial Institutions issued by SAMA (Article 23, SAMA, 2021).

UAE Loan-based CF*:* Among others, the risk governance framework of the LCF company should address conduct risk, fraud by employees and mis-selling risk (Article 6.4b, 4c, 4 g, CBUAE, 2020).

UAE Equity-based CF*:* The platform must verify that there is no fraud, deceit or harm to investors by the financing applicant (Article 6.20, UAE Government, 2022). Disclose on the platform the procedures in case there is a violation or non-commitment by the financing applicant (Article 5.7F, UAE Government, 2022). The ECF operator must develop procedures to ensure that the financing applicant fulfils its obligations towards investors, including ownership of shares (Article 6.10, UAE Government, 2022). Any errors, misleading information, data or investment risks related to financing the applicant or its projects must be immediately disclosed in the platform (Article 6.18, UAE Government, 2022). The application for financing is rejected and deleted from the platform if the applicant violates the interests of the investors or the laws and regulations (Article 6.21, UAE Government, 2022). The investor has the right to withdraw their investment decision and recover the financing amount at any time during the offering period within 5 working days of collecting the requested financing amount or if the financing applicant/operator discloses any material data, information, mistakes or changes related to the financing application, applicant or project (Article 8, UAE Government, 2022).

Table 9.2 summarises the status of 'Fair Practice and Protection from Fraud and Deception' in different sample jurisdictions.

Table 9.2 Status of fair practice and protection from fraud and deception

Countries	*Fair practice and protection from fraud and deception*	*Leximetric score*
Bahrain	Briefly covered	1
Oman	Widely covered	2
Saudi Arabia	Briefly covered	1
UAE	DCF: Briefly covered	1
	ECF: Widely covered	2

B.2. Disclosure, Transparency, Clear and Truthful Communications

Bahrain: The CBB (2022a) rulebook requires disclosing the following information on their websites: general risk warning, details of fees charged to lenders/investors and borrowers/issuers, default rates of financing-based CF and failure rates of equity-based CF, declaration of conflict of interests and rights of investors (such as withdrawal of commitments, lodging complaints or voting rights) (CFD-1.1.1, CBB, 2022a). Furthermore, the website must also have information on the eligibility criteria of the borrowers/lenders and issuers/investors, details of the safeguards in place to protect clients' money, the status of the offer if the target level of funding is not achieved, steps taken if the material position of the borrower/issuer changes, how the overdue payment or default is dealt with the governing law applicable for the transaction (CFP-1.1.7, CBB, 2022a).

When onboarding the borrowers/issuers the CFP must provide the following information: the process for offering financing or equity, the risks associated with financing or equity, the limits of funds that can be raised, the right of retail clients to withdraw offers within five working days, existence/nonexistence of secondary markets, due diligence by the platform on the offer and the relation between the borrower/issuer and platform after the closing of the offer (CFP-1.1.6, CFP-1.1.15, CBB, 2022a). Furthermore, a borrower/issuer successful in raising funds must communicate with the crowdfunding participants and provide regular updates on the business and financial position in a transparent and effective manner (CFP-2.1.7, CBB, 2022a).

Oman: CFP should have written procedures showing the rights and obligations of all parties, including the amount outstanding from the investors for participation, the operator's fees for the services rendered and a declaration by the investor being aware of the investment risk (Article 19, No. 7, CMAO, 2021). The operator has to ensure that the funding disclosure document is verified for accuracy, fairness, is not misleading and is written in simple and clear language (Article 19, No. 9, CMAO, 2021). Any errors or misleading statements and investment risk should be disclosed immediately on the platform and exercise due diligence to ensure that there is no fraudulent means or deception or damage to the investor by the funding applicant (Article 19, No. 10, 11, CMAO, 2021). If the applicant breaches the interest of the investors, the operator must stop displaying the application for funds from the platform (Article 19, No. 12). The operator should carry out awareness and education programmes continuously (Article 19, No. 16, CMAO, 2021).

The platform should prominently display relevant information such as all risk factors, rights and obligations of investors, criteria to access the platform, fees charged and other expenses imposed on investors and education materials (Article 19, No. 18, CMAO, 2021). For peer-to-peer financing, the information on the criteria of an investment to be considered a default and the processes and policies to manage the default must also be displayed (Article 36, CMAO, 2021).

Saudi Arabia: The DCF platform should clarify the nature of the business offered on the platform, the basic information on how the service works and the relationship of parties involved (Article 29, No. 1, 3, SAMA, 2021). The information provided on the platform must include how the DCF platform works, the service fees charged, eligibility criteria of the borrower and the participants, the finance amount requested and the mechanism of dealing with participants' funds in cases when the finance amount requested is not covered, the rights of the parties when there is a material change in the conditions of the borrower and the steps taken by the platform in such cases and also in cases of default (Article 29, No. 3, SAMA, 2021). Furthermore, detailed information on the institutional beneficiary or borrower must be provided which includes the project for which financing is sought, the finance amount requested and how the funds will be used, the results of the due diligence process, details on the term cost and other rights, guarantees and any restrictions, charges, fees and payment terms (Article 29, No. 4, SAMA, 2021). The platform should also provide information on the significant risks that the borrower may face, including the credit risk that can result in participants losing some or all of their money (Article 29, No. 5, SAMA, 2021).

UAE Loan-based CF: LCF companies should disclose updated terms and conditions of their business and provide necessary warnings of material risks to their clients (Article 8.23, 8.24, CBUAE, 2020). The activities of the platform should be structured in a clear, transparent manner using plain language, and sufficient details of the loan, terms of repayment and rights and obligations of the lender and borrowers should be provided within the enforceable contract (Article 8.5, 8.6, CBUAE, 2020).

The platform must provide relevant information on the borrower to lenders which must include historical and projected information on the business model and operation, financial condition, critical success factors and dependencies, borrowing and repayment terms, risks and expected default rates, control and precautionary measures, the rights of cancellation of contracts and applicable jurisdiction for disputes (Article 8.27, CBUAE, 2020). The financial situation of the borrower must be reviewed annually and any material changes communicated to the lenders (Article 8.9, CBUAE, 2020).

An LCF platform must ensure that a transparent and sufficient risk-scoring and loan-pricing system is in place, and the basis and methodology of this system must be made publicly available (Article 8.7, CBUAE, 2020). The platform must also require information on cash flow forecasts, carry out due diligence and risk assessment of the borrower within the risk-scoring process and communicate these to lenders (Article 8.8, CBUAE 2020). Information on the default rates of projects/borrowers listed on the platform must be publicly available (Article 8.7.h, CBUAE, 2020).

UAE Equity-based CF: ECF platforms must disclose information on the platform on its nature, work mechanism, services, risks, owners, legal form, capital and board (Article 5.7A, 7G, UAE Government 2022). Similarly, all disclosures of the financing applicant must be published on the platform, and the information must be verified for its accuracy and validity (Article 6.17, UAE Government, 2022). Publish all relevant information of the financing applicant 21 days before allowing investors to invest in the project (Article 6.15, UAE Government, 2022). Include all relevant information related to investments in the agreement, including the risks that investors are exposed to, such as the inability to sell or assign shares to other investors (Article 6.1, UAE Government, 2022). Provide information on the mechanisms of receiving the dividends and the rights of investors to revoke their investment decisions, and the mechanisms and difficulties to exit from projects (Article 6.2, 6.3, UAE Government,

Table 9.3 Presents the leximetric results of *disclosure, transparency, clear and truthful communications* for different countries in the sample

Countries	*Disclosure, transparency, clear and truthful communications*	*Leximetric score*
Bahrain	Widely covered	2
Oman	Widely covered	2
Saudi Arabia	Widely covered	2
UAE	DCF: Widely covered	2
	ECF: Widely covered	2

2022). All material data, information, mistakes or changes to the projects, the benefits, potential risks and the mechanism of investor exit must be disclosed by the financing applicant (Article 7.2B, 2C, UAE Government, 2022) (Table 9.3).

B.3. Suitability and Appropriateness of Investors

Bahrain: When onboarding retail clients, the CFP should assess the suitability and appropriateness of clients in terms of their knowledge, experience, financial situation and their understanding of the risks of crowdfunding (CFP-1.1.13, CBB, 2022a). Before clients can use the platform, they have to sign a self-declaration that acknowledges that they understand the risks, that they can lose their money and should invest only amounts that they can afford to lose, that they can have problems exiting from the investments and that offers are not approved by CBB (CFP-1.1.14, CBB, 2022a).

Oman: A person can donate or invest any amount in the donation and reward-based CFPs within the limits of the funding request by the applicant (Article 8, CMAO, 2021). Investors in equity-based CFP are categorised as sophisticated investors, angel investors and retail investors. While there are no restrictions on investment amounts for sophisticated investors, angel investors can invest a maximum of RO 100,000 within a 12-month period. Retail investors can invest a maximum of RO 3000 per offer/applicant and a total amount of RO 20,000 within a 12-month period (Article 9, CMAO, 2021).

Saudi Arabia: An eligible participant is defined as a natural or legal person fulfilling one or more of the following: (a). Has assets of at least

SAR 3 million; (b) currently working or has worked for at least three years in the financial sector; (c) has an internationally approved professional certificate in finance or investment; and d) has an annual income of at least SAR 600,000 in the past two years (Article 1, No. 2.7, SAMA, 2021).

UAE Loan-based CF: The process of onboarding lenders should be documented, and the LCF platform should assess the suitability of lenders and ensure that they have a clear understanding of the risks when onboarding them (Article 8.1, CBUAE, 2020). This can be done by obtaining sufficient information from the lender about their objectives and financial circumstances by using self-declared assessment questionnaire forms or equivalent means and confirming the information provided (Article 8.3, 8.7b, 8.7c, CBUAE, 2020).

Based on the information gathered, the lenders can be classified as retail or market counterparty (Article 8.4, CBUAE, 2020). The market counterparty has net assets of AED 2 million, not including their primary residence, and retail lenders are those who do not fulfil the criteria of the market counterparty (Article 1.12, CBUAE, 2020).

Equity-based CF: An investor who is not a professional investor or counterparty is limited to investing 30,000 UAE dirhams for each financing applicant and a total of 100,000 UAE dirhams on the platform (Article 6.5, UAE Government, 2022) (Table 9.4).[6]

B.4. Data Protection and Confidentiality

Table 9.4 Summarises the leximetric scores of the *suitability and appropriateness of investors* for different jurisdictions

Countries	*Suitability and appropriateness of investors*	*Leximetric score*
Bahrain	Widely covered	2
Oman	Widely covered	2
Saudi Arabia	Widely covered	2
UAE	DCF: Widely covered	2
	ECF: Briefly covered	1

[6] UAE Government (2022) defines 'Professional investor or counterparty' as 'A natural or legal person who is capable of managing its own investments by itself in accordance with the rulebook'. The law, however, does not provide the criteria.

Bahrain: Not covered.

Oman: Before getting a licence, the CFP has to declare that adequate measures are taken for information systems, data integrity and confidentiality (Article 16, CMAO, 2021). The CFP must have a written information security plan to protect the confidentiality, integrity and quality of information and technology assets by complying with information security legislation and adopting the best domestic and international practices (Article 18, No.14, CMAO, 2021).

Saudi Arabia: The DCF company must develop written policies to address the confidentiality and security of information (Article 17, No. 1, SAMA, 2021). All client documents, records and files should be updated regularly and kept in a safe and orderly manner for 10 years from the end of the relationship (Article 17, No. 5, SAMA, 2021). The platform should comply with the information security requirements and the relevant laws, regulations and instructions of SAMA (Article 18, No. 1, SAMA, 2021). All employees of the CFP must maintain the confidentiality of clients' data and transactions even after the end of service of the employee or revocation of the licence (Article 24, No. 2, 3, SAMA, 2021). The measures in place for information security and data protection should be displayed on the platform (Article 29, No. 3j, SAMA, 2021).

UAE Loan-based CF*:* An LCF company must implement necessary systems and controls to ensure the strictest standards of maintaining client information confidentiality (Article 8.17, CBUAE, 2020).

Equity-based CF*:* Not covered (Table 9.5).

B.5. Setting up Disputes/Complaints Handling Mechanism

Table 9.5 Presents the leximetric results of *data protection and confidentiality* from regulations of different countries

Countries	*Data protection and confidentiality*	*Leximetric score*
Bahrain	Not covered	0
Oman	Widely covered	2
Saudi Arabia	Widely covered	2
UAE	DCF: Briefly covered	1
	ECF: Not covered	0

Bahrain: The rulebook stipulates that the CFP should have effective and transparent procedures for fair, prompt and consistent handling of clients' complaints (CFP-1.1.11, CBB, 2022a). CFP must ensure that the terms and conditions of the contracts between parties of the crowdfunding offer are clearly stated and legally enforceable (CFP-1.6.2, CBB, 2022a).

Oman: The policies, processes and operating systems of the platform should provide an avenue of appeal against the decision of the operator (Article 18, No. 7, CMAO, 2021). The platform should prominently display information on receiving complaints and how it is handled, dispute resolution and its procedures, and contingency arrangements in the case of cessation of business (Article 19, No. 18, CMAO, 2021).

Saudi Arabia: The CFP must establish a function for handling complaints and have clear procedures to receive, document, review and respond to complaints within the time specified by SAMA (Article 24, No. 1, SAMA, 2021). Complaints and the procedures taken must be kept in special records.

UAE Loan-based CF: The LCF company should implement policies to manage disputes (Article 8.7i, CBUAE, 2020). The policies include setting up dispute handling and grievance redress mechanisms to deal with complaints of clients or other parties (Article 8.32a, CBUAE, 2020). The platform must also maintain records of the control mechanisms to address complaints and grievances for the CBUAE (Article 8.32c, CBUAE, 2020).

Equity-based CF: The SCA should be competent to receive complaints related to the activities of the CF operator and has the right to investigate any violation found through investigation (Article 9.3, UAE Government, 2022) (Table 9.6).

Table 9.6 Status of setting up disputes/complaints handling procedure

Countries	*Setting up disputes/complaints handling procedure*	*Leximetric score*
Bahrain	Widely covered	2
Oman	Widely covered	2
Saudi Arabia	Widely covered	2
UAE	DCF: Widely covered	2
	ECF: Briefly covered	1

Consumer Protection Regulations for CFPs: An Overview and Assessment

The results show some interesting features of crowdfunding regulations in the sample countries of the GCC. First, crowdfunding regulatory regimes differ in various GCC countries. CFPs are regulated by central banks in Bahrain and Saudi Arabia and by the securities commission in Oman. In the UAE, the debt-based CF is regulated by the central bank, and the equity-based CF is under the purview of the Securities and Commodities Authority. Second, except for Saudi Arabia, where only debt-based CF is allowed, all other countries allow both DCF and ECF. Furthermore, Oman also allows other forms of CF platforms, such as rewards and donations. Third, the regulatory regimes for consumer protection differ in different countries, as shown in Table 9.7. While Oman scores the best (score of 10), the ECF regulatory framework in the UAE scores the least (score of 6). However, it must be noted that the regulatory guidelines for ECF for the latter are not regulations issued by a regulatory body, but a resolution of the cabinet. The lower score of ECF in the UAE is reflective of the cabinet resolution that usually does not provide details on operational issues that regulations provide.

The results identify the strengths and weaknesses of consumer protection regimes in different countries. For example, there seems to be a gap in 'Data Protection and Confidentiality' related rules in Bahrain and ECF in the UAE. Furthermore, further detailed rules on other aspects of consumer protection, such as 'Suitability and Appropriateness of Investors' for ECF in the UAE, and 'Fair Practice and Protection from Fraud and Deception' can be provided by the CF regulations of Bahrain, Saudi Arabia and DCF in the UAE can make the CF regulations more robust.

It should be noted that differences in scores among the countries can arise due to the different approaches taken to develop regulations. While some countries provide detailed regulatory guidelines on issues arising in crowdfunding, others refer to general guidelines that they may have on these issues. For example, instead of providing details on specific fraud that can arise in crowdfunding platforms, SAMA's regulations stipulate compliance with its general instructions on financial crimes and fraud (Article 18, No. 2, SAMA, 2021). Since this approach does not require too many details, it is ranked as 'Briefly mentioned' which affects the overall scores. The implication is that dealing with the issues in regulations

Table 9.7 Summary of status of consumer protection regulatory regimes

Regulatory features	*Bahrain (DCF & ECF)*	*Oman (DCF & ECF)*	*Saudi Arabia (DCF)*	*UAE*	
				DCF	*ECF*
B.1. Fair practice and protection from fraud and deception	1	2	1	1	2
B.2. Disclosure, transparency, clear and truthful communications	2	2	2	2	2
B.3. Suitability and appropriateness of investors	2	2	2	2	1
B.4. Data protection and confidentiality	0	2	2	1	0
B.5. Setting up disputes/complaints handling procedure	2	2	2	2	1
Total for consumer protection	7	**10**	9	**8**	**6**

can enhance the overall regulatory framework for consumer protection in crowdfunding.

Conclusion

Crowdfunding is considered to be an instrument of financial inclusion, as smaller organisations that do not have access to financing from traditional legacy sources can raise funds using digital platforms. Since retail lenders/investors provide the bulk of the funds in crowdfunding, they will not be forthcoming until their rights are protected. Thus, there is a need to protect investors in the development of the CF industry. Regulations play an important role in protecting consumers and building trust in the systems. Regulators have to balance the welfare-enhancing objectives of financial innovation and the risks they pose to financial systems and consumers. The paper developed a framework to assess the regulatory regimes of CFPs related to consumer protection and examined the status in a sample of four countries (Bahrain, Oman, Saudi Arabia and UAE). Other than highlighting the differences in regulatory regimes and regulated CF activities in these countries, the results on the status of consumer/investor protection identify areas where the regulations can be strengthened to promote the growth of CFPs.

References

Aaron, M., Rivadeneyra, F., & Sohal, S. (2017). Fintech: Is this time different? A framework for assessing risks and opportunities for central banks. Bank of Canada Staff Discussion Paper, No. 2017-10, Bank of Canada, Ottawa, https://www.econstor.eu/bitstream/10419/200480/1/894585355.pdf.

Amstad, M. (2019). Regulating Fintech: Objectives, Principles, and Practices. Asian Development Bank Institute Working Paper Series 1016, Asian Development Bank Institute, Tokyo. https://www.adb.org/publications/regulating-fintech-objectives-principles-practices.

Armour, J., Deakin, S., Lele, P., & Siems, M. (2009). How do legal rules evolve? Evidence from a cross-country comparison of shareholder, creditor, and worker protection. *American Journal of Comparative Law*, 57(3), 579–629.

Arner, D.W., Barberis, J., Buckley, R.P. (2016). The Evolution of FinTech: A New Post-Crisis Paradigm. *Georgetown Journal of International Law,* 47 (4), 1271–1320.

BCBS (2016). *Guidance on the application of the Core Principles for Effective Banking Supervision to the regulation and supervision of institutions relevant to financial inclusion*. Basel Committee on Banking Supervision, https://www.bis.org/bcbs/publ/d383.pdf.

Boot, A., Hoffmann, P., Laeven, L., & Ratnovski, L. (2021). Fintech: what's old, what's new? *Journal of Financial Stability*, 53, 1–13.

Brummer, C. & Yadav, Y. (2019). Fintech and the Innovation Trilemma. *Georgetown Law Journal,* 107 (2), 235–308.

Buchanan, J., Dominic H.C., & Simon D. (2014). Empirical analysis of legal institutions and institutional change: multiple-methods approaches and their application to corporate governance research, *Journal of Institutional Economics*, 10(1), 1–20.

CBB (2020). *High-level Controls Module*, Central Bank of Bahrain. https://cbben.thomsonreuters.com/sites/default/files/net_file_store/Vol_5_Ancillary_HC_Oct_2020.pdf.

CBB (2022a). *Crowdfunding Platform Operators Module*, Central Bank of Bahrain https://cbben.thomsonreuters.com/sites/default/files/net_file_store/Vol_5_Ancillary_CFP_July_2022.pdf.

CBB (2022b). *Ancillary Service Providers Authorisation Module*. Central Bank of Bahrain. https://cbben.thomsonreuters.com/sites/default/files/net_file_store/Vol_5_Ancillary_AU_July_2022.pdf.

CBUAE (2020) *Loan-based Crowdfunding Activities Regulation*. Central Bank of the U.A.E. https://www.centralbank.ae/media/p3edqstt/2020-10-28-c-7-2020-loan-based-crowdfunding-reg-og-published2.pdf.

Chatain, P., de Willebois, E.V.D., & Bökkerink, M. (2022). *Preventing Money Laundering And Terrorist Financing A Practical Guide For Bank Supervisors,* https://openknowledge.worldbank.org/server/api/core/bitstreams/ed032775-7c7a-517d-be11-5d1d94b45a90/content.

Cicchiello, A.F. (2020). Harmonizing the crowdfunding regulation in Europe: need, challenges, and risks. *Journal of Small Business & Entrepreneurship*, 32 (6), 585–606. doi:https://doi.org/10.1080/08276331.2019.1603945.

CMAO (2021). Rules for Crowdfunding Platforms. CMA Decision No. E/153/ 2021, Capital Markets Authority of Oman.

Cooter, R. D., & Ginsburg, T. (2003). Leximetrics: Why the same laws are longer in some countries than others. Illinois Law and Economics Working Paper Series, Working Paper No. LE03-012.

Didenko, A. (2018). Regulating FinTech: Lessons from Africa. *San Diego International Law Journal*, 19 (Index 2), 311–370.

Feyen, Erik, Harish Natarajan and Matthew Saal (2023), Fintech and the Future of Finance, Market and Policy Implications, World Bank Group, Washington DC https://documents1.worldbank.org/curated/en/099450005162250110/pdf/P17300600228b70070914b0b5edf26e2f9f.pdf

FSB (2017). *Financial Stability Implications from FinTech*. Financial Stability Board. https://www.fsb.org/wp-content/uploads/R270617.pdf.

G20/OECD (2022). *G20/OECD High-Level Principles on Financial Consumer Protection*. https://www.oecd.org/daf/fin/financial-education/G20_OECD%20FCP%20Principles.pdf.

Havrylchyk, O. (2021) *Regulatory framework for the loan-based crowdfunding platforms*. OECD Economics Department Working Papers No. 1513. https://hal.archives-ouvertes.fr/hal-03201936/document.

Jenik, I., Lyman, T. & Nava, A. (2017). Crowdfunding and Financial Inclusion. CGAP Working Paper. https://www.cgap.org/sites/default/files/Working-Paper-Crowdfunding-and-Financial-Inclusion-Mar-2017.pdf.

Kirby, E., & Worner, S. (2014). *Crowd-funding: An Infant Industry Growing Fast,* Staff Working Paper No. SWP3/2014, IOSCO. https://www.iosco.org/research/pdf/swp/Crowd-funding-An-Infant-Industry-Growing-Fast.pdf.

La Porta, R., Lopez-de-Silanes, F., Shleifer, A., & Vishny, R. W. (1997). Legal determinants of external finance. *Journal of Finance*, 52, 1131–1150.

La Porta, R., Lopez-de-Silanes, F., Shleifer, A., & Vishny, R. W. (1998). Law and finance. *Journal of Political Economy*, 106, 1113–1155.

Lele, P., & Siems, M. M. (2007). Shareholder protection: A leximetric approach. *Journal of Corporate Law Studies*, 7(1), 17–50.

Meadows, M.R. (2018). The Evolution of Crowdfunding: Reconciling Regulation Crowdfunding with Initial Coin Offerings. *Loyola Consumer Law Review*, 30 (2), 272–295.

OECD (2019). Effective Approaches for Financial Consumer Protection in the Digital Age: FCP Principles 1, 2, 3, 4, 6 and 9. Directorate for Financial and Enterprise Affairs Committee on Financial Markets, https://www.oecd.org/finance/financial-education/Effective-Approaches-FCP-Principles_Digital_Environment.pdf.

Pekmezovic, A., & Walker, G. (2016). The Global Significance of Crowdfunding: Solving the SME Funding Problem and Democratizing Access to Capital. *William & Mary Business Law Review*, 7 (2), 347–458.

Petrou, M.M.R., & Al Hanai, A. (2022). Oman's Crowdfunding Regulations. *The MENA Business Law Review*, 2, 11–15. https://www.lexis.ae/wp content/uploads/2022/07/LexisNexis-MENA-Business-Law-Review-No.-02_2022.pdf.

SAMA (2020). *Rules for Engaging in Debt-Based Crowdfunding*. Saudi Arabian Monetary Authority, https://www.sama.gov.sa/en-US/Laws/FinanceRules/Rules_for_Engaging_in_Debt_Based_Crowdfunding-EN.pdf

SAMA (2021). The Updated Rules for Engaging in Debt-Based Crowdfunding, December 2021, Saudi Arabian Monetary Authority.

Siems, M. M. (2008). Shareholder protection around the world (Leximetric II). *Delaware Journal of Corporate Law*, 33, 111–147.

Thottoli, M.M. (2022). The starring role of crowdfunding in GCC: a structured literature review. *Asian Journal of Economics and Banking*, 6 (2), 155–177.

UAE Government (2022). The Cabinet The Cabinet Resolution No. (36) of 2022 Concerning Regulating Activity of the Crowdfunding Platform Operator. https://www.sca.gov.ae/assets/1ee8a9a8/the-cabinet-resolution-no-36-of-2022-concerning-regulating-activity-of-the-crowdfunding-platform.aspx

World Bank (2013). *Crowdfunding's Potential for the Developing World*. Washington, DC: World Bank. https://documents1.worldbank.org/curated/en/409841468327411701/pdf/840000WP0Box380crowdfunding0study00.pdf.

World Bank (2020a). *How Regulators Respond to Fintech Evaluating the Different Approaches—Sandboxes and Beyond*. World Bank, https://documents1.worldbank.org/curated/en/579101587660589857/pdf/How-Regulators-Respond-To-FinTech-Evaluating-the-Different-Approaches-Sandboxes-and-Beyond.pdf.

World Bank (2020b). *Capital Markets and SMEs in Emerging Markets and Developing Economies: Can They Go the Distance*. Washington DC: The World Bank. https://openknowledge.worldbank.org/handle/10986/33373.

World Bank & CCAF (2019). *Regulating Alternative Finance: Results from a Global Regulator Survey*, World Bank and Cambridge Centre for Alternative Finance. https://www.jbs.cam.ac.uk/wp-content/uploads/2020/08/2019-11-ccaf-regulating-alternative-finance-report.pdf.

World Bank and IFC (2017). *MSME Finance Gap*, World Bank and International Finance Corporation, https://documents1.worldbank.org/curated/en/653831510568517947/pdf/121264-WP-PUBLIC-MSMEReportFINAL.pdf.

World Bank (2022), Regulation and Supervision of Fintech: Considerations for EMDE Policymakers, https://openknowledge.worldbank.org/server/api/core/bitstreams/ffa8d04d-d7f2-5cc1-833f-d79a366d0940/content

CHAPTER 10

Smart Islamic Financial Engineering Towards an Integrated Digital System in the Islamic Financial Industry

Anas Ibrahim Jamous

Introduction

The Reality of the Islamic Financial Industry and Its Development in the Age of Digitalization

The Islamic financial industry has deep roots in Sharia (the Qur'an and Sunnah), but has crystallized in its modern form of institutions and tools in recent decades. The industry has succeeded in offering economically efficient financial alternatives that are increasingly globally accepted.

In light of the renaissance and intense economic competition, Islamic financial engineering has emerged as a necessary tool for finding innovative solutions and new tools that combine Shari'a guidelines and economic efficiency.

A. I. Jamous (✉)
Al-Zahraa University, Jarabulus, Syria
e-mail: anas.10045@gmail.com

K. Tsanis et al. (eds.), *Digital Finance and Transformation in the Gulf*,
https://doi.org/10.1007/978-981-92-1588-1_10

Islamic financial institutions are no longer isolated from the massive technological development; the trend towards digitization has led to the emergence of Islamic FinTech. This technology is considered an enabler and catalyst for digital financial activities, as it has allowed the emergence of many Shariah-compliant digital platforms, which has significantly boosted the growth and development of the Islamic financial industry in the era of digital transformation.

Hence, the following problem must be raised:

Research Problem

To what extent Islamic financial engineering and its compatible digital applications have succeeded in providing financial innovations that comply with Islamic Shari'a and achieve economic efficiency.

Although Islamic finance has witnessed rapid digital transformation in recent years, most existing studies focus on technological adoption or Shariah compliance frameworks in isolation. Only a limited number of works have attempted to **integrate Islamic Financial Engineering (SIFE) methodologies with the concrete design and governance of digital financial platforms**. This gap results in a lack of systematic approaches to designing, structuring, and evaluating digital Islamic financial solutions that align both with Shariah principles and with modern digital innovation practices. Addressing this gap is essential to ensure that Islamic FinTech ecosystems evolve on sound engineering, governance, and ethical foundations.

Importance of the Research

The importance of the study lies in the role played by Islamic financial engineering in innovating Islamic financial products that compete with traditional products that combine the controls of the Islamic religion with considerations of economic efficiency, contribute to the development of banking and investment services at the level of banking and financial institutions, and provide new financing mechanisms, alternatives, and solutions to get out of various economic fluctuations and crises.

Reasons for Choosing the Research (Motivations)

1. Bridging the Research Gap: The urgent need for research in the field of Islamic financial engineering, especially in the age of digitalization, given the paucity of studies that integrate the Islamic financial industry and FinTech.
2. Building an Integrated System: Providing an integrated study of digital Islamic finance tools and formulas, by identifying various global digital platforms to form an integrated system called "Smart Islamic Financial Engineering", with the aim of achieving economic efficiency.
3. Meet market demands: Helping Islamic financial institutions build a diverse portfolio of tools and products that give them sufficient flexibility to respond to extreme economic changes, similar to what traditional institutions do.

The research aims to establish the parameters of the Islamic approach in smart Islamic financial engineering.

Research Contribution

This research makes three key contributions.

First, it defines and conceptualizes Islamic Financial Engineering (SIFE) as a structured methodology for designing, synthesizing, and evaluating Shariah-compliant financial innovations within digital environments.

Second, it proposes an evaluation framework that combines SIFE principles with digital platform governance criteria, enabling a holistic assessment of innovation, compliance, and operational soundness.

Third, the study applies the proposed framework to selected cases across major segments of the Islamic digital economy—namely digital Islamic banks, Takaful platforms, Sukuk issuance systems, Waqf management applications, and Zakat distribution platforms—to demonstrate its applicability and practical value.

Research Objectives

1. Explaining the importance of Islamic financial engineering, its characteristics and its role in innovating contemporary Shariah alternatives and solutions that meet the needs of people and keep pace with technology and digital transformation.
2. Studying and characterizing some contemporary applications and digital platforms that are considered as tools for smart Islamic financial engineering.
3. Explaining the impact of financial technology in the light of the purposes of Sharia.

Research Methodology

This research employs a qualitative methodology that combines descriptive and analytical approaches to examine Smart Islamic Financial Engineering (SIFE). The descriptive component clarifies the concepts, objectives, and characteristics of SIFE, while qualitative content analysis is applied to selected digital Islamic financial platforms—such as digital Islamic banks, Takaful systems, and smart Sukuk—based on publicly available information. Data were collected from official platform websites, whitepapers, governance documents, AAOIFI standards, and selected industry reports, including the *Cambridge Global Islamic Finance Report (GIFR)* 2021. A comparative lens is used to assess how these platforms operationalize Shari'a compliance and economic efficiency. The study is subject to certain limitations, including reliance on publicly disclosed sources, lack of access to internal audit or Shari'a supervisory reports, and the diversity of regulatory jurisdictions governing the platforms.

Previous Studies

After researching, I did not find a comprehensive and complete study that brings together the pillars of the Islamic financial industry and the digital technology revolution, as most recent studies have been limited to individual platforms or a specific sector. For example, Sassi's (2018) study looked at the Finterra Waqf Chain platform for the use of blockchain in endowment assets, and Al-Amrawi's (2019) study focused on the Nasdaq Dubai Murabaha platform as a mechanism to enhance the liquidity of Islamic banks.

The paper consists of an introduction, three chapters, a conclusion, and indexes as follows:

Introduction: It includes the research problem, the importance of the research, the reasons for choosing the research, the objectives of the research, and the research methodology, and this is a statement of the research plan.

Chapter 1: The Concept of Islamic Financial Engineering.

Chapter 2: The Importance of Innovation and its Tools in the Smart Islamic Financial Engineering Industry.

Chapter 3: Digital Platforms and Technologies Compatible with Islamic Financial Engineering Regulations.

Conclusion: Includes Findings and Recommendation.

Chapter 1. The Concept of Islamic Financial Engineering

Islamic financial engineering is both ancient and new contemporary at the same time, as it is a method of innovation and development of Islamic financial transactions that dates back to the history of the Prophethood as will be seen, and it is new and contemporary in this term. With the beginning of the digital revolution and the era of digital transformation, digitization imposed its presence on all sectors, including Islamic finance and Islamic financial engineering, so digitization was added to most sciences such as digital economy, digital finance) and also smart Islamic financial engineering.

At the beginning of this study, it is necessary to identify the concept and principles of Islamic financial engineering, and then explain the entry of digitization on this science and its impact under the name of—Smart Islamic Financial Engineering.

First: Definition of Islamic Financial Engineering

It is a set of activities that includes the design, development and implementation processes of both innovative financial tools and processes, as well as the formulation of creative solutions to financing problems, all within the framework of the directives of Islamic Sharia (Saleh, 2002).

This definition indicates that Islamic financial engineering includes the following elements:

- Innovation of new financial instruments.
- Innovating new financing mechanisms.
- Devising new financing management solutions, such as managing liquidity or debt, or preparing financing formulas for specific projects that suit the circumstances surrounding the project.
- The innovations referred to earlier, whether in the instruments or financing processes, should be in accordance with the Shari'a while avoiding jurisprudential differences as much as possible, which will distinguish them from Shari'a credibility (Qandouz, 2007).

The need for financial engineering arises either in response to investment opportunities according to the aspirations of both investors and institutions, or to deal with the constraints of international competition, or to prevent risks surrounding investment activities, and in this regard, it is considered as a financial hedging tool. The objectives of financial engineering are determined according to the situation facing the institution in question (Saleh, 2002).

Second: The Emergence and Development of Islamic Financial Engineering

In reality, the Islamic financial industry has existed since the Islamic Shari'a came with its purified provisions. Perhaps the Prophet (peace and blessings of Allaah be upon him) directed Bilal al-Mazini to him, when he wanted to exchange good dates for bad dates, and the Messenger of Allaah (peace and blessings of Allaah be upon him) said to him: **"Do not do (this). Sell the collection/whole for dirhams and buy a *Janīb* (superior quality item) with dirhams"** as a sign of the importance of looking for solutions that meet economic needs without violating the rulings of sharee'ah. The basic rule concerning transactions is permissibility unless contradicted by a valid Islamic text or a firmly established religious ruling. Accordingly, the Islamic Shari'ah did not block the circle of innovation, but on the contrary, it closed the circle of the forbidden, and kept the circle of the project open to human effort in innovation and innovation.

The phenomenon of financial engineering, in a form, has existed since ancient times, and there is no doubt that the jurisprudential exits proposed by the pioneers of jurisprudential schools in trying to facilitate Muslims in their financial contracts according to the rules of Islamic Sharia do not go beyond the circle of Islamic financial engineering, and we can reach by tracing Islamic history that financial engineering has been used in many Islamic financial transactions (Qandouz, 2008).

Third: Characteristics of Islamic Products and Their Smart Engineering

Islamic products aim to combine two main characteristics: Shari'a credi bility (adherence to Shari'a and avoidance of disputes and sham contracts) and economic efficiency (achieving customers' intentions with minimal procedural costs). This combination seeks to provide ideal models for the Islamic economy.

In this context, there is a need for financial engineering to make traditional formulas more efficient. For example, Murabaha for the order and credit card can be developed from low-efficiency formulas to more efficient and credible models by transforming the relationship from direct selling or discount to a partnership between the bank and the merchant.

This shift (participation rather than selling/discounting) eliminates the costs of possession and arrest of the bank (e.g., in Murabaha), and avoids the suspicion of financial deduction on the merchant (e.g., in the case of a credit card), thus achieving an integration between legitimate credibility and economic efficiency (Al-Suwailem, 2004).

Fourth: The Importance of Islamic Financial Engineering

1. The importance of Islamic financial engineering stems from its pivotal role in meeting the needs of society and the protection of the economic system. It works to innovate and develop financing tools that are disciplined by Shari'a controls, which contributes to achieving God's pleasure and removes the embarrassment and hardship of the public by providing compatible contracts that are in line with the objectives of taxpayers in the development of money.

2. On the economic front, Islamic financial engineering represents the alternative and remedy for crises. It combines the elements of legitimate credibility and practical economic efficiency, which ensures the continuity of the Islamic system and protects its economy from being affected by suffocating crises. It also contributes to breaking the cycle of dependence on Western regimes and encourages continuous jurisprudential to adapt and develop new contracts that keep pace with global economic developments, highlighting the comprehensiveness of the Islamic economic system (Al-Anzi, 2015).

Fifth: Objectives of Islamic Financial Engineering

Islamic financial engineering has many goals, which can be summarized in the following points:

1. Creating banking institutions that are free of Shari'a violations, which enable Muslims to carry out transactions in accordance with their religious beliefs.
2. Providing credible and high-quality Islamic financial products, as a legitimate alternative to haram products.
3. Achieve economic efficiency by expanding investment opportunities, reducing transaction costs, and aligning returns, risks, and liquidity.
4. Contributing to the revival of the economy by including many of those who left projects due to their violation of Sharia, and providing stable and real financing that reduces the effects of inflation.
5. Compete with traditional banks by providing innovative and Shariah-compliant tools, mechanisms, and solutions.
6. Assist in the development of local and global financial markets, and gain recognition from international institutions.
7. Reducing investment risks by diversifying its Shariah formulas and sectors, and providing innovative Shari'a solutions to financing problems (Al-Enezi, 2015).

Chapter 2. Digital Financial Innovation and its Tools in the Industry Smart Islamic Financial Engineering

First: Definition of Financial Innovation

Financial innovation is a set of actions and measures aimed at meeting the needs of the financial community, whether by developing existing products or by designing innovative and viable alternatives within the rules and controls of Islamic Sharia (Qantaqji, 2016).

Digital technological innovation focuses on the technical aspect, i.e., the introduction of modern technology and technologies to develop Islamic financial tools and products, which is referred to as smart Islamic financial engineering.

The financial product aims to achieve financing and profitability purposes, but it differs from the traditional product (which depends on usurious interest or the sale of non-existent). An Islamic financial product is a financial compound that observes the rules and controls of Sharia, and achieves for customers purposes that satisfy their financing needs (Qantaqji, 2016).

The development of these products is one of the biggest challenges facing Islamic institutions, and the use of new digital platforms (smart financial engineering) helps in this aspect tremendously.

To achieve smart Islamic financial innovation safely and effectively, the specialist must have a combination of knowledge and skills:

Shari'a and jurisprudential knowledge: Must have a deep understanding of Islamic economics and mathematical jurisprudence, with jurisprudential faculty, jurisprudential flexibility, and adherence to fundamentalist controls.

Technical and Financial Knowledge: Learn techniques and programming rules, high mathematics, financial management sciences, banking, insurance, and market affairs.

This combination ensures the creation of tools that keep pace with the times while maintaining Islamic authenticity.

Second: Financial Innovation in Islamic History

In the early Islamic tradition, "financial innovation" was known as "tricks", and its practitioners were nicknamed "engineers", as it aimed to find solutions to financial sales and transactions. In the modern era, a distinction has been made between traditional and Islamic financial engineering, and the term "engineering" has been replaced by the term "financial innovation jurisprudence", which is part of Islamic jurisprudence of transactions and seeks to satisfy people's needs within the framework of Sharia and justice.

Innovation has always been inherent in human life, evolving from barter to monetary exchange, but deceit has led to forbidden innovations such as riba (excess on debt). In the current era of digital transformation, smart Islamic financial engineering has emerged as an inevitable step to digitize Islamic financial services and products within the Shari'a standard, as an alternative to illicit innovations.

Third: The Necessity of Digital Innovation in Islamic Financial Jurisprudence

The world is witnessing a tremendous development in digital technology that has radically impacted financial markets, and the use of this technology (digitization) has become necessary because of the speed, quality, and ability to achieve financial inclusion and accumulate savings.

Islamic jurisprudence not only calls for innovation, but also makes it a legitimate duty when the legitimate interest is only achieved by it, in accordance with the rule that "what is not done is obligatory." In this context, the fundamentalists decide that the means take the rule of their purposes. Al-Qarafi believes that what the absolute obligation is not completed without is obligatory. The means to the obligatory is obligatory. Al-Ghazali: What is not originally obligatory becomes what the absolute duty is only accomplished by means is a duty, because the duty depends on it. He also decides that "the pretext, as it must be filled, must be opened... The means of duty are obligatory, such as seeking Jumu'ah and Hajj." Al-Ghazali explains that what is not obligatory in its origin becomes obligatory according to the obligation of what is meant.

This imperative requires the adoption of the latest information and communication technologies to enable Islamic institutions to improve their performance and expand their business globally. Digital transformation is a Shariah-approved means of transforming knowledge into a resource, achieving global competitiveness, and dealing with the challenges of the era that is moving towards fully digital banking.

Fourth: Innovative Means Scale

The global financial crises have proven the traditional utility/interest criterion wrong, as it achieves benefit at the microeconomic level, but it does harm at the macroeconomic level. Therefore, Islamic law has provided general controls (such as consent and justice) and special (such as holding and tenure) to control financial innovations and ensure prosperity. The Prophet (peace and blessings of Allaah be upon him) prescribed the Bai' al-Salam, and the jurists based istisna'a on it to be among the permissible with specific controls.

By comparing Islamic and traditional innovation, it becomes clear that the following:

1. In Corporate Finance: The Industrial Revolution in the West produced good financial innovations (such as joint stock companies and the issuance premium to achieve equity between partners). In contrast, innovations that are rejected by Sharia have emerged, such as preferred stocks that set a profit in advance and forcibly deduct profits, which is an unjust withholding of profits from below, as opposed to the voluntary withholding from above that jurists have permitted (for encouragement and donation).
2. In debt: Bonds were created as a new product by dividing the riba-based debt into small amounts, but they remained in essence the borrowing of money with money in excess (riba).

Islamic innovations also turned to macro politics. The Prophet (peace and blessings of Allaah be upon him) and his successors borrowed money from the treasury as a good loan without interest. In the year of famine, Umar ibn al-Khattab (may Allah be pleased with him) also gave the rich a choice between employment (imposing a tax on the rich only) or lending the treasury in advance from zakat, so that people could choose the latter. This represents a pure, fair, and equitable financial innovation.

In contrast, governments today resort to value-added tax (sales tax), which carries its costs on consumers and leads to inflation and social injustice, and the Prophet (peace and blessings of Allaah be upon him) recommended that "no tax be imposed on the markets."

Islamic financial innovations are characterized by being constrained by the principles of justice ('Adl) and kindness (Ihsan), ensuring the interest without total imbalance. Traditional innovations are based on utility, which upsets their balances and shows their detrimental macro effects late, which is contrary to the most basic rules of strategic management.

Fifth: The Relationship between Financial Innovation and Financial Engineering

Financial engineering and financial innovation are not one thing, they are complementary processes.

Robert Merton answers this question by saying that financial engineering is a means of implementing financial innovation. It is a system approach that financial services institutions use to find better solutions to their customers' problems. It is the need that drives innovation, while innovation depends on financial engineering. Financial engineers have the experience, skills, and ability to employ complex mathematical and statistical models, which qualifies them to put these innovations into practice, to be introduced to the market as new financial tools and services (Radwan, 2005).

As for Islamic financial engineering, if financial institutions do not adopt a clear approach that takes into account Shari'a objectives and seeks to achieve the difficult equation (combining Shari'a credibility with economic efficiency), they will remain captive to imitation and emulation of traditional financial products, which may lead to them deviating from the right path.

Sixth: The Importance of Developing and Digitizing Islamic Financial Products

The importance of developing Islamic financial products through smart Islamic financial engineering allows for the development of various financial institutions and the Islamic banking system, as highlighted in the following:

1. Diversification of Sources of Profitability for Islamic Banks
2. In response to investment opportunities according to the aspirations of both investors and institutions.
3. Innovation of new Islamic banking products that support deposit attraction and increase financing capabilities.
4. Supporting the financial efficiency of both monetary and financial markets through speed and transparency reflected in the price of new products.
5. Solving the problem of immediate liquidity, and finding solutions to hedge against financial risks according to a safe method.

From the above, we see the importance of digital financial innovation and its role in the development of Islamic financial products, which contributes to the smart Islamic financial engineering industry. This is what contributed to the establishment and launch of digital platforms that operate in accordance with the principles and controls of Islamic Sharia, and I will present in the following research the most important and largest digital platforms in Islamic financial technology, and we will find that these platforms in their diversity share Islamic financial products, and can form a system and formulation compatible with the Islamic financial industry.

Chapter 3. The World's Most Popular Digital Platforms and Technologies in Islamic Finance

Introduction: The importance of financial engineering as a suitable tool for finding innovative solutions and new financial tools that combine the guidelines of Shari'a and considerations of economic efficiency is highlighted. In this particular period, when the world has witnessed tremendous radical changes, represented by the change in the management of economic resources to a free economic model, in addition to the interdependence of international financial markets due to the ICT revolution, this imposes severe competitive pressures that may be unequal for Islamic financial institutions, especially in the markets of finance, banking and financial services to continue effectively.

Taking a holistic view of the structure of the Islamic financial industry, we find that the Islamic financial industry is divided into three components:

1. Islamic Financial Institutions: These are institutions that provide financial services that comply with the provisions of the Islamic Sharia. These institutions include Islamic banks, Islamic insurance companies, Islamic investment companies, and Islamic investment funds.
2. Islamic Financial Instruments: Financial instruments designed to comply with the provisions of Shari'a. Islamic. These instruments include Islamic sukuk and Islamic capital investments.
3. Regulatory and Regulatory Authorities: These are the bodies responsible for regulating the financial industry

Islamic and ensuring its compliance with the provisions of Islamic Sharia. These include Islamic central banks and Shari'a boards.

Smart Islamic Financial Engineering is concerned with the development and innovation of the components of the Islamic financial industry, through the facilitation and digitization of financial services in Islamic banks and insurance companies, and also through the development and digital financial innovation in the Islamic Financial Instruments Division represented in Sukuk and other Islamic financial products.

In this research, the technologies and financial technology of Islamic financial institutions will be presented, and then the global platforms for Islamic financial instruments such as Sukuk and others, and then the regulatory and supervisory authorities and institutions for these platforms will be shown.

1. **Islamic Financial Institutions**:

   As we have seen, they are institutions that provide financial services that comply with the provisions of Islamic Sharia. These institutions include Islamic banks, Islamic insurance companies, Islamic investment companies, and Islamic investment funds.

Here we review digital platforms and technologies in the Islamic banking and insurance sectors.

Islamic and Islamic Investment Funds.

A. Digital Islamic Banks: The world is moving towards digitization in the banking sector, and Islamic banks, as the leader of the Islamic financial industry, see this transformation as an opportunity to enhance their activity, expand their reach, and address the requirements of their customers looking for flexible and accessible services.

This adoption of the technology began with gradual transformations and reached the model of full (virtual) digital banks. This end-to-end digital model is characterized by low operational costs, increased productivity, and improved performance, as automation reduces operational cost, and regulatory technology (RegTech) contributes to enhancing compliance with regulatory authorities. The services provided at these banks are also characterized by high transparency and ease of use.

The Islamic economy's attitude towards this transformation is positive, as digital transformation enshrines the concept of saving money (one of the purposes of Sharia), and aims to remove embarrassment and facilitate customers in application of the jurisprudential rule "hardship brings facilitation". The digital transformation of Islamic banks also contributes to enhancing financial inclusion, supports the achievement of social solidarity and distributive justice, in addition to supporting economic growth and financial stability, which is part of Islam's goals in building the earth.

Among the most important international digital Islamic banks are:

1. **Nomo Bank:** https://www.nomobank.com/ar/fixed-termdeposits

Nomo Bank is the world's first fully digital international Islamic bank, based in the UK and compliant with Sharia law. It operates under Bank of London and The Middle East (BLME), owned by Boubyan Bank (Kuwait).

The bank offers smart, technology-driven services tailored for frequent travelers, including:

- Current Accounts
- Linked accounts via **Open Banking**
- Fixed-Term Deposits
- Flexible Savings Accounts
- Real Estate Finance (Rent & Residential)

From a Sharia perspective, Nomo uses Islamic contracts such as.

Murabaha, Ijarah, and Diminishing Partnership for financing, avoiding interest-based lending. Sharia governance is ensured through BLME and Boubyan Bank's supervisory frameworks.

Economically, Nomo leverages its digital infrastructure to reduce costs, automate compliance, and facilitate account management for international clients. Socially, it promotes financial inclusion by providing accessible, Sharia-compliant banking across borders.

Overall, Nomo Bank combines advanced digital technology with Sharia compliance, economic efficiency, and international accessibility.

2. **Kestrl:** https://kestrl.io/

Kestrl is an Islamic finance application designed as an alternative to traditional banking, operating in the UK and the Middle East. It aims to make finance more accessible, transparent, and ethical for Muslims.

Key features include:

- Spending tracking, budgeting, and money management to achieve financial goals
- Educational tools to enhance understanding of Islamic finance concepts
- Comprehensive platform for easy financial management

From a Sharia perspective, Kestrl ensures all offered services and products are compliant and promotes transparency in financial dealings. Economically, it supports users in planning and managing finances efficiently, while socially, it fosters trust and financial literacy within Muslim communities.

Overall, Kestrl provides a transparent, ethical, and accessible alternative to conventional banking, aligned with Sharia principles.

The following is a presentation of these two banks.

Feature	*Nomo Bank*	*Kestrl*
Basic definition	The world's first fully digital international Islamic bank, compliant with sharia law	An Islamic finance application, an alternative to the traditional banking system, aiming to make finance more accessible and transparent for Muslims
Primary location/ Reach	A digital banking application in the **United Kingdom**	Currently available in the **United Kingdom** and the **Middle East** region

(continued)

(continued)

Feature	*Nomo Bank*	*Kestrl*
Affiliation/ Ownership	Part of Bank of London and the Middle East (**BLME**), which is owned by **Boubyan Bank** (Kuwait)	
Main goal	Designed to meet the requirements of frequent travelers to manage their money with comfort and ease through smart technological services	Aims to rebuild trust in Islamic finance by offering transparent and ethical products and services
Key services and products	– current accounts	– spending tracking, money management, budgeting, and achieving financial goals
	– links bank accounts in one place (**open banking** technology)	– offers educational tools to understand Islamic finance concepts
	– fixed-term deposits	– easy money management through a comprehensive platform
	– flexible savings account	
	– real estate Finance (rent and residential)	
Competitive advantage	Combines innovative Islamic banking services with the latest technology, offering an advanced international digital banking experience	Offers a real alternative to the traditional banking system and facilitates Islamic finance

B. Digital Islamic Insurance: It is the use of the latest technologies and innovative applications in technology and their exploitation in the insurance sector, which improves the insurance image, achieves the quality and speed of services, and helps solve the traditional problems that the insurance sector suffers from.

As in financial technology, insurance technology also seeks to use technology to provide simplified products to the largest number of customers away from the complexities of underwriting and traditional products, as despite its novelty, it has been able to prove its ability through its applications that rely on modern and innovative technology, and how to integrate it into people's daily life and traditional habits.

Insurance technology is characterized by advanced technologies and business models that rely on innovation and creativity, which made it a point of attraction for customers of all categories, as it represents strengths for it, through which it can diversify and deliver services directly to the customer without the need for an intermediary, and this direct relationship with the customer is what ensures their loyalty and desire to use these technologies and models (Mashali, 2023).

Examples of digital platforms in digital Islamic insurance

1. **Takadao:** https://takadao.io/academy

   Takadao is a FinTech company in Saudi Arabia specializing in Takaful (Islamic insurance) solutions powered by Blockchain technology. It leverages digital innovation to provide transparent, Sharia-compliant risk-sharing services.

   Key features include:

   - Decentralized Takaful products and collaborative savings Operates under Wakala (Agency) and Mudarabah (Partnership) models following AAOIFI standards
   - Blockchain-enabled transparency in insurance operations From a Sharia perspective, Takadao ensures compliance with Islamic insurance principles and AAOIFI guidelines. Economically, the platform enhances efficiency and trust in Takaful operations. Socially, it promotes equitable risk-sharing and financial inclusion in the Saudi market.

Overall, Takadao offers innovative, transparent, and Sharia-compliant Takaful solutions using advanced Blockchain technology.

2. **YukTakaful:** https://yuktakaful.com/

YukTakaful is Indonesia's first digital platform for Shariah-compliant insurance services, using mobile and web applications to enhance customer convenience.

Key features include:

- Focus on micro-insurance and community-based Takaful products
- Promotes financial and insurance inclusion in local communities
- Fully Shariah-compliant operations

From a Sharia perspective, YukTakaful adheres to Islamic insurance principles. Economically, it improves access to insurance for underserved populations. Socially, it supports community engagement and financial empowerment.

Overall, YukTakaful provides accessible, Sharia-compliant, and community-focused digital insurance solutions in Indonesia.

The following is a comparison table between the two institutions.

Feature	*Takadao*	*YukTakaful*
Basic definition	A leading FinTech company specializing in Takaful (Islamic insurance) solutions powered by blockchain technology	The first digital shariah insurance services platform in Indonesia
Headquarters	**Saudi Arabia** (Kingdom of Saudi Arabia)	**Indonesia**
Technology and model	Relies on **blockchain technology** to facilitate transparent risk-sharing (Takaful system) Uses a combination of **Wakala** (agency) and **Mudarabah** (partnership) models, following **AAOIFI** guidelines	Relies on mobile and web applications (**Insurtech**) to provide convenience to customers
Area of focus/ Motto	Specializes in decentralized insurance products and collaborative savings	Focuses on micro-insurance and community-based products to increase financial and insurance inclusion

2. Islamic Financial Instruments and Products

They are financial instruments that are designed to comply with the provisions of Islamic Sharia. These instruments include Islamic sukuk of all kinds, Islamic investments in capital, financing products, and compound financial contracts, in addition to charitable financing contracts such as endowments and zakat.

Investment Sukuk is one of the most prominent Shari'a-compliant securities, and it is defined as: "Documents of equal value that represent common shares in the ownership of objects, benefits and services or in the assets of a specific project or private investment activity, after the collection of the value of the Sukuk and the closing of the subscription door and the start of using it for what it was issued for" (Accounting and Auditing Organization website, Standard No. 17).

In traditional finance, they are usually loans or other rights receivables, while in Islamic finance, they are assets that can be negotiable according to the provisions of Islamic Shari'a and its principles, such as assets that are the subject of Ijara, and the second process is the transfer of ownership of the assets to a special purpose entity that acts as an issuer by placing them in the form of securities (sukuk), and finally the process of issuing the latter to investors, and Islamic financial sukuk takes many forms, including Ijara sukuk and participation bonds. Murabaha Sukuks, Mudaraba Sukuks, Istisna'a Sukuks, Sukuk al-Salam. Farms Sukuk

- **Smart Sukuk (Smart Contracts)**

The Islamic Fiqh Academy defined smart contracts as "a contract between two parties that is automatically executed based on the idea of peer to peer without an intermediary through a decentralized distribution network (Blockchain (1) and is done in cryptocurrencies such as Bitcoin and others" (Session, Decision 230).

Blockchain technology and smart contracts contribute to solving the complex challenges of sukuk issuance and trading. This technology allows sovereign entities or the business sector to launch smart sukuk to attract funding.

How Smart Instruments Work:

1. Technical Foundation: Smart sukuk is based on smart contracts, which are coded rules that automatically apply contract terms (such as payments and transfer of ownership) as soon as orders are received.
2. Automation and Broker Cancelation: The investor gets a smart instrument in exchange for the amount paid. Dividends, project

returns, and sukuk ownership are distributed automatically and directly through the blockchain ecosystem, eliminating the need for financial intermediaries.

3. Socio-economic objective: Smart instruments are used to finance public benefit and social projects, such as the Indonesian Blossom Finance project, which aims to finance projects in poor areas and the expansion of hospitals.

Smart Sukuk offers a solution for the development of the Islamic finance sector, combining a Shariah contractual structure with digital operational efficiency.

The following is a presentation of the most important Islamic financial products that operate according to the mechanism of smart investment sukuk, and the most important global digital platforms that issue these sukuk.

A. Smart Ijara Sukuk: (Wethaq Capital Platform)

Wethaq Capital is a digital Sukuk platform that automates the full issuance lifecycle using smart contracts on the R3 Corda blockchain. The platform focuses on **Smart Ijara Sukuk**, integrating issuers, investors, and service providers in a single ecosystem.

Key Features:

- Automated rental payments and contract execution
- High transparency through predefined smart-contract terms
- External Shari'a oversight via Shari'a Review House

Shari'a Assessment: The platform embeds Ijara requirements directly into the smart contract—asset clarity, rental terms, and ownership of usufruct—reducing gharar and strengthening compliance.

Economic Efficiency: Automation lowers operational costs, reduces reliance on intermediaries, and improves settlement speed and market accessibility.

Socio-economic Value: Supports digital transformation in Sukuk markets and expands access for smaller issuers.Wethaq offers a transparent, efficient, and Shari'a-compliant model for Smart Ijara Sukuk through blockchain-enabled automation. (Al-Hourani/Nael, 2023).

B. Smart Murabaha Sukuk

Several international platforms have emerged that issue smart sukuk based on the Murabaha formula, and I have chosen the most important of them, which are three platforms:

1. Nasdaq Dubai (Al-Amrawi, 2019)
2. Qardus/(Alzobui 2024)
3. MicroLEAP Platform (Mounir, 2022)

The following is a definition of these platforms and the most important features.

Feature	*Nasdaq Dubai Murabaha Platform*	*Qardus Platform*	*microLEAP Platform*
Definition and location	An Islamic finance platform in **Dubai** (2014) that uses Sharia-compliant certificates as the underlying asset for finance transactions	The first ethical **Islamic P2P financing marketplace** for SMEs in the **UK**	A **P2P financing platform** in **Malaysia** (2018), focused on the microfinance sector
Sharia Mechanism & Technology	Relies on **Murabaha** using tradable certificates, primarily serving Islamic banks and windows	Relies on the Islamic **commodity Murabaha** system to cover short-term operational needs	Uses the concept of **commodity Murabaha (Tawarruq)** to finance small businesses, allowing users to bypass banks

(continued)

(continued)

Feature	*Nasdaq Dubai Murabaha Platform*	*Qardus Platform*	*microLEAP Platform*
Beneficiaries and advantages	Serves Islamic banks; distinguished by high-speed Murabaha execution (within minutes) at a fixed rate	Serves SMEs and investors; its products comply with the standards of global sharia boards	Serves Malaysian small businesses and retail investors; its financing is fully sharia-compliant, and it acts as an alternative financing and investment tool

C. Smart Mudaraba Sukuk

In 2018, Blossom Finance announced the launch of the Smart Sukuk Platform for Islamic Microfinance Institutions in Indonesia. In 2019, the platform issued the world's first Islamic smart Sukuk that works through smart contracts for the benefit of the BMT Bina Ummah Foundation (a cooperative microfinance institution to support small traders and farmers in rural areas).

Financing and Performance Structuring

Shariah Mechanism: The Sukuk is based on a Shariah financing structure, which is the Mudaraba formula, based on the principle of sharing profits and losses between the issuer and the investor, and thus it is based on assets rather than debt, and involves risk-sharing.

1. Achievements: The sukuk raised IDR 715 million (equivalent to US$ 50,476 thousand at the time). At the end of 2020, the company reported a total annual return of 12.94% for investors, and was able to finance 144 individual small business owners (Al-Hourani/Nael, 2023).
2. Recognition: The company was awarded the "Best Islamic Microfinance Company" award for $$SmartSukuk technology in 2019, for using blockchain technology to reduce traditional barriers to sukuk issuance and investment (https://www.blossomfinance.com/).

Structuring the business of Mudaraba sukuk in Blossom.

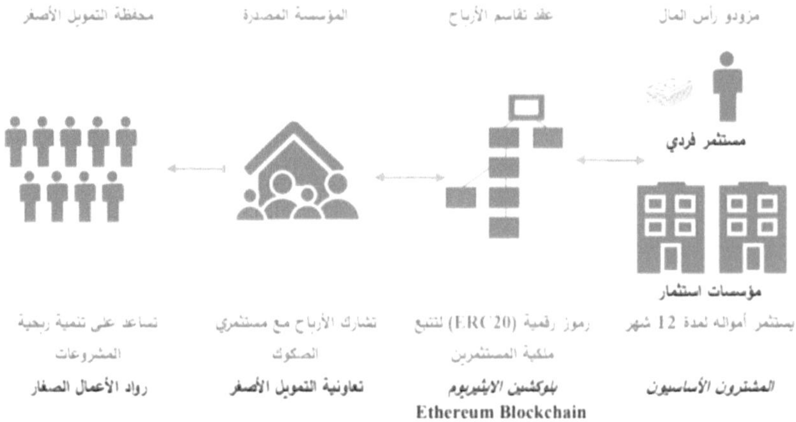

D. Smart Waqf Sukuks

Waqf is an Islamic principle that aims to confine the origin and bear fruit to promote social solidarity. But the endowment sector has faced problems with transparency and a lack of data about its management.

The solution lies in smart contracts:

A smart endowment is defined as an asset that is managed and invested through smart contracts on blockchain technology, which gives the endowment (the grantor) the ability to track the endowment history, the scope of its use, and the ways of spending it with transparency and security.

Waqf sukuk are documents of equal value issued by the Waqf Department to raise the necessary financing to invest in an existing Waqf asset (such as financing a project on an endowment land), and the profits are shared according to the financing formula used (Al-Hourani/Nael, 2023).

In short, smart contracts provide a technical mechanism to solve the challenges of traditional endowments, adding transparency and security to the management and investment processes through smart endowment sukuk.

In this product, the Finterra platform is active, and the following is a description of the mechanism of work of this platform:

Platform/Finterra Waqf Chain/

Finterra Waqf Chain is a blockchain-based platform founded in 2017 to support Shari'a-compliant digital solutions for Waqf management across Malaysia, Singapore, the UAE, and Hong Kong. The platform enables endowment institutions to manage and grow Waqf assets through diversified investment tools, offering four main transaction types: **Waqf contributions, Islamic loans, Mudaraba investments, and Sukuk issuance**. (https://mywaqf.com/).

Shari'a Assessment: The platform structures Waqf and investment contracts according to Shari'a rules, ensuring asset segregation and maintaining the perpetual nature of Waqf capital. The use of blockchain enhances transparency and traceability, reducing uncertainties related to asset ownership and fund usage.

Economic Efficiency: Finterra improves operational efficiency through digital fundraising, automated processes, and diversified investment options for Waqf institutions. Blockchain reduces administrative costs and enhances investor confidence, while enabling scalable crowdfunding models for endowment projects.

Socio-economic Value: The platform expands public participation in Waqf development and supports financing of community projects. It addresses long-standing challenges of underutilized Waqf assets by enabling more sustainable and income-generating investment structures.

Limitations: Adoption barriers include limited awareness among Waqf institution personnel regarding blockchain technology, and hesitation among some Shari'a scholars due to the novelty and incomplete regulatory clarity surrounding digital Waqf applications.

Overall: Finterra Waqf Chain offers a promising, Shari'a-compliant digital infrastructure for modernizing Waqf management, though successful expansion depends on stronger regulatory acceptance and institutional awareness.

E. Smart Contracts in Zakat

Zakat is an essential pillar and an effective tool for poverty eradication, and it has proven its effectiveness historically (such as the era of Omar bin Abdulaziz). With the rapid development of financial technology, blockchain technology and smart contracts have become a powerful tool to achieve greater efficiency and transparency in their management and distribution, in order to achieve the purposes of Shariah and the public interest.

This system enables the automation of the Zakat process and ensures its transparency through smart contract technology and blockchain, and this system includes three main parties: Zakat payers, beneficiaries, and the supervisory body.

Working Mechanism and Digitization:

1. Creation of contracts: A Zakat contract is created that specifies the amount and distribution when the zakat is paid, and a matriculation contract for each beneficiary that specifies the eligibility conditions based on the database of beneficiaries.
2. Automatic Distribution Process: The Zakat Recipient deposits

Zakat in the smart contract, which automatically verifies the conditions of the beneficiaries. When the conditions are met, the contract immediately transfers the funds to the accounts of the beneficiaries without the need for intermediaries.

Advantages and Challenges:

Challenges	*Advantages*
Initial costs: Developing and implementing the system requires significant investments in infrastructure.	Transparency and security: Recording all transactions on the blockchain ledger ensures complete monitoring and prevents tampering
Training and technology: The necessity of training users and overcoming challenges of technological compatibility and cyber threats	Efficiency and fairness: Automated distribution reduces intermediaries, increases process speed, and ensures accurate, unbiased application of conditions

This system provides an effective solution for the distribution of Zakat, combining technical efficiency with ensuring justice and Shari'a integrity.

Global Sadaqah (official website: https://globalsadaqah.com/).

Global Sadaqah is a Malaysia-based charitable crowdfunding platform, established in 2018 under Singapore's Ethis Foundation—one of the leading institutions in Islamic FinTech. The platform connects individual and institutional donors with verified charitable organizations, using Islamic social finance tools such as **Zakat, Waqf, and Qard al-Hasan** to fund social-impact initiatives. With more than 30,000 contributors across 50 countries, it supports a wide range of projects including housing, SME support, emergency relief, and endowment-based development initiatives.

Shari'a Assessment: The platform adheres to Shari'a rules governing Zakat distribution, Waqf utilization, and benevolent loans. Projects undergo Shari'a vetting to ensure proper categorization of funds and compliance with Islamic social finance principles.

Economic Efficiency: Digital crowdfunding reduces administrative costs and accelerates fundraising cycles. The platform increases transparency by clearly documenting fund flows and project milestones, which enhances donor trust and improves allocation efficiency.

Socio-economic Value: Global Sadaqah strengthens financial inclusion and global social solidarity by enabling donors worldwide to support impactful development projects. It promotes sustainable charitable models through Waqf-based initiatives and supports vulnerable communities in multiple regions.

Overall: The platform offers a transparent, Shari'a-compliant, and globally scalable model for Islamic social finance crowdfunding, effectively integrating philanthropic tools with modern financial technology.

To strengthen the analytical dimension of this study, a comparative evaluation of the major digital Islamic finance platforms examined in the research is provided below. The table synthesizes their key characteristics across technological foundations, underlying Shariah contracts, governance structures, oversight mechanisms, efficiency outcomes, and broader socio-economic objectives.

Comparative Analysis of Selected Islamic Digital Finance Platforms

Platform	*Core Technology*	*Shariah Contract/Model*	*Governance Structure*	*Shariah Oversight*	*Efficiency Gains*	*Socio-Economic Objectives*
Nomo Bank	Mobile banking, APIs	Murabaha	Centralized	Internal shariah board	Reduced operational cost; enhanced transparency	Financial inclusion; SME support
Kestrl	Blockchain; smart contracts	Mudaraba	Decentralized	External shariah advisory	Automated workflows; reduced processing time	Innovation financing; community empowerment
Takadao	Blockchain	Wakala (agency)	Decentralized	Limited shariah supervision	Faster transaction execution	Community-based risk-sharing
YukTakaful	Mobile applications	Takaful (mutual cooperation)	Centralized	Shariah supervisory board	Improved risk pooling; enhanced management	Islamic micro-insurance expansion
Blossom Finance	Blockchain; digital platform	Mudaraba; Murabaha	Centralized	Full shariah oversight	Automated profit distribution; lower cost	SME financing; financial empowerment
Wethaq	Blockchain	Sukuk issuance and settlement	Decentralized	Shariah advisory committee	Digitized issuance; automated post-trade processes	Strengthening Islamic capital market infrastructure
Nasdaq Dubai (sukuk platform)	Electronic trading; blockchain integration	Sukuk; Islamic equities	Centralized	Exchange-level shariah board	High transparency; rapid settlement	Supporting global Islamic capital flows

(continued)

(continued)

Platform	*Core Technology*	*Shariah Contract/Model*	*Governance Structure*	*Shariah Oversight*	*Efficiency Gains*	*Socio-Economic Objectives*
Qardus	Mobile platform	Qard Hasan	Centralized	Shariah advisory	Streamlined financing procedures	Enhanced financial access for individuals
Micro LEAP	Blockchain; digital marketplace	Mudaraba; Murabaha	Decentralized	Partial shariah oversight	Lower cost; automated matching	Micro-enterprise and SME development
Finterra	Blockchain	Mudaraba; Murabaha; waqf-based models	Decentralized	Full shariah supervisory board	Efficient digital fund management	Financing innovation; supporting waqf and social projects

3. Regulatory and Supervisory Authorities

They are responsible for regulating the Islamic financial industry and ensuring its compliance with the provisions of Islamic Sharia. These include Islamic central banks and Shari'a boards.

A regulatory framework must be put in place to oversee the performance of FinTech, and authorities should reduce system-specific risks and security-related threats, which calls for an effective legal and regulatory framework to avoid fraud and other risks while ensuring the confidence of investors and consumers and allow growth and development in a competitive environment, through the advancements and successes of the digital Islamic banking system.

Central banks in leading FinTech countries contribute to the development of regulatory frameworks and laws. In Singapore and Hong Kong, which are competing for FinTech leadership, the central banks of the two countries have agreed to cooperate in the field of technology that promotes cooperation between information and expertise exchange projects.

Also, in this context, some regional digital platforms and associations have emerged in an attempt to codify, develop, and support digital innovation and organize work within legal and regulatory frameworks and regulations.

The following are the most important regional FinTech centers that carry out supervision, regulation and supervision functions, which aspire to be the world's leading centers: Malaysian Digital Economy Corporation (MDEC), Dubai International Financial Technology Centre (DIFC), and Bahrain FinTech Bay (BFB).

A. **Malaysia Digital Economy Corporation** (MDEC): Malaysia Digital Economy Corporation (Official Website https://mdec.my)

MDEC is a government agency under the Ministry of Digitalization, which aims to lead Malaysia's digital economy and strengthen its position as a digital hub of the Association of Southeast Asian Nations (ASEAN). Malaysia has the advantage of having a vibrant Islamic financial industry.

MDEC stimulates growth by granting Malaysia Digital Status (Malaysia Digital Status) to eligible companies, which provides them with government incentives, rights, and privileges, as well as greater flexibility to operate and expand. As of April 2024, this status has been granted to more than 5000 companies.

B. **Dubai International Financial Centre for FinTech (DIFC)**

The Innovation Centre at the DIFC is the largest innovation community in the region and the world's leading hub for Islamic FinTech. The center is home to more than 1000 technology companies, including growth companies, digital labs, and venture capital firms. It is also home to the first and largest FinTech accelerator in the Middle East, Africa and South Asia ($$MEASA), the FinTech Hive program. The center aims to generate economic value by fostering innovation and talent. The center provides support to Islamic FinTech, insurance, and regulatory technology startups through acceleration programs, licensing, and a comprehensive and supportive regulatory framework. It is believed that Shariah-compliant FinTech could attract 150 million new banking customers over the next three years.

(Official website MDEC-Islamic-Fintech-Report-2020)

C. **Bahrain FinTech Bay (BFB)**

Bahrain FinTech Bay (BFB) was established in 2018 as a public-private partnership, aiming to build and accelerate the FinTech ecosystem.

BFB is the first and largest dedicated FinTech hub in the Middle East and Africa (MEA), holding great importance for the growth of the Islamic FinTech sector regionally and internationally. The hub receives strong support from the **Islamic banking community** in Bahrain (including eight of the largest banks as partners) and welcomes both conventional and Islamic financial solutions, leveraging Bahrain's well-developed regulatory environment and over 40 years of financial experience.

One of the important initiatives presented by Bahrain is the founder of the Bahrain Federation, which is the world's first Islamic FinTech Consortium, which is one of the leading global centers in establishing an ecosystem with the aim of promoting and developing FinTech in cooperation with government bodies, financial institutions, companies, consulting firms, universities, associations, venture capital, and startups in the field of FinTech.

The following is a definition of this federation and its importance:

Alco Bahrain Consortium (ALGO Bahrain):

The Bahrain ALGO FinTech Consortium is the world's first Islamic FinTech Consortium, established by three leading Islamic banks to manage the paradigm shift brought by FinTech innovations. Strategic objectives focus on enabling member banks to create and implement fast, low-cost FinTech solutions. The also aims to promote growth and financial inclusion by accelerating market access for sustainable services. It has an ambitious plan to roll out 15 FinTech platforms within five years, starting with a crowdfunding platform. This collaborative initiative supports Bahrain's position as a regional hub for Islamic finance and FinTech.

"The following table provides a concise comparison of regulatory and supervisory frameworks relevant to the discussed Islamic digital financial platforms."

Country /Regulator	*Licensing pathways*	*Sandbox maturity*	*Shariah governance requirements*	*Data & cybersecurity frameworks*	*Cross-border passporting*	*Dispute resolution mechanisms*
Malaysia (BNM, SC)	Clear pathways for digital banks, takaful operators, P2P, ECF; specific guidelines for sukuk and Islamic digital finance	One of the world's most mature sandboxes; well-structured and frequently updated	Mandatory shariah committees; AAOIFI-compatible standards; strong industry guidance	Strong frameworks via PDPA, BNM RMiT standards	Strong regional cooperation (ASEAN passporting for funds)	Shariah advisory council decisions are binding; arbitration + financial ombudsman
Saudi Arabia (SAMA, CMA)	Digital bank licenses, finance company licenses, crowdfunding, robo-advisory; active licensing waves	Rapidly developing; sandbox expanding since 2018	Strong—Mandatory shariah board; compliance with SAMA/CMA guidelines; AAOIFI-based	Strong cybersecurity controls (ECC, NCA, SAMA cybersecurity framework)	Some cross-border FinTech pilots; limited formal passporting	Specialized committees + courts; shariah compliance handled internally
UAE (FSRA–ADGM, DFSA–DIFC)	Clear pathways for digital banks, virtual assets, takaful, crowdfunding	Very mature—Separate sandboxes (ADGM RegLab, DIFC innovation hub)	Flexible—Shariah governance optional unless product claims shariah compliance	Advanced cybersecurity + data protection frameworks	Strong—International passporting, hubs for cross-border finance	Courts of ADGM/DIFC + arbitration centers

(continued)

(continued)

Country /Regulator	*Licensing pathways*	*Sandbox maturity*	*Shariah governance requirements*	*Data & cybersecurity frameworks*	*Cross-border passporting*	*Dispute resolution mechanisms*
Bahrain (CBB)	Dedicated rules for digital banks, crowdfunding, open banking, sukuk; strong Islamic finance regulations	One of the most active sandboxes in GCC	Mandatory shariah boards; central shariah governance framework	Comprehensive cybersecurity + data protection	Growing cross-border initiatives	CBB dispute resolution + Bahrain chamber for dispute resolution
United Kingdom (FCA)	Open banking licenses, EMI licenses, crowdfunding, investment platforms	One of the earliest and most respected sandboxes	No mandatory shariah governance; firms set their own frameworks	Strong GDPR-based frameworks	Very strong cross-border capabilities	Courts, financial ombudsman service

The comparison highlights differences in regulatory maturity and readiness. Malaysia, the UAE, and the UK have advanced sandboxes and strong data governance frameworks, while Saudi Arabia and Bahrain are rapidly developing in these areas. Shariah governance requirements vary from mandatory to optional depending on the country, and most jurisdictions provide effective dispute resolution and Shariah compliance mechanisms.

Conclusion

This research is an attempt to lay the foundations for the restructuring of Islamic financial engineering through the integration of digital technology, in order to reach an integrated system in smart Islamic financial engineering.

I. Findings (Results)

1. **Enhanced Shariah Compliance Reliability through Pre-Programmed Contracts:** Smart Sukuk platforms (e.g., Wethaq and Blossom) reveal that embedding **Shariah controls** within the code reduces **Gharar** (uncertainty) and operational errors, ensuring the automatic and compliant execution of contract terms, unlike traditional models reliant on ex-post human oversight.
2. **Increased Economic Efficiency through Automation and Reduced Intermediaries:** Cases (Nomo—microLEAP—Nasdaq Murabaha) indicate that full automation and digital verification reduce operational costs, increase the speed of contract finalization and settlements, and enhance transparency compared to traditional systems that rely on a long chain of intermediaries.
3. **Variability in the Strength of Digital Governance Across Platforms:** The comparison showed that more mature governance platforms (e.g., Nomo, Wethaq, and Global Sadaqah) possess clear mechanisms for governance, digital risk management, and operational transparency, while some emerging Takaful platforms (e.g., Takadao) lack a comprehensive institutional governance structure.
4. **Pivotal Role of Shariah Supervision in Building User Trust:** Platforms with institutionalized **Shariah supervision** (e.g., Finterra

and YukTakaful) indicate higher levels of public acceptance, versus platforms that rely on partial or external Shariah supervision, which face institutional adoption challenges.

5. **Significant Variation in Regulatory Framework Compliance Across Jurisdictions:** Comparing regulatory hubs shows that the progress of Malaysia, the UAE, and the UK in **sandboxes** and cybersecurity frameworks boosts platform growth, while other environments (Saudi Arabia and Bahrain) face challenges related to variations in Shariah and regulatory standards.
6. **Clear Social and Economic Impact of Digital Waqf and Zakat Platforms:** Cases (Finterra—Global Sadaqah) confirmed the technology's ability to improve targeting, governance of charitable funds, increase transparency, and deliver financing to vulnerable groups with higher efficiency than traditional models.

2-Recommendations

The recommendations focus on the need for Islamic financial institutions to undertake serious and coordinated digital transformation to ensure the authenticity and integrity of their products:

1. **Standardize a Unified Digital Shariah Governance Framework:** Design a unified procedural standard for coding operations (**Smart Contracts**) based on **AAOIFI** (Accounting and Auditing Organization for Islamic Financial Institutions) principles and **Maqasid al-Shariah** (Objectives of Shariah). This standard should mandate platforms to include requirements for transparency, asset segregation, and auditable records. This recommendation stems from the findings related to Smart Sukuk and the cases of Finterra and Wethaq, which demonstrated the benefit of automation in reducing **Gharar** and enhancing Shariah integrity.
2. **Mandate Formal and Shariah Testing Before Launch (Formal Verification + Shariah Review):** Integrate a **formal technical verification** process of the code with a documented **Shariah review** as a condition for full operation outside **sandbox** environments. This addresses the noted variations in governance maturity across Takaful

and market platforms (Findings: variability in governance maturity and trust).

3. **Implement Maqasid-based Key Performance Indicators (Maqasid KPIs):** Adopt a simple set of performance indicators (fairness of distribution, cost transparency, access to vulnerable groups, and contract compliance) to be included in platforms' periodic reports to enhance accountability and evaluation. This is based on the proven impact of digital Waqf and Zakat on improving targeting and transparency.
4. **Strengthen Regulatory Integration via Sandboxes and Incident Disclosure:** Encourage regulatory bodies to provide **dedicated sandbox tracks** for Islamic products, while requiring technical/ Shariah disclosure of incidents and failures. This supports cross-border scalability, as demonstrated by the comparison of regulatory hubs (Malaysia, UAE, UK).
5. **Build Hybrid Human Capabilities (Shariah–Tech–Finance):** Launch collaborative programs between universities and platforms to train personnel capable of reviewing smart contracts from both a Shariah and technical perspective (**Shariah + DevOps**), as the research showed that the lack of combined expertise is a major obstacle to sustainable innovation.

References

Al-Anzi, M. M. (2015). *Jurisprudence of Islamic financial engineering*. Alukah Network. https://www.alukah.net *(URL inferred; exact page should be verified)*.

Al-Hourani, R., & Na'el, I. (2023). Smart contracts: An applied jurisprudential study. *Bayt Al-Mashura Journal*, (20), 1–25.

Al-Amrawi, H. (2019). FinTech platforms as a mechanism to enhance the growth of the Islamic financial industry: Case study of the Nasdaq Dubai Murabaha Platform. *Journal of Strategy and Development, 9*(3), 45–63.

Al-Suwailem, S. (2004). *The industry of financial engineering: Perspectives on the Islamic methodology*. Bayt Al-Mashura Training.

Alzobui, H. (2024). The role of financial technology in the development of the Islamic financial industry in Europe: Qardus platform as a model. *Taʿamul: Journal of Islamic Economics, 3*(1), 1–18.

Cambridge GIFR. (2021). *Global Islamic finance report 2021.* Cambridge Institute of Islamic Finance.

Mashaali, M. (2023). *Financial technology and its applications in the insurance sector* (Unpublished manuscript). Faculty of Economic and Commercial Sciences. *(University name missing).*

Munir, B. A. (2022). Islamic financial technology and the digital finance revolution: The Malaysian experience. *Journal name not specified, 16*(2), 1–20.

Qanatqi, S. M. (2016). *Jurisprudence of financial innovation between verification and recklessness*. Center for Research in Islamic Transactional Jurisprudence.

Qandouz, A. (2007). Islamic financial engineering. *King Abdulaziz University Journal*, (2), 1–30.

Qandouz, A. (2008). *Islamic financial engineering between theory and practice.* Al-Risalah Publishers.

Ridwan, S. A. (2005). *Financial derivatives and their role in risk management and the role of financial engineering in manufacturing their instruments*. Dar Al-Nashr Lil-Jamiᶜat.

Saleh, A. M., & Fath Al-Rahman. (2002). Islamic money market instruments: An introduction to Islamic financial engineering. *Al-Masrafi (The Banker) Journal*, 26, Bank of Sudan.

PART III

Sustainability, Risk, and Societal Dimensions of Digital Finance

CHAPTER 11

Behavioral Dynamics and Switching Price Regimes in Electricity Markets: Implications for Green Pricing in the GCC

Pascal Stiefenhofer and Cafer Deniz

Introduction

Electricity markets differ fundamentally from conventional commodity markets. Unlike oil or wheat, electricity cannot be stored economically at scale, requires continuous real-time balancing of supply and demand, and is increasingly shaped by renewable energy integration. These features make electricity pricing unusually volatile and highly sensitive to technological, regulatory, and market design shifts. In liberalized systems, rapid

P. Stiefenhofer (✉) · C. Deniz
Department of Economics, Newcastle University, Newcastle, UK
e-mail: pascal.stiefenhofer@newcastle.ac.uk

C. Deniz
Graduate School of Healthcare Management, Royal College of Surgeons, Dublin, Ireland

Department of Economics, University of UsĄk, UsĄk, Turkey

K. Tsanis et al. (eds.), *Digital Finance and Transformation in the Gulf*,
https://doi.org/10.1007/978-981-92-1588-1_11

renewable expansion has generated persistently low and sometimes negative wholesale prices. In the Gulf Cooperation Council (GCC)—Bahrain, Kuwait, Oman, Qatar, Saudi Arabia, and the United Arab Emirates—markets have historically been insulated from such dynamics by subsidies and fossil-fuel dominance. Yet the region's accelerating energy transition suggests that similar pricing challenges are likely to emerge.

Negative prices have attracted substantial scholarly attention. [37] linked them to intertemporal price theory, while [33] showed how renewable intermittency disrupts conventional equilibrium models, producing oversupply and abrupt price collapses. [9] applied regime switching methods to capture volatility clustering, and [38] provided empirical evidence that large-scale solar penetration amplifies volatility and the frequency of negative prices. More recently, [20] emphasized that negative prices reflect not only technical conditions but also market design and institutional flexibility.

Classical accounts, however, often understate behavioral and institutional dimensions. [3] showed that prosumers—agents who both consume and produce electricity—exhibit bounded rationality, asymmetric responses to prices, and loss aversion. [35] further situated prosumers within socio-digital systems such as peer-to-peer markets and virtual power plants, where collective interactions generate nonlinear feedback. These findings imply that electricity prices cannot be explained by equilibrium models alone but require explicit attention to heterogeneity, behavioral asymmetries, and network effects.

The GCC provides a distinctive institutional setting for examining these interactions. [2] documented how subsidies historically suppressed volatility and weakened price signals.

Ref. [10] showed how fossil-fuel dominance and state control limited incentives for efficiency and diversification. More recently, [30] stressed that subsidy reforms and climate commitments are transforming the regional energy landscape. The [23] argued that fiscal pressures make reform unavoidable, while [27] emphasized the role of tariff realignment in promoting cost-reflective pricing. These studies depict a region where legacy institutions now confront decarbonization and diversification imperatives.

Renewable investment is already altering supply conditions. [6] estimated more than $100 billion in renewable investment pledges by 2030, while [24] reported that installed capacity reached 5.6 GW in 2022. [22] demonstrated that renewable growth depresses wholesale prices through the merit-order effect. [14] and [5] further showed that systems with limited flexibility and interconnection are especially prone to oversupply and negative prices. Within the GCC,

Ref. [21] described Oman's wholesale market, while [32] and [8] analyzed regional trade through the GCC Interconnection Authority. Yet, as [29] and [31] argued, absent expanded participation, real-time pricing, and demand-side flexibility, GCC markets remain poorly prepared for renewable-driven volatility.

Policy shifts add further complexity. [12] reported that subsidy cuts in Saudi Arabia are already accelerating distributed solar adoption as a hedge against rising tariffs. At the same time, [34, 40], and [13] warned that poorly designed support instruments—such as feed-in tariffs, net metering, and guaranteed dispatch—may stimulate investment while distorting price signals. The central policy challenge is therefore to scale renewables without undermining price stability or system efficiency.

Analytical tools for studying such dynamics have also evolved. [11] established the foundations of discontinuous dynamical systems, while [25] formalized sliding modes along regime boundaries. [15, 16, 17, 18] showed how small parameter changes can trigger abrupt bifurcations, cycles, and equilibrium loss. [43, 44, 45, 46, 47, 41, 42] subsequently applied Filippov systems to economics, capturing regime switching, instability, and feedback-driven oscillations. These contributions imply that electricity prices are often piecewise, threshold-driven, and path-dependent.

When combined with behavioral insights, this perspective becomes particularly powerful. [3] showed that prosumers react asymmetrically to gains and losses, generating nonlinear aggregate dynamics. Together, behavioral heterogeneity and discontinuous price formation re-cast electricity markets as regime switching systems shaped by policy thresholds, technology shocks, and heterogeneous agent responses.

Despite these advances, existing models rarely integrate behavioral asymmetries and discontinuous price dynamics within a unified analytical framework. This gap is especially pronounced in the GCC, where subsidy reform, renewable deployment, and distributed generation are destabilizing centralized fossil-fuel systems. These transformations generate sharp demand responses at tariff thresholds, midday solar surpluses, and nonlinear feedback from prosumers—precisely the dynamics that smooth equilibrium models cannot capture.

This chapter advances current debates on negative pricing, behavioral energy economics, and GCC electricity market governance in three ways. First, it provides a mechanism-based explanation of negative prices using a discontinuous dynamical framework, rather than relying exclusively on statistical regime switching models. Second, it formally embeds bounded rationality, loss aversion, and asymmetric prosumer behavior into non-smooth price dynamics, showing how behavioral biases themselves generate persistent volatility and regime coexistence. Third, it translates bifurcation parameters into policy instruments—such as tariff floors, export credits, and net-billing rules—thereby offering a governance framework for stabilizing renewable-rich electricity markets in the GCC.

Against this background, the chapter addresses four research questions:

1. How can electricity price dynamics in prosumer-influenced, renewable-integrated markets be modeled to capture both behavioral responses and discontinuous regime shifts?
2. How do bounded rationality, loss aversion, and asymmetric prosumer behavior shape the stability of positive and negative price regimes?
3. Which regulatory instruments—tariffs, export credits, and net-billing rules—act as bifurcation parameters in electricity price dynamics?
4. What are the implications of regime switching dynamics for market design and green pricing in GCC electricity markets?

Section 11.2 introduces a Filippov-type model of electricity price dynamics. Section 11.3 presents the behavioral analysis. Section 11.4 discusses GCC policy implications, and Sect. 11.5 concludes.

The Model

Electricity markets with high renewable penetration differ fundamentally from conventional commodity markets. Because electricity cannot be stored economically at scale, supply and demand must balance instantaneously. In this context, many market participants now operate as both consumers and producers. Households with rooftop solar, for example, draw electricity when local generation is insufficient but export to the grid when production exceeds demand. Conventional power plants, though typically suppliers, may at times absorb excess electricity rather than incur costly shutdowns. These role-switching dynamics are amplified under negative price regimes, where incentives are inverted and actors reconfigure strategies to minimize losses or capture arbitrage opportunities.

To capture such behavior, we construct a framework in which market dynamics change discontinuously at a critical threshold: the zero-price boundary. When prices are positive ($x > 0$), households and firms primarily act as consumers and traditional producers supply most electricity. When prices turn negative ($x < 0$), prosumers supply surplus generation while conventional producers may consume electricity to maintain system stability. The market therefore exhibits two distinct regimes separated by the zero-price threshold. Mathematically, this is represented as a Filippov system with piecewise dynamics: one regime for positive prices, another for negative prices. The full specification is given in the Appendix; here we emphasize the intuition rather than algebraic detail.

The novelty of the model lies in embedding behavioral finance into this dual-regime structure. Prosumers are not perfectly rational optimizers: they operate with bounded rationality, reference dependence, and loss aversion. For example, many households benchmark electricity costs against a "normal" bill. Prices above this baseline may trigger demand restraint, but prices below it often provoke disproportionate responses, such as accelerated battery charging, over-consumption, or delayed exports. These asymmetric responses generate nonlinear aggregate effects that reinforce or dampen price swings.

This framework also explains why markets often "hesitate" near zero prices. In practice, actors do not switch roles instantaneously at the threshold. Instead, they display inertia or ambiguity, producing what we term *grazing events*: price trajectories linger at the boundary before shifting regimes. Classical smooth models cannot capture this hesitation, but it emerges naturally in a discontinuous system with behavioral thresholds.

Over time, repeated interactions among prosumers, conventional producers, and policy incentives give rise to recurring pricing patterns. The model shows that electricity markets may converge not to a single equilibrium but to periodic regimes, such as daily cycles shaped by solar generation and cooling demand. Crucially, these regimes can shift suddenly if thresholds are crossed: a subsidy reform, a collective change in prosumer expectations, or a policy signal can push the market into a qualitatively different orbit. In mathematical terms, this is a bifurcation; in economic terms, it is a tipping point.

From a governance perspective, negative pricing should not be seen as a mere technical artifact of oversupply. Instead, it is the outcome of feedback loops among boundedly rational actors embedded in a discontinuous system. For GCC markets—where subsidy reforms, rapid solar deployment, and limited storage are converging—this means that standard forecasting models may underestimate volatility and fail to anticipate regime shifts. By contrast, the framework developed here highlights the central role of behavioral thresholds, prosumer dynamics, and policy design in shaping long-run price stability.

Formally, let $x \in \mathbb{R}\backslash\{0\}$ denote the electricity price and $q \in \mathbb{R}_{+}$ the associated quantity demanded. A household h demands energy ${q^d}_h$ when $x > 0$ and supplies energy ${q^s}_p$ when $x < 0$. Let ${q^d}_c$ denote demand from non-producing consumers and ${q^s}_p$ supply from power plants. Then for markets $i = 1, 2$, total demand is

$$q_i^s = \begin{cases} \sum\limits_h q_h^d + q_c^c, if x > 0, \\ q_c^c, if x < 0, \end{cases}$$

with linear functions

$$q_1^d = \alpha_1 - \beta_1 x(x > 0), q_2^d = -\alpha_2 - \beta_2 x(x < 0).$$

Similarly, total supply is

$$q_i^s = \begin{cases} q_p^s, if x > 0, \\ \sum\limits_h q_h^s + q_p^s, if x < 0, \end{cases}$$

with linear forms

$$q_1^s = -\gamma_1 + \delta_1 x(x > 0), q_2^s = +\gamma_2 + \delta_2 x(x < 0).$$

Price adjusts according to a Walrasian mechanism with seasonal forcing:

$$\dot{x} = \xi_i\left(q_i^d - q_i^s\right) + a_i sin(\omega_i t), i = 1, 2,$$

yielding a non-smooth periodic ODE of the form

$$\dot{x} = \begin{cases} a_1 \backslash sin(\omega_1 t) - \theta_1 x + c_1, x > 0, \\ a_2 \backslash sin(\omega_2 t) - \theta_2 x - c_2, x < 0, \end{cases}$$

with $\theta_i = \xi_i(\beta_i + \delta i)$ and $c_i = \xi_i(\pm\alpha_i - \gamma_i)$. Mathematically, the model admits discontinuous flows, grazing events, and bifurcations. Behaviorally, these correspond to hesitation at thresholds, sudden shifts in expectations, and tipping points in prosumer strategies. The existence of compact forward-invariant sets and periodic attractors can be interpreted as the formation of *behavioral equilibria*: recurring price regimes shaped by repeated, path-dependent decisions. Stability conditions on fixed points provide criteria for when these equilibria are robust to shocks, while grazing bifurcations represent policy-sensitive thresholds where markets may suddenly destabilize.

The model demonstrates that electricity markets influenced by prosumers are best understood as complex adaptive systems rather than smooth equilibrium mechanisms. They are shaped by discontinuous role-switching, psychological thresholds, and feedback effects—features that are particularly relevant to GCC electricity systems undergoing reform and rapid renewable integration. Having established the structure of the model, the next step is to examine its behavioral implications. In particular, we analyze how bounded rationality, reference dependence, and loss aversion interact with discontinuous price dynamics to generate distinct market regimes. This behavioral analysis not only connects the formal model to real-world decision-making but also illustrates how prosumer responses can amplify or stabilize volatility. For the GCC, where subsidy reforms and distributed solar adoption are changing incentives, such behavioral dynamics will play a central role in shaping the trajectory of electricity price transitions.

Behavioral Analysis

Existing electricity price models rarely capture two features that are increasingly central to renewable-rich systems: (i) behavioral feedback from prosumers and (ii) endogenous regime switching at psychologically meaningful thresholds. In this section, we demonstrate—with minimal formalism—how role-switching at the zero-price boundary ($x = 0$) interacts with bounded rationality and reference dependence to generate *persistent, endogenously sustained* price regimes. We interpret the resulting periodic orbits and bifurcations as *behavioral equilibria* and *tipping points*. Throughout, the analysis is tied directly to GCC realities such as subsidy reforms, growing solar penetration, limited storage, and evolving market rules.

Case I: Behavioral Switching and Volatile Price Regimes

In Case I, prosumers equipped with rooftop photovoltaic generation, storage, and smart-grid access alternate between consumption and supply. They consume electricity when prices are positive ($x > 0$), but when prices fall below zero, they rapidly switch to battery charging or electricity export. Centralized generators, facing high costs of ramping and shutdown, may also absorb surplus electricity at very low or even negative prices. The defining feature of this regime is the *zero-price threshold*: near this boundary, behavior is discontinuous, and small incentive changes trigger large shifts in strategies.

Expectations are anchored to household reference points such as "normal" electricity bills. Loss aversion makes prosumers disproportionately sensitive to price changes below this benchmark. As a result, they tend to hesitate just above zero—waiting for further gains—while over-reacting sharply once prices cross into negative territory by rapidly increasing demand or exports. This asymmetric response amplifies negative regimes and generates feedback loops that prolong volatility.

As the policy-sensitive parameter c_1 (representing tariffs, subsidies, or export credits) varies, the model generates multiple coexisting periodic orbits—positive, negative, and mixed. Economically, this implies that electricity markets may settle into distinct repeatable pricing patterns, with abrupt transitions ("bifurcations") caused by small policy or behavioral changes. These regime shifts are fully endogenous: no external shock is required—only the collective interaction of heuristics, expectations, and incentive design.

Case I dynamics are especially relevant for GCC systems characterized by strong midday solar peaks, weak demand-side flexibility, and limited storage capacity. Under such conditions, even modest changes to export credits, curtailment rules, or short-lived tariff adjustments can push the system into a high-volatility regime. The emergence of persistent *negative* periodic orbits highlights why prosumer compensation schemes and tariff design in the GCC must be carefully calibrated to avoid regime instability.

Case I: A Closer Technical Look

Case I provides a systematic exploration of price dynamics when both positive and negative periodic orbits are feasible. We fix $\theta_1 = \theta_2 = 0.1$, $\omega = 1$, $a = 8$, and $c_2 = 1$. Under these conditions, a negative periodic orbit necessarily exists because $c_2 = 1$ exceeds the threshold $c^* = 8/\sqrt{101} \approx 0.7960$. A positive periodic orbit exists only when $c_1 > c^\star$, opening the possibility of regime coexistence.

Figure 11.1 provides the global bifurcation map of Case I. As c_1 decreases from high values, the system transitions through regimes with two, three, five, four, three, and finally one periodic solution. Each change corresponds to a bifurcation on the zero-price manifold, where behavioral switching at the threshold reorganizes the global dynamics.

High c_1: coexistence of positive and negative orbits. For $c_1 = 10$ and $c_1 = 7$, the market supports both positive and negative periodic solutions. The separatrices (red and black trajectories) cleanly divide the basins of attraction. Long-run behavior is dominated by the positive orbit,

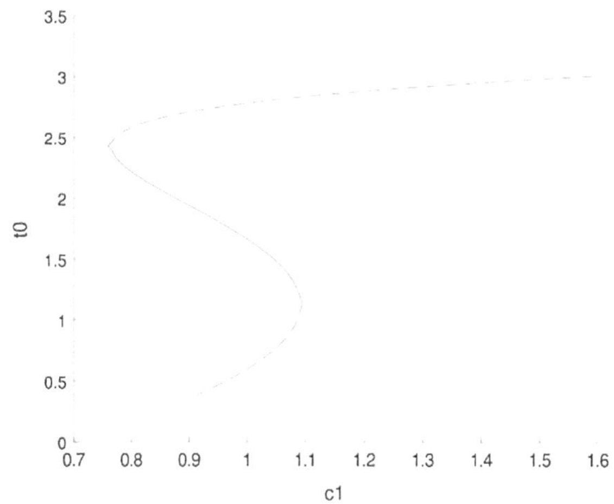

Fig. 11.1 Bifurcation diagram for Case I. The vertical axis shows electricity price deviation x, with positive values indicating surplus-price regimes and negative values deficit-price regimes. As the export-credit parameter c_1 varies, positive, negative, and mixed periodic orbits emerge and disappear through bifurcations on the zero-price threshold

although temporary sign reversals may occur due to transient behavioral switching.

Intermediate c_1: emergence of mixed orbits. At $c_1 = 5$ and $c_1 = 3$, unstable mixed orbits appear and the basin geometry becomes more intricate. Trajectories may now alternate between positive and negative states before converging. Economically, these transients correspond to hesitation above zero and overreaction below zero driven by behavioral asymmetry (Figs. 11.2, 11.3, 11.4 and 11.5).

Near-threshold c_1: multiple coexisting regimes. When $c_1 = 1.4$ and $c_1 = 0.85$, up to five periodic solutions coexist. The separatrices close on themselves, generating unstable cycles that partition the state space into intricate behavioral basins (Fig. 11.6).

Approaching the bifurcation boundary. At $c_1 = 0.77$, the positive orbit disappears, leaving only negative and mixed solutions. At $c_1 = 0.7$ and eventually $c_1 = 0.5$, only the negative periodic orbit remains stable, while separatrices continue to structure transient behavior.

Case I demonstrates the richness of endogenous regime switching generated by a single policy-sensitive parameter. The export-credit variable c_1—interpretable as tariff design or prosumer compensation—governs whether markets remain anchored in positive pricing, enter volatile coexistence, or collapse into persistent negative regimes. The geometry of the separatrices captures behavioral hesitation and abrupt switching near the zero-price threshold. From a GCC policy perspective, Case I illustrates how poorly calibrated export remuneration, weak curtailment rules, and insufficient flexibility can structurally lock markets into volatile price coexistence. Overall, Case I shows that generous export incentives combined with weak flexibility can transform negative pricing from a rare anomaly into a persistent and self-reinforcing regime (Figs. 11.7, 11.8, 11.9 and 11.10).

Case II: Anchored Dynamics without Negative Prices

In Case II, parameter values are chosen such that negative price orbits cannot arise. Formally, the parameter c_2 lies below the critical threshold required for the existence of a stable negative periodic solution. Economically, this corresponds to a market in which tariff structures, export remuneration, and dispatch rules are designed so that prices—while potentially volatile in the short run—remain strictly positive in the long-run. Occasional mixed behavior may still occur near the zero threshold,

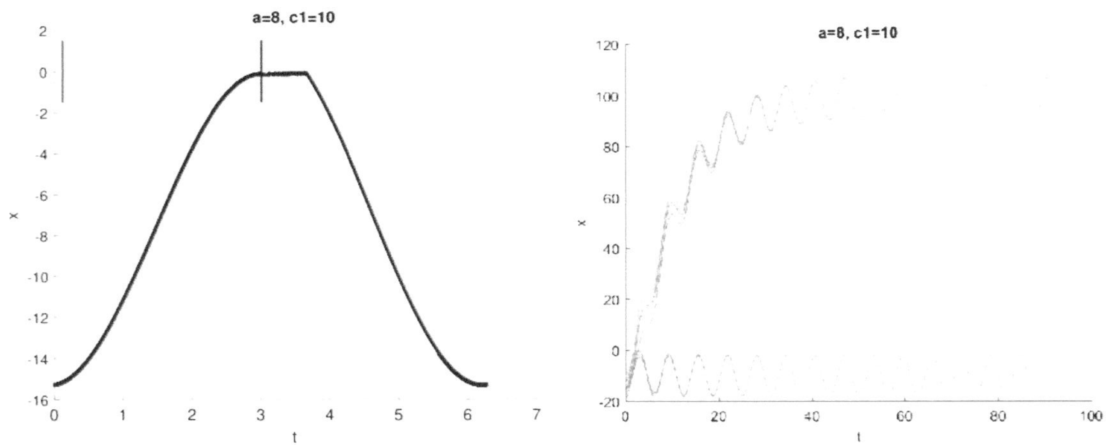

Fig. 11.2 $c_1 = 10$: stable coexistence of positive and negative periodic price regimes with clear separation of basins of attraction

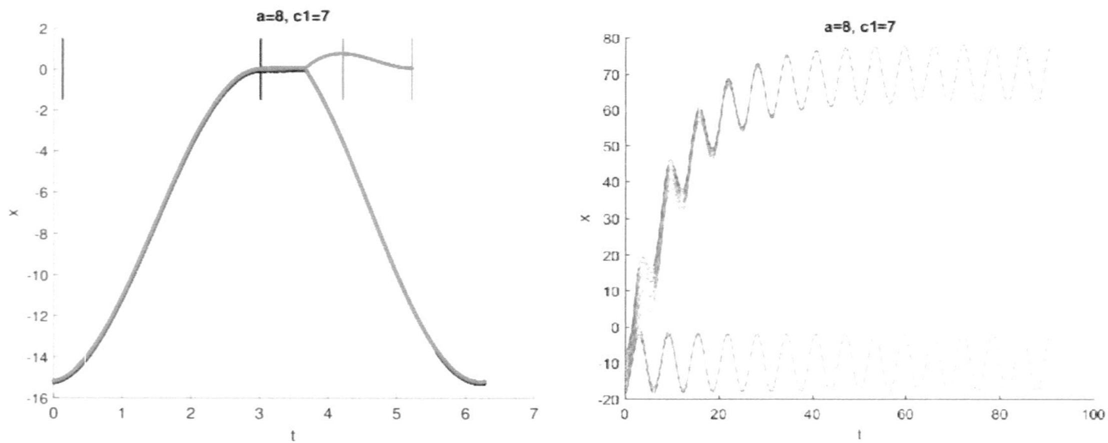

Fig. 11.3 $c_1 = 7$: coexistence persists, but folded separatrices permit temporary transitions from positive to negative price regimes

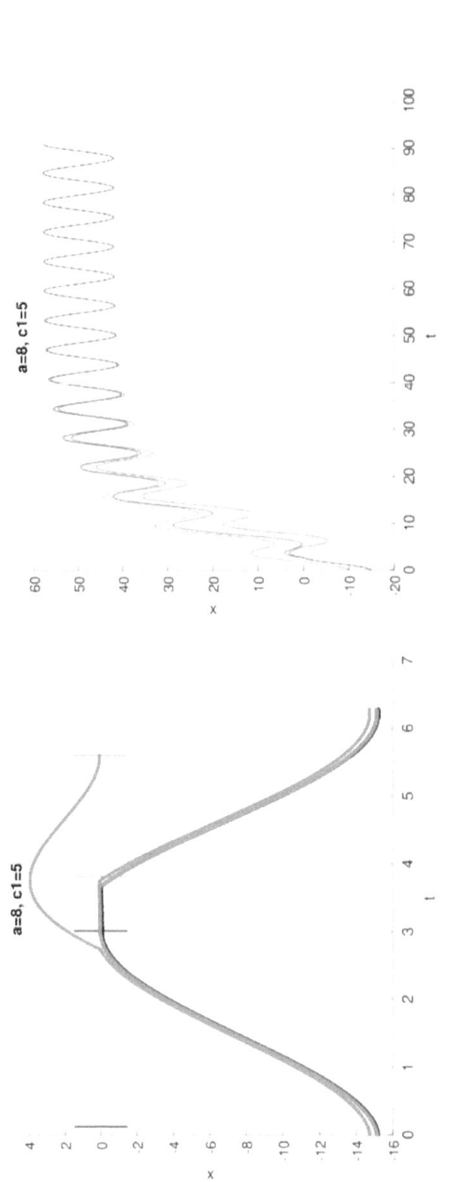

Fig. 11.4 $c_1 = 5$: unstable mixed periodic orbit generates complex short-term switching between positive and negative price regimes

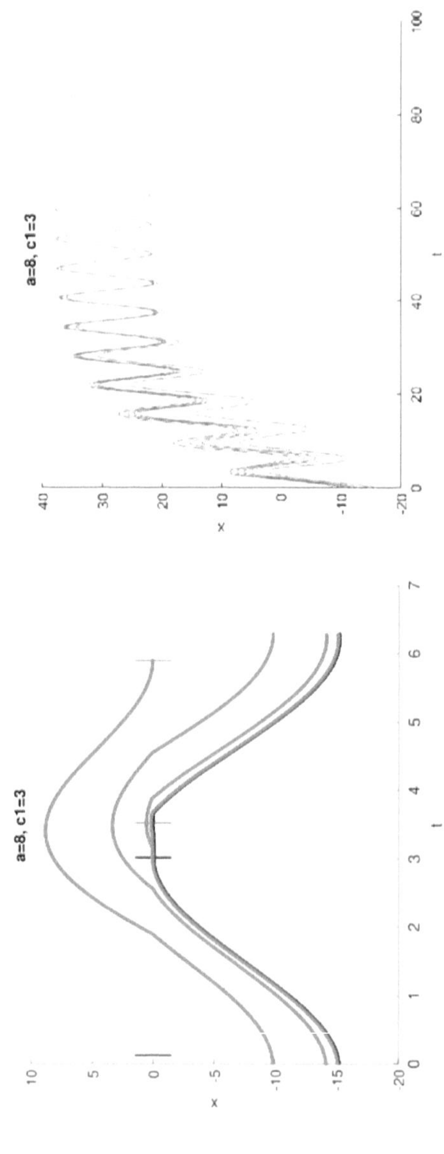

Fig. 11.5 $c_1 = 3$: intersecting separatrices create multiple mixed solutions and highly sensitive regime dependence

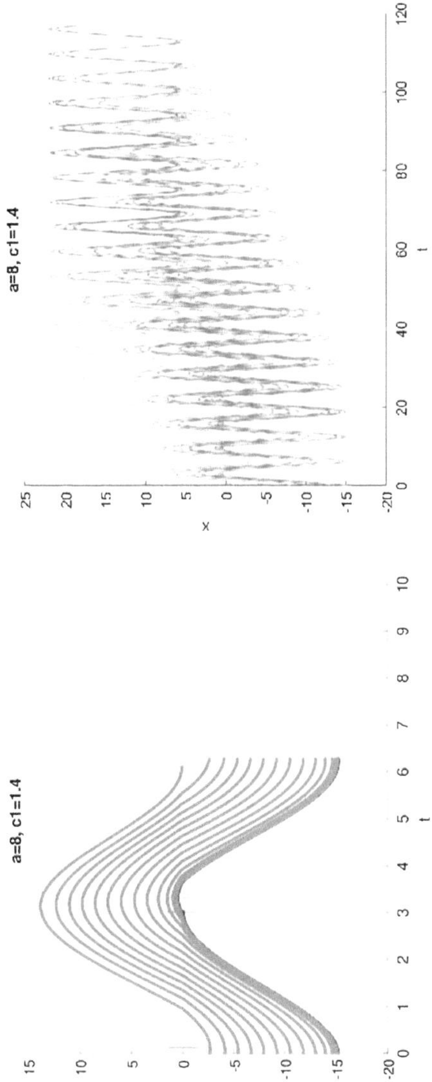

Fig. 11.6 $c_1 = 1.4$: unstable mixed orbit divides positive and negative basins into finely segmented regions

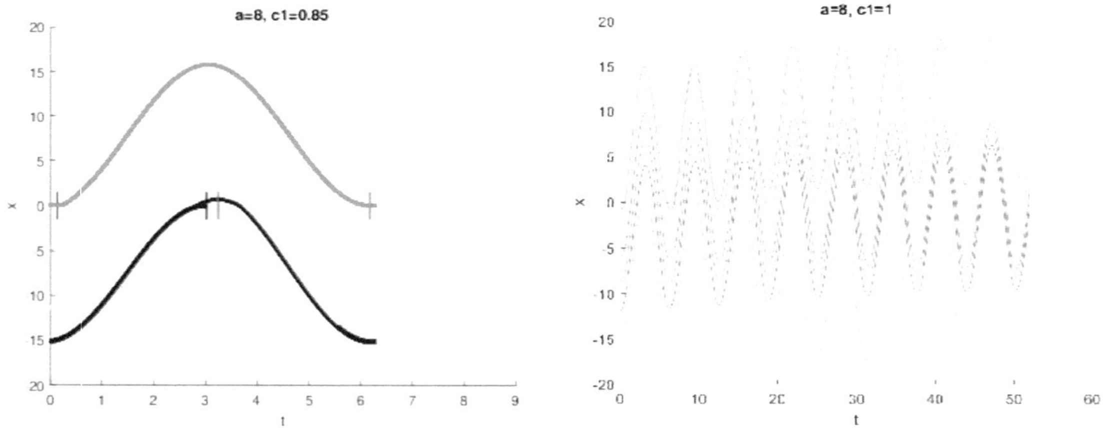

Fig. 11.7 $c_1 = 0.85$: coexistence of three stable periodic regimes (positive, negative, mixed) and one unstable mixed orbit

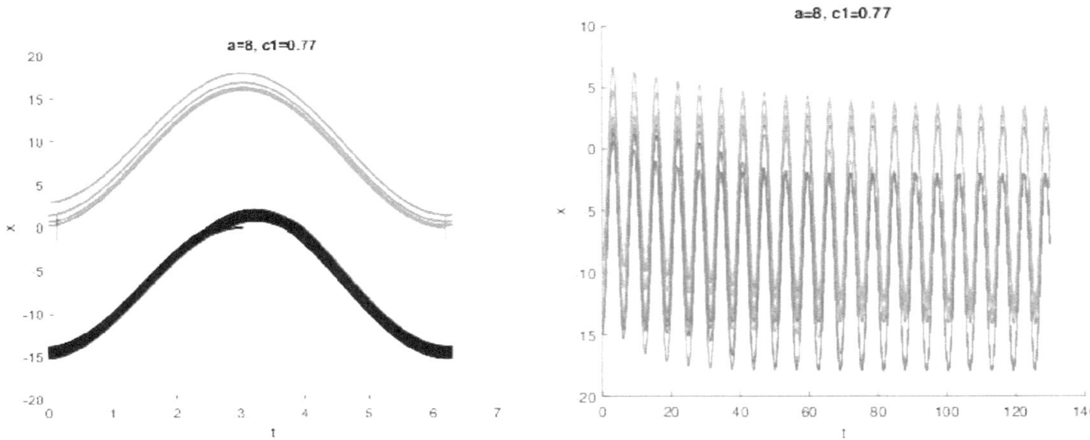

Fig. 11.8 $c_1 = 0.77$: collapse of the stable positive orbit; dominance of mixed and negative price regimes

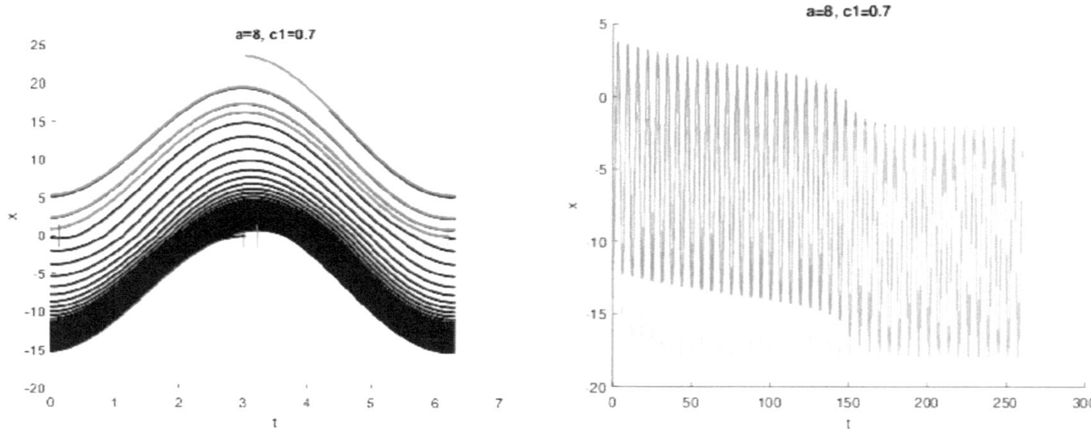

Fig. 11.9 $c_1 = 0.7$: layered separatrices with only the negative periodic attractor remaining stable

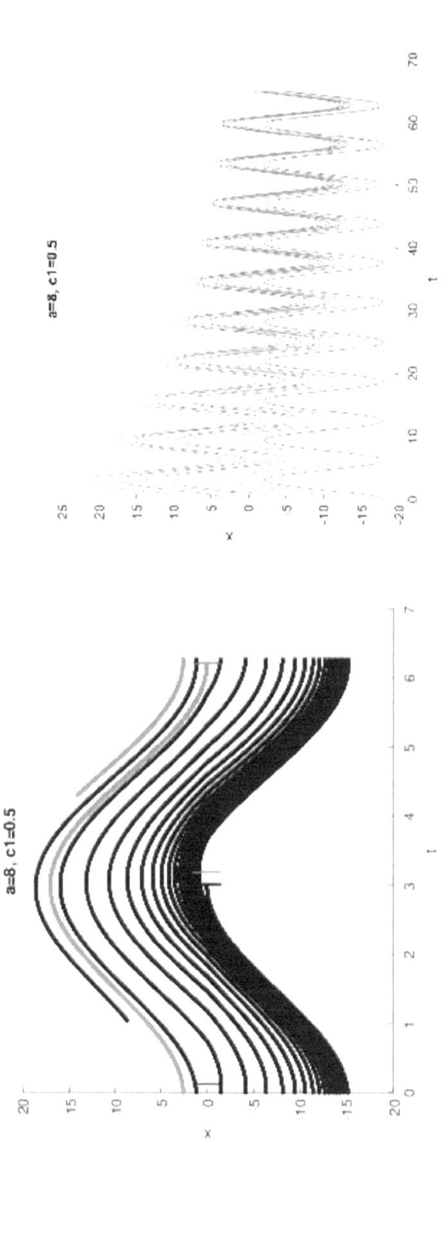

Fig. 11.10 $c_1 = 0.5$: full stabilization on the negative periodic orbit; separatrices govern only transient adjustments

but the system is structurally prevented from collapsing into persistent negative pricing.

In this environment, expectations become *anchored* around positive price levels. Prosumers no longer behave as opportunistic switchers but instead act as forward-looking optimizers who smooth bills and manage storage across longer horizons. Stable reference points dampen over-reaction and herding tendencies, as predicted by behavioral economics [26, 39]. Rather than reacting sharply to small fluctuations, agents adopt trend-following or mean-reversion heuristics that reinforce stability. Role reversals between consumption and export remain possible but are less frequent and far less disruptive, consistent with evidence that consumers in regulated or semi-regulated electricity systems adjust gradually to price signals [28, 4].

Mathematically, the system admits a *stable positive periodic orbit*. For certain values of c_1, this may coexist with a mixed orbit, but a purely negative orbit is ruled out by construction. As a result, systemic volatility is lower and regime transitions are smoother than in Case I. The long-run attractor corresponds to a behaviorally "quiet" market state: endogenous discontinuities remain present, but they no longer destabilize the overall trajectory. This mechanism formalizes earlier observations from European and U.S. power markets that calibrated export rules, storage incentives, and flexibility deployment can limit both the frequency and the depth of negative price episodes [22]. In the model, policy settings that keep incentives below the bifurcation threshold effectively suppress destabilizing regime switches.

Case II closely mirrors the reform trajectory currently pursued across much of the GCC. In Saudi Arabia and the United Arab Emirates, tariff reforms have gradually moved electricity prices toward cost-reflective levels while preserving strictly positive pricing structures to safeguard investment confidence [29, 36]. Dubai's *Shams Dubai* program and Oman's *Sahim* rooftop initiative are specifically designed to stimulate distributed solar uptake while containing volatility through regulated net-billing and interconnection standards [19]. In model terms, these frameworks restrain the export-credit parameter c_1 while simultaneously strengthening flexibility through grid access, limiting the possibility of regime entry into negative price dynamics. The analysis therefore implies that, with disciplined export remuneration, storage procurement, and transparent curtailment policies, GCC markets can sustain rapid renewable growth without triggering destabilizing price reversals. Overall, Case

II demonstrates that when export incentives are restrained and flexibility is deployed in parallel with renewable expansion, negative price regimes are structurally excluded and electricity price dynamics remain stably anchored.

Comparative Insights and GCC Policy Levers

The two cases together illustrate how prosumer behavior and discontinuous switching around the zero-price threshold can determine whether markets remain stable or drift into volatility. In statistical models such as Markov regime switching, researchers have long observed the coexistence of regimes and sudden transitions in electricity prices [9, 38, 20]. Our framework complements this work by adding behavioral microfoundations: it explains not only *that* regimes appear, but also *why* they emerge or disappear, depending on how agents interpret thresholds and incentives. On the technology side, the literature shows that the merit-order effect of renewables depresses wholesale prices as penetration grows, raising the likelihood of negative hours [22], while limited interconnection and flexibility exacerbate oversupply events [14, 5]. In the GCC, subsidies and administered tariffs historically suppressed such dynamics [2, 10], but current reforms and ambitious renewable build-out [30, 23, 27] are creating precisely the discontinuities that our model is designed to explore.

Policy levers and their modeled effects

- *Export remuneration and netting rules* (c_1, c_2). International experience shows that feed-in tariffs, net metering, and guaranteed dispatch accelerate uptake but can distort market signals if too generous [40, 34, 13]. In our framework, such policies widen the space for mixed or negative regimes by over-rewarding prosumer exports. Moving toward capped net-billing, as some GCC states are considering, narrows incentives near the zero threshold, reducing overreaction while still encouraging adoption.
- *Storage incentives and flexibility markets* (thresholds near $x = 0$). Systems with greater storage, demand response, and interconnection exhibit shorter and fewer negative price episodes [14, 5]. In model terms, these investments shrink the domain of negative or mixed orbits and anchor the system on $x > 0$. For GCC policymakers, requiring flexibility capacity alongside solar procurement

and strengthening regional trade through GCCIA interconnection are practical ways to apply this lever [32, 8].

- *Curtailment and dispatch rules* (amplitude of periodic forcing). Guaranteed dispatch without balancing flexibility amplifies swings and increases volatility [22]. Transparent curtailment with compensation, by contrast, dampens the oscillations in our model and reduces the persistence of negative regimes. This design choice is especially relevant for GCC markets introducing competitive procurement.
- *Real-time pricing and demand response* (agents' heuristics). Literature on peer-to-peer markets and digital coordination highlights how clearer, faster price signals reduce herding and overreaction [35]. In our model, such mechanisms narrow the "grazing" band around zero, making hesitation and sudden bursts less likely. For the GCC, experiments with wholesale spot platforms (e.g., Oman's market) provide the infrastructure for such signals [21], while reform strategies increasingly emphasize demand-side participation [29, 31].

If renewable capacity expands faster than flexibility, or if export credits remain too generous, markets may exhibit Case I dynamics: volatile coexistence of regimes, abrupt switches, and strong behavioral asymmetries. This is a real risk given the speed of solar deployment [24] and the incentive effects of subsidy reform [12]. By contrast, reforms that pair PV rollout with storage and demand response, move from net metering to net-billing, and leverage interconnection capacity are more likely to produce Case II dynamics: anchored positive prices, smoother adjustments, and lower volatility. In this sense, policy choices act as bifurcation parameters: poorly sequenced reforms can push markets into instability, while calibrated design can keep them on a stable path [23, 27, 30].

This analysis brings together three strands that are often treated separately: (i) empirical studies on volatility clustering and negative prices [9, 38, 20]; (ii) market design work on merit-order effects, curtailment, and incentive structures [22, 40, 34, 13]; and (iii) behavioral perspectives on prosumer decision-making and socio-digital coordination [35, 3]. By embedding these insights in a discontinuous (Filippov) framework, we provide a micro-founded way of identifying when regimes emerge, persist, or vanish, and translate those conditions into actionable governance levers for GCC electricity markets.

Implications for GCC Countries

The gap identified earlier—the absence of behavioral feedback and endogenous regime switching in conventional electricity price models—has direct resonance in the GCC. Subsidy reforms, rapid solar deployment, limited storage, and evolving market rules create precisely the threshold conditions under which prosumer heuristics can tip systems abruptly from stable to volatile regimes. In the broader literature, the merit-order effect of renewables has been shown to depress wholesale prices as penetration grows, sometimes inducing negative price episodes [22]. Policy instruments such as feed-in tariffs and guaranteed dispatch can stimulate renewable uptake but, if poorly calibrated, also risk suppressing prices or destabilizing dispatch. Similar concerns apply to net metering and export remuneration schemes, which can widen volatility if not sequenced with flexibility investments [40]. Market design therefore functions as a threshold mechanism determining whether systems converge to stability or drift into oscillation [34].

Empirical studies further show that volatility clustering is shaped by limited storage and inflexible generation [5]. In Spain, oversupply amplified by renewables and weak interconnection produced sharp price dips and increased curtailment [14]. Markov regime switching models document the coexistence of high- and low-volatility regimes in power markets but lack behavioral micro-foundations [9]. More recent evidence shows that transitions are often triggered by nonlinear dynamics at zero-price thresholds [38], with European day-ahead markets exhibiting regime persistence and sudden transitions consistent with bifurcation behavior [20].

Behavioral economics helps explain why such transitions are amplified. Prospect theory shows that agents evaluate outcomes relative to reference points, leading to asymmetric responses near thresholds [26]. Herding and overreaction further amplify volatility when expectations are weakly anchored [39]. Prosumers exhibit precisely these features: bounded rationality, reference dependence, and loss aversion drive heterogeneous responses to price signals [3].

GCC-focused research confirms the policy relevance of these mechanisms. Tariff reforms, renewable integration, and gradual liberalization are already reshaping incentives in ways that can either stabilize or destabilize pricing regimes [29]. These features make GCC markets especially exposed to the dynamics captured in our model—but also uniquely positioned to benefit from governance frameworks that explicitly manage behavioral thresholds.

From Model to Policy: Design Levers, Regimes, and Sequencing

Our framework highlights four drivers of regime behavior and their policy analogues:

- Threshold incentives near $x = 0$ (regime shifts): export remuneration / net-billing rules, curtailment compensation, and temporary price floors or collars [40, 34].
- Adjustment intensity to imbalances (speed of response): RTP granularity, imbalance charging, gate-closure timing, automated demand response triggers [5, 38].
- Amplitude of periodic forcing (solar and cooling cycles): PV build-out pacing, must-run constraints, and cooling-efficiency standards [14, 22].
- System flexibility (surplus absorption): utility-scale storage, behind-the-meter batteries, demand response, and GCCIA interconnection [32, 8].

See Table 11.1.

Anchored positivity (Case II analogue). Negative price orbits are ruled out by design through restrained export remuneration and flexibility deployed in parallel with solar. Outcomes include lower volatility, fewer role reversals, anchored expectations, and reduced risk premia [29, 36]. *Volatile coexistence (Case I analogue).* Positive, negative, and mixed regimes coexist; small design shifts trigger large swings. This arises when generous export credits and weak curtailment rules allow PV to outpace storage and demand response [22].

Key steps include: (1) diagnosing regime position using zero-crossing event studies; (2) pacing solar with storage and DR procurement; (3) tuning export remuneration via capped net-*billing* rather than full net metering [40, 34]; (4) sharpening price signals through short settlement and automated DR [38, 5]; and (5) deploying temporary guardrails and GCCIA balancing during build-out phases [32, 8]. These steps

Table 11.1 Policy levers mapped to model mechanisms and behavioral responses

Model driver	*GCC policy levers*	*Expected effect (Behavioral lens)*
Threshold at $x = 0$	Net-*billing* (caps), export credits, curtailment pay, floors/collars	Fewer regime flips; less hesitation and herding near zero
Adjustment intensity	RTP intervals, imbalance charges, gate-closure, DR automation	Narrows grazing band; smoother corrections
Forcing amplitude	PV pacing, must-run limits, cooling/EE codes	Shallower midday dips; weaker mixed/negative orbits
Flexibility	Storage auctions, BTM batteries, TOU + automation, GCCIA trades	Absorbs oversupply; anchors prices positive

BTM = Behind-the-meter; TOU = Time-of-use; EE = Energy efficiency

are consistent with evidence that policy acts as a bifurcation parameter [9, 20].

Country Applications and Monitoring: A Compact Roadmap

Since 2018, Saudi Arabia has implemented sharp electricity tariff reforms as part of fiscal consolidation and energy price rationalization, while simultaneously accelerating distributed solar adoption as households hedge against rising bills [12]. In model terms, tariff reform shifts the demand-side threshold, while emerging rooftop solar introduces export-credit effects analogous to c_1. If solar expansion is matched by storage auctions and demand response aggregation, a Case II anchored regime can be sustained. If not, abrupt regime switching becomes likely [4, 1, 29].

Dubai's *Shams Dubai* net metering framework provides a concrete example of how export-credit design shapes stability. Net metering at the retail tariff has stimulated rooftop PV but also creates the precise surplus-injection channel represented by c_1. As deployment scales, stability depends on explicit net-billing caps, interconnection limits, and storage linkage. This positions Dubai to lock in an anchored regime if flexibility is scaled in parallel [19, 36].

Oman's wholesale electricity market (WEM) is the most advanced spot-pricing system in the GCC [21]. Real-time price formation closely corresponds to the model's continuous adjustment channel θ. As renewable penetration increases, the WEM becomes the natural testbed for behavioral–discontinuous dynamics. Without commensurate storage and DR, the system risks drifting into volatile coexistence; with flexibility, it can anchor prices despite variable renewables.

Distributed generation remains nascent. Here, the model suggests prioritizing capped net-billing, time-varying export credits, and early public-sector storage (airports, campuses, hospitals) to stabilize early adoption and prevent premature negative-price regimes [8].

Four indicators are especially actionable: (i) threshold asymmetry around zero prices; (ii) zero-crossing frequency; (iii) volatility-normalized curtailment; and (iv) the flexibility adequacy ratio. Policy experiments—including export-credit ladders, automated DR defaults, and standard-offer storage contracts—can directly test how fast mixed or negative orbits contract once flexibility is deployed [22].

The comparative evidence shows that volatile pricing is not technologically predetermined but institutionally mediated. Saudi Arabia and the UAE demonstrate how sequenced reform and flexibility mandates can sustain anchored regimes, while Oman illustrates both the promise and risks of early liberalization. Kuwait, Bahrain, and Qatar underscore the importance of careful entry design. Across all cases, export credits, curtailment rules, tariffs, and storage mandates operate as bifurcation parameters governing whether GCC electricity markets converge to stability or drift into volatility.

Limitations and Directions for Future Research

This chapter develops a stylized, mechanism-based framework for understanding electricity price regime switching under behavioral and institutional discontinuities. As with any analytical model, its scope is defined by explicit assumptions and analytical boundaries that should be acknowledged.

Model Assumptions and Analytical Boundaries

First, the model is intentionally stylized and abstract. Parameters governing behavioral responses, supply–demand adjustment, and policy thresholds are not empirically calibrated but chosen to illustrate qualitative regime switching mechanisms. As a result, the model is not designed for short-term price forecasting or quantitative welfare evaluation.

Second, the framework is deterministic and does not explicitly include stochastic shocks from weather variability, fuel price uncertainty, or demand fluctuations. While periodic forcing captures renewable intermittency in a stylized manner, real-world electricity systems exhibit random disturbances that may interact with regime switching in complex ways.

Third, investment dynamics, endogenous capacity expansion, and strategic market power are not modeled. The analysis focuses on short- to medium-run price formation under given technological and regulatory conditions rather than on long-run equilibrium outcomes.

Finally, the behavioral representation captures bounded rationality and loss aversion in aggregate form but does not explicitly model heterogeneous learning, expectation formation, or network-based interactions among prosumers.

Directions for Future Research

Several avenues for future research follow directly from these limitations. A first priority is empirical calibration using high-frequency wholesale and retail price data from GCC electricity markets, particularly from reform-oriented systems such as Saudi Arabia, the UAE, and Oman. Such calibration would allow for quantitative validation of regime switching thresholds and behavioral asymmetries.

Second, the framework can be extended to stochastic Filippov systems to incorporate random renewable output fluctuations, demand shocks, and fuel price volatility. This would enable systematic analysis of how noise interacts with policy-induced thresholds and behavioral responses.

Third, integrating the discontinuous behavioral model into agent-based or market simulation platforms would allow for richer representations of heterogeneous prosumers, storage adoption, and distributed generation. This would also permit the evaluation of alternative tariff structures and export-credit regimes under realistic system constraints.

Finally, future work could embed the price dynamics framework into welfare-optimized regulatory design, allowing for the joint assessment of price stability, investment incentives, and distributional effects under different green pricing regimes.

Together, these extensions would strengthen the empirical grounding and policy operationality of the behavioral–discontinuous framework developed in this chapter.

Conclusion

This chapter has argued that electricity price dynamics in renewable-integrated systems cannot be adequately understood through classical smooth models that assume rational agents and stable equilibria. By introducing a Filippov-type framework enriched with behavioral insights, we have shown how prosumers, guided by bounded rationality, reference dependence, and loss aversion, contribute to discontinuous switching around the zero-price threshold. The resulting dynamics are better described as regime-dependent trajectories—positive, negative, or mixed—rather than as convergence toward a single equilibrium.

Two stylized cases illustrate the possibilities. In Case I, the coexistence of positive, negative, and mixed regimes produces volatility, sudden transitions, and heightened uncertainty. In Case II, anchored dynamics exclude persistent negative prices, stabilizing expectations and reducing systemic risk. The distinction between these regimes highlights a central point: volatility in green electricity prices is not an inevitable by-product of renewable growth, but a design-dependent outcome shaped by behavioral thresholds and institutional choices.

Applied to the GCC context, the model offers new perspectives on ongoing debates about subsidy reform, renewable expansion, and market liberalization. Earlier work has shown that administered tariffs and fossil-based generation historically muted price signals in the region [7, 28], while more recent studies document how fiscal pressures and climate goals are driving reform and diversification [1, 36, 30]. Our framework adds that these reforms act as *bifurcation parameters*: export remuneration schemes, curtailment rules, and tariff adjustments determine whether markets stabilize in anchored regimes (Case II) or drift into volatile coexistence (Case I). Research on the GCC Interconnection Authority further emphasizes the stabilizing role of regional integration [8, 32], which in our model corresponds to shrinking the domain of negative or mixed trajectories.

The governance implications are therefore clear. Policymakers in the GCC face a dual challenge: advancing ambitious renewable targets while safeguarding system stability. Our analysis suggests that this balance can be achieved if reforms are sequenced carefully, incentives are calibrated to avoid destabilizing thresholds, and flexibility is scaled in lockstep with solar expansion. Policy experiments such as net-billing pilots [19], automated demand response trials [3], and storage standard-offer programs [22] provide low-regret pathways to test and refine interventions. As [29] stresses, reforms in the region require both technical adaptation and institutional innovation, and our model offers a lens for identifying the tipping points where governance design makes the difference between volatility and stability.

More broadly, the chapter contributes to the literature by bridging discontinuous dynamical systems with behavioral economics and energy policy. It extends statistical accounts of negative prices and volatility clustering [9, 38, 20] by offering a behavioral micro-foundation for regime switching, and it situates these insights in the applied setting of GCC electricity reforms.

Looking forward, further research should calibrate the model with empirical data from GCC markets as reforms deepen, explore stochastic extensions to capture shocks, and test predictive power in regulatory sandboxes. Embedding behavioral-dynamical insights into governance processes can help ensure that the Gulf's energy transition is not only ambitious but also stable, efficient, and resilient.

In conclusion, the dynamics of green electricity prices are shaped as much by institutions and behavior as by technology. By recognizing policy as a bifurcation lever, and by treating prosumers not as anomalies but as central actors, GCC countries can design electricity markets that turn volatility into stability, and uncertainty into a managed pathway toward sustainable growth.

References

1. Al-Asaad, H. K. (2009). Electricity power sector reform in the GCC region. *The Electricity Journal*, 22(9), 58–64. https://doi.org/10.1016/j.tej.2009.08.013.
2. Al-Faris, A. R. F. (2002). The demand for electricity in the GCC countries. *Energy Policy*, 30(2), 117–124.
3. Almeida, C., Madaleno, M., & Robaina, M. (2021). Psychological barriers in the electric market: Study applied to the Nord Pool market. *Review of Behavioral Finance*, 13(5), 584–609. https://doi.org/10.1108/RBF-05-2020-0099.
4. Al-Sheikh, H., & Alghamdi, A. (2021). Household electricity demand and

the impact of tariff reform in Saudi Arabia. *Energy Economics*, 95, 105127.
5. Bushnell, J., & Novan, K. (2017). Review of the economics literature on US electricity re-structuring. *Unpublished manuscript*, Department of Economics, University of California at Davis, Davis, CA.
6. Carbon Credits. (2025). Gulf countries bet big: $100B for renewables to slash emissions by 20%. Available at: https://carboncredits.com/gulf-countries-bet-big-100b-for-renewables-to-slash-emissions-by-20/.
7. El-Katiri, L. (2014). *A Roadmap for Renewable Energy in the Middle East and North Africa*. Oxford Institute for Energy Studies, MESP paper MEP 6. https://doi.org/10.26889/9781907555909.
8. El-Katiri, L. (2011). Interlinking the Arab Gulf: Opportunities and challenges of GCC electricity market cooperation. *Oxford Institute for Energy Studies*, OIES Paper EL-10. https://doi.org/10.26889/9781907555299.
9. Fanone, E., Gamba, A., & Prokopczuk, M. (2013). The case of negative day-ahead electricity prices. *Energy Economics*, 35, 22–34. https://doi.org/10.1016/j.eneco.2011.12.006.
10. Fattouh, B., & El-Katiri, L. (2012). Energy subsidies in the Middle East and North Africa. *Energy Strategy Reviews*, 2(1), 108–115.
11. Filippov, A. F. (1988). *Differential Equations with Discontinuous Righthand Sides*. Mathematics and Its Applications (Soviet Series). Dordrecht: Kluwer Academic Publishers.
12. Financial Times. (2025). Saudi businesses turn to solar power as kingdom cuts energy subsidies. Available at: https://www.ft.com/content/f6dc634b-6ad8-4011-999a-a3d966542446.
13. Ganhammar, K. (2019). The effect of regulatory uncertainty in green certificate markets: Evidence from the Swedish–Norwegian market. *Energy Policy*, 158, 112583. https://doi.org/10.1016/j.enpol.2021.112583.
14. Gelabert, L., Labandeira, X., & Linares, P. (2011). An ex-post analysis of the effect of renewables and cogeneration on Spanish electricity prices. *Energy Economics*, 33, S59–S65. https://doi.org/10.1016/j.eneco.2011.07.027.
15. Giesl, P. (2007). On the determination of the basin of attraction of a periodic orbit in two-dimensional systems. *Journal of Mathematical Analysis and Applications*, 335(1), 461–479. https://doi.org/10.1016/j.jmaa.2007.01.069.
16. Giesl, P. (2008). Construction of a local and global Lyapunov function using radial basis functions. *IMA Journal of Applied Mathematics*, 73(5), 782–802.
17. Giesl, P. (2009). On the determination of the basin of attraction of periodic orbits in three- and higher-dimensional systems. *Journal of Mathematical Analysis and Applications*, 354(2), 606–618. https://doi.org/10.1016/j.jmaa.2009.01.027.

18. Giesl, P. (2019). Computation of a contraction metric for a periodic orbit using meshfree collocation. *SIAM Journal on Applied Dynamical Systems*, 18(3), 1536–1564. https://doi.org/10.1137/18M1220182.
19. Griffiths, S., & Mills, R. (2019). Potential of rooftop solar photovoltaics in the energy system evolution of the United Arab Emirates. *Energy Strategy Reviews*, 9, 1–7. https://doi.org/10.1016/j.esr.2015.11.001.
20. Halbru¨gge, S., Schott, P. A., & Weibelzahl, M. (2023). Negative electricity prices as a signal for lacking flexibility? On the effects of demand flexibility on electricity prices. *International Journal of Energy Sector Management*. https://doi.org/10.1108/IJESM-12-2021-0005.
21. Hasan, S., Al-Aqeel, T., Al-Badi, A., Bhatt, Y., & Al-Badi, M. (2019). Oman electricity sector: Features, challenges and opportunities for market integration. *King Abdullah Petroleum Studies and Research Center*, pp. 1–32.
22. Hirth, L. (2013). The market value of variable renewables: The effect of solar and wind power variability on their relative price. *Energy Economics*, 38, 218–236.
23. International Monetary Fund. (2015). Energy price reforms in the GCC—What can be learned from international experience? *IMF Policy Paper*, November 2015. Available at: https://www.imf.org/external/np/pp/eng/2015/111015b.pdf.
24. International Renewable Energy Agency (IRENA). (2023). Renewable energy markets: GCC 2023. *IRENA Market Report*. Available at: https://www.irena.org/Publications/2023/Dec/Renewable-energy-market-analysis-GCC.
25. Ito^, F. (1979). A Filippov solution of a system of differential equations with discontinuous right-hand side. *Economics Letters*, 4, 349–354.
26. Kahneman, D., & Tversky, A. (1979). Prospect theory: An analysis of decision under risk. *Econometrica*, 47(2), 263–291.
27. King Abdullah Petroleum Studies and Research Center (KAPSARC). (2018). Electricity market integration in the GCC and MENA: Imperatives and challenges. *KAPSARC Discussion Paper*. Available at: https://www.kapsarc.org/our-offerings/publications/electricity-market-integration-in-the-gcc-and-mena-imperatives-and-challenges.
28. Krane, J. (2019). *Energy governance in Saudi Arabia: An assessment of the kingdom's resources, policies, and climate approach*. Unpublished report.
29. Krane, J., & Monaldi, F. (2021). Oil prices, political instability, and energy subsidy reform in MENA oil exporters. *Center for Energy Studies, Baker Institute for Public Policy, Rice University*.
30. Krane, J. (2024). Fuel and electricity pricing and subsidies in the GCC states. *Asian Energy Studies*, 10(2), 123–145.
31. Luciani, G. (2019). Framing the economic sustainability of oil economies. In G. Luciani & T. Moerenhout (eds.), *When can oil economies be deemed*

sustainable? The Political Economy of the Middle East. Singapore: Palgrave Macmillan. https://doi.org/10.1007/978-981-15-5728-6_2.
32. Mollet, P., Al-Mubarak, I., Efird, B., Al Muhanna, S., & Al-Ubaydli, O. (2018). *Assessment of the political feasibility of developing a GCC power market*. KAP-SARC. Available at: https://www.kapsarc.org/wp-content/uploads/2018/10/KS-2018-DP39-Assessment-of-the-Political-Feasibility-of-Developing-a-GCC-Power-Mapdf.
33. Nicolosi, M. (2010). Wind power integration and power system flexibility – An empirical analysis of extreme events in Germany under the new negative price regime. *Energy Policy*, 38(11), 7257–7268.
34. Pahle, M., Schill, W.-P., Gambardella, C., & Tietjen, O. (2016). Renewable energy support, negative prices, and real-time pricing. *The Energy Journal*, 37(01), 147–169. https://doi.org/10.5547/01956574.37.SI3.MPAH.
35. Parag, Y., & Sovacool, B. K. (2016). The rise of the prosumer: How grid-connected individuals are transforming the electricity system. *Nature Energy*, 1(4), 1–4. https://doi.org/10.1038/nenergy.2016.32.
36. Sanfilippo, A., Vermeersch, M., & Bermudez Benito, V. (2024). Energy transition strategies in the Gulf Cooperation Council countries. *Energy Strategy Reviews*, 55, 101512. https://doi.org/10.1016/j.esr.2024.101512.
37. Schneider, S. (2011). Power spot price models with negative prices. *The Journal of Energy Markets*, 4(4), 77–102. https://doi.org/10.21314/JEM.2011.079.
38. Seel, J., Millstein, D., Mills, A., Bolinger, M., & Wiser, R. (2021). Plentiful electricity turns wholesale prices negative. *Applied Energy*, 298, 100073. https://doi.org/10.1016/j.adapen.2021.100073.
39. Shiller, R. J. (2003). *Irrational Exuberance*. Princeton: Princeton University Press.
40. Steffen, B. (2020). Estimating the cost of capital for renewable energy projects. *Energy Economics*, 88, 104783. https://doi.org/10.1016/j.eneco.2020.104783.
41. Stiefenhofer, P., & Giesl, P. (2019). A global stability theory of nonsmooth periodic or-bits: Example I. *Applied Mathematical Sciences*, 13(11), 511–520. https://doi.org/10.12988/ams.2019.9463.
42. Stiefenhofer, P., & Giesl, P. (2019). A local stability theory of nonsmooth periodic orbits: Example II. *Applied Mathematical Sciences*, 13(11).
43. Stiefenhofer, P., & Giesl, P. (2019). Switching regimes in economics: The contraction mapping and the ω-limit set. *Applied Mathematics*, 10(7).
44. Stiefenhofer, P., & Giesl, P. (2019). Exponentially asymptotically stability of nonsmooth periodic orbits: The contraction mapping and the ω-limit set. *Nonlinear Analysis and Differential Equations*.

45. Stiefenhofer, P., & Giesl, P. (2019). Economic periodic orbits: A theory of exponential asymptotic stability. *Nonlinear Analysis and Differential Equations*, 7(1), 9–16.
46. Stiefenhofer, P. (2020). Economic stability of non-smooth periodic orbits in the plane: Omega limit sets Part I. *Nonlinear Analysis and Differential Equations*, 8(1), 41–52. https://doi.org/10.12988/nade.2020.91121.
47. Stiefenhofer, P. (2020). Economic stability of non-smooth periodic orbits in the plane: Omega limit sets Part II. *Nonlinear Analysis and Differential Equations*, 8(1), 53–65. https://doi.org/10.12988/nade.2020.91122.

CHAPTER 12

The Future of Gulf Finance: Converging Signals from Fintech and Green Markets

Mehmet Sahiner

Introduction

The Gulf Cooperation Council (GCC) countries are undergoing a profound structural transformation of their financial systems. As part of broader economic diversification strategies, the region is embracing two interlinked trajectories: the institutionalisation of green finance and the proliferation of financial technology (fintech). These dual agendas are no longer merely parallel developments; they are increasingly converging in policy intent, market behaviour, and institutional design. This paper examines the nature of that convergence, focusing on how digital finance infrastructure is shaping the evolution of green finance, and vice versa, in GCC economies.

M. Sahiner (✉)
School of Business, University of Dundee, Dundee, UK
e-mail: msahiner001@dundee.ac.uk

Faculty of Economics and Administrative Science, University of Yalova, Yalova, Turkey

K. Tsanis et al. (eds.), *Digital Finance and Transformation in the Gulf*,
https://doi.org/10.1007/978-981-92-1588-1_12

Each member state has launched long-term strategic frameworks, such as Saudi Arabia's Vision 2030, the UAE's Vision 2050, and Oman's Vision 2040, that prioritise environmental sustainability and technological innovation as pillars of post-oil economic resilience. These policy roadmaps place financial market transformation at the core of national reform agendas. At the same time, GCC countries are responding to global trends in climate finance and digital disruption, increasingly positioning themselves as laboratories for techno-economic experimentation.

Green finance, broadly defined as the mobilisation of capital for projects with measurable environmental benefits, has experienced rapid acceleration in the region. By mid-2024, cumulative green bond and sukuk issuance exceeded $35 billion (PwC, 2024), with sovereign wealth funds and state-linked entities, such as Saudi Arabia's Public Investment Fund (PIF), Masdar, and DEWA, playing pivotal roles in large-scale climate-aligned investments (PIF, 2023). These initiatives reflect both reputational and structural imperatives: to meet net-zero targets, attract ESG-conscious capital, and construct resilient infrastructure amid rising climate risks (Flammer, 2021). Parallel to this green shift, the fintech landscape in the GCC has witnessed a surge in regulatory support, investment inflows, and market uptake. Regulatory sandboxes have been established across all six countries, with Bahrain (2017) and the UAE (via ADGM and DIFC) leading initial experimentation (Khan et al., 2023). Saudi Arabia's fintech sector has expanded from a dozen firms in 2018 to over 200 in 2023, fuelled by government-backed initiatives such as Fintech Saudi (SAMA, 2023). Fintech in the GCC now spans digital payments, wealthtech, open banking, distributed ledger systems, and AI-driven compliance tools (Yusoff et al., 2025; Schueffel, 2016; Thakor, 2020; Liu et al., 2024).

These two movements, toward green and toward digital, have been mainly analysed in isolation. The literature on fintech adoption has focused on diffusion dynamics, regulatory environments, and financial inclusion (Musleh Alsartawi, 2024; Hornuf & Schwienbacher, 2018; Rau, 2020). Research on sustainable finance has emphasised capital allocation, ESG disclosures, and institutional commitment to climate goals (Al-Kubaisi & Abu Khalaf, 2025; Flammer, 2021). Yet the growing academic consensus suggests that fintech is not merely a parallel track but an enabling infrastructure for the next generation of sustainable finance (Siddik et al., 2023; Aysan et al., 2023).

Several studies suggest that digital technologies have the potential to enhance transparency, reduce transaction costs, and expand participation in ESG markets. Blockchain systems provide tamper-proof traceability of green bond proceeds (Reyes & Scholz, 2019; Chen et al., 2023; Malamas et al., 2024), thereby mitigating the risk of greenwashing, a key concern for institutional investors. AI and big data tools are improving the granularity and frequency of ESG performance reporting (Berg et al., 2020; Krueger et al., 2020; Alshahmy & Sahiner, 2024). Crowdfunding platforms and tokenised green assets are democratising access to sustainable investment opportunities (Carè et al., 2025), allowing smaller investors and communities to participate in transition finance. Fintech thus becomes a structural enabler of ESG ambition, particularly in contexts where traditional financial intermediaries have limited coverage or where governance systems prioritise real-time monitoring and cross-border capital flows. In this sense, the convergence of green and digital finance may not be incidental, but systemic: it reflects a reordering of financial priorities and mechanisms in response to both domestic transformation goals and global market pressures.

While this hypothesis has been theorised in the European and East Asian contexts, it remains underexplored in the Gulf region. The GCC's institutional architecture presents unique features that mediate the digital–green interaction: strong state presence in the financial sector, nascent ESG standardisation, varying levels of Sharia-compliant finance integration, and differentiated fintech maturity across member states (Beck et al., 2023; Zetzsche et al., 2020; Aysan et al., 2023). These dynamics make the GCC a compelling setting for studying convergence under conditions of top-down policy coordination and fast-moving technological adoption.

Empirically, however, there is limited evidence on whether this convergence is occurring, and if so, how: Do fintech innovations shape market-level volatility and systemic risk in the same way as conventional macro drivers like oil? Are clean energy indices and fintech benchmarks emerging as new transmission hubs in regional financial networks? Do national green finance strategies explicitly integrate digital tools into their regulatory or operational logic?

To answer these questions, this paper employs a mixed-methods design that combines financial econometrics with computational text analysis. First, we estimate a time-varying parameter vector autoregression (TVP-VAR) model to analyse the dynamic connectedness between 13 variables representing fintech indices (e.g., blockchain, digital finance), green finance proxies (e.g., clean energy), commodity benchmarks (e.g., crude oil, natural gas), and GCC equity markets. This model captures evolving spillover relationships and identifies how the role of each variable as a transmitter or absorber of shocks changes over time. The connectedness framework builds on prior work that examines volatility transmission across asset classes, including cryptocurrencies, energy markets, and ESG-linked securities (Gong et al., 2021).

Second, we complement this quantitative analysis with Latent Dirichlet Allocation (LDA) topic modelling of sustainable finance frameworks issued by GCC governments and institutions. This allows us to inductively identify recurring themes, such as regulatory ambition, transparency, climate mitigation, or digital infrastructure, and assess how prominently fintech-related concepts are embedded in official sustainability narratives. Topic modelling enables systematic cross-country comparison and reveals latent structure in the discursive construction of green finance.

By triangulating market behaviour with policy discourse, we contribute to three literatures. First, we extend the financial connectedness literature by demonstrating that fintech and green indices are not peripheral but increasingly central to volatility dynamics in the Gulf. Second, we offer novel evidence that sustainable finance in the region is being framed in ways that explicitly or implicitly rely on digital enablers, highlighting a discursive convergence that mirrors market trends. Third, we contextualise these developments within the institutional environment of the GCC, providing insights into how state-led development strategies are reshaping financial systems through both digital and sustainability lenses.

Conceptually, this paper contributes to the theory of financial transformation under conditions of institutional convergence. It suggests that in emerging financial systems, convergence is not merely a technological inevitability but a strategic choice shaped by governance models, policy design, and market signalling. Fintech becomes not just a tool for financial inclusion or efficiency, but a structural element in the construction of future-ready, sustainable finance regimes.

This study follows a mixed-methods framework grounded in comparative institutional economics and policy analysis. It combines quantitative financial econometrics with textual policy analysis to trace how institutional structures and policy narratives interact with market-level dynamics. This approach enables a dual understanding, capturing both systemic financial behaviour and the institutional logic that shapes the convergence of fintech and green finance.

The remainder of the paper proceeds as follows. Section "Methodology" presents the empirical methodology, including the TVP-VAR model and the LDA-based topic modelling approach. Section "Data Description" describes the dataset and variable construction. Section "Empirical Results" presents the empirical findings. Section "Conclusion" concludes with implications for financial governance, regulatory coordination, and future research on digital–green convergence in emerging markets.

Methodology

Empirical Methodology

To examine the evolving linkages between fintech innovation, green finance, commodity markets, and regional equities in the Gulf Cooperation Council (GCC), we employ a Time-Varying Parameter Vector Autoregression (TVP-VAR) model. This approach is well-suited to analysing dynamic systems, particularly where structural changes and nonlinear dependencies are expected. Compared to the traditional connectedness framework of Diebold and Yilmaz (2012), the TVP-VAR model offers several advantages, including the elimination of arbitrary rolling-window selection, minimisation of information loss, and greater robustness to outliers and volatility clustering (Koop & Korobilis, 2014; Antonakakis et al., 2020).

Analytically, the study is grounded in an institutional political-economy perspective, operationalised through a "Regulatory–Technology Interface" model. This framework views the financial system as a co-evolving interaction between regulatory institutions, technological innovation, and market behaviour. The institutional dimension captures how state-led governance structures, such as Vision 2030 programmes and national green finance frameworks, shape financial incentives and risk distribution. The technological dimension reflects how the adoption of fintech and digital infrastructure alters systemic transmission mechanisms.

The mixed-methods design, combining the TVP-VAR model with textual topic modelling, directly reflects this analytical stance. The econometric analysis captures the dynamic market responses within the regulatory–technology interface, while the textual analysis uncovers how institutional narratives and policy discourses legitimise these structural shifts. Together, these methods form a coherent framework that links systemic market behaviour to institutional evolution, consistent with comparative institutional economics reasoning.

The model estimates a multivariate VAR with time-varying coefficients and covariances using a Bayesian forgetting-factor algorithm. This allows the parameter estimates to update recursively, assigning more weight to recent observations and enabling the model to adapt to new regimes or events without pre-specifying structural breaks.

The baseline specification is a first-order TVP-VAR model expressed as:

$$y_t = A_t y_{t\in-1} +_{t,t} \epsilon \sim N(0, \Sigma_t), \tag{12.1}$$

$$vec(A_t) = vec(A_{t-1}) + v_t, v_t \sim N(0, R_t), \tag{12.2}$$

where y_t is a vector of $N \times 1$ endogenous variables at time t, A_t is the time-varying coefficient matrix, and ϵ_t and v_t are innovations to the residuals and state dynamics, each with time-varying covariance matrices Σ_t and R_t, respectively. The model is estimated with a Minnesota prior, and lag order is determined using the Bayesian Information Criterion (BIC) on a constant-parameter VAR. A single lag was found sufficient for removing autocorrelation in the residuals, consistent with daily data.

To evaluate systemic connectedness, we derive a Time-Varying Vector Moving Average (TVP-VMA) representation:

$$y_t = \sum_{j=0}^{\infty} \psi_{j,t} \epsilon_{t-j}, \tag{12.3}$$

where $\psi_{j,t}$ represents a time-dependent matrix of dimension $N \times N$ capturing the dynamic moving average parameters. The Generalised Forecast Error Variance Decomposition (GFEVD) is then computed at each point in time and at a 10-day forecast horizon:

$$\theta_{ij}(H) = \frac{(\Sigma_t)_{jj}^{-1} \sum_{h=0}^{H} \left((\psi_h \Sigma_t)_{ij} \right)^2}{\sum_{h=0}^{H} \left(\psi_h \Sigma_t \psi_h' \right)_{ii}}, \tag{12.4}$$

where $\theta_{ij}(H)$ quantifies the contribution of shocks originating from variable j to the forecast error variance of variable i over a horizon of H steps ahead. To ensure comparability, these variance shares are normalised:

$$\tilde{\theta}_{ij}(H) = \frac{\theta_{ij}(H)}{\sum_{k=1}^{N} \theta_{ik}(H)} \tag{12.5}$$

such that the total of all elements sums to N, thereby maintaining consistency within the variance decomposition framework. From the GFEVD, we compute directional connectedness measures for each variable j:

$$\begin{aligned} C_{i \to j}(H) &= \sum_{j \neq i} \tilde{\theta}_{ji}(H), \\ C_{j \to i}(H) &= \sum_{j \neq i} \tilde{\theta}_{ij}(H). \end{aligned} \tag{12.6}$$

nd the net directional connectedness:

$$C_i(H) = C_{i \to j}(H) - C_{j \to i}(H), \tag{12.7}$$

In this context, a positive $C_i(H)$ implies the variable contributes more to the volatility of others than it receives, while a negative value suggests the opposite. Finally, the Total Connectedness Index (TCI), capturing the share of system-wide forecast error variance arising from cross-variable shocks, is defined as:

$$TCI_t(H) = \frac{N}{N-1} \sum_{i=1}^{N} C_{i \to j}(H) = \frac{N}{N-1} \sum_{i=1}^{N} C_{j \to i}(H). \tag{12.8}$$

The TCI ranges from 0 to 100%, with higher values indicating stronger cross-market integration and more intense spillover effects.

For visualisation, we construct spillover network graphs, where each node represents a market or index, and directed edges are weighted by the intensity of connectedness (as measured by normalised FEVD values).

Thicker arrows denote stronger transmission. We also track the temporal evolution of the TCI, identifying periods of heightened integration corresponding to geopolitical, financial, or technological shocks.

The TVP-VAR model is implemented in Python, using Bayesian VAR libraries with a discounted forgetting factor for recursive estimation. Diagnostic checks include the Jarque–Bera test for normality, ERS test for unit roots, Ljung-Box Q-tests for serial correlation, and ARCH tests on squared residuals to identify conditional heteroskedasticity. These tests guide any necessary transformations and ensure the suitability of the return series for VAR estimation.

Lastly, we complement the dynamic connectedness analysis with a thematic content analysis of green finance policy frameworks across the GCC. This mixed-methods approach enables us to interpret quantitative results in light of ongoing regulatory developments, fintech innovation diffusion, and regional sustainability initiatives.

Topic Modelling of Policy Narratives

To examine how green finance frameworks across the GCC reflect themes related to financial technology, regulatory ambition, and sustainability, we apply Latent Dirichlet Allocation (LDA), an unsupervised probabilistic topic modelling technique. LDA identifies latent semantic structures within a corpus by modelling each document as a mixture of topics, and each topic as a distribution over words (Blei et al., 2003). This allows for inductive discovery of recurrent themes across diverse national frameworks without requiring prior labels.

The corpus comprises sustainable finance documents from all six GCC countries, including sovereign green bond frameworks, ESG strategy reports, and regulatory guidance issued between 2018 and 2024. Prior to modelling, all documents were pre-processed using standard natural language processing (NLP) techniques: punctuation and stop words were removed, tokens were lowercased, and only alphabetic words were retained. We further filtered the vocabulary using English dictionary validation to exclude spurious or non-semantic terms, improving topic interpretability.

The model was implemented in Python using the gensim library. The number of topics (K) was selected based on a trade-off between coherence scores and conceptual distinctiveness; a five-topic solution was retained.

We used symmetric Dirichlet priors for both document-topic and word-topic distributions. For each topic, the most probable terms were extracted and qualitatively labelled based on thematic coherence (e.g., "Framework Credibility," "Climate Mitigation," "ESG Governance").

This analysis enables a systematic comparison across countries, highlighting differences in how fintech, regulation, and sustainability are integrated into national green finance discourse. The topic modelling results serve as a qualitative complement to our empirical connectedness analysis, providing interpretive context on how institutional narratives may align with observed market dynamics.

Data Description

This study draws on a novel dataset composed of high-frequency financial indicators, sector-specific indices, and policy documents to investigate the evolving interdependencies between fintech, green finance, and traditional economic drivers in the Gulf Cooperation Council (GCC) region. The empirical analysis is based on daily data spanning the period from June 8, 2018, to September 13, 2024. To account for structural shifts associated with the COVID-19 shock, the sample is divided into two conceptually distinct phases. The first phase (*Period 1*) spans the pre-COVID and COVID periods, from June 8, 2018, to January 1, 2021, comprising 135 daily observations. The second phase (*Period 2*) represents the post-COVID period, from January 8, 2021, to September 13, 2024, and consists of 194 daily observations. This temporal division captures both the immediate disruption of the pandemic and the subsequent acceleration in digital financial adoption and green finance initiatives across the GCC. The early 2021 breakpoint aligns with the global vaccine rollout, economic reopening, and regional policy shifts emphasising sustainability and fintech innovation.

We construct a balanced panel of 13 daily time series variables encompassing four major domains: Fintech innovation, Green finance and sustainability, Commodity prices, and GCC stock market performance. All financial data are sourced from Bloomberg and Refinitiv Eikon, with prices and indices converted to daily log returns to ensure stationarity and focus the analysis on short-run interdependencies and shock transmission. A detailed classification of these assets is presented in Table 12.1.

Table A1 in the Appendix reports the descriptive statistics of the daily return series across the two subsamples. For each series, we present the

Table 12.1 Description of selected assets

Ticker	*Name*	*Description*
BDCI	S&P Business Development Company Index	Index tracking the performance of major cryptocurrencies and blockchain-related assets. Reflects trends in digital asset markets
KLEDGER	S&P Kensho Distributed Ledger Index	Equity index composed of global companies active in blockchain and distributed ledger technologies. Captures institutional fintech innovation
GFI	STOXX Global Fintech Index	Composite index covering fintech firms worldwide. Measures broader fintech sector performance, including digital finance adoption
Natural Gas	S&P GSCI Natural Gas	Commodity index tracking natural gas prices. Represents energy market dynamics relevant to GCC economies
Crude Oil	S&P GSCI Crude Oil	Benchmark index for global crude oil prices. Core macroeconomic driver for GCC financial conditions
Copper	S&P GSCI Copper	Price index for copper. Acts as a proxy for global industrial demand and renewable energy infrastructure activity
GCEI	S&P Global Clean Energy Index	Stock index of leading clean energy companies. Serves as a measure of green finance and ESG investment sentiment
Bahrain	Bahrain All Shares Index	National equity index for Bahrain
Kuwait	Boursa Kuwait All-Share Index	Broad-based equity index for Kuwait's financial market
Saudi (KSA)	Tadawul All Share Index	Main stock market index for Saudi Arabia. Captures market-level financial activity in the region's largest economy
Qatar	Qatar Stock Market (QE) Index	Primary equity index for Qatar
Oman	The Muscat Securities Market Index	Oman's principal stock index
UAE	FTSE ADX General Index	UAE's main equity index, covering major listed firms in Abu Dhabi. Reflects broader financial market trends in the UAE

mean, variance, skewness, excess kurtosis, and results from normality and stationarity diagnostics. The Elliott-Rothenberg-Stock (ERS) unit root test confirms that the majority of the return series are stationary, validating their use in the TVP-VAR framework. Additionally, Jarque–Bera statistics strongly reject the null of normality at the 1% level across nearly all variables, highlighting the presence of asymmetry and fat tails, features typical of high-frequency financial data. Evidence of autocorrelation is assessed using the Ljung-Box Q(10) test, while volatility clustering is evaluated using the ARCH-LM $Q^2(10)$ test. These diagnostics justify our return-based specification and the use of a time-varying volatility model.

In addition to quantitative data, the analysis integrates institutional and policy documents that contextualise market developments within national frameworks. To capture the regulatory and sustainability environment shaping fintech–green finance convergence, the study briefly outlines key initiatives across major GCC economies. These are summarised below in a comparative table of regulatory sandboxes, ESG frameworks, and fintech hubs.

Empirical Results

We present our empirical findings by combining both static and dynamic connectedness analyses. These results are based on a 13-variable TVP-VAR model applied to two sub-periods: (i) the Pre-/During-COVID period (*Period 1*) (June 2018—January 2021) and (ii) the Post-COVID period (*Period 2*) (January 2021—September 2024). We complement these with regression outputs and a mixed-methods thematic analysis of green finance frameworks to contextualise the convergence of fintech and green finance in the GCC.

Static Connectedness Analysis

Figures 1a and 1b present the network visualisations of static connectedness for the two periods, and Table 12.2 summarises the corresponding variance decompositions. During the *Period 1* the overall system was only moderately integrated, with a Total Connectedness Index (TCI) of 50.65%, indicating that nearly half of the forecast error variance was attributable to cross-market spillovers. On the other hand, in *Period 2*, the TCI increased to 54.87%, suggesting a more interconnected financial environment. This jump reflects the growing interdependence between

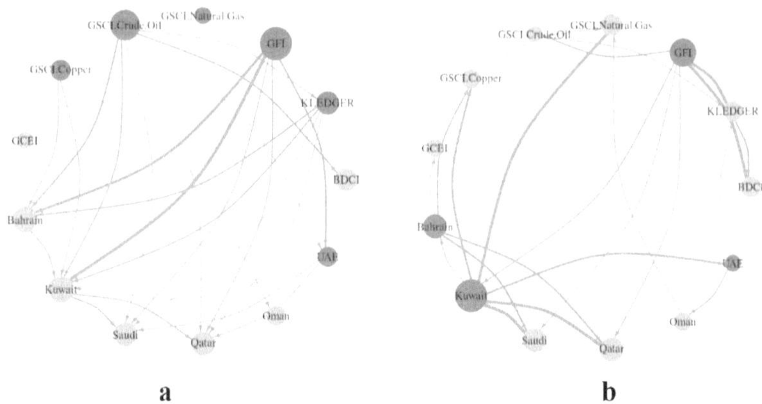

Fig. 12.1 (a) and (b) Static net pairwise connectedness for period 1 and period 2, respectively

fintech, green finance, and GCC equity markets in the post-pandemic landscape.

Table 12.3 further reveals that fintech-related variables, particularly GFI, became more influential in Period 2. For instance, GFI's "TO" spillovers increased substantially from 93.76% in Period 1 to 95.68% in Period 2, while KLEDGER's influence declined to 46.89%. Thus, rather than both fintech indices becoming more influential, GFI assumed an outsized role as a systemic shock emitter post-COVID, while KLEDGER's centrality declined.

Traditional commodities such as crude oil and natural gas, which were strong transmitters in Period 1 (with values of 100.36% and 17.01%, respectively), experienced a marked decline in their relative influence in Period 2. Crude oil's influence decreased to 47.76%, while natural gas remained nearly unchanged at 17.56%. These patterns suggest a rebalancing of systemic risk dynamics away from energy commodities toward new macro-financial drivers, particularly fintech and equity market variables, consistent with post-pandemic digitalisation and green finance narratives. Meanwhile, Bahrain, Kuwait, and the UAE consistently acted as net recipients of spillovers. However, Kuwait's net connectedness experienced a dramatic role reversal, rising from 53.71% in Period 1 to + 83.18% in Period 2, the highest net transmitter score in the system. This reversal implies that Kuwait shifted from a passive market absorbing

Table 12.2 Comparative overview of GCC fintech and green finance frameworks

Country	*Regulatory sandbox/ Fintech hub*	*ESG/Green finance framework*	*Key institutional initiatives*
Saudi Arabia	SAMA Sandbox (2017); Fintech Saudi	PIF Green Bond Framework (2023); Vision 2030 FSDP	National fintech strategy; ESG disclosure mandates
UAE	ADGM RegLab; DIFC Innovation Hub	UAE Sustainable Finance Framework (2021); Net Zero 2050	Blockchain-based green bonds; digital ESG reporting
Qatar	QCB Fintech Sandbox; QFC Fintech Circle	Qatar National Vision 2030; ESG Disclosure Guidelines (2022)	Sustainable finance taxonomy; green lending incentives
Bahrain	CBB Regulatory Sandbox (2017)	NBB ESG Framework (2023); Economic Vision 2030	Islamic green-fintech experimentation; SME inclusion
Kuwait	CBK Fintech Unit & Sandbox (2019)	NBK ESG Framework; Kuwait Vision 2035	Regtech pilots; sustainable banking integration
Oman	CBO Fintech Framework (2023); Innovation Hub	Oman Green Finance Framework; ESG Disclosure Guidelines (2022); Vision 2040	Open banking; ESG-aligned investment policies

volatility to a key node generating shocks across the regional financial network. Similar, albeit more moderate transitions were observed for Bahrain (net: + 33.25% to + 37.70%) and UAE (–26.47% to + 0.15%). Energy markets, though still influential, lost ground as net transmitters. For instance, crude oil's net connectedness fell from + 37.56% in Period 1 to –0.70% in Period 2, and natural gas declined from –6.56% to –27.34%, indicating their waning systemic importance in the post-COVID structure.

In terms of total connectedness (TCI), the network exhibited increased overall interdependence, rising from 52.17% in Period 1 to 54.87% in Period 2, consistent with tighter cross-asset linkages in the post-pandemic environment. This finding aligns with prior literature suggesting that

Table 12.3 Static connectedness

Period 1 (June 8, 2018—January 1, 2021)

	BDCI	*KLEDGER*	*GFI*	*Natural Gas*	*Crude Oil*	*Copper*	*GCEI*	*Bahrain*	*Kuwait*	*Saudi*	*Qatar*	*Oman*	*UAE*	*FROM*
BDCI	65.15	8.01	4.44	1.34	7.52	2.39	0.49	5.88	0.73	0.64	0.64	2.09	0.68	34.85
KLEDGER	6.10	38.21	21.13	0.87	18.25	4.86	0.25	3.78	1.82	0.52	0.52	1.25	2.44	61.79
GFI	4.86	19.18	35.65	2.99	19.60	4.85	0.47	4.58	1.70	0.56	0.56	1.58	3.42	64.35
Natural Gas	2.81	6.04	2.38	76.42	5.18	0.29	0.19	1.92	0.36	0.65	0.65	2.13	0.98	23.58
Crude Oil	5.65	17.85	21.06	1.99	37.21	5.08	0.32	5.93	1.93	0.52	0.52	0.46	1.49	62.79
Copper	3.30	9.62	9.46	1.66	9.88	47.99	0.36	4.70	4.76	2.92	2.92	0.70	1.73	52.01
GCEI	0.92	1.21	1.77	1.59	1.67	0.46	79.32	1.35	1.41	3.98	3.98	0.51	1.80	20.68
Bahrain	5.63	5.79	4.64	1.74	10.63	1.64	1.44	64.56	0.58	0.57	0.57	0.31	1.91	35.44
Kuwait	4.82	7.17	10.18	0.38	12.16	4.79	0.56	29.09	26.05	0.17	0.17	0.69	3.77	73.95
Saudi	0.56	0.77	0.86	0.60	0.54	2.48	0.58	1.21	1.08	43.81	43.81	1.58	2.12	56.19
Qatar	0.56	0.77	0.86	0.60	0.54	2.48	0.58	1.21	1.08	43.81	43.81	1.58	2.12	56.19
Oman	0.97	3.11	5.72	2.40	1.62	3.82	0.27	0.45	1.78	1.18	1.18	71.10	6.41	28.90
UAE	2.61	8.86	11.26	0.86	12.77	2.34	1.37	8.59	3.01	1.06	1.06	1.56	44.67	55.33
TO	38.79	88.37	93.76	17.01	100.36	35.47	6.87	68.70	20.24	56.58	56.58	14.44	28.87	626.04
Inc.Own	103.94	126.58	129.41	93.44	137.56	83.47	86.20	133.25	46.29	100.40	100.40	85.54	73.53	cTCI/TCI
NET	3.94	26.58	29.41	−6.56	37.56	−16.53	−13.80	33.25	−53.71	0.40	0.40	−14.46	−26.47	52.17/48.16
NPT	6.00	10.00	10.00	5.00	11.00	4.00	1.00	8.00	4.00	5.00	4.00	4.00	6.00	

Period 2 (January 8, 2021—September 13, 2024)

	BDCI	*KLEDGER*	*GFI*	*Natural Gas*	*Crude Oil*	*Copper*	*GCEI*	*Bahrain*	*Kuwait*	*Saudi*	*Qatar*	*Oman*	*UAE*	*FROM*
BDCI	56.95	18.56	17.27	0.25	2.86	0.51	0.33	0.41	1.26	0.20	0.20	1.11	0.07	43.05
KLEDGER	9.52	34.82	25.66	0.13	8.54	0.96	4.02	2.34	3.52	0.40	0.40	2.52	7.18	65.18
GFI	0.82	9.09	62.96	0.22	13.43	2.86	4.32	2.46	0.96	0.90	0.90	0.50	0.58	37.04
Natural Gas	1.33	0.45	1.60	55.11	3.24	9.10	0.30	3.41	17.64	0.92	0.92	5.65	0.32	44.89
Crude Oil	0.57	2.51	22.41	2.59	51.53	0.43	4.47	0.73	8.75	0.42	0.42	2.89	2.29	48.47
Copper	0.81	1.16	1.43	3.84	1.19	52.88	0.67	12.02	17.92	3.42	3.42	0.56	0.69	47.12
GCEI	0.80	3.99	1.87	2.06	3.53	1.37	73.37	4.61	3.13	0.15	0.15	0.70	4.27	26.63
Bahrain	0.50	0.67	2.80	0.29	2.02	4.08	0.14	46.11	22.91	2.07	2.07	2.89	13.45	53.89
Kuwait	0.24	0.14	8.09	1.83	7.63	6.28	0.90	16.81	45.38	1.60	1.60	1.50	8.01	54.62
Saudi	0.24	1.39	6.58	2.09	1.75	2.80	0.26	13.13	18.16	24.88	24.88	1.17	2.67	75.12
Qatar	0.24	1.39	6.58	2.09	1.75	2.80	0.26	13.13	18.16	24.88	24.88	1.17	2.67	75.12
Oman	3.32	4.61	0.98	0.19	0.99	0.36	0.66	5.98	4.69	1.03	1.03	65.43	10.74	34.57
UAE	0.72	2.93	0.42	1.96	0.81	1.70	1.68	16.57	20.69	0.90	0.90	3.52	47.22	52.78
TO	19.11	46.89	95.68	17.56	47.76	33.24	18.00	91.59	137.80	36.89	36.89	24.16	52.93	658.49
Inc.Own	76.05	81.70	158.64	72.66	99.30	86.12	91.36	137.70	183.18	61.77	61.77	89.58	100.15	cTCI/ TCI
NET	−23.95	−18.30	58.64	−27.34	−0.70	−13.88	−8.64	37.70	83.18	−38.23	−38.23	−10.42	0.15	54.87/ 50.65
NPT	8.00	6.00	9.00	4.00	7.00	4.00	5.00	8.00	11.00	1.00	2.00	6.00	7.00	

Notes The table presents the static connectedness matrices for the system variables across two sub-periods: Period 1 (June 8, 2018—January 1, 2021) and Period 2 (January 8, 2021—September 13, 2024). These estimates are derived from a time-varying parameter vector autoregression (TVP-VAR) model with a lag order of 1, selected based on the Bayesian Information Criterion (BIC). The analysis is based on daily data, comprising 135 observations for Period 1 and 194 observations for Period 2. The "TO" and "FROM" columns indicate the total spillovers transmitted to and received from all other variables in the system, respectively. In line with the existing literature, the forecast horizon is set at $H = 10$

financialisation and digitalisation trends have heightened market interconnectivity in the aftermath of global crises (Yiming et al., 2024; Kayani et al., 2024).

Dynamic Connectedness Analysis

To complement the static analysis and better understand the temporal evolution of systemic risk transmission, we conduct a dynamic spillover analysis using the TVP-VAR framework. Figures 12.2 and 12.3 illustrate the Total Connectedness Index (TCI) and net total directional connectedness for each variable over Periods 1 and 2, respectively. As shown in Fig. 2a (Period 1), the TCI fluctuates between 50 and 55%, with a notable surge around early 2020, a period coinciding with the onset of the COVID-19 pandemic. This pattern suggests heightened co-movement across the system during crisis conditions, aligning with recent findings that global shocks increase cross-market interdependencies (Gong et al., 2021; Abdullah et al., 2023). Following this peak, the TCI stabilises at elevated levels through 2020, indicating persistent spillover effects during the pandemic recovery phase.

In contrast, Fig. 2b (Period 2) presents a different dynamic. The TCI begins at a relatively lower level (~37%) in early 2021 but gradually rises and peaks around early 2023, reaching approximately 41–42%, before tapering slightly toward the end of the sample. This delayed peak reflects a more gradual systemic integration, likely associated with the post-COVID acceleration of digitalisation, monetary policy normalisation, and increased geopolitical uncertainty (e.g., interest rate hikes, debates over the energy transition, and regional conflicts). The TCI's moderate elevation over time reinforces the notion of a structurally tighter, though less volatile, system compared to the COVID-19 shock phase.

Figures 3a and 3b further decompose the dynamic net total directional connectedness to identify the changing roles of each variable as either net transmitters or net receivers over time. In Period 1, GFI and KLEDGER both display increasing transmitter roles, particularly during and after the pandemic shock in early 2020, reflecting their growing influence on the broader system. Notably, GFI's transmitter role persists and intensifies toward the end of the period, consistent with its rising "TO" contribution in the static table. BDCI also begins as a net absorber but shifts into a modest transmitter role by late 2020, potentially due to the growing momentum of digital finance.

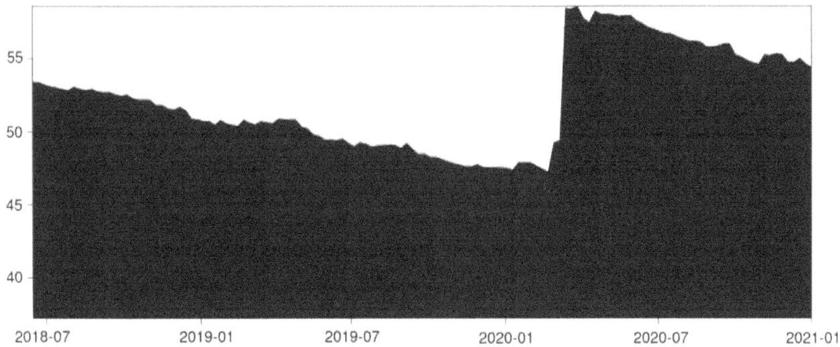

a. Total Connectedness Index (Period 1)

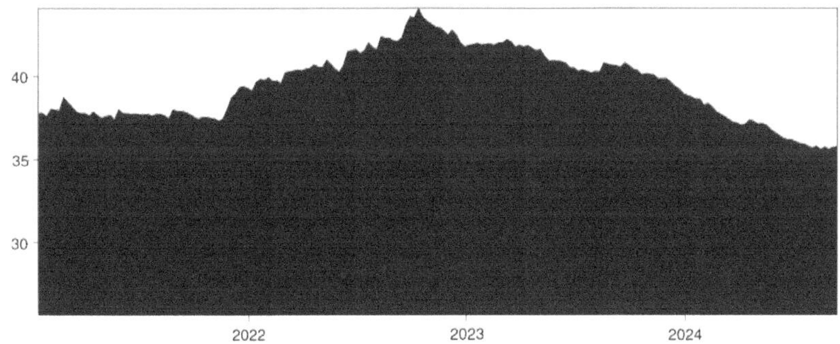

b. Total Connectedness Index (Period 2)

Fig. 12.2 (a) Total connectedness index (Period 1) (b) Total connectedness index (Period 2)

Among regional markets, Kuwait and the UAE show clear directional asymmetries. Kuwait transitions from a mild net receiver to a moderate transmitter by late 2020, supporting its sharp role reversal in the static net connectedness score (+83.18% in Period 2 vs. –53.71% in Period 1). The UAE remains largely a net receiver across Period 1, but this role begins to erode post-2020. Other GCC markets such as Qatar, Saudi Arabia, and Oman show relatively stable absorption roles throughout the period.

In Period 2 (Fig. 3b), the dynamics appear less volatile but more structured. GFI continues to dominate as a persistent net transmitter, reinforcing its critical role in volatility propagation post-COVID. Crude oil and natural gas, which exhibited strong transmission and influence roles during shocks in Period 1, shift to more neutral or net recipient

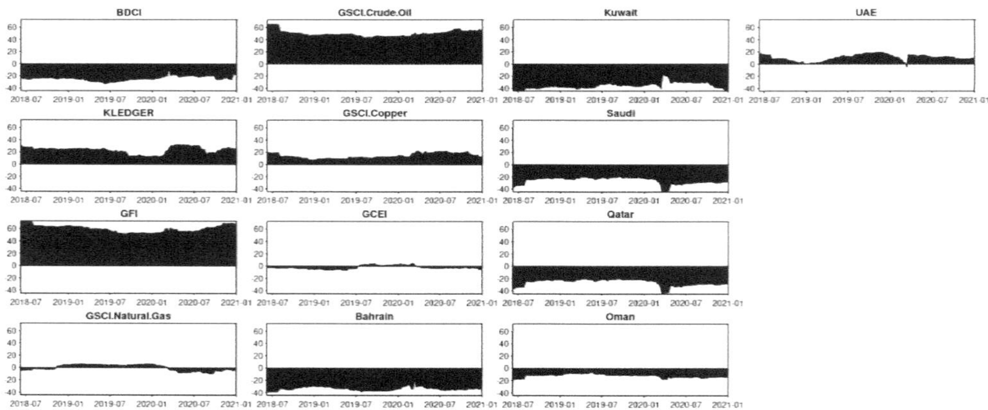

Fig. 12.3 (a) Dynamic net total directional spillovers (Period 1) (b) Dynamic net total directional spillovers (Period 2)

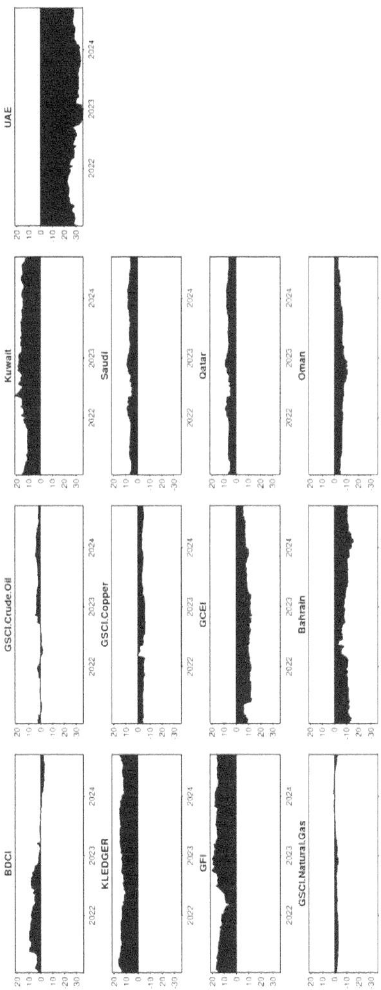

Fig. 12.3 (continued)

positions, confirming the de-emphasis of energy drivers in a digitally oriented post-pandemic market environment. Interestingly, Kuwait sustains its transmitter status throughout Period 2, consistent with its sharply positive static net score. UAE, however, transitions back to a net receiver role, although with less magnitude than in Period 1, indicating greater integration into global volatility cycles but still relatively low propagation. Bahrain and Qatar maintain relatively stable absorption dynamics, while Saudi Arabia appears neutral throughout the period, neither transmitting nor absorbing significantly.

Topic Modelling and Textual Analysis of GCC Green Finance Frameworks

To deepen the interpretation of our empirical findings, we conduct a topic modelling analysis using Latent Dirichlet Allocation (LDA) on official green and sustainable finance frameworks from six GCC countries. This approach reveals five dominant thematic clusters that reflect the policy and institutional narratives underpinning green finance in the region. When triangulated with our connectedness results, these textual insights provide important context for understanding the rising interplay between fintech and green finance across the Gulf. The LDA results are summarised in Table 12.4, while a visual representation of key terms in each country's narrative is shown in Fig. 12.4.

A central observation is the emphasis on framework credibility and international alignment (Topic 2), present in the documents of Oman, Bahrain, and Saudi Arabia. These frameworks closely follow ICMA and LMA principles, underscoring a policy commitment to transparency, standardisation, and investor trust. This finding complements our empirical result that fintech indices, often associated with digital transparency and real-time monitoring, are becoming more influential in GCC financial markets. It suggests that the demand for accountability in sustainable finance may be driving openness to fintech tools such as blockchain-based tracking of proceeds or AI-powered ESG reporting systems.

Institutional ESG governance (Topic 1) also features prominently, particularly in Kuwait and Bahrain, where frameworks are driven by banks and sovereign institutions. This top-down approach to sustainability aligns with the growing spillover effects observed from fintech-related indices, such as GFI, as internal ESG commitments within financial institutions may incentivise investments in ESG-oriented digital platforms. Moreover, the presence of advanced mitigation narratives (Topic 3) in Saudi Arabia and the UAE, emphasising hydrogen, carbon capture, and

Table 12.4 LDA topics in GCC green finance frameworks

Country	*LDA Topic(s)*	*Interpretation and Topic summary*
Oman	Topic 2	Emphasizes ICMA/LMA-aligned framework architecture, with strong focus on international standards, use-of-proceeds reporting, and post-issuance transparency
Saudi Arabia	Topics 2 + 3	Combines technical rigour (Topic 2) with ambitious mitigation efforts (Topic 3), including hydrogen, carbon capture, and net-zero targets
Bahrain (NBB)	Topics 2 + 1	Merges framework credibility (Topic 2) with institutional ESG governance (Topic 1), highlighting board-level oversight and ESG-linked performance integration
Kuwait (NBK)	Topic 1	Focuses on internal ESG strategy (Topic 1), especially within banks, reflecting early-stage ESG adoption led by institutional leadership
Qatar	Topic 4	Prioritises regulatory infrastructure (Topic 4), including green taxonomies, Central Bank guidelines, and sustainability-linked lending criteria
UAE	Topics 3 + 4	Blends advanced climate mitigation (Topic 3) with enabling regulatory frameworks (Topic 4), consistent with the UAE's dual focus on technology leadership and policy alignment

Note Topics are derived using Latent Dirichlet Allocation (LDA) topic modeling across official green finance frameworks from six GCC countries

Fig. 12.4 Country-specific word clouds of green finance frameworks

net-zero targets, reflects the region's ambition to position itself as a leader in climate innovation. These technology-intensive strategies likely require alternative financing mechanisms. Our dynamic connectedness results, which show an increasing influence from fintech indices post-2020, support the notion that fintech is playing a greater role in channelling capital toward such frontier projects.

In parallel, regulatory infrastructure and sustainable finance taxonomies (Topic 4) are especially pronounced in Qatar and the UAE, suggesting a growing role for state-led definitions and oversight. This institutional emphasis on rule-setting mirrors the evolving supervisory interest in integrating digital tools (e.g., RegTech and SupTech) to monitor ESG compliance. Finally, while social inclusion and infrastructure resilience (Topic 0) is less dominant overall, its appearance signals that green finance in the GCC is broadening to incorporate elements of equitable development. Thematic convergence between social sustainability and green finance aligns with fintech's potential to democratise financial access, particularly via crowdfunding or mobile-enabled financing for SMEs and local infrastructure. A related dimension concerns the intersection with Islamic finance principles, which remain foundational to the region's financial architecture. The primary challenge here lies less in jurisprudential interpretation than in governance and financial engineering adaptation, specifically, integrating Sharia-compliant instruments within emerging digital finance ecosystems. For example, recent pilots in Sukuk tokenisation demonstrate how blockchain-based platforms can enhance transparency and traceability in Islamic bond issuance, aligning ethical finance objectives with digital innovation and sustainability goals.

Taken together, the topic modelling findings reveal a coherent narrative: the increasing market role of fintech in the GCC is not incidental, but rather reflects a deeper strategic alignment between sustainability objectives, technological innovation, and institutional frameworks. The convergence of these domains, evident in both policy discourse and market behaviour, suggests that fintech is becoming a structural enabler of the region's green transition.

Conclusion

This study examined the convergence of fintech and green finance in the GCC, revealing a clear post-COVID shift from parallel development to strategic integration. Before 2020, fintech and green finance evolved in relative isolation, with Gulf financial markets primarily driven by oil. Our empirical results indicate that, in the post-pandemic period, fintech and green indices have become significantly more influential in GCC markets. Time-varying connectedness and regression analyses demonstrate that variables such as blockchain equity indices and clean energy stocks now shape market dynamics alongside traditional drivers, indicating a diversification of systemic influences.

Complementing this, our topic modelling of national green finance frameworks shows that GCC countries are embedding themes of transparency, innovation, and institutional governance into their sustainable finance strategies. Frameworks increasingly emphasise international alignment (ICMA), regulatory oversight, and advanced mitigation technologies—areas where fintech applications, such as blockchain, digital crowdfunding, and AI-based ESG analytics, are particularly relevant. The convergence is not incidental but reflects a broader policy trajectory linking financial innovation with sustainable development under national transformation plans.

This convergence has important implications. For policymakers, it calls for integrated oversight and targeted support for green fintech initiatives. Practical steps could include establishing a GCC-wide Fintech Council to coordinate regulatory sandboxes and data standards; developing harmonised ESG–Islamic finance taxonomies to ensure comparability and integrity across jurisdictions; and promoting cross-listing of tokenised green sukuk to deepen liquidity and attract diverse investors. Strengthening collaboration between regulators and industry through public–private RegTech and SupTech sandboxes would further enhance supervisory innovation and ESG compliance monitoring. For financial institutions, it opens new avenues for digitally enabled green finance products, while raising the bar on transparency and ESG data management. At the macro level, fintech provides scalable tools to mobilise private capital for sustainable projects, thereby reinforcing economic diversification goals across the region.

In short, the Gulf is emerging as a testbed for fintech-enabled green finance. The integration of these domains is measurable in both policy design and market behaviour. If sustained, this convergence could position the GCC as a leader in building a digitally driven, climate-aligned financial ecosystem.

Appendices

See Table A1.

Table A1 Summary statistics

Period 1 (June 8, 2018—January 1, 2021)						
	BDCI	*KLEDGER*	*GFI*	*Natural Gas*	*Crude Oil*	*Copper*
Mean	1.02	0.545	0.467	0.117	0.933	−0.446
Variance	92.978	22.798	12.066	43.744	18.538	55.909
Skewness	−0.632***	−0.221	−0.482**	0.513**	−0.824***	−0.653***
	(0.004)	(0.277)	(0.022)	(0.016)	(0.000)	(0.003)
Ex.Kurtosis	2.561***	1.205**	6.587***	2.182***	6.330***	5.668***
	(0.000)	(0.020)	(0.000)	(0.001)	(0.000)	(0.000)
JB	45.544***	9.201***	247.413***	32.448***	238.916***	188.919***
	(0.000)	(0.010)	(0.000)	(0.000)	(0.000)	(0.000)
ERS	−1.325	−5.204***	−5.767***	−3.254***	−4.437***	−4.459***
	(0.188)	(0.000)	(0.000)	(0.001)	(0.000)	(0.000)
Q(10)	5.254	4.202	10.101*	5.821	5.459	13.617**
	(0.468)	(0.632)	(0.067)	(0.389)	(0.439)	(0.012)
Q2(10)	2.018	42.438***	63.209***	5.701	24.034***	108.772***
	(0.936)	(0.000)	(0.000)	(0.405)	(0.000)	(0.000)
Period 2 (January 8, 2021—September 13, 2024)						
	BDCI	*KLEDGER*	*GFI*	*Natural Gas*	*Crude Oil*	*Copper*
Mean	0.591	0.238	0.031	0.341	−0.349	0.412
Variance	77.793	100.606	8.661	71.922	16.725	25.281
Skewness	−0.274	0.598***	0.450**	−0.066	0.243	0.489***
	(0.114)	(0.001)	(0.011)	(0.701)	(0.160)	(0.006)
Ex.Kurtosis	1.711***	0.553	0.905**	0.042	0.252	3.390***
	(0.001)	(0.117)	(0.029)	(0.715)	(0.359)	(0.000)

Period 2 (January 8, 2021—September 13, 2024)

	BDCI	*KLEDGER*	*GFI*	*Natural Gas*	*Crude Oil*	*Copper*
JB	25.817***	13.885***	13.020***	0.151	2.393	99.572***
	(0.000)	(0.001)	(0.001)	(0.927)	(0.302)	(0.000)
ERS	−3.762***	−6.564***	−2.364**	−4.936***	−1.712*	−6.517***
	(0.000)	(0.000)	(0.019)	(0.000)	(0.089)	(0.000)
Q(10)	8.734	4.388	4.270	9.921*	7.083	13.126**
	(0.124)	(0.602)	(0.621)	(0.073)	(0.245)	(0.015)
Q2(10)	2.633	8.911	24.627***	6.394	31.017***	4.853
	(0.869)	(0.115)	(0.000)	(0.318)	(0.000)	(0.529)

Period 1 (June 8, 2018—January 1, 2021)

	GCEI	*Bahrain*	*Kuwait*	*Saudi*	*Qatar*	*Oman*	*UAE*
Mean	0.002	0.137	0.15	0.105	0.105	−0.186	0.113
Variance	1.342	2.776	5.493	7.482	7.482	2.686	6.238
Skewness	−0.587***	−2.515***	−2.010***	−1.284***	−1.284***	−1.000***	−1.762***
	(0.006)	(0.000)	(0.000)	(0.000)	(0.000)	(0.000)	(0.000)
Ex.Kurtosis	1.509***	15.003***	13.207***	6.386***	6.386***	6.033***	11.782***
	(0.008)	(0.000)	(0.000)	(0.000)	(0.000)	(0.000)	(0.000)
JB	20.411***	1397.967***	1064.118***	264.495***	264.495***	225.530***	844.416***
	(0.000)	(0.000)	(0.000)	(0.000)	(0.000)	(0.000)	(0.000)
ERS	−5.082***	−1.299	−3.847***	−3.133***	−3.133***	−5.120***	−4.578***
	(0.000)	(0.196)	(0.000)	(0.002)	(0.002)	(0.000)	(0.000)
Q(10)	17.947***	14.926***	11.246**	3.930	3.930	7.182	13.039**
	(0.001)	(0.006)	(0.039)	(0.676)	(0.676)	(0.236)	(0.016)
Q2(10)	15.517***	1.931	12.019**	7.206	7.206	6.931	14.881***
	(0.004)	(0.944)	(0.026)	(0.234)	(0.234)	(0.260)	−0.006

(continued)

Table A1 (continued)

Period 2 (January 8, 2021—September 13, 2024)							
	GCEI	*Bahrain*	*Kuwait*	*Saudi*	*Qatar*	*Oman*	*UAE*
Mean	−0.015	0.161	0.144	0.184	0.184	0.154	0.337
Variance	0.61	1.251	2.225	4.435	4.435	1.867	3.111
Skewness	−1.300***	−0.331*	−0.655***	−0.173	−0.173	0.752***	0.355**
	(0.000)	(0.058)	(0.000)	(0.313)	(0.313)	(0.000)	(0.043)
Ex.Kurtosis	6.853***	3.223***	2.626***	1.004**	1.004**	1.920***	1.842***
	(0.000)	(0.000)	(0.000)	(0.020)	(0.020)	(0.001)	(0.001)
JB	429.757***	86.580***	68.901***	9.030**	9.030**	47.574***	31.165***
	(0.000)	(0.000)	(0.000)	(0.011)	(0.011)	(0.000)	(0.000)
ERS	−4.849***	−4.264***	−5.262***	−4.811***	−4.811***	−7.084***	−2.512**
	(0.000)	(0.000)	(0.000)	(0.000)	(0.000)	(0.000)	(0.013)
Q(10)	13.558**	10.048*	7.669	3.170	3.170	11.555**	3.360
	(0.012)	(0.068)	(0.194)	(0.795)	(0.795)	(0.033)	(0.767)
Q2(10)	14.010***	58.604***	4.473	10.710**	10.710**	11.066**	7.175
	(0.009)	(0.000)	(0.589)	(0.050)	(0.050)	(0.042)	−0.237

Notes ***, **, and * indicate statistical significance at the 1%, 5%, and 10% levels, respectively. Values in parentheses report corresponding p-values. Skewness is tested using D'Agostino's method (1970), and kurtosis is assessed following the approach of Anscombe and Glynn (1983). Overall normality is evaluated using the Jarque–Bera test (1980). The ERS statistic refers to the unit root test developed by Elliott, Rothenberg, and Stock (1996). The Q(20) and Q(20) statistics are based on the weighted portmanteau tests proposed by Fisher and Gallagher (2012), applied to residuals and squared residuals, respectively

References

Abdullah, Mohammad, Mohammad Ashraful Ferdous Chowdhury, and Zunaidah Sulong. "Asymmetric efficiency and connectedness among green stocks, halal tourism stocks, cryptocurrencies, and commodities: Portfolio hedging implications." *Resources Policy* 81 (2023): 103419.

Al-Kubaisi, Mohammed Khalifa, and Bashar Abu Khalaf. "Climate Governance, ESG Reporting, and the Firm Performance: Does It Matter More for Europe or the GCC?." *Sustainability* 17, no. 9 (2025): 3761.

Alshahmy, Suliman, and Mehmet Sahiner. "Enhancing the Issuance and Monitoring of Sustainable Finance Instruments through AI." In *Artificial Intelligence, Finance, and Sustainability: Economic, Ecological, and Ethical Implications*, pp. 217–241. Cham: Springer Nature Switzerland, 2024.

Antonakakis, N., Chatziantoniou, I., & Gabauer, D. (2020). Refined measures of dynamic connectedness based on time-varying parameter vector autoregressions. *Journal of Risk and Financial Management, 13*(4), 84.

Aysan, A. F., Disli, M., Ng, A., & Ozturk, H. (2023). Fintech and Islamic finance: Digitalization, development, and sustainability. *Journal of International Financial Markets, Institutions and Money, 86*, 102707. https://doi.org/10.1016/j.intfin.2023.102707

Beck, T., Chen, T., Lin, C., & Song, F. M. (2023). Financial innovation: The bright and dark sides. *Journal of Banking & Finance, 146*, 106700. https://doi.org/10.1016/j.jbankfin.2023.106700

Berg, F., Koelbel, J. F., & Rigobon, R. (2020). Aggregate confusion: The divergence of ESG ratings. *Review of Finance, 24*(6), 1315–1344. https://doi.org/10.1093/rof/rfaa031

Blei, David M., Andrew Y. Ng, and Michael I. Jordan. "Latent dirichlet allocation." *Journal of Machine Learning Research* 3, no. Jan (2003): 993–1022.

Carè, Rosella, Rabia Fatima, Massimiliano Cerciello, and Simone Taddeo. "Exploring the Landscape of Green Crowdfunding: Trends, Themes, and Insights from a Bibliometric Review." *Finance Research Letters* (2025): 107143.

Chen, Y., Li, Y., Wu, S., & Luo, J. (2023). Blockchain in green finance: Evidence from green bond markets. *Journal of Corporate Finance, 78*, 102341. https://doi.org/10.1016/j.jcorpfin.2023.102341

Diebold, F. X., & Yilmaz, K. (2012). Better to give than to receive: Predictive directional measurement of volatility spillovers. *International Journal of Forecasting, 28*(1), 57–66.

Fisher, T. J., & Gallagher, C. M. (2012). New weighted portmanteau statistics for time series goodness of fit testing. *Journal of the American Statistical Association, 107*(498), 777–787.

Flammer, Caroline. "Corporate green bonds." *Journal of Financial Economics* 142, no. 2 (2021): 499–516.

Gong, Xu, Yun Liu, and Xiong Wang. "Dynamic volatility spillovers across oil and natural gas futures markets based on a time-varying spillover method." *International Review of Financial Analysis* 76 (2021): 101790.

Hornuf, L., & Schwienbacher, A. (2018). Market mechanisms and funding dynamics in equity crowdfunding. *Journal of Corporate Finance, 50*, 556–574. https://doi.org/10.1016/j.jcorpfin.2017.08.009

Kayani, Umar, Mirzat Ullah, Ahmet Faruk Aysan, Sidra Nazir, and Josephine Frempong. "Quantile connectedness among digital assets, traditional assets, and renewable energy prices during extreme economic crisis." *Technological Forecasting and Social Change* 208 (2024): 123635.

Khan, Habib Hussain, Shoaib Khan, and Abdul Ghafoor. "Fintech adoption, the regulatory environment and bank stability: An empirical investigation from GCC economies." *Borsa Istanbul Review* 23, no. 6 (2023): 1263–1281.

Koop, G., & Korobilis, D. (2014). A new index of financial conditions. *European Economic Review, 71*, 101–116.

Krueger, P., Sautner, Z., & Starks, L. T. (2020). The importance of climate risks for institutional investors. *Review of Financial Studies, 33*(3), 1067–1111. https://doi.org/10.1093/rfs/hhz137

Liu, Qianhua, Ka-Ching Chan, and Ranga Chimhundu. "Fintech research: systematic mapping, classification, and future directions." *Financial Innovation* 10, no. 1 (2024): 24.

Malamas, Vangelis, Thomas K. Dasaklis, Veni Arakelian, and Gregory Chondrokoukis. "A blockchain framework for digitizing securities issuance: the case of green bonds." *Journal of Sustainable Finance & Investment* 14, no. 3 (2024): 569–595.

Musleh Alsartawi, Abdalmuttaleb. "The diffusion of financial technology-enabled innovation in GCC-listed banks and its relationship with profitability and market value." *Journal of Financial Reporting and Accounting* (2024).

Public Investment Fund (PIF). *Green Bond Impact Assessment: For Eligible Green Uses of Proceeds under the PIF Green Bond Framework.* September 2023. https://www.pif.gov.sa/. (accessed May 16, 2025).

PwC Middle East. *Green Financing Gathers Pace.* April 2024. https://www.pwc.com/m1/en/publications/middle-east-economy-watch/april-2024/green-financing-gathers-pace.html.

Rau, P. R. (2020). Law, trust, and the development of crowdfunding. *Management Science, 66*(5), 2046–2062. https://doi.org/10.1287/mnsc.2019.3320

Reyes, C., & Scholz, P. (2019). Blockchain and the future of green finance. *Journal of Sustainable Finance & Investment, 9*(2), 115–127. https://doi.org/10.1080/20430795.2018.1548446

Saudi Central Bank (SAMA). *Fintech Strategy and Sandbox Overview.* 2023. https://www.sama.gov.sa/en-US/Regulatory%20Sandbox/Documents/Regulatory_Sandbox_Framework_English-NOV2020.pdf (accessed May 16, 2025).

Schueffel, Patrick. "Taming the beast: A scientific definition of fintech." *Journal of Innovation Management* 4, no. 4 (2016): 32–54.

Siddik, Abu Bakkar, Md Nafizur Rahman, and Li Yong. "Do fintech adoption and financial literacy improve corporate sustainability performance? The mediating role of access to finance." *Journal of Cleaner Production* 421 (2023): 137658.

Tang, Pengzhu, Houyun Ma, Yuanyuan Sun, and Xiaowan Xu. "Exploring the role of Fintech, Green Finance and Natural Resources towards Environmental Sustainability: A study on ASEAN economies." *Resources Policy* 94 (2024): 105115.

Thakor, Anjan V. "Fintech and banking: What do we know?." *Journal of financial intermediation* 41 (2020): 100833.

Yiming, Wang, Liu Xun, Muhammad Umair, and Assilova Aizhan. "COVID-19 and the transformation of emerging economies: financialization, green bonds, and stock market volatility." *Resources Policy* 92 (2024): 104963.

Yusoff, Abdul Karim Mohamed, Heather Webb, and Seen Seery. "UAE's Strategic Initiatives to Boost FinTech: Investment, Regulation, and Innovation in the MENA Region." In *The Palgrave Handbook of FinTech in Africa and Middle East: Connecting the Dots of a Rapidly Emerging Ecosystem*, pp. 1–25. Singapore: Springer Nature Singapore, 2025.

Zetzsche, D. A., Buckley, R. P., Arner, D. W., & Barberis, J. N. (2020). Decentralized finance. *Journal of Financial Regulation, 6*(2), 172–203. https://doi.org/10.1093/jfr/fjaa010

CHAPTER 13

The Impact of Fintech Innovations and Financial Inclusion on Banks' Cyber Risk in GCC

Ilinka Antova

Introduction

The rapid expansion of digital financial services has transformed payment systems and financial inclusion dynamics across both advanced and emerging economies. As fintech penetration deepens, the resilience of financial infrastructures to cyber incidents has become a central policy concern. The GCC countries are at the forefront of this transition, pursuing ambitious digitalization agendas while facing rising exposure to operational and cyber risks.

While a substantial literature examines cybersecurity in global financial institutions, there is relatively limited empirical work on the intersection between fintech-driven financial inclusion and cyber incident frequency

I. Antova (✉)
University of Sofia "St Kliment Ohridski", Sofia, Bulgaria
e-mail: ilinkaantova@yahoo.ca

K. Tsanis et al. (eds.), *Digital Finance and Transformation in the Gulf*,
https://doi.org/10.1007/978-981-92-1588-1_13

in the GCC context. This study addresses that gap by analyzing the relationship between financial inclusion, measured primarily through digital-payment participation, and reported cyber incidents in GCC economies, benchmarked against advanced digital ecosystems such as the United Kingdom, Singapore, and Malaysia.

The chapter contributes to emerging research linking financial inclusion, innovation, and cybersecurity resilience in developing financial systems. By contrasting GCC patterns with mature markets, it highlights how institutional development shapes the balance between financial inclusion growth and cyber risk stability.

The remainder of the chapter is structured as follows: Sect. 2 reviews the relevant literature, Sect. 3 outlines the data and methodology, Sect. 4 presents the empirical analysis and discussion, and Sect. 5 concludes.

Literature Review

Cyber Risk in Financial Institutions

Although limitations persist in the availability and quality of data on cyber incidents (Bouveret, 2018), academic interest in cyber risk within the banking sector has expanded substantially. Cyber risk is increasingly acknowledged as a critical risk driver in the financial industry (Bank of England, 2024; Frost & Sharpio, 2021). It is frequently characterized as a "known unknown" tail risk (Aldasoro et al., 2022), the most significant threat to financial institutions (Pollmeier et al., 2023), and a systemic risk to the broader financial system (Kashyap & Wetherilt, 2019; Kaffenberger et al., 2017).

A significant proportion of successful cyberattacks are concentrated in advanced economies, with the United States accounting for the largest share (Bouveret, 2018). Such incidents have the potential to trigger contagion effects across financial institutions (Baldwin et al., 2017; Crosignani et al., 2023; Eisenbach et al., 2022). Aldasoro et al. (2022) observe that the financial impact of cyber incidents tends to scale with the size of the affected institution. However, Bouveret (2018) finds no direct relationship between firm size and losses among U.S. financial institutions, noting that smaller institutions often experienced the most severe losses. Moreover, large-scale cyberattacks in the financial sector tend to be associated with relatively low average costs (Aldasoro et al., 2022). Phishing, skimming, data breaches, and other security incidents are generally among the most costly types of cyberattacks (Aldasoro et al., 2022). Theft and denial-of-service (DoS) attacks are among the most prevalent threats targeting bank deposits (Duffie & Younger, 2019). One prominent example includes the theft of USD 81 million from the Bangladesh Central Bank's account at the Federal Reserve Bank of New York (Rubenfeld, 2019).

Operational Risk and Fintech-Driven Exposure

In a broader context of operational risk, Chernobai et al. (2011) find that breaches in internal controls are among the leading causes of high-magnitude operational loss events. Additionally, Curti et al. (2019) and Shih et al. (2000) report a positive correlation between the size of financial institutions and the scale of operational losses incurred. Such risk events can have significant negative implications for bank revenues (Cummins et al., 2006; Gillet et al., 2010; Sturm, 2013). In recent years, operational risk has gained increasing significance in the banking sector, driven by the accelerating pace of digitalization, the expansion of financial inclusion, and the broader adoption of advanced technologies. While comprehensive cybersecurity frameworks are now common among large multinational financial service providers and in developed markets, smaller and mid-sized institutions, particularly those based in developing economies, continue to face significant preparedness gaps (Baur-Yazbeck et al., 2019). As highlighted by Ozili (2018), the spread of digital technologies like mobile money has coincided with more frequent and severe cyber-attacks, raising concerns about data security and user privacy. On the other hand, the use of robust authentication systems by digital banks has a significant positive effect on enhancing customer protection (Ahmed et al., 2024).

Cyber Risk and Financial Inclusion

Previous research on financial inclusion has explored diverse themes, including its implications for financial stability (Cull et al., 2012; Hannig & Jansen, 2010; Neaime & Gaysset, 2018), its contribution to economic development (Ghosh, 2013; Sarma & Pais, 2011), and its relationship with economic growth (Kim et al., 2018; Mohan, 2006; Ulrich-Diener & Spacek, 2021). Scholars have also investigated the role of microfinance and financial institutions in broadening access (Ghosh,

2013; Marshall, 2004), the influence of financial innovation and technological progress on expanding inclusion (Donovan, 2012; Gabor & Brooks, 2017; Ozili, 2018, 2019), and by providing quicker and lower-cost services for underserved (Naumenkova et al., 2019).

As noted by Demirgüç-Kunt et al. (2017), few studies have analyzed the link between financial inclusion and inequality at the country level. According to Ouma et al. (2017), the diffusion of mobile-phone technology has enabled new financial services that promote household saving and increase the value of deposits. Evidence from 49 countries presented by Chinoda & Kwenda (2019) confirms that mobile innovation strengthens financial inclusion. In Southeast Asia, the combination of high internet penetration and a vibrant fintech sector has similarly supported access to financial services for unbanked groups (Al-Mudimigh & Anshari, 2020; Ozili, 2020). In general, the degree of financial inclusion both shapes and is shaped by factors such as financial innovation, poverty incidence, financial-sector stability, macroeconomic conditions, financial literacy, and the regulatory environment, all of which vary across national contexts (Ozili, 2020).

Further, privacy and incident response are seen as one of the biggest cybersecurity issues in the GCC region (Positive Technologies, 2024). As per McKinsey & Company (2023) around 62% of surveyed companies in GCC region utilize AI at least in one business unit, that is more in comparison to the rest of the world. But the utilization in financial sector is less than the overall usage in the region (McKinsey & Company, 2023). As per Shafeeq & Beg (2019), cyber incidents do not necessarily cause financial exclusion but can diminish the use of digital financial services, indirectly constraining the progress of digital financial inclusion.

GCC or Emerging Market Perspectives

Several studies indicate that cyber risk is not yet adequately integrated into enterprise risk management frameworks (Lovejoy et al., 2019; Pollmeier et al., 2023). This misalignment is often exploited by cybercriminals, who take advantage of organizational indecisiveness (Boehm et al., 2019). Two primary approaches to cybersecurity risk management have emerged: the "risk-based" and the "maturity-based" models. Among these, the risk-based approach has demonstrated greater effectiveness in mitigating enterprise-level risks (Boehm et al., 2019). In addition, Facchinetti et al.

(2020) propose a novel methodology employing ordinal data to construct a cyber risk criticality index.

In the context of the GCC, where financial digitalization has accelerated through national fintech strategies and Vision 2030 reforms, cyber risk management remains unevenly institutionalized. Emerging markets in general face similar challenges: fragmented governance structures, limited cyber disclosure practices, and nascent incident-reporting systems (Vergara Cobos, 2024). These characteristics result in risk dynamics that differ from those observed in advanced economies, where cybersecurity considerations are more formally integrated into prudential supervision frameworks. In addition, shifted clients' preference toward digital products and services, higher third-party involvement, social engineering attacks and talent shortage could lead to increased operational risk in banks in GCC region (Proven Solutions, 2024). While strengthening legal frameworks and enforcing appropriate penalties for digital-banking offenses can support customer protection and uphold the integrity of the digital-banking sector (Ahmed et al., 2024).

Methodology

Data Sources and Variables

The empirical analysis integrates two complementary datasets that together capture both the scale of financial digitalization and the associated cyber risk exposure. The first dataset consists of reported cyber incidents affecting the finance sector across GCC and comparator economies between 2014 and 2025, interpolated, gathered from Center for International & Security Studies, University of Maryland (2025). The second dataset derives from the World Bank Global Findex Database (2025), which reports cross-country indicators of financial inclusion and digital-payment usage at five survey waves: 2011, 2014, 2017, 2021, and 2024. Each indicator measures the percentage of adults aged 15 and above who (i) own a formal financial account, (ii) made or received a digital payment, or (iii) hold a mobile-money account. These variables represent core dimensions of fintech diffusion and inclusion depth. Because Findex data are collected intermittently, annual series for 2014–2025 were constructed using linear interpolation between observed survey years.

Data Harmonization and Preprocessing

Country identifiers were harmonized to maintain consistency across datasets (e.g., various spellings of the United Kingdom were unified). The combined panel was standardized into an annual frequency spanning 2014–2025, interpolated. Missing data points were filled through linear interpolation, and negative or implausible interpolated values were truncated at zero. This process preserved internal consistency while retaining the natural temporal variation of observed series. The interpolation formula is expressed as follows:

$$x_t^* = x_{t-1} + (x_{t+1} - x_{t-1}) \times (t - (t-1)) / ((t+1) - (t-1)) \quad (13.1)$$

where x^*_t represents the interpolated value for year t, and x_{t-1} and x_{t+1} denote the nearest observed values before and after the missing observation. This linear method assumes a constant rate of change between two observed points and is appropriate where annual variation is gradual.

Analytical Framework

The analytical strategy combines descriptive, comparative, and inferential elements. Descriptive statistics summarize the distributional features of incident frequency and digital-payment penetration across countries. Comparative visualization through scatterplots and time-series lines enables identification of structural contrasts between GCC and comparator economies. The inferential stage applies ordinary least squares (OLS) regression to estimate the marginal association between fintech adoption and reported cyber incident counts. The OLS approach was chosen for its interpretability and efficiency in small-to-medium samples, allowing the estimation of directional relationships rather than causal inference. Heteroskedasticity robust standard errors were employed to address variance non-uniformity across cross-sections. Diagnostic checks were performed to verify linearity, residual normality, and absence of multicollinearity among regressors.

Estimation and Statistical Equations

Incident frequencies were normalized relative to adult population size to ensure comparability across economies of differing scales. The incident rate ($I_{(c,t)}$) per 100,000 adults is computed as:

$$I_{(c,t)} = \left(N_{(c,t)}/P_{(c,t)}\right) \times 100,000 \quad (13.2)$$

where $N_{(c,t)}$ denotes the number of incidents recorded for country c in year t, and $P_{(c,t)}$ represents its adult population. The normalized rate enables cross-national comparison independent of demographic size. Statistical association between fintech adoption and cyber exposure is then estimated through a bivariate OLS regression model:

$$I_{(c,t)} = \alpha + \beta F_{(c,t)} + \varepsilon_{(c,t)} \quad (13.3)$$

where $I_{(c,t)}$ is the dependent variable representing incident frequency or rate, $F_{(c,t)}$ is the share of adults who conducted digital payments, α is the intercept, β measures the marginal effect of fintech adoption, and $\varepsilon_{(c,t)}$ is an error term capturing unobserved influences. The sign and statistical significance of β indicate whether increased digital-payment adoption correlates with greater or reduced incident exposure. Additionally, graphical diagnostics were used to validate regression assumptions and interpret nonlinear tendencies visually.

To assess the robustness of the financial inclusion-cyber risk relationship, supplementary regressions were performed. The regression analysis examines the association between financial sector cyber incidents and multiple dimensions of financial inclusion derived from the World Bank's Global Findex Database (2025). Three indicators are employed: (i) Made or received a digital payment (% adults), (ii) Account ownership at a financial institution (% adults), and (iii) Mobile-money account (% adults). Each variable captures a distinct dimension of financial inclusion: from formal institutional participation to alternative digital ecosystems.

To test robustness, separate bivariate OLS regressions were estimated for each indicator using heteroskedasticity-robust (HC1) standard errors. Models were run on the pooled sample and on GCC and comparator subsamples to explore structural heterogeneity. The coefficients reflect within-country variation over time rather than cross-sectional differences in absolute incident levels. Accordingly, a negative coefficient indicates that, as financial inclusion deepens, the growth rate or relative frequency of reported cyber incidents tends to moderate, rather than implying that high inclusion economies experience fewer total events.

This distinction is critical because advanced economies typically record more incidents in absolute terms due to broader digital footprints and more comprehensive disclosure requirements. The analysis therefore interprets financial inclusion-cyber incidents relationships as relative stabilizations of incident dynamics, consistent with institutional learning and control maturation effects.

Regression diagnostics confirmed that residual distributions and variance-inflation factors (VIFs) remained within acceptable thresholds across pooled and subgroup samples.

Limitations

Several limitations are acknowledged. First, the availability and accuracy of cyber incident data vary across jurisdictions, leading to potential under-reporting in emerging markets relative to mature economies. Second, the linear interpolation method, while maintaining continuity, may smooth out short-term volatility and obscure sudden surges in incident activity. Third, the OLS model captures association rather than causality; therefore, results should be interpreted as indicative rather than deterministic. Nonetheless, the analytical framework remains valuable for cross-country comparisons and for exploring systemic patterns linking fintech inclusion to cyber risk evolution. In addition, data availability limits statistical power; reported incidents may be undercounted.

Use of Generative AI tools

ChatGPT (GPT-5 Thinking) was used as an assistive tool for the study analysis, and figure/table templates.

IV. Analysis and Findings

GCC Bank Cyber Incidents vs. Other Countries

This section examines cyber incidents in the finance industry using a Center for International & Security Studies, University of Maryland (2025) dataset: 2014-Q2 2025. To avoid scale distortion from the U.S., comparisons exclude the United States. The non-GCC set in this file consists of the United Kingdom, Singapore, and Malaysia. Within the GCC, incidents are recorded for United Arab Emirates, Saudi Arabia, Qatar, Oman, and Kuwait; Bahrain has no entries and is therefore missing from the analysis. All results refer to incident counts rather than loss magnitudes and are presented in Fig. 13.1.

Fig. 13.1. Top ten trends in GCC (*Source* Center for International & Security Studies, University of Maryland, 2025)

Descriptive patterns

1. Overall weight of GCC incidents is low but persistent.
   Using the year-by-year decomposition, the GCC's share of reported incidents averages ~3% across the sample, with visible oscillations and several zero-incidence years. Peaks occur sporadically (e.g., 2015), driven by one-off events rather than a structural rise.
2. Concentration within the GCC.
   Incidents cluster in the UAE and, to a lesser extent, Saudi Arabia. Qatar, Oman, and Kuwait appear only intermittently. This concentration is consistent with those markets' larger, more internationally connected financial centers and faster adoption of digital financial services.
3. Comparators show broader and steadier activity.
   The United Kingdom exhibits the largest and most consistent year-on-year activity among the non-GCC comparators, with multiple active event subtypes in any given year. Singapore shows a moderate, recurring pattern; Malaysia appears episodic.

Event subtypes

The combined multi-panel figure based on event subtype indicates clear structural differences: Within the GCC financial industry cyber incidents, Exploitation of Application Server is the most frequent subtype, followed by External Denial of Service. Other subtypes (e.g., data-attack variants, message manipulation, network or end-host exploitation) appear, but at materially lower frequencies and typically as one-off spikes.

GCC profile (ranked)

- Exploitation of Application Servers (most common).
  This subtype recurs across multiple years in the available dataset and is particularly visible in markets with more advanced digital-finance ecosystems, especially the United Arab Emirates. Within the GCC sample, these incidents represent the most frequently observed pattern and predominantly affect internet-facing application services, consistent with exploitation of weaknesses in web and application layers.
- External Denial of Service (second most frequent).

External DoS incidents constitute the second most common subtype in the dataset and appear in episodic waves, often aligned with identifiable campaigns rather than continuous background activity. In the GCC context, they target public-facing banking services and are temporally clustered, which is consistent with campaign-driven disruption focused on operational interruption rather than persistent, stealthy compromise of data.

- Other Subtypes (infrequent).

  Data-centric compromises and other non-infrastructure subtypes appear only sporadically in the GCC portion of the dataset, and multi-vector combinations are not observed in the recorded GCC incidents. This pattern supports the view that, within this sample, the regional threat landscape is dominated by infrastructure- and availability-oriented vectors, while data-centric and complex blended attack chains play a comparatively limited role.
- United Kingdom

  The United Kingdom exhibits a broad and relatively complex incident portfolio across multiple observed years, encompassing data-compromise events, application-server exploitation, network-level attacks, message manipulation, and both internal and external denial-of-service incidents. Multi-vector cases, such as concurrent exploitation of application servers and end hosts, are recurrently observed in the dataset, indicating the presence of more sophisticated campaigns and coordinated activity within targeted environments. This pattern is consistent with the United Kingdom's highly digitized financial sector, where extensive interconnectivity and layered service architectures provide both operational efficiencies and an expanded attack surface.
- Singapore and Malaysia

  The incident profile for Singapore shows a consistent presence of financial-sector events over the observed period, with many cases involving data compromise and occasional episodes of application-layer exploitation. This mix aligns more closely with sustained adversarial interest in data-rich systems than with persistent degradation of core infrastructure services. Malaysia, by contrast, exhibits a more episodic trajectory. A notable cluster in 2014, largely composed of sensor-related exploitation, is followed by smaller subsequent bursts in which application-server attacks become more prominent. Data-compromise incidents remain comparatively limited in the available dataset, suggesting that Malaysia's exposure has been more function-specific and temporally concentrated than broadly systemic.

Implications. In the financial sector, incidents in the GCC are concentrated in application-layer breaches and external denial-of-service attacks, whereas comparator markets, particularly the United Kingdom, display greater subtype diversity and more complex multi-vector campaigns. For banks in the GCC, this suggests that strengthening application-layer security and enhancing resilience to high-volume denial-of-service attacks is likely to mitigate a substantial share of observed risk. In more mature markets, by contrast, effective risk mitigation typically requires broader, layered defenses spanning network and messaging layers, together with robust controls designed to address complex, composite attack patterns.

Actor perspective

As presented in Fig. 13.2, across the GCC, Criminal actors account for the largest share (50.0%; 6 of 12), followed by Hacktivists (33.3%; 4 of 12). Nation-state and Undetermined categories each make up 8.3% (1 of 12); Hobbyist cases are absent. Thus, the GCC profile is criminal-led, with a substantial secondary hacktivist component. In comparison, the non-GCC sample is heavily criminal-dominated (87.9% Criminal; 9.1% Hacktivist; 1.5% Hobbyist; 1.5% Nation-state). Relative to these benchmarks, the GCC shows less criminal dominance and a higher hacktivist share, even though criminals remain the largest actor category within the GCC.

Country detail within the GCC reinforces this pattern: the UAE exhibits the most diversified mix (Criminal 42.9%, Hacktivist 28.6%, Nation-state 14.3%, Undetermined 14.3%; HHI = 0.306), while Saudi Arabia is hacktivist-concentrated (100%). Qatar, Oman, and Kuwait each have one recorded incident (criminal), which inflates concentration metrics and warrants cautious interpretation. Criminal incidents are led by Exploitation of Application Server (4 of 6), with the remainder Data Attack (2 of 6). No criminal-attributed DDoS appears in the GCC slice (GCC DDoS is hacktivist-driven in this dataset).

By GCC country.

- United Arab Emirates: criminal activity is Exploitation of Application Server (3).
- Qatar: Exploitation of Application Server (1).

Fig. 13.2. Actors type by country (share percentage, all years) (*Source* Center for International & Security Studies, University of Maryland, 2025)

- Oman: Data Attack (1).
- Kuwait: Data Attack (1).
- Saudi Arabia: no criminal incidents recorded (hacktivist only).
- Bahrain: no entries in the file.

Comparison with the rest (non-GCC). Criminal activity is broader: still dominated by Exploitation of Application Server (32 occurrences), but also including Data Attack (8), External Denial of Service (6), Exploitation of End Hosts (5), Exploitation of Sensors (4), and smaller numbers of network-infrastructure exploitation, message manipulation, internal denial-of-service, and related multi-vector combinations (e.g., application-server plus end-host or network). In short, the GCC's criminal profile is narrow and application-centric, whereas non-GCC criminal activity shows a wider portfolio that includes end-host compromise, some criminal-attributed DoS, and mixed-technique campaigns. Within the GCC, all hacktivist activity manifests as External Denial of Service, concentrated in Saudi Arabia and the UAE. By contrast, hacktivist activity in the UK remains primarily External DoS but includes smaller counts of Internal DoS and undetermined cases.

Cyber Risk and Data Security in GCC

Public sector in UAE is exposed to around 50 000 cyberattacks daily (Positive Technologies, 2024). UAE (with 40%) and Saudi Arabia (with 26%) are the countries of higher interest among cyber hackers in GCC region (Positive Technologies, 2024). The most popular categories of interest by hackers are: Data (33%), Access (21%) and DDoS (10%) & Carding (10%) (Positive Technologies, 2024). Further, the most popular industry data between hackers in the region is for finance (Positive Technologies, 2024). In 2023 there was a rise in the interest in credit card info data: for companies up to 6% increase and up to 16% for individuals (Positive Technologies, 2024). Further, financial institutions in United Arab Emirates encounter the highest number of cyber incidents followed by financial institutions in Saudi Arabia (presented in Fig. 13.3).

As per Khaitan (2024) First Abu Dhabi Bank, RAKBANK and Mashreq Bank possibly encountered DDoS attacks in 2024. Another bank in UAE encountered a six-day DDoS attack in 2024 with 4.5 million requests per second and by being 70% of the time under attack (Lemos, 2024). The DDoS attacks in H1 2024 increased by 70% in comparison to H1 in 2023 (Positive Technologies, 2024). Qatar National Bank in

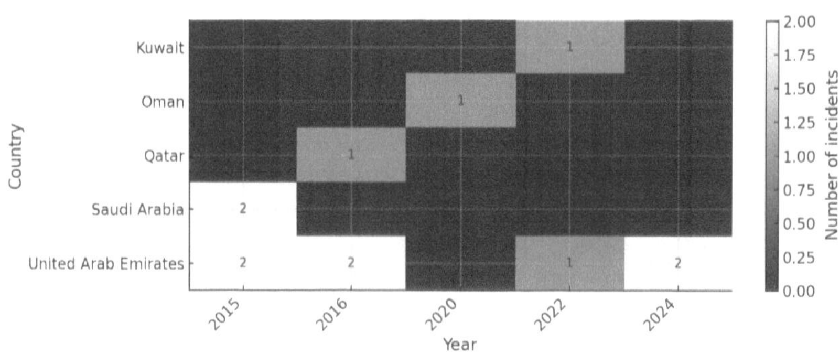

Fig. 13.3 Cyber incidents in financial sector in GCC by country 2015–2024 (*Source* Center for International & Security Studies, University of Maryland, 2025)

April 2016 suffered an extreme cyberattack, by which PINs, passwords and names of a huge number of customers including Al-Jazeera journalists and members of the ruling al-Thani family, were revealed and posted to a Cryptome website (Lago, 2021). The second most prevalent cyber-attack in GCC region during the period 2016–2024 was DDoS (presented in Fig. 13.4).

Reflection DDoS attacks (presented in Fig. 13.5) are executed based on application-layer protocols through the use of transport layer protocols as: transmission control protocol (TCP), user datagram protocol (UDP) or through their combination. TCP attacks mainly include: MSSQL, SSDP, etc., while UDP attacks include: CharGen, NTP and TFTP (presented in Fig. 13.5). Attacks like DNS, LDAP, NETBIOS, SNMP, and PORTMAP can be executed both TCP or UDP (presented in Fig. 13.5). The exploitation-based attacks can be executed through TCP and UDP. TCP attacks include: SYN flood, while UDP attacks include: UDP flood and UDP lag (presented in Fig. 13.5). In UDP flood attack a large amount of UDP pockets are transmitted to the target for to cause network exhaustion leading to system crash, in SYN floods

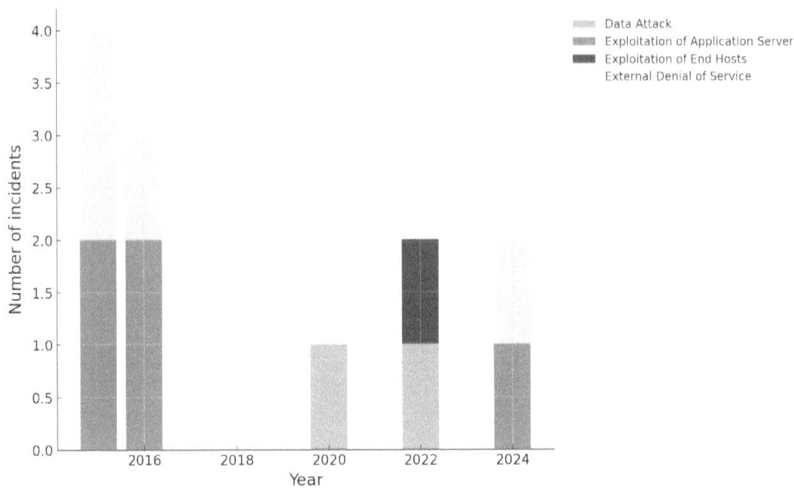

Fig. 13.4. Type of cyber-attacks in the financial sector in GCC 2015–2024 (*Source* Center for International & Security Studies, University of Maryland, 2025)

server resources are demolished by utilizing TCP-three-way handshake (Sharafaldin et al., 2019). And with UDP-Lag attack the connection between the server and the client is distort (Sharafaldin et al., 2019). Their usual detection can be done by the classification use of normal and abnormal flow in a network (Reddy et al., 2021). DDoS attacks are characterized with rapid expansion and complexity, which make them difficult to be detected, while outright the network resources and prohibiting the target servers to support the valid users (Salih & Abdulrazaq, 2024). Their usual detection can be done by the classification use of normal and abnormal flow in a network (Reddy et al., 2021). Real-time packet monitoring of network traffic could be seen as one of the solutions to prevent against DDoS attacks. Convolutional Neural Networks (CNN) are discrete feed-forward class of deep learning well suited for data processing. Multiple convolutional layers are systematically packed within the CNN framework. Each layer is capable of identifying complex patterns.

Further, around one third of the companies in the Middle East attacked with ransomware in 2020, paid a ransom (Lago, 2021). Paid, but not recover data due to a ransomware attack is slightly higher in GCC region in comparison to the world, while recovered data without paying ransom in GCC region is slightly lower in comparison to the rest of the world (presented in Table 13.1). There was a 600% increase in the

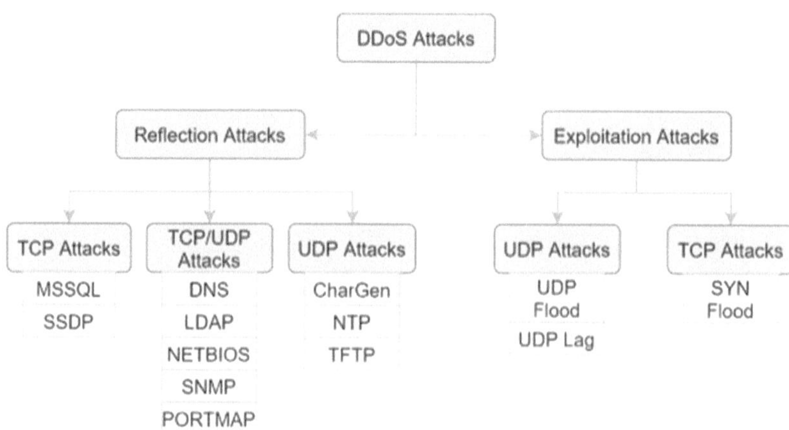

Fig. 13.5. The distribution of DDoS attack (*Source* Salih & Abdulrazaq, 2024)

Table 13.1. Ransomware attacks and recovery options in EMEA and the World in 2023 (*Source* Veeam, 2024)

Region	*Paid and able to recover their data from the attack (%)*	*Paid but could not recover data (%)*	*Recover without paying ransom (%)*
EMEA	54	28	14
World	54	27	15

phishing attacks in MENA region during the first quarter of 2020 (Lago, 2021).

Over 90% of the ransomware victims believe that the ransom by itself is not the only significant financial impact on the organization from the attack (Veeam, 2024). On average the ransom accounts for only 29% of the overall financial impact from an attack (Veeam, 2024). Only 45% of the organizational backup storage in EMEA is immutable (Veeam, 2024). While a secure backup is one of the best strategies against ransomware (Veeam, 2024).

There was a 358% increase in malware attacks in 2020 in comparison to 2019 (AAG, 2025).

The most successful malware attack in GCC region was Remote Access Trojan (RAT) both in Q3 2023–Q2 2024 and in Q3 2022–Q2 2023 periods, followed by spyware (presented in Fig. 13.6). New versions of RAT can easily be accepted as legitimate applications, allowing them to circumvent antivirus programs and remain undetected for a longer period (Positive Technologies, 2024).

The global average cost of a data breach amounted to USD 4.88 million in 2024 from USD 3.86 million in 2018, that is the biggest increase since COVID-19 (presented in Fig. 13.7). More than 50% of the organizations that were affected in 2024 by data breaches have cyber security personal shortage (IBM, 2024). Around 35% of the breaches were related to shadow data, that is also longer to be identified in comparison to data stored in just one type of environment (presented in Table 13.2).

Malicious attacks in comparison to other vectors, were the costliest ones in 2024 with an average of USD 4.99 million (IBM, 2024). Around 46% of the breaches are related to customer personal data (IBM, 2024). Data breaches related to stolen or compromised credentials usually experience the longest time to identify and contain: 292 days (IBM, 2024). As

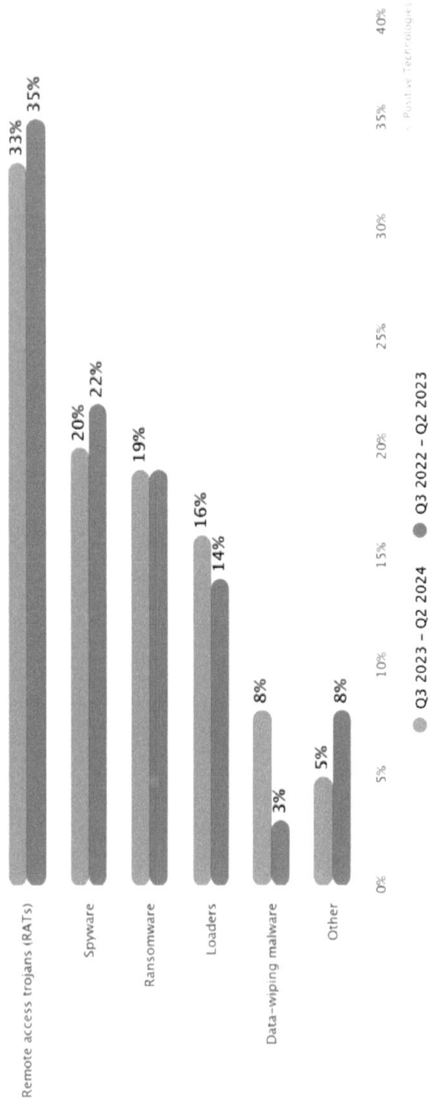

Fig. 13.6. Types of successful malware attacks in GCC (*Source* Positive Technologies, 2024)

Fig. 13.7. Global average total cost of a data breach (in USD millions) (*Source* IBM, 2024)

Table 13.2. Type of environment data breaches (*Source* IBM, 2024)

Type of environment	*Multiple types of environments (%)*	*Public cloud (%)*	*Premises (%)*	*Private cloud (%)*
Data breaches	35	25	20	15

Table 13.3. Time from data breach to client notification (*Source* Author's compilation, based on Nebraska Attorney General data, 2025)

metric	*min_days*	*median_days*	*mean_days*	*max_days*	*p90_days*
breach → discovery	0	145	136.7777778	383	263.7
discovery → notify	1	47	105.1818182	435	303.8
breach → notify	118	212	235.2363636	424	357.8

presented in Table 13.3 the mean days between breach and discovery by financial institutions in Nebraska are longer than the mean days between discovery and clients' notification.

Middle East is the region that incurred the highest costs for data breaches in 2024 with an increase of 8.7% from the previous year (IBM, 2024; Lago, 2021). Financial industry is the industry with the second highest cost of a data breach in 2024 after healthcare, with an increase of 3.05% from the previous year (presented in Fig. 13.8). The mean time to identify and contain data breach had its peak during the COVID-19 pandemic and in 2024 it returned to 2017 level (IBM, 2024).

Fintech Inclusion Analysis: GCC vs Comparators, and Within-GCC

This analysis uses Global Findex indicators. Bahrain is excluded for consistency with prior analyses. Values are linearly interpolated to form an

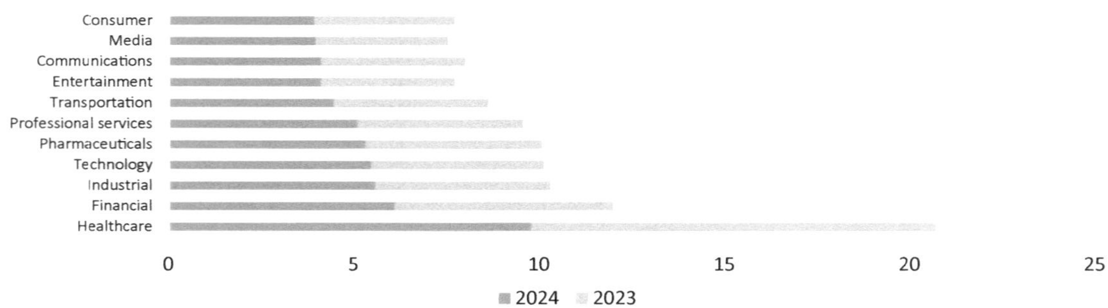

Fig. 13.8. Cost of a data breach by industry (Excerpt) (*Source* IBM, 2024)

annual series (2014–2025). The study compares GCC economies with comparators and examines within-GCC variation.

Figure 13.9 shows a persistent but modestly narrowing gap between GCC economies and mature comparator countries. Comparator economies start at around the low-80s in 2014 and rise to just above 90% of adults by 2021. GCC economies begin in the mid-60s in 2014 and increase to the mid-70s by 2021, with the steepest gains between 2014 and 2017 and more gradual growth thereafter. The gap falls slightly over the period, indicating gradual, though incomplete, convergence as GCC digital-payment infrastructure and adoption deepen.

Figure 13.10 shows the cross-sectional distribution of digital-payment inclusion among GCC economies, using the most recent available observation for each country. Qatar is omitted from the figure owing to a lack of comparable data. The data reveal notable intra-regional heterogeneity. The UAE, Saudi Arabia and Kuwait form a high-adoption cluster, with roughly three-quarters of adults (around 75–77%) making or receiving digital payments. These high levels are consistent with comprehensive national digital strategies and the rollout of modern payment infrastructures. Oman records the lowest inclusion level, at about 60%, reflecting later-stage policy adoption and a smaller market scale. Overall, the bar chart indicates that, although digital-payment usage is generally high across reporting GCC economies, substantial variation persists within the bloc, underscoring the role of domestic policy sequencing, financial-literacy initiatives and sustained public–private collaboration.

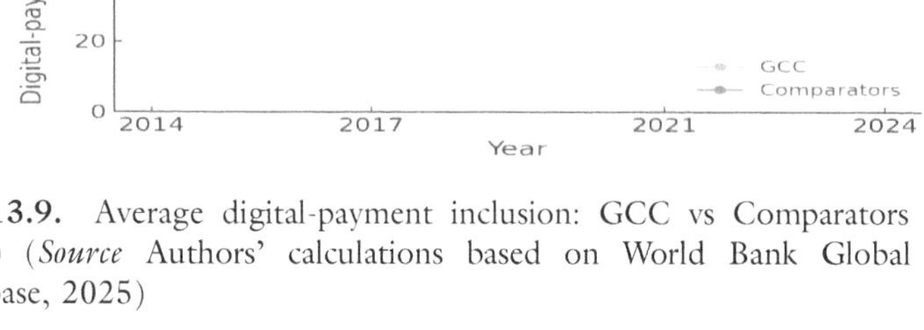

Fig. 13.9. Average digital-payment inclusion: GCC vs Comparators (2014–2024) (*Source* Authors' calculations based on World Bank Global Findex Database, 2025)

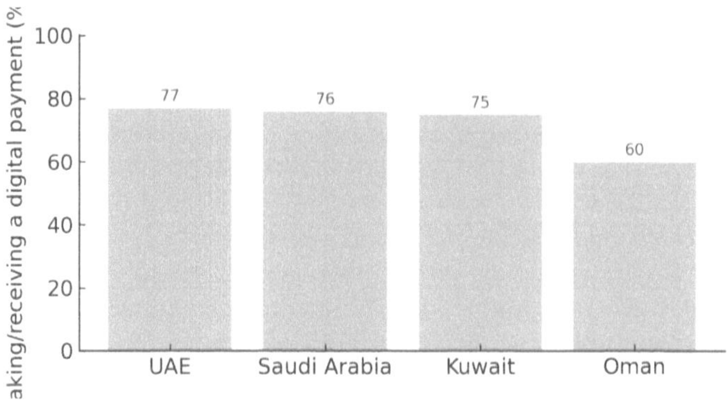

Fig. 13.10. Within-GCC digital-payment inclusion, 2024 (*Source* Authors' calculations based on World Bank Global Findex Database, 2025)

Figure 13.11 depicts the evolution of digital-payment inclusion across reporting GCC economies from 2014 to 2025, using linear interpolation between survey years. Series are shown for four countries with available data (United Arab Emirates, Saudi Arabia, Kuwait, and Oman); Qatar is excluded owing to a lack of comparable observations. The trajectories indicate an overall increase in digital-payment usage over the period, although the pace and stability of this progress differ across economies.

The United Arab Emirates begins at a relatively high inclusion level, around 76% in 2014, rising to the mid-80s by 2017 before easing back and stabilizing in the high-70s from 2021 onward. This pattern suggests a high but mature level of usage, with saturation among digitally active consumers rather than a reversal in adoption. Saudi Arabia shows the most substantial and continuous growth, increasing from just over 50% in 2014 to the mid-70s by 2024, in line with the rapid rollout of national payment initiatives and the Vision 2030 financial-sector program. Kuwait climbs from the mid-60s to around 75% by 2017 and remains broadly stable thereafter, consistent with an early but steady adoption phase. Oman's series lies close to 60% throughout, reflecting slower structural change and should be interpreted with caution given the limited underlying data.

Table 13.4 reports annual group averages of digital-payment usage for GCC and comparator economies, based on linear interpolation between available Global Findex survey years. The table confirms that comparator economies consistently exhibit higher inclusion levels than their GCC

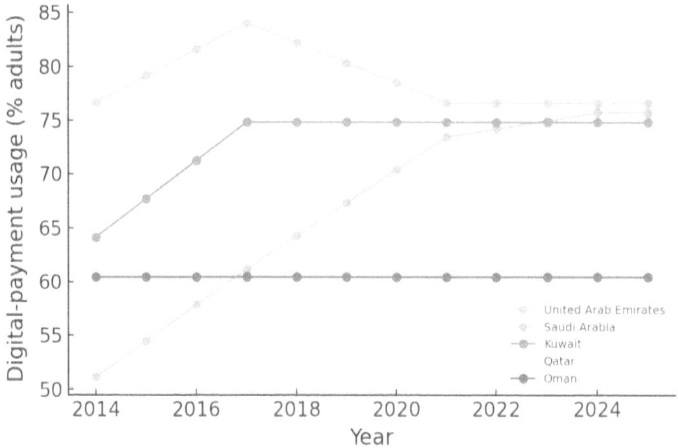

Fig. 13.11. Within-GCC inclusion trends by country (2014–2025, interpolated) (*Source* Authors' calculations based on World Bank Global Findex Database, 2025)

peers: comparator usage rises from about 83% of adults in 2014 to just over 91% in 2021, before easing in the 2024 observation. GCC economies start from lower levels, at around 64% in 2014, but increase to roughly 75% by 2021. Over this period the GCC group gains about 11 percentage points, compared with an increase of around 8 points in comparator economies, indicating somewhat faster relative growth from a lower base.

The temporal pattern in Table 13.4 shows that the main phase of convergence occurs between 2014 and 2021, after which the series flatten or decline slightly, reflecting the limitations of the most recent data point and the smaller set of reporting countries in 2024. Even so, the interpolated averages highlight that digital-payment adoption has become an entrenched trend in both groups, with GCC economies gradually narrowing, but not yet closing, the gap with more advanced comparators.

Table 13.5 summarizes descriptive statistics for GCC countries over the 2014–2025 interpolated period, quantifying the patterns shown in Fig. 13.11. Mean inclusion rates range from about 60% in Oman to just under 80% in the United Arab Emirates, and the cross-country standard deviation of these means is around 8 percentage points, indicating that differences within the GCC are substantive rather than marginal.

Table 13.4. Group averages by year (digital-payment usage, % adults) (*Source* Authors' calculations based on World Bank Global Findex Database, 2025)

Year	*Comparators*	*GCC*
2014	83.29	63.98
2015	83.99	67.10
2016	84.68	70.22
2017	85.38	73.35
2018	86.81	73.77
2019	88.24	74.19
2020	89.67	74.61
2021	91.10	75.03
2022	86.56	72.72
2023	82.01	70.40
2024	77.47	68.08
2025	77.47	68.08

Median values track closely with means, suggesting relatively symmetric trajectories rather than growth driven by a small number of outlier years.

The table also shows that three of the four reporting GCC economies (United Arab Emirates, Kuwait, and Saudi Arabia) exhibit clear increases between their minimum and maximum values over the period, pointing to broad-based digital advancement. Oman's series, by contrast, remains essentially flat at around 60%. Taken together, the heterogeneity in levels and volatility underscores the importance of domestic policy design, institutional maturity, and innovation capacity as determinants of fintech participation within the region.

Figure 13.12 plots the coefficient of variation (CV) of digital-payment inclusion across GCC and comparator economies for the survey years 2014, 2017, and 2021, with an additional GCC observation for 2024.

Table 13.5. Within-GCC descriptive statistics for digital-payment inclusion (2014–2025, interpolated) (*Source* Authors' calculations based on World Bank Global Findex Database, 2025)

Country	*Mean*	*Median*	*Min*	*Max*	*Std*
United Arab Emirates	78.79	77.58	76.61	84.04	2.66
Kuwait	73.04	74.83	64.12	74.83	3.57
Saudi Arabia	66.72	68.85	51.12	75.72	8.82
Oman	60.44	60.44	60.44	60.44	0.0
Qatar	nan	nan	nan	nan	Nan

The CV measures the relative dispersion of country-level inclusion rates within each group. For the GCC, cross-country heterogeneity is high in 2014 (CV around 0.20), declines to roughly 0.16 by 2017 and compresses sharply to a very low level in 2021, before rising again in 2024 as lower-usage economies enter the sample. Comparator economies also show a decline in dispersion, with the CV falling from just above 0.20 in 2014 to slightly above 0.10 by 2021. These patterns suggest some convergence within both groups over time, although GCC dispersion is more volatile and remains non-negligible by the end of the period.

Figure 13.13 traces the evolution of digital-payment inclusion in GCC economies and advanced comparator markets between 2014 and 2024, with each country's level expressed as a percentage of the frontier in that year (the highest inclusion rate among Singapore, the United Kingdom and Malaysia, normalized to 100). In 2014, GCC economies range from roughly one-half (Saudi Arabia) to about four-fifths (United Arab Emirates) of the frontier. Over time, GCC countries with available data

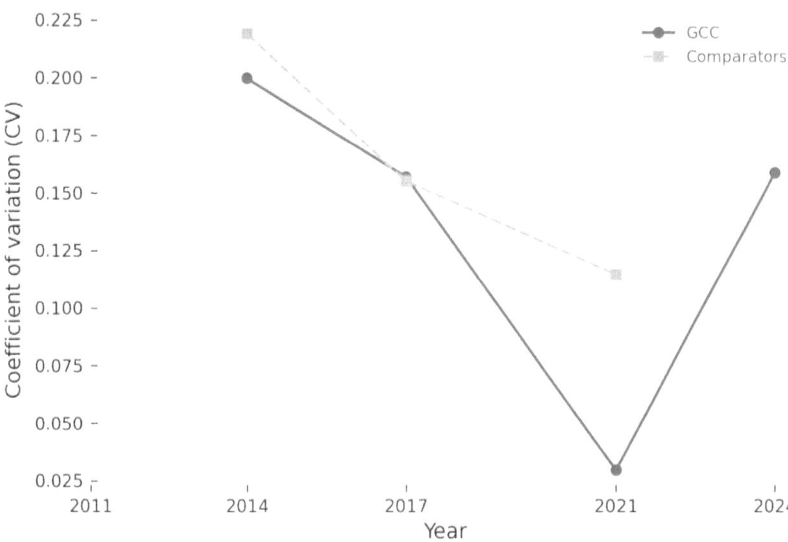

Fig. 13.12. Coefficient of variation in digital-payment inclusion, GCC and comparator economies, 2011–2024 (*Source* Authors' calculations based on World Bank Global Findex Database, 2025)

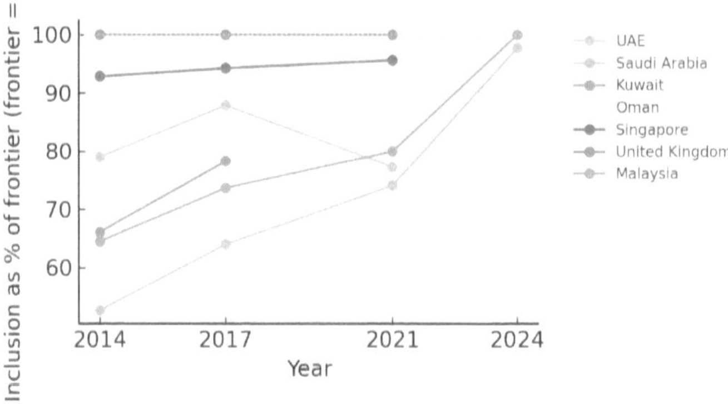

Fig. 13.13 Digital-payment inclusion relative to comparator frontier (frontier = 100), GCC and comparator economies, 2014–2024 (*Source* Authors' calculations based on World Bank Global Findex Database, 2025, *Note* The digital-payment frontier in each year is defined as the highest inclusion level observed among the three comparator economies (Singapore, United Kingdom, Malaysia); the country at the frontier is set to 100, and all other series are expressed as a percentage of that level. Solid lines denote GCC members; dashed lines denote comparator economies. The dotted horizontal line marks the 100 benchmark. Qatar is omitted owing to a lack of comparable data.)

move closer to the advanced-economy benchmark: Saudi Arabia in particular rises from just over 50% of the frontier in 2014 to almost full convergence by 2024, while Kuwait, the UAE (by 2021) and Oman cluster around three-quarters to four-fifths of frontier levels. Qatar is absent from the figure owing to a lack of comparable data.

Among comparator economies, the United Kingdom defines the frontier through 2021, with Singapore just below and Malaysia converging upward over time, ultimately becoming the frontier country in 2024. The joint display highlights both the catch-up of several GCC economies toward the advanced-economy frontier and the remaining gap for some members, setting the stage for the subsequent analysis of how these inclusion dynamics relate to cybersecurity exposure.

Integration of Financial Inclusion Metrics

Table 13.6 reports Pearson correlation matrices between the annual incident rate in the finance sector (incidents per 100,000 population) and three financial inclusion indicators: made or received a digital payment (% adults), account ownership at a financial institution (% adults), and mobile-money account (% adults). Correlations are shown for the pooled sample of GCC and comparator economies, and separately for each group. In the pooled panel, the correlations between the incident rate and the inclusion indicators are small in magnitude and generally negative, with very weak negative associations for digital payments and account ownership and a somewhat stronger negative association for mobile-money usage. Within the GCC subsample, the incident rate is modestly positively correlated with digital payments and account ownership, but moderately negatively associated with mobile-money usage, which itself is strongly negatively correlated with the other inclusion indicators. By contrast, in the comparator group the incident rate is moderately negatively correlated with both digital payments and account ownership and weakly negatively correlated with mobile money, while the three inclusion measures are strongly positively correlated with one another. Overall, the matrices suggest no single systematic linear relationship between financial inclusion levels and reported cyber incident intensity across all settings; the associations are modest, vary in sign across subsamples, and should be interpreted as descriptive rather than causal.

Table 13.7 reports the results of bivariate OLS regressions linking the annual incident rate in the finance sector (incidents per 100,000 population) to three financial inclusion indicators: (i) made or received a digital-payment (% adults), (ii) account ownership at a financial institution (% adults), and (iii) mobile-money account (% adults). The regressions are estimated separately for the pooled sample, GCC economies and comparator economies using heteroskedasticity-robust (HC1) standard errors. The slope coefficient captures the marginal association between each inclusion measure and the incident rate, while the intercept corresponds to the fitted rate when the respective inclusion variable is close to zero.

In the pooled panel, the estimated coefficients on digital payments and account ownership are small but consistently positive, whereas the coefficient on mobile-money usage is negative. The magnitudes of all slopes remain economically modest, and only the digital payments and mobile-money coefficients approach conventional significance levels (at around the 10% threshold), with R^2 values below 0.06. This suggests that variation in basic inclusion measures explains only a limited share of the

Table 13.6. Correlation matrices (cyber incidents vs financial inclusion variables) (*Source* Authors' calculations based on World Bank Global Findex Database, 2025 & Center for International & Security Studies, University of Maryland, 2025)

Variable	*incidents_per_100k*	*digital_payments*	*account_ownership*	*mobile_money*	*sample*
incidents_per_100k	1.000	−0.090	−0.074	−0.239	Pooled
digital_payments	−0.090	1.000	0.918	−0.063	Pooled
account_ownership	−0.074	0.918	1.000	−0.251	Pooled
mobile_money	−0.239	−0.063	−0.251	1.000	Pooled
incidents_per_100k	1.000	0.242	0.353	−0.415	GCC
digital_payments	0.242	1.000	0.894	−0.675	GCC
account_ownership	0.353	0.894	1.000	−0.906	GCC
mobile_money	−0.415	−0.675	−0.906	1.000	GCC
incidents_per_100k	1.000	−0.443	−0.442	−0.173	Comparators
digital_payments	−0.443	1.000	0.985	0.401	Comparators
account_ownership	−0.442	0.985	1.000	0.263	Comparators
mobile_money	−0.173	0.401	0.263	1.000	Comparators

observed cross-country and intertemporal variation in incident intensity, even when the sample is pooled.

Within the GCC subsample, the point estimates for account ownership and digital payments are again positive, while the coefficient on mobile-money usage is negative and statistically significant at the 5% level. The corresponding R^2 for the mobile-money regression (around 0.17) is the highest, but still indicates only moderate explanatory power.

For the comparator economies, the regressions yield small positive coefficients for account ownership and digital payments and a small negative coefficient for mobile-money usage; none of these coefficients are statistically significant and the R^2 values remain very low. Taken together,

Table 13.7. OLS regressions: cyber incidents—financial inclusion variable (robust SE) (*Source* Authors' calculations based on World Bank Global Findex Database, 2025 & Center for International & Security Studies, University of Maryland, 2025)

Variable	*incidents_per_100k*	*digital_payments*	*account_ownership*	*mobile_money*	*sample*
incidents_per_100k	1.000	−0.090	−0.074	−0.239	Pooled
digital_payments	−0.090	1.000	0.918	−0.063	Pooled
account_ownership	−0.074	0.918	1.000	−0.251	Pooled
mobile_money	−0.239	−0.063	−0.251	1.000	Pooled
incidents_per_100k	1.000	0.242	0.353	−0.415	GCC
digital_payments	0.242	1.000	0.894	−0.675	GCC
account_ownership	0.353	0.894	1.000	−0.906	GCC
mobile_money	−0.415	−0.675	−0.906	1.000	GCC
incidents_per_100k	1.000	−0.443	−0.442	−0.173	Comparators
digital_payments	−0.443	1.000	0.985	0.401	Comparators
account_ownership	−0.442	0.985	1.000	0.263	Comparators
mobile_money	−0.173	0.401	0.263	1.000	Comparators

the results suggest that normalized cyber incident rates do not exhibit a strong or uniform linear relationship with simple measures of financial inclusion, even in more advanced financial systems.

Overall, the OLS results in Table 13.7 provide tentative, descriptive evidence on the association between financial inclusion and cyber incident intensity. Given the small sample sizes, very modest effect sizes, limited explanatory power, and the fact that most coefficients fail to attain standard significance thresholds, the estimates should not be interpreted as causal. Rather, they underscore the need for richer empirical models and additional structural covariates to capture the financial inclusion-cyber risk nexus more fully.

Table 13.8 summarizes the simple Pearson correlations between the annual incident rate in the finance sector (incidents per 100,000 population) and three financial inclusion indicators drawn from the Global Findex Database. The coefficients indicate modest positive associations between the cyber incident rate and the two account-based measures of financial inclusion: the Pearson correlation is about 0.16 for formal account ownership and about 0.18 for digital-payment usage. By contrast, the correlation between the incident rate and mobile-money account penetration is negative, at roughly −0.24. None of these bivariate correlations are statistically significant at conventional levels, reflecting both the small sample size and the substantial influence of other unobserved factors on cyber incident-financial inclusion dynamics.

Taken together, the results in Table 13.8 suggest that higher levels of basic formal financial inclusion and digital-payment usage tend to coincide with somewhat higher reported cyber incident rates in the finance sector, whereas greater reliance on mobile-money accounts is weakly associated with lower incident intensity. However, the magnitudes remain modest and the relationships are far from deterministic. These simple correlations should therefore be interpreted as descriptive patterns rather than evidence of causal effects.

Table 13.9 reports Pearson correlation coefficients between the annual cyber incident rate in the financial sector (incidents per 100,000 population) and three financial inclusion indicators, reported separately for GCC economies and comparator countries.

In the GCC group, the cyber incident rate exhibits modest positive correlations with account ownership and digital-payment usage, with coefficients of approximately 0.26 and 0.20, respectively. By contrast, the

Table 13.8. Correlation between cyber incidents and financial inclusion Indicators (*Source* Authors' calculations based on World Bank Global Findex Database, 2025 & Center for International & Security Studies, University of Maryland, 2025)

Indicator	*Pearson r*
Bank or similar financial institution account (% age 15+)	0.16
Made or received a digital payment (% age 15+)	0.18
Mobile–money account (% age 15+)	−0.24

Table 13.9 Correlation Coefficients by Market Group (*Source* Authors' calculations based on World Bank Global Findex Database, 2025 & Center for International & Security Studies, University of Maryland, 2025)

Indicator	*GCC (r)*	*Comparators (r)*
Account ownership (% age 15+)	0.26	0.16
Digital payments (% age 15+)	0.20	0.23
Mobile money accounts (% age 15+)	−0.41	−0.17

correlation with mobile-money account penetration is negative and relatively larger in magnitude, at about −0.41, and approaches conventional significance levels.

Among comparator economies, the corresponding coefficients are also small in absolute value. The incident rate is weakly positively correlated with account ownership (around 0.16) and digital-payment usage (around 0.23), and weakly negatively correlated with mobile-money account penetration (around −0.17). None of these correlations are statistically significant at standard thresholds, and they point to only a loose association between headline financial inclusion levels and reported cyber incident intensity.

Conclusion

This chapter has examined how the evolution of financial inclusion in GCC economies relates to patterns of cyber incidents in the financial sector, benchmarked against a small set of advanced comparator markets. On the financial inclusion side, the evidence points to clear, but incomplete, convergence by GCC economies. On the cyber risk side, the incident data reveal distinct structural profiles across regions. In the GCC sample, cyber incidents are dominated by exploitation of internet, facing application servers and external denial-of-service attacks, with a notable hacktivist component and a relatively narrow set of technical subtypes. Comparator markets, particularly the United Kingdom, display broader subtype portfolios and more multi-vector campaigns, combining data compromise, end-host exploitation, network attacks and various forms of message manipulation.

A central question of the chapter was whether deeper financial inclusion is associated with higher or lower cyberincident intensity. Once incident counts are normalized by population, the answer remains necessarily cautious. The correlation matrices (Tables 13.6, 13.8, and 13.9) and the bivariate OLS regressions (Table 13.7) show that incident rates per 100,000 people have only weak linear associations with standard financial inclusion indicators. In the pooled sample, incident rates are modestly positively correlated with account ownership and digital-payment usage and modestly negatively correlated with mobile-money penetration, but the magnitudes are small and the relationships are not statistically robust. Within the GCC and comparator groups, most coefficients remain small and statistically insignificant, with low explanatory power. The main exception is a more pronounced negative association between mobile-money usage and cyber-incident rates in GCC economies, which is statistically significant but still explains only a limited share of variation. Taken together, these patterns do not support any strong claim that expanding financial inclusion mechanically reduces (or increases) cyber incidents; rather.

The broader implication is that the financial inclusion-cyber risk nexus is mediated by institutional and structural factors that sit beyond headline Findex measures. Regulatory design, supervisory capacity, incident reporting obligations, technology architectures, and the maturity of risk management practices all shape how additional users and transactions translate into observed cyber exposure. Advanced comparator markets combine high inclusion saturation with dense governance and disclosure frameworks; GCC economies, by contrast, are still building these institutional layers as they expand digital access. The weak and mostly non-robust empirical links identified here are therefore best interpreted as descriptive markers of a co-evolution process, the negative association between mobile-money usage and incident rates in GCC economies suggests that the way mobile-money systems are deployed may be one channel through which cyber risk is managed, although this pattern remains only suggestive and not causal.

Finally, the analysis highlights several avenues for further research. The small country set, limited time span and reliance on aggregate incident counts constrain the statistical power and scope of inference. Future work could exploit micro-level data (for example, institution-level incidents and controls), richer regulatory indicators and alternative normalization schemes (such as incidents per transaction or per active account) to capture cyber intensity more precisely. Extending the country sample beyond the GCC and the three comparators used here would also help assess how general these patterns are across different regulatory and technological contexts. Taken together, the results suggest that financial inclusion and cyber resilience are co-evolving dimensions of financial modernization, but the strength, sign, and timing of their interaction are ultimately determined by the quality of governance and the depth of institutional preparedness, rather than by financial inclusion metrics alone.

References

AAG. (2025). The latest 2025 cyber-crime statistics (updated April 2025). The Latest Cyber Crime Statistics (updated April 2025) | AAG IT Support

Ahmed, F., Hussain, A., Khan, S. N., Malik, A. H., Asim, M., Ahmad, S., & El-Affendi, M. (2024). Digital risk and financial inclusion: Balance between auxiliary innovation and protecting digital banking customers. *Risks*, *12*(8), 133. https://doi.org/10.3390/risks12080133

Aldasoro, I., Gambacorta, L., Giudici, P., & Leach, Th. (2022). The drivers of cyber risk. *Journal of Financial Stability*, 60. https://doi.org/10.1016/j.jfs.2022.100989

Al-Mudimigh, A., & Anshari, M. (2020). Financial Technology and Innovative Financial Inclusion. In Financial Technology and Disruptive Innovation in ASEAN (pp. 119–129). IGI Global. Available at: https://www.igi-global.com/chapter/financial-technology-and-innovative-financial-inclusion/231127

Baldwin, A., Gheyas, I., Ioannidis, C., Pym, D., & Williams, J. (2017). Contagion in cyber security attacks. *Journal of the Operational Research Society*, *68*(7), 780–791. https://doi.org/10.1057/jors.2016.37

Bank of England. (2024). Systemic risk survey results—2024 H1. Systemic Risk Survey Results - 2024 H1 | Bank of England

Baur-Yazbeck, S., Frickenstein, J., Medine, D. (2019). Cyber security in financial sector development. Challenges and potential solutions for financial inclusion. November. World bank. CGAP. Giz. On behalf of Federal Ministry for Economic Cooperation and Development. World Bank Document

Boehm, J., Curcio, N., Merrath, P., Shenton, L., Stăhle, T. (2019). The risk-based approach to cybersecurity. The approach to risk-based cybersecurity | McKinsey

Bouveret, A. (2018). Cyber risk for the financial sector: a framework for quantitative assessment. IMF Working Paper WP/18/143. Cyber Risk for the Financial Sector: A Framework for Quantitative Assessment (imf.org)

Center for International & Security Studies, University of Maryland. (2025). Cyber events database. Cyber Events Database Home | Center for International and Security Studies at Maryland

Chernobai, A., Jorion, P., & Yu, F. (2011). The determinants of operational risk in US financial institutions. *Journal of Financial and Quantitative Analysis*. 46, 1683–1725

Chinoda, T., & Kwenda, F. (2019). Do mobile phones, economic growth, bank competition and stability matter for financial inclusion in Africa? *Cogent Economics & Finance*, 7(1).

Cull, R., Demirgüç-Kunt, A., & Lyman, T. (2012). Financial Inclusion and Stability: What Does Research Show? Consultative Group to Assist the Poor, 71305, 1–3

Curti F., Frame, W.S., & Mihov, A. (2019). Are the largest banking organizations operationally more risky? Available at SSRN 3210206.

Crosignani, M., Macchiavelli, M., Silva, A. F. (2023). Pirates without borders: The propagation of cyberattacks through firms' supply chains. *Journal of Financial Economics*, 147 (2), 432–448. https://doi.org/10.1016/j.jfineco.2022.12.002

Cummins, J.D., Lewis, C.M., & Wei. R. (2006). The market value impact of operational loss events for US banks and insurers. *Journal of Banking & Finance*. 30, 2605–2634.

Demirgüç-Kunt, A., Klapper, L., & Singer, D. (2017). Financial Inclusion and Inclusive Growth: A Review of Recent Empirical Evidence. World Bank Policy Research Working Paper. https://doi.org/10.1596/1813-9450-8040

Ulrich-Diener, F., & Spacek, M. (2021). Digital transformation in banking: A managerial perspective on barriers to change. Sustainability. 13. 2032. https://doi.org/10.3390/su13042032.

Donovan, K. (2012). Mobile money for financial inclusion. *Information and Communications for development*, 61(1), 61–73

Duffie, D., Younger, J. (2019). Cyber Runs: How a Cyber Attack Could affect U.S. Financial Institutions. Hutchins Center Working Paper No 51. WP51-Duffie-Younger-2.pdf (brookings.edu)

Eisenbach, Th. M., Kovner, A., Lee, M. J. (2022). Cyber risk and the U.S. financial system: A pre-mortem analysis. *Journal of Financial Economics*, 145 (3), 802–826. https://doi.org/10.1016/j.jfineco.2021.10.007

Facchinetti, S., Giudici, P. & Osmetti, S.A. (2020). Cyber risk measurement with ordinal data. *Stat Methods Appl* 29, 173–185. https://doi.org/10.1007/s10260-019-00470-0

Frost, J., Sharpio, J. (2021). Cyber attacks "the biggest risk in banking". The Australian Financial Review, March 30. Cyber attacks 'the biggest risk in banking' (afr.com)

Gabor, D., & Brooks, S. (2017). The digital revolution in financial inclusion: international development in the fintech era. *New Political Economy*, 22(4), 423–436

Gillet, R., Hubner, G., & Plunus, S. (2010). Operational risk and reputation in the financial industry. *Journal of Banking & Finance* 34, 224–235.

Ghosh, J. (2013). Microfinance and the challenge of financial inclusion for development. *Cambridge journal of economics*, 37(6), 1203–1219

Hannig, A., & Jansen, S. (2010). Financial inclusion and financial stability: Current policy issues. Asian Development Bank Institute Working Paper, No. 259, 1–29.

IBM. (2024). Cost of a Data Breach Report. Cost of a Data Breach Report 2024

Kaffenberger, L., Kopp, E., & Wilson, C. (2017). Cyber Risk, Market failures, and Financial Stability. 17–185. International Monetary Fund.

Kashyap, A.K., & Wetherilt, A. (2019). Some Principles for Regulating Cyber Risk. In AEA Papers and Proceedings, v 109, 482–87.

Kim, D. W., Yu, J. S., & Hassan, M. K. (2018). Financial inclusion and economic growth in OIC countries. *Research in International Business and Finance*, 43, 1–14

Khaitan, A. (2024). Anonymous Sudan attacks UAE banks: cybersecurity breach raises concerns. March. UAE Banks Cyber Attack By Anonymous Sudan: Threat For GCC Finance

Lago, C. (2021). The biggest data breaches and cyberattacks in the Middle East. CIO. May. The biggest data breaches and cyberattacks in the Middle East | CIO

Lemos, R. (2024). Pro-Palestinian actor levels 6-day DDoS attack on UAE bank. July. Pro-Palestinian Actor Levels 6-Day DDoS Attack on UAE Bank

Lovejoy, K., Hartkopf, L., Randolph, M., George, A., Chambers, R., Petrisky, D. (2019). The risky six: Key questions to expose gaps in board understanding of organizational cyber resilience. Global perspectives and insights. The Institute of Internal Auditors and Ernst & Young. An IIA & EY Report: "The Risky Six: Key questions to expose gaps in board understanding of organizational cyber resiliency" (theiia.org)

Marshall, J. N. (2004). Financial institutions in disadvantaged areas: a comparative analysis of policies encouraging financial inclusion in Britain and the United States. *Environment and Planning A*, 36(2), 241–261

McKinsey & Company. (2023). The state of AI in GCC countries - and how to overcome adoption challenges May. State of AI in the Middle East's GCC countries | McKinsey

Mohan, R. (2006). Economic growth, financial deepening, and financial inclusion. Download citation of Economic growth, financial deepening and financial inclusion

Naumenkova, S., Mishchenko, S., & Dorofeiev, D. (2019). Digital financial inclusion: Evidence from Ukraine. *Investment Management & Financial Innovations*, 16(3), 194–205.

Neaime, S., & Gaysset, I. (2018). Financial inclusion and stability in MENA: Evidence from poverty and inequality. *Finance Research Letters*, 24, 230–237

Nebraska Attorney General. (2025). Data breach public search. Data Breach Public Search: AGO - Attorney General's Office

Ouma, S. A., Odongo, T. M., & Were, M. (2017). Mobile financial services and financial inclusion: Is it a boon for savings mobilization? *Review of development finance*, 7(1), 29–35

Ozili, P.K. (2020). Financial inclusion research around the world: a review. *Forum for Social Economics*. 50(4):457–479. https://doi.org/10.1080/07360932.2020.1715238

Ozili, P. K. (2019). Blockchain Finance: Questions Regulators Ask. Disruptive Innovation in Business and Finance in the Digital World (International Finance Review, Vol. 20), Emerald Publishing Limited

Ozili, P. K. (2018). Impact of digital finance on financial inclusion and stability. *Borsa Istanbul Review*, 18(4), 329–340

Pollmeier, S., Bongiovanni, I., & Slapničar, S. (2023). Designing a financial quantification model for cyber risk: A case study in a bank. *Safety Science*, 159, https://doi.org/10.1016/j.ssci.2022.106022

Positive technologies. (2024). GCC Countries and the Cybercriminal Services Market (2023 - 2024 report). September. GCC countries and the cybercriminal services market (2023–2024 report)

Proven Solutions. (2024). The growth of AI solutions for banking in GCC: top trends. November. The Growth of AI Solutions for Banking in the GCC: Top Trends - Proven Solution

Reddy, K. P., Kodati, S., Swetha, M,. Parimala, M., & Velliangiri, S. (2021). A hybrid neural network architecture for early detection of DDOS attacks using deep learning models. 2nd International Conference on Smart Electronics and Communication (ICOSEC), Trichy, India. https://doi.org/10.1109/ICOSEC51865.2021.9591969.

Rubenfeld, S., (2019). Bangladesh Bank Sues Filipino Lender in U.S. Court Over hack Heist: the New York Fed is Assisting Bangladeshi Central bank with the Lawsuit. Wall Street Journal, February. Bangladesh Bank Sues Filipino Lender in U.S. Court Over Hack Heist - WSJ

Salih, A. A., Abdulrazaq, M.B. (2024). Cybernet model: A new deep learning model for cyber DDoS attacks detection and recognition. *Computers, Materials and Continua*. 78(1), 1275–1295, https://doi.org/10.32604/cmc.2023.046101

Sarma, M., & Pais, J. (2011). Financial inclusion and development. *Journal of international development* 23(5), 613–628

Shafeeq, M., & Beg, S. (2019). Cyber risk: A hindrance to financial inclusion? *JETIR*, 6 (5). https://www.jetir.org/papers/JETIR1905023.pdf

Sharafaldin, I., Lashkari, A. H., Hakak S., & Ghorbani A. A. (2019). Developing Realistic Distributed Denial of Service (DDoS) Attack Dataset and Taxonomy. Developing-Realistic-Distributed-Denial-of-Service-DDoS-Attack-Dataset-and-Taxonomy.pdf

Shih, J., Samad-Khan, A., & Medapa, A. (2000). Is the size of an operational loss related to firm size. *Operational Risk*, 2, 21–22.

Sturm, P. (2013). Operational and reputational risk in the European banking industry: The market reaction to operational risk events. *Journal of Economic Behavior & Organization* 85, 191–206

Veeam. (2024). Ransomware Trends 2024. Executive Summary. EMEA edition. PowerPoint Presentation

Vergara Cobos, E. (2024). Cybersecurity Economics for Emerging Markets. Washington, DC: World Bank. https://doi.org/10.1596/978-1-4648 2120-2

CHAPTER 14

Banking System Goes Digital: Acceptance of Fintech Services by Households of Saudi Arabia

Abul Hassan

Introduction

The Fintech, as a term, incorporates information technology (IT) has recently gained fascination on a wide scale, highlighting the visible transformation of the financial industry (Ali et al., 2018). In an increasingly digitized world, Saudi Arabia has been a late entrant in the FinTech space. However, the rapid pace of FinTech's progress in Saudi Arabia bewilders stakeholders, including bankers. Also the term 'FinTech' relates to the services sector of various high-tech start-ups that offer innovative digital and business platform models. The digital transformation of the financial sector has not only revolutionized digitized business processes and models

This Research involves Human Participants.

A. Hassan (✉)
School of Business, King Faisal University, Hofuf, Saudi Arabia
e-mail: hassan@kfu.edu.sa

K. Tsanis et al. (eds.), *Digital Finance and Transformation in the Gulf*,
https://doi.org/10.1007/978-981-92-1588-1_14

but has also established new services and products. For instance, there has been significant growth in digital trading and advisory systems, machine learning and artificial intelligence, peer-to-peer (P2P) mobile payment and lending systems, crowdfunding, and various forms of digital money (such as Bitcoin and other crypto assets). Digital networks are no longer just an added or affordable way to interact with consumers; they represent a substantial and constantly increasing number of retail and corporate clients globally.

While Saudi Arabia may be behind some developing nations in terms of FinTech application, it possesses all the necessary factors for an effective FinTech business. A notable example is the mobile payments marketplace, where nearly 60% of Saudi Arabian households currently utilize internet banking and mobile applications. Conversely, many developed and developing countries have already embraced digital advisory and trading systems, as well as alternative digital currencies, including Bitcoin and other crypto assets. These significant variations in the adoption of digital applications in financial services necessitate a thorough assessment of the underlying causes for the differing levels of acceptance across nations and the implementation of measures to enhance customer acceptance in Saudi Arabia.

The Technology Acceptance Model (TAM), suggested by Davis (1989), states that a customer's intention to accept a newly developed technology is influenced by its perceived effectiveness and ease of use. Recent research has applied the TAM to predict the adoption of Fintech cryptocurrencies payments in the Netherlands (Jonker, 2019) and e-commerce (Smith et al., 2014), among other services. However, several studies, such as Gomber et al. (2017) and Liu et al. (2020), emphasize that for improved regulatory efficiency and meeting customer needs, the financial markets should introduce Fintech. Also, Minto et al. (2017) and Haddad and Hornuf (2019) argue that customer convenience alone cannot solely be attributed to the increasing attractiveness of innovative services and technologies in the financial service industry. They suggest that a customer's behavioral and cognitive factors will also influence the acceptance of FinTech products. Specifically, they propose expanding the TAM model to include the assessment of perceived risk and trustworthiness to address customer concerns regarding privacy and security in digital banking. Therefore, the growth of FinTech appears to be more complex, and customer willingness to adopt these services extends beyond the mere aspect of being more appealing and affordable.

Lack of satisfaction and trust are often the primary reasons why individual consumers choose to switch to banks or consider FinTech as their primary service provider (Manrai and Manrai, 2007; Maier, 2016). If FinTech can deliver higher levels of consumer satisfaction through improved services, reduced fees and rates, faster and more flexible processes, and transparent operations, they can capitalize on consumers' dissatisfaction with traditional competitors and increase their market share (Maier, 2016).

It is believed that understanding the acceptance of innovation in the investment sector by individual consumers is becoming an increasingly significant factor (Manrai and Manrai, 2007, Hassan & Raimi, 2025), for example, in measuring the financial stability implications of Fintech (FSB, 2017), among other consequences. The unbundling of banking services by various firms utilizing digital systems, and the adoption of fully digital banking systems by individual consumers, is an understudied and overlooked topic. Given the lack of research from an emerging economy perspective, addressing this theoretical and empirical research gap could significantly enhance the understanding of FinTech adoption.

Objectives of the Study

In order to examine customers' choices regarding the adoption of digital banking services and what motivates them to switch to FinTech, this study will address the following objectives:

(i) To identify the types of firms employing digital techniques in Saudi Arabia.
(ii) To investigate and identify the reasons for customer adoption or reluctance to accept digital banking services.
(iii) To determine the FinTech services (such as digital lending and credit through P2P lending, mobile banking, cryptocurrency and blockchain, trading of stocks, insurance, etc.) that are likely to be adopted.
(iv) To assess the level of comfort and trust that households have with innovative technologies and evaluate the overall impact on their decision to switch to FinTech.

Literature Review

The growth of FinTech has made a significant impact on the conventional banking sector. FinTech involves a broad selection of mobile applications, including payment of loan requests, wealth management, money transfers, insurance transactions, crowdfunding, and investment management (Chen et al., 2019). The essential field of FinTech, utilizing technological advances, encompasses business operations, banking transactions including payments and connectivity, monetization, securitization, asset and risk management (Chen et al., 2019). Towards advancement in smartphones, cloud computing, machine learning, big data, artificial intelligence, and blockchain have redesigned the dynamics of FinTech in the financial field, creating new opportunities and addressing legal concerns (Puschmann, 2017; KPMG, 2020).

FinTech services are now widely available, opening up new business opportunities for banks, non-banking financial organizations, telecommunications companies, and related industries. However, the adoption of FinTech poses technological challenges due to several factors. While ease of use influences the adoption of FinTech services, social influences have a negative effect, as stated by Singh et al. (2021). In their study, Singh et al. (2020) found that customers' intention to adopt FinTech services is primarily determined by perceived advantages, although social effects can also have a negative impact. Another study by Ali et al. (2021) observed that customers' perception of benefits and risks has a significant and positive influence on FinTech acceptance. Additionally, perceived benefits have a key and positive effect on trust, while perceived risks have a negative effect on trust. There is a strong positive and important relationship between trust and the intention to adopt Islamic FinTech (Ali et al., 2021). Moreover, socio-economic status and demographic factors provide better support in understanding the heterogeneity in the acceptance of FinTech platforms (Krishna and Krishna, 2020).

It may be noted that the inherent biases within the banking and finance industries can result in subjective lending decisions (Dobbie et al., 2021). Mortgage lenders, for instance, impose higher fees and interest rates, limiting the affordability for a small number of customers. However, adopting FinTech algorithms may mitigate this issue, as technology offers advantages in avoiding certain incidental costs associated with traditional mortgage markets. Moreover, the use of advanced financial technologies and data provides superior capabilities for screening borrowers (Berg et al., 2021).

Previous studies have also examined the use of FinTech by investigating people's intentions to use this technology in banking operations (Rodrigues et al., 2016). Considering the widespread availability of FinTech services, some studies have assessed FinTech implementation by surveying households. This study analyzes consumers' bank switching behavior and aims to explore the increasing importance of individual customers' perception of innovation acceptance in the financial sector. This includes evaluating investment stability and the implications of using FinTech (FSB, 2017), among other factors. The unbundling of banking functions by various companies using digital techniques, as well as the implementation and utilization of fully digital banking systems by customers, remains an under-researched area. Therefore, this study contributes to the nascent FinTech literature by investigating the factors that lead consumers to accept fully digital banking services and encourage them to switch to FinTech services.

Database and Methodology

The data used in this study were obtained from a house-to-house survey of 700 households conducted between January 2, 2022, and March 29, 2022, across some important locations such as Damamm, Jeddah, Riyadh, and surroundings of these cities in Saudi Arabia. We deliberately chose these locations based on our specific study need which may be termed as purposive sampling. The objective was to examine the determining factors influencing the inclination of Saudi Arabian households to switch from conventional/Islamic banking to FinTech services. After removing incomplete questionnaires and instances of missing or omitted values for certain variables, a total of 349 (291 male and 58 female) usable and definitive filled-in questionnaires were finalized.

The survey questionnaire included data on savings behavior, individual investments, the financial and economic conditions of households, as well as socio-economic and demographic variables. Additionally, we gathered information from respondents regarding their financial awareness and self-assessed levels of risk tolerance. The results indicate that three primary dimensions—transparency, financial expertise, and trust—significantly influence households' decisions to either remain with conventional retail banking systems or switch to FinTech services. Specifically, households with lower levels of trust, higher levels of financial knowledge, and a preference for more transparency exhibit a higher probability of switching. Conversely, households' perceptions of prices do not appear to influence the likelihood of switching. For a detailed description of the survey and the questionnaire pertaining to all the variables included in the study, please refer to Appendix A.

Since a high level of correlation was found among the survey items, this study employed Principal Component Analysis (PCA). PCA is a technique used to reduce the dimensionality of a dataset, increasing interpretability while minimizing information loss. The PCA in this study identified three factors: social milieu, saving attitude, and financial skill/expertise. The steps taken to perform the PCA are as follows:

Step 1: Standardize the dataset and calculate the covariance matrix.
Step 2: Find the eigenvalues and eigenvectors.
Step 3: Arrange the eigenvalues.
Step 4: Form the feature vector.
It may be mentioned here that PCA and logistic regression are employed together they serve distinct yet complementary function in data analysis. PCA is often used as a prepossessing step to enhance the performance and efficiency of a subsequent logistic regression model rather than an alternative to it. In the PCA analysis, the eigenvalues that are above 1 explain 60.44 percent of the variance in the ten times (as seen in Table 14.2). The factor loadings range from 0.48, indicating the possession (ownership) of investment products, to 0.73, indicating the level of education.

This study primarily focuses on the choice factors that determine the propensity of Saudi Arabian households to switch from the traditional banking system (both conventional and Islamic banks) to FinTech services. The dependent variable immediately indicates the ability of a private household to transition and use FinTech. This dummy variable is equal to 1 if individual consumers are willing to terminate an existing relationship with a traditional bank/Islamic bank and establish a new one by adopting a FinTech service. In the survey, we obtained the first principal component, 'social milieu,' from the survey responses. We asked households questions related to socio-demographic and economic attributes, such as income, education, and employment status. Our proxy for 'financial knowledge or expertise' includes an additional principal component comprising a set of indicators of financial expertise.

Our set of decision factors and control variables has been obtained from a household-level survey conducted by the General Authority of Statistics, specifically the Household Income & Expenditure survey of Saudi Arabia (2020). The assessment of financial literacy in Saudi Arabia has been collected from various studies, such as KPMG (2020) and Al-Rahahleh (2022), as well as from the Annual Report on the Financial Sector Development Program 2021 (Vision 2030, Kingdom of Saudi Arabia). These surveys served as baseline assessments of individual wealth and financial knowledge among households in the Kingdom of Saudi Arabia. To ensure a comprehensive assessment of 'savings attitude', this study calculates a composite variable that combines two elements: general behavior and savings rate. This composite variable accounts for 12 percent of the variation between the two elements.

Empirical Findings

Characteristics of Household

Descriptive statistics of this study are shown in Table 14.1. The age of the survey respondents ranged from 18 to 70 years, with an average age of 32 years. Our database consisted of 291 males and 51 females. A relatively high percentage of respondents, 23.33%, held a university degree, with a few having PhD degrees (1.5%) as their highest educational qualification. The average net income was less than SAR 8000, indicating a relatively high level of trust. Furthermore, the empirical analysis reveals significant variations in the measurement of transparency and price conditions. While individuals tend to be price-sensitive, the level of transparency appears to be of great importance to them. Additionally, it is worth mentioning that individuals in our sample consider themselves to have above-average levels of financial awareness. Interestingly, survey participants correctly answered two out of three financial awareness-related questions regarding compounding interest rates, diversification of securities based on basic principles, Islamic financial product selection, and the impact of inflation on financial principles. However, on average, they reported owning less than a quarter of the surveyed financial products.

One of the major aims of this study is to measure the intention of Saudi Arabian households to adopt services offered by FinTech and determine the extent to which households are eager to use FinTech services. Surprisingly, more than 35 percent of respondents stated that they were

Table 14.1 Descriptive statistics

	Observation	*Mean*	*Standard deviation*	*Minimum*	*Maximum*
Possible Use of FinTech	349	0.33	0.47	0.00	1.00
Respondent's age	349	32,14	12.11	20.00	60.00
Gender					
Male	291	1.52	0.52	1.00	2.00
Female	58	1.11	0.49	1.00	1.00
Education qualification	349	5.11	2.27	1.00	9.22
Employment	349	0.71	0.52	0.00	1.00
Household Net income	349	7.45	1.46	1.00	6.99
Self-assessment trust	349	4.55	2.17	0.00	9.98
Self-assessment price	349	4.99	1.95	0.00	9.99
Self-assessment transparency	349	7.99	1.58	2.99	9.98
Self-assessment risk	349	4.70	2.17	0.00	9.99
Self-assessment patience	349	5.49	2.41	0.00	9.98
Self-assessment fin. knowledge	349	2.95	1.22	1.01	4.98
Preference of financial products					
- Islamic financial products	349	4.30	2.22	1.00	4.67
-Conventional financial products	349	3.35	2.01	1.00	3.94
Savings behavior	349	3.44	1.02	1.00	
Saving rate	349	2.55	1.52	1.00	6.99
Financial literacy	349	0.92	0.29	0.00	1.00
Knowledge on finance products	349	0.52	0.13	0.08	0.85

willing to do so. These findings support the hypothesis of this study, which suggests that the rise of online banking services and the emergence of other online financial intermediaries have a negative impact on traditional banking businesses. Consequently, there is an increase in customer migration from traditional banks to FinTech.

Table 14.2 Key factor analysis

	Factor1 Social atmosphere	*Factor 2 Financial Skill*	*Factor 3 Saving mind-set*
Saving behavior	0.026	−0.011	0.751
Saving rate	−0.017	−0.001	0.711
Education level	0.786	−0.007	−0.132
Employment	0.594	−0.116	0.091
Household net income	0.759	0.085	1.151
Self-assessment finance knowledge	0.003	0.617	0.116
Financial literacy	0.002	0.654	−0.236
Knowledge on Islamic finance products	0.109	0.534	0.161
Ownership investment products	0.191	0.499	0.074

Deciding Factors for Picking up Financial Services Institutions

The study employed a logistic regression analysis to examine the survey data, as we are interested in determining which variables have an effect on the propensity to choose a different banking system. To accomplish this, we calculated three separate binary logistic regression models.

(1) The initial model includes only the three control variables and factors.
(2) The second model examines the influence of the questionnaire respondent's self-valuation, transparency, price, and risk.
(3) The third model combines elements from both previous models. This combination allows us to draw conclusions about whether the effects of variables change when additional descriptive variables are included in the study.

Table 14.3 presents the results of the regression analysis. Firstly, it was observed that older participants or respondents had a lower probability of switching to FinTech. This finding aligns with the common belief that younger generations are more attracted to digital technological advancements. Additionally, the impact of social milieu, which represents social pressure to conform to certain actions or opinions, has been recognized in the literature (Rahi et al., 2019). It is assumed that communication and discussions among young people or with friends about emerging technologies, such as FinTech, may influence their adoption. The influence of social norms is significant in various countries, as seen in the adoption of mobile technology services across different age groups in the UK (Choudrie et al., 2018). These results are consistent with the findings of a study conducted by Junger and Mietzner (2020). The actions, comments, and perceptions of family members, colleagues, and friends regarding the use of technology play a crucial role in shaping individuals' decisions.

Table 14.3 Regression Findings

Models	*Odds ratio (1)*	*SE*	*Odds ratio (2)*	*SE*	*Odds ratio(3)*	*SE*
Age of respondents	0.96	(0.03)	0.99**	(0.03)	0.97**	(0.03)
Gender	0.97	(0.27)	0.76	(0.27)	0.91	(0.28)
Social milieu factor	0.97	(0.28)	–	–	0.90	(0.25)
Financial expertise factor	2.11***	(0.23)	–	–	2.12***	(0.23)
Saving attitude factor	0.84	(0.24)	–	–	0.81	(0.24)
Self-assessment trust	–		1.15**	(0.07)	1.14***	(0.08)
Self-assessment transparency	–		1.41**	(0.09)	1.43***	(0.11)
Self-assessment price	–		0.98	(0.07)	0.96	(0.08)
Self-assessment patience	–		1.05	(0.06)	1.03	(0.06)
Self-assessment risk	–		1.15**	(0.07)	1.08	(0.06)
Constant	1.25	(0.62)	0.05***	(1.15)	0.04***	(1.23)
Observations	349		349		349	
Log likelihood	382.72		375.641		360.61	
Cox & Snell R^2 (CS)	0.065		0.079		0.115	
Nagelkerke R^2 (N)	0.091		0.161		0.159	

Another important aspect related to the self-assessment variable is "transparency," where customers who prioritize transparency in banking services are more likely to switch to FinTech. Transparency reduces information asymmetries, enabling consumers to thoroughly evaluate prices and services. This becomes significant as customers become increasingly concerned about the credibility of financial guidance, especially when it comes to financial obligations. For example, Ferdaous and Rahman (2021) highlight the challenges of reliable financial guidance in Bangladesh. They point out that incentive structures can introduce biases in financial advice, leading to the promotion and sale of products that may not align with the needs of retail consumers.

Studies conducted by KPMG Saudi Arabia (2020) and Al-Rahahleh (2022) have highlighted the challenges in ensuring consistent financial advice in Saudi Arabia. These studies have also pointed out that incentive structures may introduce biases in financial guidance, leading to the promotion and sale of financial products that may not necessarily meet the requirements of retail customers. Therefore, transparency can serve as a significant differentiating factor that influences consumer behavior in switching to FinTech. Additionally, transparency can also serve as a trust-building measure, particularly when firms provide assurances regarding privacy and security. Regarding security, it is worth noting that the Cybersecurity program in Saudi Arabia, as emphasized by Vision 2030 Kingdom of Saudi Arabia (2021), plays a crucial role in protecting online banking customers and financial institutions. It contributes to the development of specialized cybersecurity capabilities in the financial sector, enhancing its ability to safeguard this vital pillar. In light of this, it becomes evident that security concerns have a substantial impact on clients' intention to adopt a potentially risky technology in Saudi Arabia.

The anticipation of potential losses associated with the implementation of technology is referred to as perceived risk (Pavlou, 2003). Communication systems, including those in the digital sector, inherently carry risks. Similarly, there is a possibility of financial loss when using FinTech services. Therefore, customers may express reluctance to adopt FinTech services due to these perceived risks. Various aspects of perceived risk exist in the digital sector, such as concerns regarding time, privacy, opportunity costs, and monetary aspects. Empirical evidence has shown the impact of perceived risk on the adoption of FinTech services, including mobile payment, as demonstrated by studies conducted by Ferdous and Rahman (2021) and Chopdar et al. (2018).

One of the significant contributions of this study is the analysis of logit regression from the perspective of a developing economy, taking into account perceived risk. This analysis is based on the theories of technology adoption and consumer behavior, providing a comprehensive understanding of consumers' intention to accept FinTech in an economy like Saudi Arabia. Consistent with previous studies, including the work of Junger and Mietzner (2020), the findings from the regression analysis are influenced by various factors such as different technologies and social context (Handoko, 2020; Al-Saedi et al., 2020; Palau-Samme et al., 2019). In the context of Saudi Arabia, this study contributes to the existing body of knowledge by addressing certain gaps observed in the utilization of FinTech.

Regarding financial advice, Kramer (2016) observes that individuals who have a high level of trust in others are more likely to seek expert assistance. Customers have also become accustomed to engaging in personal communication with their bank advisors. As they may not typically experience this type of interaction with FinTech, there is a greater likelihood that they will remain with their current banks. Consistent with this, it has been found that individuals with a higher level of trust in others are less likely to switch to FinTech. Specifically, consumers who are more skeptical than trusting have an estimated probability of 80% or higher of switching to FinTech, while those with a high degree of trust have a probability of 70% or lower of switching. (The predicted probability method involves calculating predicted outcomes for each individual exposure scenarios and then averaging these predicted outcomes. This yields a population level (marginal) probability that accurately reflects the co-founder distribution in the target population) Another one possible explanation for this finding could be the inherent skepticism of retail consumers towards traditional banks (Hassan & Raimi, 2025). Skeptical consumers are more likely to question the service providers, while individuals who are more self-assured may not consider switching to FinTech as they trust the services provided by their current banks. Trustworthiness and trust, therefore, play a crucial role in the acceptance of FinTech services by customers and can be based on knowledge or developed through previous customer experiences and interactions with others.

According to Table 14.3, it is evident that households with a higher level of financial literacy are more likely to switch to FinTech. The positive impact of financial literacy and expertise on the probability of households switching service providers can be attributed to two main reasons. Firstly, households with a strong interest in financial investments tend to have a higher level of financial literacy, enabling them to understand financial products more effectively. Secondly, individuals with a greater degree of financial knowledge are better equipped to navigate various financial products. They have a broader understanding of the banking products being offered and can discern which offers perform better. In contrast, households with lower financial literacy may struggle to differentiate between different offers. This finding is supported by the empirical analysis conducted by Shahzad et al. (2018), which demonstrated a positive relationship between perceived trustworthiness, literacy, and awareness of bitcoins in Canada. Based on these findings, it can be concluded that households with higher financial literacy are more inclined to switch to FinTech, as they are particularly interested in the innovative products and solutions offered by FinTech.

However, contrary to the findings of this study, a study conducted by Pala-Samumell et al. (2019) indicated that higher banking fees can potentially drive customers to switch their banks. As a result, the coefficient of the "price" variable in our models does not show significance. This study reveals that households with higher price elasticity have an average anticipated probability of around 70% of switching service providers, while it is slightly below 70% for households who consider themselves to be price inelastic. The minimal variation suggests that price sensitivity does not have a significant impact on the probability of an individual household switching from a bank to FinTech.

Contrary to the study conducted by Jensen (2012), the results of this study indicate that the price of financial services is not typically a decisive factor in the choice between FinTech and conventional financial institutions. Other factors may also play a role in the decision-making process. However, FinTech is often characterized by its appealing offers. It should be noted that this attribute may not be relevant to all individuals and certainly not to all contemporary business service providers. In summary, since price alone does not appear to significantly influence the likelihood of switching, traditional financial institutions or banks should avoid engaging in harmful price competition and instead differentiate themselves through the provision of excellent customer service offerings.

Conclusion

This research provides empirical evidence regarding the factors that can lead customers to switch at least a portion of their financial services from conventional finance to financial technology setups. It is found that over 33% of our survey respondents/participants expressed their willingness to transition from a conventional provider to a FinTech, indicating that these innovative digital financial service providers have the potential to capture a significant market share from traditional financial institutions. One of the driving factors behind this shift in market share towards FinTech is the higher level of customer satisfaction experienced with their service offerings.

Hence, for conventional financial institutions to differentiate themselves from FinTech, they need to focus on innovative business models, investments in digital offerings, and improved service quality. Generally, customer satisfaction with incumbent institutions appears to be quite low. In particular, by reducing information asymmetries and increasing transparency, customers can make more informed decisions about prices and services, which may decrease their inclination to switch to FinTech. However, there are significant differences between non-users and users of FinTech technology across countries. The empirical survey results emphasize that perceived transparency, reliability, trust, and financial literacy are the most important factors influencing the adoption of FinTech products. The results also indicate that in the Saudi Arabian context, the price of financial or banking services is not typically a decisive criterion when choosing between FinTech and conventional financial institutions, highlighting the greater importance of convenience as a differentiating factor for customers rather than prices.

Regarding the FinTech landscape in Bangladesh, Ferdaous and Rahman (2021) note that digital payment services, crowdfunding, peer-to-peer (P2P) lending, and digital investment advisory services like robo-advisors have emerged as major segments. Particularly, the rapidly growing digital financial advisory services address the need for greater transparency, as services like robo-advisory and price comparison make certain banking transactions and related services more transparent to clients. However, clients may require adequate resources, financial knowledge, and capacity to utilize financial and FinTech advisory services effectively. In the Saudi Arabian context, our results indicate that financial literacy or knowledge plays a significant role in P2P investing. Additionally, our study shows that interest rates are relatively low in P2P lending platforms, suggesting that clients are less price-sensitive when it comes to FinTech lending services. However, compared to other areas of finance, there is an upward trend in P2P lending activities in Saudi Arabia. Regarding digital payment and banking services, it is found that financial literacy is increasing in Saudi Arabia as these firms are generally highly valued. Moreover, higher financial knowledge also increases the likelihood of adoption and usage of FinTech in lending and payment services.

In general, our study's findings align well with the current state of FinTech service adoption in Saudi Arabia. Therefore, this research can provide valuable insights for policymakers, households, and practitioners, contributing to a better understanding of the innovative adoption of financial services by individual customers. However, given the diverse range of business models within the FinTech industry, the overall recommendation for policymakers and industry stakeholders is to strive towards reducing consumers' perceived risk and enhancing their trust in digital technologies and FinTech services. To address clients' concerns regarding FinTech products and services, policymakers should prioritize ensuring adequate consumer protection measures, promoting transparency and comparability, and enhancing knowledge about digital financial services. These efforts will help build trust and confidence among consumers, fostering a conducive environment for the growth and adoption of FinTech in the financial sector.

The overall contributions of this research are diverse and can be classified into the areas of theory, practice, and policy. This study provides valuable insights for policymakers, practitioners, and households, enabling a better understanding of the adoption of financial innovations by individual clients. Additionally, this research examines the influence of age, gender, and education level on the intention of Saudi customers to adopt FinTech. It offers valuable knowledge to enhance the understanding, growth, and utilization of FinTech innovations in Saudi Arabia. However, this research also has a few limitations. Firstly, it relies on logit regression analysis and three different binary logistic regression models. As the first study on FinTech adoption behavior in Saudi Arabia, further research is needed to either support or challenge the findings of this study. Secondly, the current research focuses solely on the adoption behavior of end-users of FinTech products, and it would be beneficial to explore the perspectives of business owners and intermediaries. Lastly, future studies should also investigate the moderation and mediation effects of other factors not considered in the models employed, as there is a significant literature gap regarding FinTech adoption in Saudi Arabia.

Funding Acknowledgement The author acknowledges the funding of this project from the Deanship of Scientific Research, Vice Presidency for Graduate Studies and Scientific Research, King Faisal University, Saudi Arabia (Grant No.KFU261589)

Conflicts of Interest Author declares no conflict of interest.

Appendix-A: Explanations of Variables

Variables	*Description*	*Coding*
Endogenous Variables		
Using FinTech in financial transaction	Are you already using FinTech in financial transaction?	Yes = 1
Sociodemographic Characteristics		
Highest academic qualifications	Your highest academic qualifications	No education completion = 0 Currently schooling = 1 Vocational training completed (apprenticeship) = 2 Associate degree from community college = 3 Technical college = 3 School for master craftsmen or engineers completed = 4 Bachelor's degree from University = 5 Master's degree from University = 6 Technical master degree from university = 7 PhD = 8
Employment	Are you currently employed?	Yes = 1
Marriage status	Are you married?	Yes = 1

(continued)

(continued)

Variables	*Description*	*Coding*
Net Income of the Households	What is your monthly net income?	<SAR2500 = 1 2500–5000 = 2 5000–10,000 = 3 10,000–15,000 = 4 15,000–20,000 = 5 20,000–30,000 = 6 40,000 or more = 7
Self-assessment		
Self-assessment -trust	How do you view yourself: Are you in general a person who trusts others or do you tend to distrust people?	I don't trust others fully = 1 I trust other fully = 5
Self-assessment -transparency	How do you view yourself: Do you react sensitively (elastically) to price changes?	I don't responds at all to price changes + 1 I react strongly for every price changes = 5
Self-assessment-risk	How do you view yourself: Are you in general a risk-taking person or do you try to avoid risks?	- I am not at all willing to take risk = 1 I am very willing to take risks = 5
Self-assessment-patience	How do you view yourself personally: Are you in general a person who is patient or do you tend to be impatient?	I am very impatient = 1 I have patient = 5
Self-assessment-literacy on financial matters	Do you agree with this statement? "I am very interested in financial matters and keep myself informed about potential investment opportunities."	Completely disagree in the matters = 1 Completely agree +
Financial Characteristics		
Client's saving behavior	Which of the statements best describes the saving patterns of your household?	I donot require to save = 0 I am not saving because there is no saving after household expenses = 1 I save something if there is something left to save = 2 I save every month = 3 I determine the amount depending on the financial situation = 4 I regularly save a certain amount = 5

(continued)

(continued)

Variables	*Description*	*Coding*
Rate of saving of the clients	How big is the share you save from your monthly income?	<5% = 1 5–10% = 2 10–15% = 3 15–20% = 4 20–30% = 5 30–40% = 6 40% Above = 7
Expertise on financial products	Projected knowledge about financial products Please hint which of the following financial products do you still hold? current account, credit card, prepaid payment card, mobile payment account, shares, consumer credit, unsecured bank loan, mortgage, insurance, pension fund Islamic financial products	No understanding and buying of products = 0 Understanding and buying of products = 1
Islamic Financial knowledge	Do think in Islamic investments decision, how important? Not important / Important What you think that investing in shariah compliant share of one company is less risky than investment in a fund holding shariah compliant share of similar company	Responses are wrong/ negative = 0 Responses are positive/ right = 1

(continued)

(continued)

Variables	*Description*	*Coding*
Proprietorship of investment products	Which of the following investment products are in your possession? –investments in non-publicly traded companies pension plan –savings accounts –savings and loan agreements –stocks/bonds –sukuk –mutual funds –REITs (Real estate investment trust) –Islamic investments	Possession of no product = 0 Possession of any of the products = 1

References

Ali, R; Beck R; and Smits, M (2018). Fintech and transformation of the financial industry, *Electron Markets.* 4, 235–243

Ali, M; Raza, S; Khamis, B; Pua, C and Amin, H (2021). How Perceived Risk Benefit and Trust Determine User Fintech Adoption: A New Dimension for Islamic Finance, *Foresight ,23(4), 403–420*

Al-Rahahleh, N (2022), Financial Literacy Levels Among Saudi Citizens Access Budgeting, Savins, Investment, Debt and Insurance Dimension, *Journal of Risk and Financial Management,* 15, 582–595

Al-Saedi, K; Al-Imran, M Ramaya, T and Abusham, E (2020). Developing a general extend UTAUT model for M-payment adoption, *Technology in Society*, 62, 121–132

Berg, T; Fuster, A and Puri, M (2021), Fintech Lending, NBER Working Paper No. 29421, National Bureau of Economic Research, Cambridge (US)

Chen, M.A; Wu, Q and Yang, B (2019). How valuable is Fintech innovation? *Review of Financial Studies*, 32(5), 2062–2106

Chopdar, P; Korfiatis, N; Shivakumar, V and Lytras, M (2018). Mobile shopping apps adoption and perceived risks: A cross-country perspective utilizing the United Theory of Acceptance and Use of technology, *Computers in Human Behaviour*, 86 (9). 109–128

Choudrie, J; Junior, C; MaKenna, B and Richter, S (2018). Understanding and conceptualizing the adoption, use and diffusion of mobile banking in older adults: a research agenda and conceptual framework, *Journal of Business Research*, 88, 449–465

Davis, F.D. (1989). Perceived usefulness, perceived ease of use, and user acceptance of information technology. *MIS Q*. 13 (3), 319–339.

Dobbie, W, Libberman, A; Paravisi, D and Pathamia, V(2021). Measuring Bias I Consumer Lending, *Review of Economic Studies*, 88 (6), 2799–2832

Ferdaous, J and Rahaman, M (2021). Banking Goes Digital : Unearthing the Adoption of Fintech by Bangladeshi Households, *Journal of Innovation in Business Studies*, 1(1), 7–42

FSB (2017), Financial Stability Implications from FinTech. Financial Stability Board. ULR: https://www.fsb.org/2017/06/financial-stability-implications-from-fintech//.

Gomber, P; Koch, J and Siering (2017). Digital Finance and FinTech Current Research and Future Research Direction, *Journal of Business Economics*,87(5), 537–580

Haddad, C and Hornuf (2019). The mergence of the global fintech market: Economic and Technological Determinants, *Small Business Economics*, 53(1), 81–105

Handoko, B (2020). UTAUT2 Model for Entrepreneurship Students on Adopting Technology. A per presented in the International Conference on Information Management and Technology (pp.191–196) organised by IEEE, New Jersey, United States

Hassan, A and Raimi, L (2025). "Leveraging Qard Hasan as a Financing Mechanism for Entrepreneurship at the Botom of the Pyramid : A Systematic Review". *Journal of Cultural Analysis and Social Change*, 10(2), 3095–3111. https://doi.org/10.64753/jcasc.v10i2.2061

Jensen, J (2012). Shopping Orientation and Online Travel Shopping The Role of Travel Experience, *International Journal of Tourism Research*, 14(1), 56–70

Jonker, N (2019). What drives the adoption of crypto-payments online retailers, *Electronic Commerce and Business Applications,* 35, 56–69

Junger, M and Mietzner, M (2020). Banking goes digital: The adoption of FinTech Services by German Households, *Finance Research Letters*, 34, 1–8

Kramer, M (2016). Financial Literacy, Confidence and Financial Advice Seeking, *Journal of Economic Behaviour and Organisation*, 131, 198–217

KPMG in Saudi Arabia. (2020). Household Savings: An Analysis of Household Savings in Saudi Arabia. Available online: https://home.kpmg/sa/en/home/insights/2020/05/household-savings.html

Krishna, B and Krishna, S (2020). Explaining Variation in Adoption of Fintech Products and Services Among Citizens: A Multilevel Model. A paper presented in the International Conference on Transfer and Diffusion of IT (pp. 541–552), Cambridge: Springer

Liu, J; Li, X and Wang, S (2020). What have we learnt from 10 years of fintech research? A Scientometric analysis, *Technological Forecasting and Social Change*, 7, 155–164

Maier,E (2016). Supply and demand of crowd-lending platform: connecting small and medium size enterprise browsers and customer investors, *Journal of Retail Consumers Services,* 21 (4), 143–153

Manrai, L and Manrai, A (2007). A field study of consumers switching behaviour for banks service, *Journal of Retail Consumers Services*, 14(3), 208–215

Minto, A; Voelkerling, M and Wulff, M (2017). Separating apples from oranges identifying threats to financial stability originating from FinTech. Capital Market Law Journal, 12(4), 428–426

Pala-Saumell, R; Forgas-Coll, S; Sanchez-Garcia, J and Robres, E (2019). Users acceptance of mobile apps for restaurants: An expanded and extended UTAUT-2, *Sustainability*, 11(4), 34–49

Pavlou, P (2003).Consumer acceptance of electronic commerce: Integrating trust and risk with the technology acceptance model, *International Journal of Electronic Commerce*, 7(3),101–134

Puschmann, T (2017). *Fintech, Business and Information System Engineering*, 59(1).69–76.

Rahi, S; Mansour, M; Alghizzawi, M & Alnaser, F (2019). Integration of UTAUT model in internet banking adoption context, *Journal of Research in Interactive Marketing*, 13(3), 411–435

Rodrigues, G; Sarabdeen, J and Balasubramanian, S (2016). Factors that influence consumer adoption of e-government services in UAE: A UTAUT model perspective. *Journal of Internet Commerce*, 15(1), 1939

Shahzad, F; Xiu, G' Wang, J; and Shahbaz, M (2018). An empirical investigation on the adoption of cryptocurrency among the people of mainland China, *Technol. Society*, 55, 33–40

Singh, S; Sahni, M and Kovid, R (2020). What Drives Fintech Adoption? A Multimethod Evaluation Using Adapted Technology Acceptance Model, Managerial Decision, 58(8), 1675–1697.

Singh, S; Sahni, M and Kovid, R (2021). Exploring Antecedents of Fintech Adoption Using Adapted Technology Acceptance Model, In Advances in System Engineering, (pp. 337–352). Singapore: Springer

Smith, A; Synowka, D and Smith, A (2014). E-commerce quality and adaptive elements of e-ticketing and sporting events, *International Journal of Business Information System,* 15(4), 450–457

Vision 2030 Kingdom of Saudi Arabia (2021) Financial Sector Report Program, retrieved from: https://www.vision2030.gov.sa/media/vsdfctvv/financial-sector-development-program-annual-report-2021.pdf

CHAPTER 15

The Impact of Fintech on Islamic Finance and Capital Markets in Qatar Using Network Analysis

Ahmet Faruk Aysan and Muhammad Fazlurrahman Syarif

Introduction

The digital transformation of financial services has ushered in an era of rapid innovation, with financial technology (fintech) reshaping how capital is mobilized, transactions are executed, and financial inclusion is advanced. Globally, the Islamic-fintech segment alone is projected to expand from US$137 billion in transaction volume in 2022/23 to US$306 billion by 2027—an average annual growth rate of 17%—underlining the sector's accelerating dynamism and its pivotal role in serving faith-based financial markets (IFAAS 2024). Within this broader

A. F. Aysan (✉) · M. F. Syarif
College of Islamic Studies, Hamad Bin Khalifa University, Qatar Foundation, Al-Rayyan, Qatar
e-mail: aaysan@hbku.edu.qa

M. F. Syarif
e-mail: musy33188@hbku.edu.qa

K. Tsanis et al. (eds.), *Digital Finance and Transformation in the Gulf*,
https://doi.org/10.1007/978-981-92-1588-1_15

landscape, Qatar has emerged as a leading hub for Islamic-fintech innovation. According to the Global Islamic Fintech (GIFT) Report 2023/24, Qatar's Islamic-fintech market was valued at US$2.1 billion in 2022/23 and is forecast to nearly double to US$4 billion by 2027. The same report ranks Qatar as the eighth most conducive ecosystem globally for Islamic-fintech development, reflecting supportive regulation, robust infrastructure, and a growing pool of talent.

Despite Islamic finance's entrenched position in Qatar—exemplified by Qatar Islamic Bank's 43% share of the country's Islamic banking sector and its status as the nation's largest Sharia-compliant lender—the ways in which fintech enterprises interface with traditional Islamic financial institutions, regulatory bodies, payment schemes, and capital-market venues remain insufficiently mapped. Existing studies have largely concentrated on fintech's impact on financial inclusion or systemic-risk modelling, employing network-centric approaches to identify central actors and contagion pathways. However, a focused examination of the structural relationships that underpin Qatar's Islamic-fintech ecosystem has not yet been undertaken.

Furthermore, the role of FinTech extends to addressing significant barriers to financial inclusion in Qatar. Emerging technologies can enhance access for underbanked populations, enabling individuals and small businesses to engage with financial services that match with their ethical standards. Research indicates that the use of FinTech can reduce transaction costs significantly, making financial services more accessible to low-income users (Elomari 2023; Majid and Mawaddah 2022). In developing economies, many of which are located in the MENA region, these benefits are crucial for stimulating economic growth and improving living conditions (Saba et al. 2019).

In the context of network analysis, the interconnectivity facilitated by FinTech platforms is essential for developing robust Islamic financial ecosystems. By harnessing data analytics, financial institutions can better understand consumer behaviour and enhance their service offerings, ultimately promoting a more competitive environment within the Islamic finance sector (Ajouz and Abuamria 2023; Kharrat et al. 2023). Such analysis allows institutions to identify potential risks and opportunities, tailoring products to meet the demands of diverse market segments. Moreover, as Islamic finance practices integrate with global FinTech innovations, cross-border banking and investment opportunities are becoming increasingly viable, which can enhance liquidity and market depth in Qatar (Glavina et al. 2021; Selim 2020).

This paper addresses that gap by applying network analysis to the Qatar context. We assemble a comprehensive dataset of formal partnerships, co-partnership agreements, and regulatory linkages among key actors: Islamic banks (e.g., Qatar Islamic Bank, Masraf Al Rayan, Qatar International Islamic Bank), the Qatar Central Bank, digital-payment schemes (Visa, NPCI/UPI), fintech start-ups (PayLater, Noqoody, Fatora, among others), and capital-market entities (Qatar Stock Exchange). Through the construction of adjacency matrices and the generation of network graphs, we calculate centrality measures (degree strength, betweenness, eigenvector) and detect community structures to identify (1) principal "hub" institutions, (2) bridging entities that facilitate regulatory or operational interfaces, and (3) peripheral actors that may represent emerging or niche service providers.

To date, no study has integrated these disparate threads into a systematic network analysis of Qatar's Sharia-compliant digital-finance landscape. By constructing detailed adjacency matrices, generating network graphs, and computing centrality and community-detection metrics, this paper fills that gap. In doing so, it extends the literature on fintech network structures to a high-growth, Islamic-finance hub, offering both theoretical insights and policy-relevant findings for strengthening digital-finance ecosystems in comparable jurisdictions.

By elucidating these relational patterns, our study highlight on how fintech innovations are integrated into Qatar's Islamic finance and capital-markets infrastructure, highlighting strategic partnerships, regulatory dependencies, and potential areas for policy intervention. The insights generated herein not only contribute to the literature on fintech–Islamic finance convergence but also offer practical guidance for regulators, financial institutions, and fintech entrepreneurs seeking to navigate and strengthen Qatar's rapidly evolving digital-finance ecosystem.

This study is guided by the following research questions: (1) Which institutions and fintech start-ups occupy the most central positions within Qatar's Islamic-fintech network? (2) To what extent do regulatory bodies and capital-market venues act as bridges between traditional Islamic banks and emergent fintech firms? and (3) How fragmented is the broader fintech landscape, and what implications does this have for strategic ecosystem development?

In order to answer these questions, we posit three hypotheses. First, we hypothesize that Qatar Islamic Bank (QIB) will emerge as the primary hub—exhibiting the highest degree, betweenness, and eigenvector centrality—reflecting its dominant market share and extensive partner ecosystem. Second, we hypothesize that regulatory-backed fintech (e.g., PayLater) will serve as critical bridges between commercial banks and the Qatar Central Bank, demonstrating elevated betweenness relative to purely private start-ups. Third, we hypothesize that a substantial subset of niche fintech providers will remain peripheral—forming isolated singleton communities with low connectivity—indicating opportunities and challenges for deeper sector integration.

Situated within the wider GCC push to embed fintech and digitalization at the core of post-hydrocarbon economic strategies, Qatar offers a theoretically informative and policy-relevant case for examining Islamic-fintech ecosystem design. Existing Islamic-fintech studies have largely focused on customer adoption, financial inclusion, or high-level regulatory initiatives, without systematically unpacking the meso-level network structures that connect regulators, incumbent Islamic banks, payment schemes, and start-ups in a single jurisdiction. By centring on Qatar's Islamic-fintech ecosystem and explicitly modelling its relational architecture, this study contributes in three ways: (i) it extends network-analysis approaches—thus far applied predominantly to conventional banking and cross-border payment systems—to a Sharia-compliant, bank-centric environment; (ii) it links national and GCC-level digital-transformation agendas to the concrete pattern of partnerships and regulatory linkages observed in practice; and (iii) it generates empirically grounded indicators and benchmarks that can inform ecosystem design in other Islamic-finance hubs. These contributions position the paper at the intersection of Islamic finance, digital transformation, and network theory, and highlight its relevance beyond the Qatar context.

The remainder of this paper is organized as follows. Section "Literature Review" reviews the relevant literature on fintech and network analysis. Section "Methodology" details the data collection process and network-analysis methodology, including the construction of adjacency matrices, the selection of centrality measures, and community-detection procedures. Section "Result and Discussion" presents the results of our network graphs, heatmaps, and co-partnership analyses, accompanied by a discussion that interprets the empirical findings in light of our hypotheses. Finally, section "Conclusion" concludes with a summary of key insights, policy implications for regulators and financial institutions in Qatar, and suggestions for future research directions aimed at strengthening a more cohesive and resilient Islamic-fintech ecosystem.

Literature Review

The literature on fintech and its intersection with Islamic finance spans three main strands: (1) network-analysis approaches to financial ecosystems, (2) content analysis of Islamic fintech, and (3) country-level studies—of which Qatar remains underexplored.

Network-Analysis

Network analysis has become critical tools across multiple disciplines, enabling the exploration and visualization of complex interrelationships within various systems. This response synthesizes multiple sources to detail the methodologies, applications, and advancements in network analysis approaches.

The realm of biological research demonstrates a significant impact from network analysis, particularly through methods such as network-based pathway analysis. This approach is directed at understanding intricate biological processes such as disease mechanisms, where biological pathways play crucial roles. For instance, Zhang et al. (2016a, 2016b) highlight three stages of pathway analysis that evolve from simple enrichment analysis to more complex network-based methods, enhancing our understanding of multifactorial diseases, notably cancers. Complementing this, Patel et al. (2010) utilize network analysis to identify critical pathways associated with intestinal cancer, emphasizing how robust statistical methods can refine the understanding of protein-protein interactions to separate true from false signals in biological networks. The integration of network analysis in biological systems has therefore proven invaluable as it enables researchers to distil large datasets into actionable biological insights (Naqvi et al. 2023).

In the social sciences, network analysis methods serve to explain the structures and dynamics of social phenomena. Social network analysis (SNA) has been adapted to various contexts, including criminology, where it aids in understanding criminal networks and their operational dynamics (Rossy and Morselli 2017). This method evolves from traditional approaches to include advanced techniques that analyze the flow of information and connections among actors, thereby offering novel insights into societal interactions. Mills (2017) emphasizes that SNA within archaeology and other fields promotes a relational approach, focusing on the ties between actors that delineate social relationships, further indicating the breadth of SNA applications (Zhou 2023).

The application of network analysis also extends into areas such as transportation and economic systems. For example, Gaspar et al. (2023) apply network analysis to assess changes in Advanced Driver Assistance Systems (ADAS) through over-the-air updates, showcasing the method's capability in assessing technology interconnectivity and complexity. Similarly, financial systems have leveraged network approaches for analyzing correlations among various financial entities to better understand market dynamics during crises, as indicated by Kazemilari and Mohamadi (2018) focus on correlation networks that emerged from statistical physics perspectives. This implies a critical intersection of network-analysis methods with economic modelling, contributing to more resilient economic forecasting.

Moreover, probabilistic models and advanced statistical techniques have enriched network analysis further. Scharbarg et al. (2009) demonstrate that probabilistic modelling provides insights into system behaviour under various operational conditions, particularly within the context of avionics networks. These models can illuminate the complexities of interactions in highly technical fields, where traditional statistical approaches may fall short (Bauer et al. 2010).

Content Analyses in Islamic Fintech

Content analyses in Islamic fintech provide critical insights into the development, challenges, and future direction of financial technology within the framework of Islamic finance. The integration of fintech into Islamic finance has sparked significant academic interest, resulting in various methodological approaches to literature reviews, bibliometric analyses, and thematic analyses. This synthesis of content analyses from diverse studies illustrates how they contribute to our understanding of this evolving field. For instance, Pratiwi et al. (2023) utilized bibliographic coupling and content analysis methodologies to visualize the interconnections among literature on Islamic crowdfunding and fintech, allowing researchers to identify significant research streams and topical orientations within this sector. Maniam (2024) systematic literature review (SLR) employing PRISMA guidelines offered a detailed analysis of determinants influencing the adoption of Islamic fintech, emphasizing the critical role of Sharia compliance as a persistent challenge for its growth.

Bibliometric analyses, as demonstrated by Alshater et al. (2022) and Pahlevi (2022), have been instrumental in identifying trends and the growth trajectory of Islamic-fintech research. Alshater et al. (2022) utilized statistical methods to present publication trends, while Pahlevi (2022) mapped Islamic corporate governance, highlighting rapid expansion and competition among Islamic financial institutions globally. These studies emphasize both quantitative growth and the relevance of thematic areas that warrant further exploration.

Concurrent to bibliometric studies, thematic and content analyses have revealed critical challenges facing advancements in Islamic fintech, particularly concerning Sharia compliance. For instance, Irfan and Rusmita (2023) highlight operational efficiency and regulatory frameworks as pivotal elements that influence the adoption of fintech solutions, while Hasan et al. (2020) have pinpointed Sharia compliance as a significant barrier to growth.

Qatar's Islamic-Fintech Ecosystem

Qatar's Islamic-fintech ecosystem is rapidly evolving, driven by a combination of traditional Islamic banking principles and innovations introduced by modern financial technology. As an emerging hub for Islamic finance, Qatar is strategically positioned within the Gulf Cooperation Council (GCC), leveraging its substantial economic resources and commitment to developing a competitive Islamic finance sector.

The integration of fintech within Islamic finance in Qatar presents numerous opportunities to enhance financial inclusion, optimize operations, and promote economic growth. According to Kismawadi (2024), Islamic fintech can effectively facilitate financial inclusion across the GCC, ensuring that underserved populations have access to financial services, which is vital for economic development. The role of Islamic banks in Qatar's economy is significant, as they contribute to overall economic growth by mobilizing deposits and financing various economic activities. This is further supported by research illustrating that Islamic finance is a critical component of the country's economic diversification strategies (Shawtari et al. 2023).

Qatar's Central Bank (QCB) has established a national strategy aimed at creating a favourable ecosystem for fintech innovations. This framework supports traditional banking sectors as well as emerging fintech models that adhere to Sharia principle. The QCB's initiative aims to enhance the digitalization of financial services, which is crucial for modernizing the Islamic financial landscape in the country. Furthermore, research has indicated that fintech advancements can significantly improve the efficiency and profitability of traditional Islamic banking (Elomari 2023).

The incorporation of digital platforms in Islamic insurance models, such as Takaful, exemplifies how fintech can create better accessibility and operational efficiency. Moreover, the competitive landscape of Qatar's Islamic finance sector is bolstered by evolving customer preferences for digital solutions. Recent analyses indicate that Qatar is actively positioning itself to compete with established Islamic finance markets in places like Malaysia and the UAE by promoting its fintech capabilities (Tlemsani 2015; Ali et al. 2019). This competitive strategy includes strengthening an environment conducive to blockchain technology adoption, which has shown promise in solving issues associated with trust and transaction efficiency in the Islamic finance space (Dahdal et al. 2020; Ibrahim and Truby 2021). Blockchain's capabilities to enhance transparency and security resonate well with Islamic finance's ethical requirements, thereby creating an effective synergy between traditional values and cutting-edge technology (Antova and Tayachi 2020).

However, challenges remain in maximizing the potential of Islamic fintech in Qatar. Stakeholder insights collected through qualitative research highlight concerns around regulatory frameworks, market readiness, and the necessity for continuous innovation (Supriadi et al. 2023). The successful integration of fintech within the Islamic finance sector requires addressing these challenges through robust government policies that encourage innovation while ensuring compliance with Islamic law.

Although global reports rank Qatar among the top ten most conducive environments for Islamic fintech—citing robust infrastructure, favourable regulation, and talent development—academic studies at the country level remain scarce. Industry reports (Global Islamic Fintech Report 2023/24) highlight Qatar's strengths across market size, regulatory-sandbox frameworks, and capital availability, yet they stop short of empirically mapping the relationships among banks, regulators, payment operators, fintech start-ups, and capital-market venues. A handful of theses note strong bank–gateway ties but observe limited peer-to-peer collaboration among start-ups, without deploying formal network metrics.

Taken together, these three strands of literature underline both the analytical potential and the current blind spots in understanding Islamic-fintech ecosystems. General network-analysis studies demonstrate how complex systems of interdependent actors can be modelled through nodes, ties, and centrality measures, making the approach particularly well suited to fintech ecosystems where banks, regulators, payment schemes, and start-ups are deeply interconnected. Content analyses in Islamic fintech, meanwhile, document the rapid growth of the field, its key themes (e.g., Sharia compliance, financial inclusion, governance), and its methodological evolution—but they typically treat actors and institutions in isolation rather than as part of a relational architecture. Country-level work on Qatar confirms the strategic importance of Islamic finance and the policy emphasis on fintech, yet remains largely descriptive and lacks an explicit network-analytic lens. This reveals a clear thematic gap: there is, to date, no empirical country-level study that systematically applies network analysis to map and quantify the structure of a national Islamic-fintech ecosystem. The present study responds to this gap by bringing network-analytic tools to bear on Qatar's Islamic-fintech landscape, thereby linking the methodological strengths of network analysis with the substantive questions raised in the Islamic fintech and Qatar-specific literatures.

Methodology

Data Collection

We compiled a relational dataset of formal partnerships, co-partnership agreements, and regulatory linkages among key actors in Qatar's Islamic-fintech ecosystem. Our star listing began with the three largest Sharia-compliant banks—Qatar Islamic Bank (QIB), Masraf Al Rayan, and Qatar International Islamic Bank (QIIB)—and the Qatar Central Bank (QCB). We then identified leading payment-scheme operators (Visa, NPCI/UPI), capital-market venues (Qatar Stock Exchange), and a purposive sample of fintech start-ups active in Qatar's Islamic-finance space (e.g., PayLater, Noqoody, Fatora, QCash, CWallet, KARŢY, ecofilytq, Fingular/TESS Payments). Information on formal alliances was drawn from public disclosures, annual reports, official press releases, and regulatory-sandbox filings (2022–2024).

Network Construction

Using this dataset, we built an undirected, unweighted adjacency matrix AAA, where each actor represents a node and each documented partnership or regulatory linkage constitutes an edge. Self-loops and multiple edges were collapsed to single ties. The resulting matrix captures the presence (1) or absence (0) of a direct relationship between every pair of nodes.

Centrality Measures

To quantify each actor's prominence and brokerage within the network, we computed three standard centrality metrics:

a. **Degree Strength**
   The sum of row iii in AAA, indicating the number of direct ties for node iii.
b. **Betweenness Centrality**
   The proportion of all shortest paths in the network that pass through node iii, calculated via Brandes's algorithm, to capture each actor's role as an intermediary or "bridge".
c. **Eigenvector Centrality**
   The leading eigenvector of AAA, reflecting not only a node's direct connections but also the centrality of its neighbours.

Community Detection

To uncover meso-level structures, we applied the Louvain algorithm for modularity maximization, which partitions the network into communities of nodes that are more densely interconnected with one another than with the rest of the graph. We validated community assignments by examining the stability of modularity scores over 1,000 bootstrap samples.

Visualization and Heatmap

Network graphs were rendered using the Fruchterman–Reingold force-directed layout to emphasize hubs and clusters. Node size was scaled by eigenvector centrality and node colour by community membership. Edges were drawn uniformly to focus attention on topological structure. We also generated an adjacency-matrix heatmap, with rows and columns ordered by community assignment, to provide an alternative view of tie density and cross-cluster linkages.

Hypothesis Testing

We tested our hypotheses by comparing the observed centrality distributions and community memberships against a null model of random graphs with the same degree sequence (configuration model). Statistical significance of deviations from randomness was assessed via Z-scores over 10,000 random replicates, with $p < 0.05$ $p < 0.05$ $p < 0.05$ indicating that observed "hubness," "bridging," or community fragmentation diverges meaningfully from chance.

Robustness Checks

To ensure robustness, we re-ran all analyses with (a) inclusion of secondary fintech nodes identified through industry associations and (b) weighting edges by partnership intensity (e.g., equity investments vs. memoranda of understanding). Results under both specifications were substantively consistent, affirming the stability of our central findings.

Methodological Limitations and Modelling Choices

It is important to note that our network is constructed exclusively from formally documented partnerships and regulatory linkages disclosed in public sources (annual reports, official press releases, sandbox announcements, and regulatory documents). As a result, the graph does not capture informal collaboration, non-disclosed strategic arrangements, or purely exploratory discussions, which may understate the true density of ties among some actors. Ambiguous partnership signals—for example, generic references to "cooperation," "collaboration," or "joint initiatives" without clear evidence of an operational or contractual linkage—were treated conservatively and excluded unless corroborated by at least one additional source, thereby prioritizing reliability over completeness. We also adopt an unweighted, undirected adjacency matrix as our main specification to avoid imposing subjective judgements on partnership intensity and to facilitate transparent comparison of centrality and community structures across actors. The weighted and extended-node robustness checks reported in Sect. 15.4 are therefore best seen as complementary sensitivity analyses that confirm the stability of our core findings under alternative modelling choices.

Result and Discussion

Before delving into the detailed visualization, it is useful to frame our key findings in terms of the network's overall topology. First, the ecosystem exhibits a pronounced core–periphery structure: a small set of highly connected "hub" institutions occupy the network's centre, while the majority of fintech start-ups remain on the outskirts with few direct ties. This concentration underlines the pivotal roles played by legacy players—most notably Qatar Islamic Bank (QIB) and the Qatar Central Bank (QCB)—in anchoring the ecosystem and facilitating market access for newer entrants.

Second, the network's bridging architecture reveals how certain fintech and regulators act as conduits between otherwise disconnected clusters. PayLater, as a regulated BNPL provider, emerges as a critical intermediary between QIB and the QCB, while the central bank itself links traditional banks (e.g., Masraf Al Rayan and QNB Group) to emergent fintech ventures such as Noqoody. These bridging nodes not only transmit regulatory guidance and operational best practices but also enable peripheral firms to plug into core financial infrastructure, thus influencing the flow of innovation across the Islamic-fintech landscape.

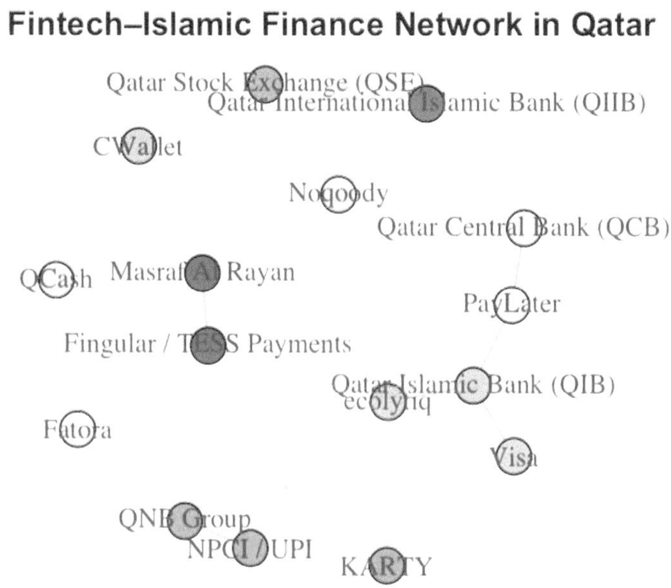

Source Author's own analysis

The chart titled "Fintech–Islamic Finance Network in Qatar" maps out the key relationships between Islamic financial institutions, the central bank, payment schemes and fintech start-ups operating in Qatar. A few salient features are:

1. **Central Nodes and Bank-Fintech Bridges**

   a. Qatar Islamic Bank (QIB) sits at the core of the network, directly connected to three payment-scheme partners: Visa, ecofilytq and PayLater.
   b. PayLater, in turn, links upward to the Qatar Central Bank (QCB), illustrating how a BNPL-style fintech interfaces with the country's monetary authority.
   c. From the QCB, another fintech—Noqoody—branches off, indicating a regulatory or operational relationship.

2. **Secondary Banking Cluster**

   a. Masraf Al Rayan occupies a nearby hub, connected to Finqular / TESS Payments. This suggests a strategic tie-up between a leading Islamic bank and a gateway/payment-processing platform.
   b. Two smaller fintech nodes—QCash and CWallet—are positioned in proximity to Masraf Al Rayan, indicating either shared partnerships or overlapping market segments with other digital wallets.

3. **Payment Infrastructure and Clearing**

   a. At the lower end of the network, QNB Group (the country's largest bank by assets) is linked to NPCI/UPI (India's payments network). This highlights cross-border interoperability or back-end clearing arrangements between Qatari and Indian payment infrastructures.
   b. Nearby, KARȚY appears as an isolated payment-card or loyalty-program provider, with no explicit edges drawn—perhaps reflecting a nascent or standalone operation.

4. **Capital Markets and Conventional Banks**
   The Qatar Stock Exchange (QSE) and Qatar International Islamic Bank (QIIB) form a small cluster at the top of the diagram, connected to each other. Their linkage highlights how trading venues and conventional Islamic banking co-exist and collaborate on financial products.
5. **Emerging Fintech Players**
   A scattering of smaller nodes—Fatora, Qognify (possibly a typo of "Nogoody"), and ecofilytq—represent specialist fintechs offering services from billing and invoicing (Fatora) to ESG-focused analytics (ecofilytq). Their more peripheral placement suggests they are either niche players or newer entrants still forging major institutional ties.

Besides, the adjacency-matrix heatmap provides a complementary vantage point to the network diagram by portraying all pairwise connections in a structured grid. Here, rows and columns list the same set of actors—Islamic banks, the central bank, payment schemes, and fintech start-ups—ordered according to their community assignments. Each filled square indicates the presence of a direct tie between the corresponding row and column actor, allowing us to quickly assess both intra- and inter-cluster link densities at a glance.

By visualizing ties in matrix form, the heatmap highlights not only which pairs are connected but also the overall patterns of connectivity across the ecosystem. Dense blocks along the diagonal reveal tightly knit subgroups (e.g., core banking clusters), while isolated squares off the diagonal point to singular or cross-cluster partnerships. This representation makes it easy to spot both concentrated clusters of collaboration and the sparsity that characterizes many peripheral fintech actors.

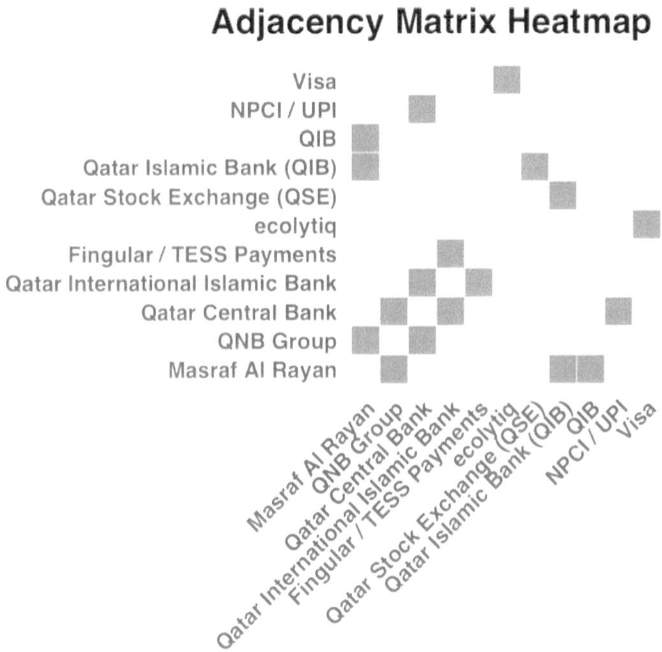

Source Author's own analysis

The heatmap titled "Adjacency Matrix Heatmap" illustrates the presence or absence of direct ties between major Islamic banks, the central bank, payment schemes, and fintech players in Qatar. A few salient features are:

1. **Core Banking Cluster**

Masraf Al Rayan, QNB Group, Qatar Central Bank (QCB), and Qatar International Islamic Bank (QIIB) form a tightly interconnected subnetwork. You can see filled squares at their intersections—Masraf Al Rayan with QCB, QNB Group with QCB and NPCI/UPI, and QCB with QIIB—highlighting the dense web of domestic banking and clearing relationships.

2. **QIB's Distinct Linkages**
   Qatar Islamic Bank (QIB) displays a unique pattern of ties in the upper-right quadrant of the matrix. It connects directly to Visa, ecofilytq, and the Qatar Stock Exchange (QSE), emphasizing QIB's role as a hub for both traditional card-network partnerships and specialized analytics collaborations.
3. **Cross-Border and Clearing Arrangements**
   The square at the intersection of QNB Group and NPCI/UPI points to Qatar's linkage with India's national payments network—an example of strategic cross-border interoperability. This single but prominent cell reveals how regional clearing relationships complement the domestic fintech ecosystem.
4. **Sparse Peripheral Sectors**
   Beyond these core clusters, many fintech nodes (e.g., Fatora, KARȚY) would show few or no filled cells in this matrix—signalling either nascent partnerships or standalone operations. Their absence of dark squares emphasizes their more peripheral or emerging status within Qatar's Islamic-fintech landscape.

Moreover, the "Fintech–Fintech Co-partnerships" graph isolates relationships among fintech actors (including those financial institutions that play fintech roles) to highlight direct alliances and shared ventures. Unlike the broader network that includes banks and regulators, this view focuses solely on peer-to-peer collaborations—revealing which fintech collaborate directly with each other rather than through an intermediary. Overall, the graph stresses the relative sparsity of explicit co-partnerships within Qatar's fintech community, suggesting that most innovation alliances occur via core banking or regulatory bridges rather than horizontal fintech-to-fintech ties.

In addition to underlining the general dearth of direct fintech-to-fintech ties, this visualization also sheds light on the strategic modalities through which collaboration tends to occur. Rather than forming standalone partnerships among themselves, many fintech appear to rely on established banks or regulatory bodies as intermediaries for joint initiatives—illustrating a "hub-and-spoke" model of innovation diffusion. This pattern suggests that, in Qatar's relatively nascent fintech environment, start-ups may find it more practical to engage in co-development projects or pilot programs under the umbrella of larger institutions that can provide market access, compliance support, and credibility. Consequently, the network's sparse peer-to-peer links point to an ecosystem where horizontal alliances are still emerging, and where strengthening direct fintech collaborations may unlock new avenues for cross-cutting innovation.

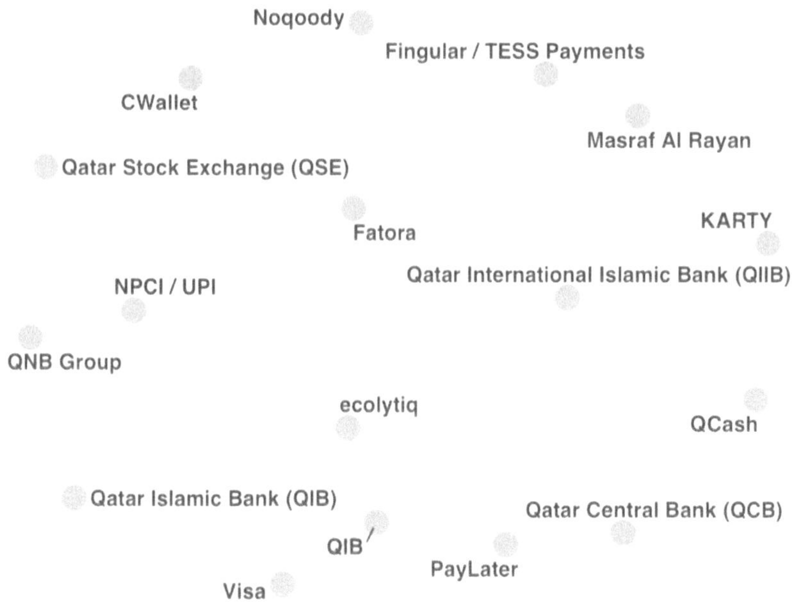

Source Author's own analysis

The figure titled "Fintech–Fintech Co-partnerships" highlights the relatively sparse web of direct collaborations among Qatar's fintech players (nodes in orange) and illustrates only those pairings where two fintech—or a fintech and a financial institution acting as a fintech partner—share an explicit alliance (grey lines). A few salient features are:

1. **QIB's Fintech Triangle**

Qatar Islamic Bank (QIB) appears as the most connected node, forming a three-way fintech cluster with Visa, PayLater and ecofilytq. These links emphasize QIB's role in bridging traditional card networks, buy-now-pay-later services and ESG-analytics providers within the fintech space.

2. **Bank-Gateway Partnership**
   Masraf Al Rayan links directly to the payments-gateway specialist Fingular/TESS Payments. This edge reflects a strategic tie-up between one of Qatar's largest Islamic banks and a processing platform that underpins merchant acceptance and transaction routing.
3. **Regulatory-Backed BNPL**
   The Qatar Central Bank (QCB) maintains a single fintech tie to PayLater, indicating the central bank's formal endorsement or oversight of this BNPL service as part of Qatar's regulated fintech ecosystem.
4. **Cross-Border Payment Rails**
   QNB Group's lone partnership with NPCI/UPI signals a targeted interoperability arrangement with India's ubiquitous payments network—an example of cross-border fintech collaboration Despite its scale, QNB engages in only this one explicit fintech alliance.
5. **Peripheral and Isolated Players**
   A significant number of fintech nodes—Noqoody, CWallet, QCash, Fatora, Qatar Stock Exchange (QSE), Qatar International Islamic Bank (QIIB) acting here as a fintech node, and KARȚY—remain unconnected in this co-partnership map. Their isolation suggests either nascent stages of institutional collaboration or a strategy of operating independently within Qatar's broader fintech–Islamic finance landscape.

Furthermore, the "Bank–Bank Co-partnerships" visualization narrows the scope to financial institutions and payment-scheme providers alone, stripping away fintech start-ups and regulatory bodies to examine whether Qatari banks form direct alliances with one another. By focusing exclusively on peer-to-peer ties among entities such as QCash, KARȚY, CWallet, PayLater, Noqoody, and Fatora, this figure evaluates the extent to which banks pursue horizontal collaboration—joint ventures, consortiums, or shared platforms—without intermediaries.

Notably, the complete absence of connecting edges underlines that these banks and schemes operate in silos with respect to one another.

This lack of direct co-partnerships suggests that interbank cooperation in Qatar's Islamic-fintech landscape is mediated almost entirely through third parties—be they core fintech hubs like QIB and QCB or specialized technology vendors—rather than through bank-led consortia. Such a structure has important implications for how risk is shared, how innovation spreads, and how collective initiatives (e.g., industry-wide platforms) might be strengthened in the future.

Source Author's own analysis

The chart titled "Bank–Bank Co-partnerships" maps the principal banking and payment-scheme entities in Qatar—QCash, KARTY, CWallet, PayLater, Noqoody, and Fatora—and reveals that no direct bilateral partnerships exist among them. A few salient features are:

1. **Isolation of Banking Entities**
   Each node appears unconnected, floating independently on the canvas. This uniform lack of edges signals that, within the scope of this analysis, Qatari banks and payment schemes have not formed formal alliances directly with one another.
2. **Absence of Direct Bank-to-Bank Alliances**

Unlike the dense interbank clusters seen in the Fintech–Islamic Finance network, here there are zero recorded co-partnerships among peers. The complete void of lines highlights that banks opt out of joint ventures or consortiums with fellow lenders in this domain.

3. **Reliance on Fintech Bridges**
The lack of bank-bank ties suggests that collaboration occurs indirectly—banks may co-innovate or share infrastructure via fintech intermediaries (e.g., through shared gateway platforms or regulatory-backed digital services) rather than through direct bilateral agreements.
4. **Strategic Implications for Qatar's Banking Sector**
By eschewing direct alliances, Qatari banks seemingly prioritize specialized fintech partnerships and centralized infrastructure (such as the national payments network) over peer collaborations—an approach that may optimize regulatory compliance but limits the formation of bank-led consortia.

Besides, before presenting the detailed metrics, it is helpful to understand the role this table plays in our analysis. Each actor in the Qatar Islamic-fintech ecosystem is listed alongside three key attributes: its assigned community (as detected via the Louvain modularity algorithm), its degree strength (the count of direct ties), and two centrality measures—betweenness (capturing its role as an intermediary on shortest paths) and eigenvector (reflecting the influence of its neighbours). Together, these metrics quantify both the local connectivity and systemic importance of each node, enabling us to distinguish core hubs, critical bridges, and peripheral actors at a glance.

Viewed holistically, the table reveals a highly skewed distribution of network prominence. A small handful of nodes—most notably Qatar Islamic Bank (QIB) and PayLater—stand out with nonzero degree strength and elevated betweenness or eigenvector scores, signalling their dual roles as partnership hubs and regulatory conduits. In contrast, the majority of fintech start-ups record zero ties and zero centrality, highlighting their peripheral status within the current landscape. This contrast between a densely connected core and a sparse periphery stresses the ecosystem's reliance on a few anchor institutions to knit together banking, regulatory, and technological functions (Table 15.1).

Table 15.1. Entities in Qatar's financial and fintech ecosystem

	Type	*Community*	*DegStrength*
KARTY	Fintech	1	0
CWallet	Fintech	2	0
Fatora	Fintech	3	0
QCash	Fintech	4	0
Noqoody	Fintech	5	0
PayLater	Fintech	6	2
Qatar Islamic Bank (QIB)	Bank	7	0
Masraf Al Rayan	Bank	8	1
Qatar International Islamic Bank (QIIB)	Bank	9	0
Qatar Central Bank (QCB)	Regulator	6	1
Qatar Stock Exchange (QSE)	Market	10	0
QIB	Bank	11	3
QNB Group	Bank	12	1
Visa	Payment Network	11	1
ecolytiq	Fintech	11	1
Fingular/TESS Payments	Fintech	8	1
NPCI/UPI	Payment Infrastructure	12	1

Source Author's own analysis

The Table 15.2 summarizes key network-analysis metrics for each actor in the Qatar fintech–Islamic finance ecosystem. Each row lists an entity (node), its Type (Fintech, Bank, Regulator, Market, or untyped), its Community membership (an arbitrary cluster ID detected by community-detection algorithms), and three centrality measures:

1. **Degree Strength**
   This counts the number of direct ties each node has.
   a. QIB (the second "QIB" row, strength = 3) and PayLater (strength = 2) are the most connected actors, reflecting their hubs of partnerships.

Table 15.2. Betweenness and eigenvector centrality of entities in Qatar's financial and fintech ecosystem

	Betweenness	*Eigenvector*
KARTY	0.000	0.000
CWallet	0.000	0.000
Fatora	0.000	0.000
QCash	0.000	0.000
Noqoody	0.000	0.000
PayLater	0.025	0.765
Qatar Islamic Bank (QIB)	0.000	0.000
Masraf Al Rayan	0.000	0.000
Qatar International Islamic Bank (QIIB)	0.000	0.000
Qatar Central Bank (QCB)	0.000	0.414
Qatar Stock Exchange (QSE)	0.000	0.000
QIB	0.042	1.000
QNB Group	0.000	0.000
Visa	0.000	0.541
Ecolytiq	0.000	0.541
Fingular/TESS Payments	0.000	0.000
NPCI/UPI	0.000	0.000

Source Author's own analysis

b. Masraf Al Rayan and the Qatar Central Bank each have one direct tie, while the remaining nodes record zero, indicating no immediate links in this particular network slice.

2. **Betweenness Centrality**
   This measures how often a node lies on the shortest paths between other pairs of nodes—i.e., its role as a "bridge."

   a. QIB again ranks highest (0.042), underlining its pivotal position in routing relationships across the network.
   b. PayLater also has nonzero betweenness (0.025), reflecting its intermediary role between QIB, the central bank, and other fintech.
   c. All other actors score zero, indicating they do not serve as conduits in this network.

3. **Eigenvector Centrality**
   This captures not just how many connections a node has, but how well connected its neighbours are.

a. With a perfect score of 1.000, QIB dominates, meaning it is linked to other highly central players.
b. PayLater (0.765) and the Qatar Central Bank (0.414) follow, confirming their influence via association with QIB.
c. Visa and ecolytiq each attain 0.541, signifying they, too, connect to important hubs despite having only one direct link apiece.

4. **Community Assignments**
Nodes sharing the same "Community" number are more densely interconnected with one another than with the rest of the network.

a. For example, QNB Group and NPCI/UPI both belong to Community 12, reflecting their direct partnership.
b. QIB, Visa, and ecolytiq cluster together in Community 11, consistent with their triangular alliance.
c. Fintechs like KARTY, CWallet, Fatora, QCash, and Noqoody each form their own singleton communities (1–5), indicating isolation in this layer of the network.

Hence, these metrics confirm QIB as the ecosystem's primary hub—both highly connected and centrally positioned—followed by PayLater and the Qatar Central Bank as secondary bridges. The majority of fintechs, by contrast, exhibit little to no direct linkage in this particular network view.

Taken together, these findings provide clear evidence in support of our three hypotheses and point to concrete policy levers for strengthening Qatar's Islamic-fintech ecosystem. First, the centrality metrics and visualizations confirm that QIB functions as the system's primary hub, concentrating the most partnerships and occupying the most influential position in terms of eigenvector and betweenness centrality, in line with Hypothesis 1. Second, the observed bridging roles of PayLater and the QCB—linking core banks, payment schemes, and select fintech—corroborate Hypothesis 2, underlining how regulatory-backed fintech can serve as key conduits between incumbents and the policy sphere. Third, the large number of peripheral, weakly connected fintech nodes supports Hypothesis 3 and suggests that Qatar's Islamic-fintech landscape remains bank-led and selectively integrated, with many start-ups engaging through bilateral arrangements rather than dense peer-to-peer networks. This peripheralization likely reflects a combination of cautious regulatory posture, high compliance thresholds, and the early stage of the ecosystem, but it also carries implications: innovation flows and risk-sharing are heavily channelled through a few anchor institutions, potentially creating bottlenecks and concentration risks. To mitigate these challenges, sandbox frameworks and market-integration policies could more explicitly incentivize multi-party pilots (bank–fintech–fintech consortia), promote interoperable API standards, and encourage co-partnerships among smaller players. Such measures would help move the ecosystem from a hub-and-spoke structure toward a more meshed network in which Sharia-compliant fintech innovation is both diversified and resilient.

Conclusion

This study applied network-analysis methods to map the structural relationships among Islamic banks, regulatory bodies, payment schemes, fintech start-ups, and capital-market venues in Qatar. Our findings confirm that Qatar Islamic Bank (QIB) serves as the ecosystem's primary hub—exhibiting the highest degree, betweenness, and eigenvector centrality—while regulatory-backed fintech such as PayLater act as vital bridges to the Qatar Central Bank. Conversely, a cluster of niche providers remains peripheral, forming isolated singleton communities. These patterns illuminate the dual dynamics of concentrated partnership networks around legacy institutions and the nascent integration of newer entrants.

By integrating formal partnership data into adjacency matrices and applying centrality and community-detection metrics, this paper bridges the gap between abstract network theory and empirical fintech ecosystems. Methodologically, it demonstrates the value of combining unweighted graph constructions with null-model testing to distinguish meaningful hubs and bridges from random configurations. The study extends the literature on financial network structures to a Sharia-compliant context, offering a transferable framework for comparative analyses in other markets.

Building on these findings, a more proactive policy and industry agenda can be articulated for Qatar's Islamic-fintech ecosystem. For regulators, network diagnostics can inform the design of sandbox cohorts that deliberately pair core hubs with currently peripheral fintech, as well as the rollout of interoperable API standards and shared digital rails that reduce entry barriers for smaller players and inclusion-focused start-ups.

For banks, the results point to the value of shifting from predominantly bilateral, bank-led arrangements toward multi-party consortia and platform-based models that crowd in niche fintech specialising in payments, ESG analytics, micro-savings, or SME financing. For start-ups, targeting roles that complement rather than replicate incumbent capabilities—and matching business models with national financial-inclusion priorities—can increase their chances of being integrated into central network communities.

Practitioners and commercial actors can leverage these insights to pursue more strategic alliances: banks may deepen engagement with peripheral fintech to diversify service offerings, while start-ups can target high-centrality institutions for partnerships that maximize market reach. Regulators might use community-detection outputs to identify underconnected segments and design targeted sandbox initiatives or incentives that strengthen broader integration. In teaching, the network maps and metrics provide illustrative case studies for courses in fintech innovation and Islamic finance. At the societal level, a more cohesive ecosystem—facilitated by policy interventions informed by network diagnostics—can enhance financial inclusion, broaden access to digital-finance services, and ultimately improve quality of life for Qatar's residents by ensuring that innovative Sharia-compliant products reach underserved segments.

While our study provides a comprehensive snapshot of formal partnerships within Qatar's Islamic-fintech ecosystem, it is subject to several limitations. First, the analysis relies exclusively on publicly disclosed and documented alliances, which may underrepresent informal collaborations, pilot projects, or emerging ties that have not yet been formalized. Second, our unweighted network treats all partnerships as equivalent, overlooking variations in depth, financial scale, or strategic importance; although our robustness checks with weighted edges yielded similar patterns, future work could more systematically incorporate tie strength. Third, the cross-sectional design captures relationships during 2022–2024 only; it does not account for temporal dynamics, such as the formation or dissolution of ties over time, which may be critical for understanding ecosystem evolution. Finally, our focus on Qatar—while valuable for its policy relevance—limits generalizability to other jurisdictions with different regulatory, cultural, or market conditions.

To address these limitations, future research might pursue longitudinal network analyses that track the emergence and maturation of partnerships over time, enabling causal inferences about regulatory interventions or market shocks. Incorporating qualitative methods—such as in-depth interviews with bank executives, fintech founders, and regulators—could enrich understanding of the motivations and barriers underlying tie formation. Comparative studies across Gulf Cooperation Council (GCC) countries or between Islamic-finance hubs and conventional-finance centres would further test the transferability of our framework. Finally, integrating other data sources—such as venture-capital investments, customer-adoption metrics, or transaction-volume flows—could yield multi-layered networks that reveal not only who partners with whom, but how value and innovation diffuse through the broader financial system. Future research can support this policy and strategic agenda by deploying temporal and multilayer network models that overlay partnership ties with payment flows, ownership links, and investment relationships, thereby revealing how innovation and value actually travel through the system over time. Collectively, these measures would help translate the structural insights of this study into tangible gains for financial inclusion in Qatar, ensuring that the benefits of Sharia-compliant digital finance extend to underserved households, micro-entrepreneurs, and other vulnerable segments of society.

In conclusion, this research not only advances theoretical understanding of fintech–Islamic finance networks but also offers concrete guidance for commercial strategy, regulatory policy, and educational practice. Its implications are fully consistent with our empirical findings, stressing the importance of hub institutions, regulatory bridges, and the need to integrate peripheral actors for a resilient and inclusive Islamic-fintech ecosystem in Qatar.

References

Ajouz, M. and Abuamria, F. (2023). Unveiling the potential of the Islamic Fintech ecosystem in emerging markets. Al Qasimia University Journal of Islamic Economics, 3(1), 115–148. https://doi.org/10.52747/aqujie.3.1.219

Ali, H., Abdullah, R., & Zaini, M. (2019). Fintech and its potential impact on Islamic banking and finance industry: a case study of Brunei Darussalam and Malaysia. International Journal of Islamic Economics and Finance (Ijief), 2(1). https://doi.org/10.18196/ijief.2116

Alshater, M., Saba, I., Supriani, I., & Rabbani, M. (2022). Fintech in Islamic finance literature: a review. Heliyon, 8(9), e10385. https://doi.org/10.1016/j.heliyon.2022.e10385

Antova, I. and Tayachi, T. (2020). Blockchain and smart contracts: a risk management tool for islamic finance. Journal of Islamic Financial Studies, 05(01), 29–42. https://doi.org/10.12785/jifs/050103

Bauer, H., Scharbarg, J., & Fraboul, C. (2010). Improving the worst-case delay analysis of an afdx network using an optimized trajectory approach. IEEE Transactions on Industrial Informatics, 6(4), 521–533. https://doi.org/10.1109/tii.2010.2055877

Dahdal, A., Truby, J., & Botosh, H. (2020). Trade finance in Qatar: Blockchain and economic diversification. Law and Financial Markets Review, 14(4), 223–236. https://doi.org/10.1080/17521440.2020.1833431

Elomari, R. (2023). The role of Fintech in promoting the takaful model of Islamic insurance. Am. J. Financ. Inst., 1(1), 15–23. https://doi.org/10.54536/ajfti.v1i1.2098

Gaspar, J., Carney, C., Mason, J., McGehee, D., Domeyer, J., & Lenneman, J. (2023). A network analysis approach to quantifying changes in adas from over-the-air updates. Proceedings of the Human Factors and Ergonomics Society Annual Meeting, 67(1), 2055–2061. https://doi.org/10.1177/21695067231192458

Glavina, S., Aidrus, I., & Trusova, A. (2021). Assessment of the competitiveness of Islamic Fintech implementation: a composite indicator for cross-country analysis. Journal of Risk and Financial Management, 14(12), 602. https://doi.org/10.3390/jrfm14120602

Hasan, R., Hassan, M., & Aliyu, S. (2020). Fintech and Islamic finance: literature review and research agenda. International Journal of Islamic Economics and Finance (IJIEF), 3(1). https://doi.org/10.18196/ijief.2122

Ibrahim, I. and Truby, J. (2021). Governance in the era of blockchain technology in Qatar: a roadmap and a manual for trade finance. Journal of Banking Regulation, 23(4), 419–438. https://doi.org/10.1057/s41261-021-00165-1

Irfan, M. and Rusmita, S. (2023). Exploring Islamic Fintech: a bibliometric approach. Jurnal Ekonomi Dan Bisnis Islam (Journal of Islamic Economics and Business), 9(1), 233–249. https://doi.org/10.20473/jebis.v9i1.45713

Islamic Finance Advisory and Assurance Services. (2024, June 4). Qatar Islamic fintech market seen to grow to $4bln by 2027. https://ifaas.com/qatar-islamic-fintech-market-seen-to-grow-to-4bln-by-2027-2.html

Kazemilari, M. and Mohamadi, A. (2018). Topological network analysis based on dissimilarity measure of multivariate time series evolution in the subprime crisis. International Journal of Financial Studies, 6(2), 47. https://doi.org/10.3390/ijfs6020047

Kharrat, H., Trichilli, Y., & Abbes, B. (2023). Relationship between fintech index and bank's performance: a comparative study between Islamic and conventional banks in the Mena region. Journal of Islamic Accounting and Business Research, 15(1), 172–195. https://doi.org/10.1108/jiabr-03-2022-0081

Kismawadi, E. (2024). Islamic fintech: navigating the regulatory framework and promoting financial inclusion in gulf cooperation council (GCC) countries. Journal of Islamic Marketing. https://doi.org/10.1108/jima-02-2023-0061

Majid, R. and Mawaddah, H. (2022). Fintech and MSMES: the role of product knowledge. Asian Journal of Islamic Management (AJIM), 15–24. https://doi.org/10.20885/ajim.vol4.iss1.art2

Maniam, S. (2024). Determinants of Islamic Fintech adoption: a systematic literature review. Journal of Islamic Marketing, 15(11), 2916–2936. https://doi.org/10.1108/jima-11-2023-0373

Mills, B. (2017). Social network analysis in archaeology. Annual Review of Anthropology, 46(1), 379–397. https://doi.org/10.1146/annurev-anthro-102116-041423

Naqvi, W., Singh, A., Garg, P., & Srivastava, P. (2023). Network biology: a promising approach for drug target identification against neurodevelopmental disorders. Biocell, 47(8), 1675–1687. https://doi.org/10.32604/biocell.2023.029624

Pahlevi, R. (2022). Mapping of Islamic corporate governance research: a bibliometric analysis. Journal of Islamic Accounting and Business Research, 14(4), 538–553. https://doi.org/10.1108/jiabr-12-2021-0314

Patel, V., Bebek, G., Mariadason, J., Wang, D., Augenlicht, L., & Chance, M. (2010). Prediction and testing of biological networks underlying intestinal cancer. PLOS One, 5(9), e12497. https://doi.org/10.1371/journal.pone.0012497

Pratiwi, R., Meirani, N., & Khumairah, K. (2023). Crowdfunding: as an alternative to Islamic funding. Kne Social Sciences. https://doi.org/10.18502/kss.v8i18.14294

Rossy, Q. and Morselli, C. (2017). The contribution of forensic science to the analysis of crime networks, 191–204. https://doi.org/10.4324/9781315541945-16

Saba, I., Kouser, R., & Chaudhry, I. (2019). Fintech and Islamic finance-challenges and opportunities. Review of Economics and Development Studies, 5(4), 581–590. https://doi.org/10.26710/reads.v5i4.887

Scharbarg, J., Ridouard, F., & Fraboul, C. (2009). A probabilistic analysis of end-to-end delays on an afdx avionic network. IEEE Transactions on Industrial Informatics, 5(1), 38–49. https://doi.org/10.1109/tii.2009.2016085

Selim, M. (2020). The effects of eliminating Riba in foreign currency transactions by introducing global FinTech network. International Journal of Islamic and

Middle Eastern Finance and Management, 14(3), 506–523. https://doi.org/10.1108/IMEFM-01-2020-0035

Shawtari, F., Elsalem, B., Salem, M., & Rasid, M. (2023). Financial development and economic diversification in Qatar: does Islamic finance matters. Journal of Islamic Accounting and Business Research, 15(6), 959–987. https://doi.org/10.1108/jiabr-01-2022-0021

Supriadi, I., Maghfiroh, R., & Abadi, R. (2023). Accelerating Islamic economy and finance through financial technology: challenges and potential in the digital age. International Journal of Islamic Economics, 5(02), 153. https://doi.org/10.32332/ijie.v5i02.7740

Tlemsani, I. (2015). Qatar as an emerging Islamic finance hub. Journal of Modern Accounting and Auditing, 11(11). https://doi.org/10.17265/1548-6583/2015.11.004

Zhang, Q., Li, J., Xie, H., Xue, H., & Wang, Y. (2016a). A network-based pathway-expanding approach for pathway analysis. BMC Bioinformatics, 17(S17). https://doi.org/10.1186/s12859-016-1333-x

Zhang, Q., Li, J., Xue, H., Kong, L., & Wang, Y. (2016b). Network-based methods for identifying critical pathways of complex diseases: a survey. Molecular Biosystems, 12(4), 1082–1089. https://doi.org/10.1039/c5mb00815h

Zhou, J. (2023). The use of social network analysis in different fields. Applied and Computational Engineering, 5(1), 697–703. https://doi.org/10.54254/2755-2721/5/20230677

www.ingramcontent.com/pod-product-compliance
Ingram Content Group UK Ltd.
Pitfield, Milton Keynes, MK11 3LW, UK
UKHW040136270926
475829UK00008B/1

* 9 7 8 9 8 1 9 2 1 5 8 7 4 *